T0347264

The Impact of European Integration on Regional Structural Change and Cohesion

The integration of Eastern Europe into the EU has widespread implications both in terms of an increase in trade and mobility and in relation to concerns regarding the widening of regional disparities. In this new book, economic integration is interpreted as a relocation of resources across sectors and space; the authors analyse empirically the changes of regional specialization over a period of two decades, observing its causes and consequences.

The authors argue that the resulting challenge to both regional and social cohesion in the enlarged European Union may require a reorientation of cohesion policy at European, national and local levels. Disaggregated national data sets with respect to both the sectoral and spatial levels are combined with an analysis of both regional structural change and the role of foreign direct investment in this process.

This book will be of great interest to postgraduate students and researchers interested in international trade and regional economics as well as policy makers engaged with regional and structural changes at both a European and national level.

Christiane Krieger-Boden is a Research Associate at the Kiel Institute for the World Economy in Germany. **Dr Edgar Morgenroth** is a Senior Research Officer at the Economic and Social Research Institute in Dublin. **Dr George Petrakos** is a Professor of Spatial Economics at the University of Thessaly in Greece.

Routledge studies in the European economy

The Impact of European Integration on Regional Structural Change and Cohesion

**Edited by Christiane Krieger-Boden,
Edgar Morgenroth and George Petrakos**

Routledge
Taylor & Francis Group

LONDON AND NEW YORK

First published 2008
by Routledge
2 Park Square, Milton Park, Abingdon, Oxon, OX14 4RN

Simultaneously published in the USA and Canada
by Routledge
270 Madison Ave, New York NY 10016

Routledge is an imprint of the Taylor & Francis Group, an informa business

Transferred to Digital Printing 2008

© 2008 Selection and editorial matter, Christiane Krieger-Boden, Edgar Morgenroth and George Petrakos; individual chapters, the contributors

Typeset in Times by Wearset Ltd, Boldon, Tyne and Wear

All rights reserved. No part of this book may be reprinted or reproduced or utilised in any form or by any electronic, mechanical, or other means, now known or hereafter invented, including photocopying and recording, or in any information storage or retrieval system, without permission in writing from the publishers.

British Library Cataloguing in Publication Data
A catalogue record for this book is available from the British Library

Library of Congress Cataloging in Publication Data
A catalog record for this book has been requested

ISBN10: 0-415-40024-4 (hbk)
ISBN10: 0-203-93482-2 (ebk)

ISBN13: 978-0-415-40024-4 (hbk)
ISBN13: 978-0-203-93482-1 (ebk)

Contents

Illustrations

Figures

Maps

Tables

Contributors

Maria Giovanna Bosco is Researcher at the Istituto Regionale di Ricerca della Lombardia (IReR) and Assistant Researcher at the Bocconi University, both in Milan, and a consultant at KPMG. Her main research interests are FDI, regional economics and international taxation. Her main publications include "Does foreign investment contribute to technological spillovers and growth? A panel data analysis of Hungarian firms", *Transnational Corporations*, Vol. 10, No. 1, UNCTAD, April 2001; "Innovation, R&D and technology transfer: policies towards a regional innovation system. The case of Lombardy", *European Planning Studies*, September 2007.

Bernd Brandl is Assistant Professor of Industrial Sociology at the University of Vienna. His research focus is on industrial relations, labour market issues and empirical methods. His publications include: "Industrial relations, social pacts and welfare expenditures", *British Journal of Industrial Relations*, Vol. 43: 635–58, 2005 (with F. Traxler).

Georgios Fotopoulos, PhD, is a tenured Assistant Professor of Applied Microeconomics in the Department of Economics at the University of Patras, Greece. He has studied Economics at the University of Athens, and holds an MSc in Regional Science from the University of Reading and a PhD from the London School of Economics and Political Science. His research interests are around applied industrial economics and regional economics, and his research can be found in various academic journals including the *Journal of Regional Science, Economics Letters, International Journal of Industrial Organization, Environment and Planning A* and *Regional Studies*.

Christian Fölzer is Head of the Department of Economics of Schienen-Control, Vienna. His research interests focus on regional economics and transport economics. His publications include: "Dasein oder nicht dasein-das ist hier die Frage. Die Daseinsvorsorge im Verkehrswesen", *Wirtschaftspolitische Blätter*, 343-52, 2005.

Anna Iara is Staff Economist at The Vienna Institute for International Economic Studies (WIIW). Before 2005, she was Research Fellow at the Center for European Integration Studies (ZEI) at the University of Bonn. In her research Anna Iara focuses on applied econometrics, regional economics, labour markets and migration in Central and Eastern Europe. In these fields she has published research articles in refereed journals, edited volumes and working paper series. She holds a Master of Arts degree in economics from the Central European University, Budapest, and a Master of Science degree in geography from the University of Bonn.

Dimitris Kallioras, PhD, holds a doctoral degree from the University of Thessaly, Department of Planning and Regional Development. He is also a Research Fellow at the South and East European Development Center. His main research interests include regional economics, transition economics, economic growth, cross-border cooperation and economic integration. He has published many articles in international journals and books and he has participated in many European and national research projects.

Eva Kippenberg studied Economics at the University of Bonn and obtained her MSc in 2001. She was Junior Fellow at the Center for European Integration Studies (ZEI) in Bonn, Germany, her main research topic being the effects of foreign direct investment on the Czech economy. Publications include "Sectoral linkages of foreign direct investment firms to the Czech economy", *Research in Business and Finance*. Today, she works at a consulting firm.

Christiane Krieger-Boden is Research Associate at the Kiel Institute for the World Economy in Kiel, Germany. She holds a Master degree in economics by the University of Münster/Westf. Her main research interests include regional effects of European integration, regional effects of subsidies and economics of border regions. She has worked as consultant to German ministries, the European Commission and the IMF. Publications in books, national and international journals concern inter alia studies in cross-border relations, chances and risks of the European Monetary Union for countries and regions, problems of the German reunification process and the review and assessment of German and European regional policy.

Edgar Morgenroth, PhD, is a Senior Research Officer at the Economic and Social Research Institute in Dublin. His research interests include economic growth, international trade, economic geography and public economics. His recent publications include papers on the regional productivity trends, the impact of demographic factors on regional growth in Ireland, spillover effects of public infrastructure and the impact of the EU Structural Funds. He has also recently published a major study on public investment priorities for Ireland.

George Petrakos, PhD, is Professor of Spatial Economic Analysis at the University of Thessaly, Department of Planning and Regional Development. He is also Director of the South and East European Development Center (SEED). His research interests include urban and regional economics, development, transition economics, Balkan studies and international economic relations. He has published several books and a large number of articles in international journals. Recent publications include: *Integration, Growth and Cohesion in an Enlarged European Union*, Springer, 2004 (with J. Bradley and J. Traistaru), *Regional Development in Greece*, Kritiki, 2004 (with Y. Psycharis, in Greek), *The Development of the Balkan Region*, Ashgate, 2001 (with S. Totev) and *Integration and Transition in Europe: the Economic Geography of Interaction*, Routledge, 2000 (with G. Maier and G. Gorzelak).

Laura Resmini is Associate Professor of Economics at the Università della Valle d'Aosta, Aosta, Italy, and Senior Researcher at ISLA, Centre for Latin American and Transition Country Studies at Bocconi University, Milan, Italy. She hold a *Dottorato di ricerca* (Italian PhD programme) in Economics, a Certificate of International Studies (specialisation in International Economics) from the Graduate Institute of International Studies, Geneva and a BA in Economics and Social Sciences from Bocconi University. Research interests regard economic integration, foreign direct investments, and economics of transition. Her recent publications include studies on the determinants and impact of FDI in transition countries. She has participated in several European research networks both as team leader and senior researcher. She also serves as referee for several academic journals, including the *European Economic Review*, *Transnational Corporation*, the *Journal of Comparative Economics*, and *Comparative Economic Studies*. She is member of the editorial board of *Scienze Regionali*, the *Italian Journal of Regional Science* and *Economic System*.

Tamás Szemlér, PhD, an economist-teacher, is Senior Research Fellow at the Institute for World Economics of the Hungarian Academy of Sciences. His main research and education fields are the structure, changes and prospects of the budget of the enlarged European Union (EU), with special emphasis on structural policy-related issues, as well as the role of French–German relations in the European integration process. He obtained his PhD with his thesis in this latter topic in 2001 at the Budapest University of Economics and Public Administration.

Stoyan Totev, PhD, is Senior Research Fellow at the Institute of Economics, Bulgarian Academy of Sciences, Department of Regional and Sectoral Studies. He is an economist, with his MSc in Statistics and his PhD in Econometrics from the University of National and World Economy, Sofia. He has done research and published on topics including: regional economics; industrial and agriculture policy; comparative economics; cross-border cooperation; Balkan countries economic relations; and investment policy. He coordinated several Phare ACE Projects and participated as a principal partner in more than 30 EU and other international projects. Stoyan Totev is delivering lectures on statistical methods as Associated Professor at Sofia University and other universities in Bulgaria. Some of his main publications are the books: *The Development of the Balkan Region*, Aldershot, Ashgate (with Petrakos, eds); *Potential for Cross-border Economic Development in* *the Nis-Skopje-Sofia Triangle*, East–West Institute (with M. Boyadjieva, eds). Recent papers include: "Economic relations in South Eastern Europe: the intra-regional FDI point of view" *Economic Studies*; "Industrial policy in the process of accession", *Iconomica*; "Comparative analysis of the process of regional specialization and concentration in the framework of EU", *Economic Investigation*; "Economic performance and structures in Southeast Europeans Countries, Albania, Bulgaria, FYR of Macedonia and Greece", *Eastern European Economics*.

Iulia Traistaru-Siedschlag, PhD, is Senior Research Officer and Head of the Centre for International Macroeconomic Analysis at the Economic and Social Research Institute in Dublin. She specialises in International Economics and Quantitative Economic Methods. Her key areas of expertise include structural change and macroeconomic adjustment in the context of economic and monetary integration; economic growth, nominal and real convergence; international transmission of business cycles; modelling of trade integration and trade policy; and applied econometrics. Her research has been published in books and in leading international journals such as *Open Economies Review, Kyklos, Labour Economics*, and *Journal of International Business and Economy*. She has received several research awards and fellowships from private and public organisations including *Il Sole 24 Ore,* the British Council, University of Warwick and the European Commission. In 2004 she received the *Best Paper Award* from the International Business and Economy Conference in San Francisco for her research on location of manufacturing in Central and Eastern Europe in the context of increased economic integration. She has been a consultant to the European Commission, European Central Bank, World Bank, Inter-American Development Bank, and the World Economic Forum.

Anna Wisniewski has worked as a Research Fellow at the Institute for World Economics at the Hungarian Academy of Sciences since 2000, and she is a PhD student at the Corvinus University of Budapest at the Faculty of International Economics. Her main research interests include: Poland in the European Union; economic and political developments with special attention to monetary and fiscal issues: regional development: and tax policy and Eastern relations.

Foreword

The ongoing European integration represents an ambitious process without historical precedent and, largely, a story of overwhelming success. Yet, even after several rounds of deepening and widening the European Union, there is still much uncertainty and even doubt at any further integration step. In particular, concerns refer to a change of the international and interregional division of labour, by which some less-developed regions might run a risk of brain draining and some developed regions might be affected by "out-migration" of jobs to low-income regions. Research in this field is therefore of high social relevance – and, besides, it is also attractive to the researcher, given the natural-experiment nature of the European integration process.

This book brings together the research results of a project analysing the impact of deepening and widening the European Union on the intra-European division of labour. This research project entitled "The impact of European integration and enlargement on regional structural change and cohesion" (EURECO) was undertaken with financial support from the European Community's 5th Research and Technological Development Framework Programme, which is gratefully acknowledged. The overall scientific objective of the project was to identify and explain in a cross-country analysis the impact of European integration and enlargement on regional structural change and cohesion, on the basis of detailed national data sources. The huge research effort this meant required a large team of contributors. Besides the authors of this volume, the editors like to thank Eckhardt Bode, Natalie Lubenets, Rüdiger Soltwedel and Andrea Szalavetz for valuable research contributions that entered this book one way or another, and Carlo Altomonte, Frank Bickenbach, John Bradley, Jürgen von Hagen, Andras Inotai, Ronald Moomaw and Peter Nijkamp for inspiring comments and suggestions at various stages of the project. Above all, we like to thank Iulia Traistaru-Siedschlag as the coordinator of the EURECO project for her sedulous engagement in bringing the project to success and thus providing the base for this book. Any responsibility for the results in the book, however, remains with the authors.

Christiane Krieger-Boden, Edgar Morgenroth and George Petrakos

1 Regional structural change and cohesion in the enlarged European Union

An introduction

Christiane Krieger-Boden and Iulia Traistaru-Siedschlag

In January 2007, with the accession of Bulgaria and Romania, the second round of the Eastern enlargement of the European Union (EU) has been completed, the first round of which was realised in May 2004 with the accession of Cyprus, the Czech Republic, Estonia, Hungary, Lithuania, Latvia, Malta, Poland, Slovakia and Slovenia. This is the most recent integration step in a series of subsequent steps since the foundation of the European Economic Community in 1957, other important steps being the Northern enlargement in 1973 admitting Denmark, Ireland and the United Kingdom, the Southern enlargement in 1981 and 1986 admitting Greece, Spain and Portugal, the Single Market Programme (SMP) in 1993, the EFTA enlargement in 1995 admitting Austria, Finland and Sweden, and the completion of the Economic and Monetary Union (EMU) in 1999. As before, this new advance of integration is likely to increase trade and factor mobility thereby intensifying interregional competition and affecting the interregional division of labour within the enlarged EU.

Over the past two decades there has been a growing interest in the analysis of spatial implications of economic integration via trade and foreign direct investment. The explanation for this increased interest is both theory and policy related. On the one hand, new theoretical trade and growth models offered new insights. Both traditional trade and growth models, based on constant returns to scale and perfect competition, as well as more recent models of economic geography and endogenous growth theory, based on increasing returns to scale and imperfect competition, interpret economic integration essentially as a reallocation of resources across sectors and space, and expect it to result in increasing specialisation of regional production structures. While these changes bring about aggregate efficiency gains, these gains may not be evenly distributed across space and sectors. In particular, the new theories describe the emergence or strengthening of an explicit core–periphery pattern with widening regional disparities. The continuing economic pressure from globalisation, increasing competition and restructuring within particular sectors could aggravate such asymmetric effects on regions. Since sectors tend to be concentrated in particular regions, industry-specific shocks could become region-specific shocks, and could pose a challenge to both regional and social cohesion.

On the other hand, although regional diversity is nothing new in Europe, the concern among policy-makers and the public about such uneven impact of economic integration on European regions has been growing: the deepening of economic integration is expected to result in winners and losers among the different regions. As achieving better economic and social cohesion is one of the European Union's priorities, the enlarged European Union may thus require a reorientation of cohesion policy at European, national and local levels for at least three reasons. First, the uneven distribution of the gains from integration may have a long-term impact on welfare. Second, the related regional structural change may imply short-term adjustment costs. Third, the integration-induced increase of regional specialisation may escalate the probability of industry-specific asymmetric shocks, which in turn has an impact on the net benefits of the European Monetary Union. All these impacts may affect the economic cohesion at the EU and national levels.

To get reliable information on the relevance of such concerns empirical studies in this field are essential. There are already several studies, most of them cross-country, in particular for EU-15 countries. However, the changes of detailed production structures at a regional level in the context of economic integration have been little investigated so far.

This book brings together the research results of a project on the impact of deepening and widening the European Union on regional structural change and cohesion.[1] The overall scientific objective of this project was to identify and explain in a cross-country analysis the impact of European integration and enlargement on regional structural change and cohesion. The analysis provides empirical evidence about the relationship between industrial location, regional specialisation and regional income per capita in the context of increased integration in the enlarged EU.

Our contribution to the literature is threefold: first, we bring novel empirical evidence on spatial implications of integration from EU-27 regions. Second, we use disaggregated national data sets with respect to both the sectoral and spatial levels, including firm-level data and comparable EU-27 data sets. The lack of disaggregation in the few previous studies severely reduces their usefulness for policy analysis since specialisation is a very localised phenomenon and cannot be picked up at the national level or macro-region level. Third, we combine the analysis of regional structural change with an analysis of the role of foreign direct investment in this process, fostering or dampening the agglomeration of economic activities.

After the theoretical and methodological background of our analysis is set out in this first chapter, the actual empirical evidence is presented in a series of country studies in Chapters 2 through 12. Chapter 13 investigates the spatial distribution of foreign direct investment (FDI) and the impact of this distribution on economic activity in the EU member states. Lessons and policy implications drawn from our analysis are discussed in the final chapter.

This introductory chapter is organised as follows: first, we discuss the common theoretical framework used in the chapters included in this book. Further, we explain the methodology applied in the country studies to uncover regional structural change including measures of polarisation, industrial concentration and regional specialisation. Next, we give an overview of empirical literature on regional structural change in the EU and discuss own calculations of measures of polarisation, regional specialisation and industrial concentration in EU-15 and EU-27. Finally, we present a brief overview of the remainder chapters.

Theoretical framework

Depending on their underlying assumptions, existing international trade theories point to different explanations for the location of economic activities and specialisation patterns across space. Thus, *traditional trade theory* (Ricardo, 1817; Heckscher, 1919; Ohlin, 1933) assumes perfect competition, homogenous products and constant returns to scale and focuses on differences in relative production costs, termed comparative advantage, as an explanation for the spatial distribution of economic activities. Assuming no trade costs, trade liberalisation is associated with a concentration of economic activities according to the comparative advantage of countries or regions.

Although relevant for a significant proportion of trade, comparative advantage fails to explain recent trends in trade and location of economic activities, such as trade between countries with similar economic structures and endowments and the uneven industrial development in developing countries (Venables, 1996). During the 1980s, new trade models were developed to explain intra-industry trade taking account of imperfect (monopolistic) competition, differentiated products produced under increasing returns to scale and trade costs (Krugman, 1980; Helpman and Krugman, 1985; Krugman and Venables, 1990). In particular, these models, known as *new trade theory*, point to the geographical advantage of large markets in attracting industries with increasing returns to scale.

More recent trade theory contributions, known as *new economic geography* models (Krugman, 1991a, 1991b; Krugman and Venables, 1995; Venables, 1996) point to the endogeneity of the advantage of large markets in attracting economic activities and focus on labour mobility and input-output linkages of firms as factors driving the spatial agglomeration of firms and economic activities. The implications for the location of economic activities in the context of falling trade barriers depend on the degree of economic integration given by the interplay between trade costs, market size and factor costs. Falling trade costs are associated with the disproportionate location of increasing returns activities in the large country (region) – the "core", while the constant returns activities will locate in the small country (region) – the "periphery". However, when trade costs are sufficiently low, factor costs gain importance and drive some firms to move back to the periphery where they can benefit from lower production costs. The relationship between spatial concentration of economic activities and trade costs takes an inverted U-shape. When tariffs are very high, competition in product markets is driving the location of economic activities, while very low tariffs imply that competition in factor markets become the driving force of the spatial distribution of economic activities (Ottaviano and Puga, 1998).

The upshot of this review of trade models is that all effects of integration depend crucially on the relative strength of centripetal and centrifugal forces and on the point of departure. Economic integration could ultimately bring about convergence of income per capita levels. Yet, if the centripetal forces were too strong to be balanced, or if integration came to a standstill at an intermediate stage of integration, the emergence and persistence of high regional disparities could remain a possible outcome. However, any expectation derived from theory depends on the empirical relevance of this theory.

The objective of this book is to provide empirical evidence and help to answer the following questions:

- What is the impact of European integration on regional specialisation and its change?
- What is the impact of regional specialisation on regional performance?
- What kind of region is affected by the structural change, and in what way?
- Is there evidence pro or contra the NEG predictions of integration jeopardising regional cohesion?

Measuring concentration and specialization[2]

The analyses of this book are mainly based on descriptive statistics, and the workhorse method applied is the measurement of polarisation, concentration and specialisation. This section will give a brief overview of the measures used in the present volume: on the industrial specialisation of regions (henceforth labelled "regional specialisation",) on the regional concentration of industries (henceforth labelled "industrial concentration",) and on the polarisation, which is a combined measure including both concentration and specialisation. If not indicated otherwise, the following discussion will concentrate on measures of regional specialisation for expositional convenience. The corresponding measures of industry concentration are obtained by just switching the indices for regions (r) and industries (i).

All measures covered are discrete measures. They measure the "dissimilarity" of the distribution of a population (e.g. workers in a region) across a finite set of mutually exclusive characteristics (e.g. the workers' affiliations to industries) from a predetermined reference distribution (e.g. the distribution of workers across industries in the EU as a whole).[3] They determine, for each industry, a value for the deviation between the region in question and the reference.[4] These deviations are "aggregated" over all industries into a scalar – the specialisation measure. Any such measure can be characterised by the *projection function* describing the assumed underlying type of distribution, the region- and industry-specific *weights* by which the observations are aggregated and finally the *reference distribution* as the benchmark to which an actual regional distribution is compared (Bickenbach and Bode, 2006).

The reference characterises the state of "no" or "no unusual specialisation" and constitutes the benchmark of the analysis. Two kinds of reference distributions will be used in the subsequent chapters, the uniform distribution, and the distribution of employment observed at a higher-level spatial aggregate such as a country or the EU. Using the uniform distribution as a reference implies that any deviation of observed industry shares from the average across all industries is interpreted as specialisation. This reference has frequently been used as a "neutral" reference in the measurement of income inequality. It allows for abstracting from differences between individuals in their abilities and opportunities for generating income. Measures using the uniform distribution as a reference are usually labelled "absolute measures" (see Haaland *et al.*, 1998). By contrast, using the distribution of employment observed at a higher-level spatial aggregate such as a country or the EU as reference implies assessing the extent and/or evolution of structural dissimilarity among the constituent spatial subunits of a country or the EU. This reference allows for controlling for a variety of external determinants of the structural composition of a regional economy, such as the general level of economic development, general comparative advantages, the regulatory framework and other institutional or political factors, or – in a dynamic perspective – global technological progress and global shocks. Measures using an observed distribution at the country or EU level as a reference are usually labelled "relative measures".[5]

The measures of regional specialisation and industry concentration used in the present volume are:

1 the coefficient of specialisation (frequently labeled "Krugman index");
2 the Herfindahl index;
3 the absolute Theil index;
4 the relative Theil index;
5 the topographic Theil index.

The coefficient of specialisation and the Herfindahl index are used here only as measures of regional specialisation; the topographic Theil index is a measure especially of industry concentration. The measures are defined as follows:

1 The **coefficient of specialization** for region r (CS_r) – also labeled "Krugman index" or "index of dissimilarity" – is defined as:

$$CS_r = \sum_{i=1}^{I} |l_{ir} - l_i|, \ 0 \leq CS_r \leq 2(1 - li^*). \tag{1}$$

$l_{ir} (= L_{ir}/L_r = L_{ir}/\Sigma_i L_{ir})$ denotes industry *I*'s share in total employment in region *r*, and l_i the same industry's share in total employment in the reference economy; and $l_i^* = \min_i l_i$ the employment share of the smallest industry in the reference economy.[6] The interpretation of the CS is easy and intuitive: A value of, say, $CS_r = 0.2$ means that a share of at least one tenth ($1/2 \cdot 0.2$) of a region's total work-force has to change sectors in order to get an employment distribution that exactly corresponds to the reference distribution. The CS is symmetric around zero in $l_{ir} - l_i$: an industry-specific deviation, $l_{ir} - l_i$, of a given absolute magnitude affects the measure to the same extent, irrespective of whether the industry is over- or underrepresented in region r. Another feature is that the CS is invariant against splitting up an industry into two parts – as long as the ratio l_{ir} / l_i is the same in both sub-industries. A potential shortcoming may, however, be that it is insensitive against shifts of employment among over- or underrepresented indus-tries, respectively: in contrast to most other measures, the CS does not change if employment shifts from, say, one underrepresented industry to another underrep-resented industry – as long as that industry remains underrepresented relative to the reference distribution.

2 The **Herfindahl index** of regional specialisation (H_r) is defined as:

$$H_r = \sum_{i-1}^{I} \left(l_{ir}\right)^2, \ 1/I \le H_r \le 1. \tag{2}$$

The Herfindahl index has no explicit reference distribution. By squaring the industries' employment shares, it is easily dominated by the biggest industries while smaller industries affect it only marginally. In contrast to the CS, the Herfindahl index is sensitive to splitting up an industry into two parts; its value changes even it the two sub-industries are identical.

3 The **absolute Theil index** (T^A) is defined as:

$$T_r^A = \frac{1}{I} \sum_{i=1}^{I} \frac{l_{ir}}{1/I} \ln\left(\frac{l_{ir}}{1/I}\right) = \sum_{i=1}^{I} l_{ir} \ln\left(I \cdot l_{ir}\right), \ 0 \le T_r^A \le \ln I. \tag{3}$$

The absolute Theil index compares the sectoral distribution of employment within the region r to the uniform distribution. Any deviation from the refer-ence share $1/I$ is deliberately interpreted as specialisation. The Theil index, which is a member the Generalised Entropy (GE) class (with sensitivity para-meter $\alpha \to 1$), meets specific axioms which define desirable characteristics of inequality measures (see Cowell, 1995; Litchfield, 1999, among others). Most notably, it is additively decomposable into components measuring the dissimi-larities within and between groups of industries. This feature may, for example, be useful for investigating the specialisation patterns within the manufacturing and the service sectors on the one hand, and between manufac-turing and services on the other. The Theil index is not symmetric around zero. It puts more emphasis on underrepresented industries, characterised by $l_{ir} < 1/I$.[7]

4 The **relative Theil index** (T^R) is defined as (Brülhart and Träger, 2005):

$$T_r^R = \sum_{i=1}^{I} l_i \frac{l_{ir}}{l_i} \ln\left(\frac{l_{ir}}{l_i}\right)$$
$$= \sum_{i=1}^{I} l_{ir} \ln\left(\frac{l_{ir}}{l_i}\right), \quad 0 \le T_r^R \le \ln(1/l_i^*). \tag{4}$$

Again, $l_i^* = \min_i l_i$ denotes the employment share of the smallest industry in the reference economy. As the right-hand side in the first row in (4) indicates, the relative (weighted) Theil index differs from the absolute (unweighted) Theil index (3) in two respects:

1   It compares each region-industry share (l_{ir}) to the corresponding share (l_i) in a reference economy rather than to the uniform value $1/I$, and;
2   it weighs each resulting summand by the industry-specific employment shares in the reference economy (l_i) rather than by $1/I$.

As argued by Brülhart and Träger (2005), and discussed in some more detail in Bickenbach and Bode (2006), the industry-specific weights, l_i, can be interpreted as reflecting the relative frequencies of sectoral activities at the level of individual workers: each worker in the reference economy, rather than each industry, enters the relative weighted measure with the same a priori weight. As a consequence, for given industry-specific deviations (l_{ir}/l_i), industries with larger shares in the reference are assigned higher weights than industries with smaller shares.

5 A variant of the relative Theil index, which may be used for analysing industry concentration, is the so-called **"topographic" Theil index**, defined by Brülhart and Träger (2005) as:

$$T_i^{TOP} = \sum_{r-1}^{R} a_r \frac{\lambda_{ir}}{a_r} \ln\left(\frac{\lambda_{ir}}{a_r}\right)$$
$$= \sum_{r=1}^{R} \lambda_{ir} \ln\left(\frac{\lambda_{ir}}{a_r}\right), \quad 0 \le T_i^{TOP} \le \ln(1/a_r^*). \tag{5}$$

a_r ($= A_r/A$; $r = 1, \ldots, R$) denotes region r's share in the total area covered by all R regions under investigation. In (5), an industry is overrepresented in regions where its employment density is higher than on average in the reference economy, i.e. $L_{ir}/A_r > L_r/A$ or, equivalently, $\lambda_{ir} > a_r$. Similar to (4), each region-specific deviation λ_{ir}/a_r is weighted by the region's relative size so as to assign the same weight to each square kilometer – rather than to each region.

6 A further useful species of measures are **polarisation measures** that evaluate industrial concentration and regional specialisation within an economy

simultaneously (Bickenbach and Bode, 2006). Polarisation measures are so far not very common in economic literature but better known from the sociological literature (used, for instance, in the analysis of racial segregation). Formally, they are straightforward generalisations of the proportionality measures discussed above. Rather than one row or column of the (IxR) matrix of region-industry employment, the polarisation measures evaluate all elements of the matrix. Polarisation measures can be calculated on the basis of most of the above-mentioned indices. In the following, two polarisation measures (T^{POL}) are defined based on the relative weighted Theil index, one describing the polarisation of the whole EU in one single scalar (6), the other describing the polarisation of a country C(7):

$$T_{EU}^{POL} = \sum_{i=1}^{I} l_i \sum_{r=1}^{R} l_r \frac{l_{ir}}{l_{EU}} \ln\left(\frac{l_{ir}}{l_{EU}}\right), \ 0 \le T_{EU}^{POL} \le \ln(1/l_i^*). \tag{6}$$

$$T_c^{POL} = \sum_{i=1}^{I} l_i \sum_{r=1}^{R_c} \frac{l_r}{l_c} \frac{l_{ir}}{l_c} \ln\left(\frac{l_{ir}}{l_c}\right), \ 0 \le T_c^{POL} \le \ln(1/l_i^*). \tag{7}$$

l_i , l_r , l_c, and l_{EU} denote the reference employment shares (usually the weighted averages) for an industry i, a region r, a country c or the EU as a whole. $l_{ir}^* = \min_{ir} l_{ir}$ denotes the employment share of the smallest region-industry unit in the reference economy. It is the charm of this measure that it allows decomposing the single overall characterisation of the EU (or country c) into its components to find out whether an actual degree of European polarisation originates from a similar polarisation of all countries and their regions across all industries, or rather by the extraordinary specialisation of a single country or region, or the specific concentration of a single industry. Such exercise allows then, to classify the subsequent results on specialisation and concentration within the countries analysed.

Compound results for EU-25 countries

While the country studies in Chapters 2 through 12 below will focus mainly on regional specialisation from a national perspective, this section will put the specialisation and concentration patterns of European countries and regions into a broader European perspective. The analysis of the structures and evolutions of regions on the background of a common, European benchmark facilitates comparisons across regional borders, and allows for assessing the relative strengths of local and national factors influencing the observed specialisation patterns.

Literature overview

The specialisation of EU regions in the course of increasing European integration has been an outstanding field of empirical research since the pioneering study by Molle (1980). The existing empirical studies differ in various respects (Table 1.1): they use different indicators, different aggregates for the reference distributions (total economy or manufacturing), different levels of sectoral disaggregation,

Table 1.1 Survey of empirical studies on specialisation and concentration

Authors	Geographical unit	Aggregate	Variable	Period	Indicator	Results
EU member states						
Hufbauer and Chilas, 1974	EU member states	Manufacturing industries	Employment	1960–1970	Shares	Specialisation +
Amiti, 1999	EU member states	65 manufacturing industries	Prod., empl.	1968–1990	Gini, σ[a]	Specialisation +, concentration +
Brülhart, 2001	EU member states	Manufacturing industries	Employment, trade	1972–1996	Gini, IIT[b]	Specialisation +, concentration + slowing down, yet single market concentration effect on spec. industries
Brülhart, 1998	EU member states	Manufacturing industries	Employment, trade	1980–1990	Gini, IIT[b], loc. coeff.	Specialisation +, localisation of IRS industries, concentration of labour intensive industries +
Midelfart-Knarvik et al., 2000	EU member states	Manufacturing industries	Production, trade	1980–1995	Krugman, Gini	Specialisation +, concentration +, at slow pace, as result of discrepant processes
Dohse et al., 2002	EU member states	20 manufacturing industries	Employment	1980–1995	Krugman	Specialisation + in 1980s, mixed evidence thereafter
Aiginger and Davies, 2000	EU member states	99 manufacturing industries	Production	1985–1998	Entropy index	Specialisation +, after 1992: ++, concentration +, after 1992: −−
Aiginger et al., 1999	EU member states	Manufacturing industries	Prod., empl., trade	1988–1998	Composite[c]	Specialisation +, concentration −
EU regions						
Molle, 1980	EU NUTS 2 regions	Large sectors	Employment	1950–1975	Krugman, loc. coeff.	Specialisation −
Molle, 1995	EU NUTS 2 regions	17 large sectors	Employment	1950–1990	Krugman, loc. coeff.	Specialisation −, concentration −
Krieger et al., 1985	F, D, I and UK NUTS 2	35–45 manufacturing industries	Employment	1970–1980	Shares	Specialisation −, concentration −
Brülhart, 1998	EU NUTS 2 regions	Manufacturing industries	Employment	1976–1985	Gini	Specialisation −, concentration −, localisation in periphery (mean reversion)

continued

Table 1.1 continued

Authors	Geographical unit	Aggregate	Variable	Period	Indicator	Results
EU member states						
Barrios and Strobl, 2004	EU NUTS 2 regions	Large sectors	Prod., empl.	1972–1995	Dumais[d]	Concentration +, yet by mean reversion and random industrial mobility
Brülhart and Träger, 2005	EU NUTS 2 regions	Large sectors	Prod., empl.	1975–2000	Theil, loc. coeff.	Concentration of manufacturing + (not in central regions), concentration of services +
Ezcurra *et al.*, 2004	EU NUTS 2 regions	17 sectors	Production	1977–1999	Krugman	Specialisation –, after 1990: +; convergence of specialisation
Paluzie *et al.*, 2001	Spanish NUTS 3 regions	30 manufacturing industries	Employment	1979–1992	Gini	Specialisation –, concentration –, both very slightly
Waniek, 1995	EU NUTS 2 regions	Large sectors	Employment	1980–1990	Absolute figures	Specialisation –, concentration –
Paci and Usai, 2000	EU NUTS 2 regions	11 manufacturing industries	Employment	1980–1990	RPA[e]	Concentration of innovative activities +
Hallet, 2000	EU NUTS 2 regions	17 large sectors	Production	1980–1995		Specialisation –
Möller, 2000	German NUTS 3 regions	Manufacturing industries	Employment	1987–1996	Shares	Specialisation –, concentration –
Leitner, 2001	EU NUTS 1 regions	10 manufacturing industries	Prod., empl.	1987–1998	CV[f], Gini	Concentration +, after 1992: –
Südekum, 2006	German NUTS 3 regions	28 sectors	Employment	1993–2001	Gini	Specialisation –, stable since 1997, concentration +, mixed evidence reg. modern industries
Akgüngör and Falcioğlu, 2005	Turkish NUTS 2 regions	22 manufacturing industries	Employment	1992–2001	Gini	Specialisation +, concentration–

Notes
a Standard deviation of locational coefficients.
b Intra-industry trade indices.
c Drawn from seven indexed indicators, i.e., Herfindahl, Krugman, concentration ratio, shares, standard deviation of shares, locational coefficients, Gini.
d Similar to Krugman, applying squares instead of absolute values.
e Revealed productive advantage.
f Coefficient of variation.

different geographical units, and different economic indicators (e.g. production, trade, employment). In spite of this considerable heterogeneity in the methods and data employed in the studies, the results are rather homogeneous and straight-forward across all studies.

To the extent that there are differences in the results, these can be attributed mainly to differing selections of areas and/or sectoral aggregates for investigation: the results for countries differ frequently from those for regions, and the results for specialisation across industries within the manufacturing sector differ from those for specialisation across sectors relative to the entire economy. By contrast, the specific time periods under investigation, the economic indicators, or the preferred specialisation measures appear to have a rather limited influence on the results.

Although specialisation patterns usually change at a fairly slow pace (Midelfart-Knarvik *et al.*, 2000), and the directions and magnitudes of their changes differ considerably between individual regions and countries under investigation, a few general trends can be observed:

- First, the division of labour has deepened between *European member states* as a whole, at least within their manufacturing sector; their specialisation has *increased* (Hufbauer and Chilas, 1974; Amiti, 1999; Brülhart, 1998, 2001; Midelfart-Knarvik *et al.*, 2000; Dohse *et al.*, 2002; Aiginger and Davies, 2000; Aiginger *et al.*, 1999).[8]
- Second, the specialisation of *European regions* across sectors (agriculture, energy, manufacturing, construction, services) as well as within the manu-facturing sector has tended to *diminish* since the 1980s (Hallet, 2002; Barrios and Stobl, 2004; Brülhart and Träger, 2005; Ezcurra *et al.*, 2004; Paluzie *et al.*, 2001; Paci and Usai, 2000; Möller, 2000; Leitner, 2001).

Specialisation and concentration results

Some of our research results on specialisation and concentration in a EU-wide perspective partly confirm and partly contradict these findings from other studies. Throughout the 1980s, we find that polarisation in the EU, as the combination of regional specialisation and industrial concentration, has decreased or remained constant (depending on whether measured in relative or in absolute terms). Begin-ning with the 1990s, however, the trend changed, and the process of diminishing polarisation has stopped. This development over the 1990s seems to accrue pri-marily from an increase of the concentration of large sectors, specifically, from an increase of the concentration of agriculture. This will be shown in what follows.

All own figures have been calculated on the basis of Theil indices for the polarisation, specialisation and concentration of total employment across regions and industries within the EU. As far as relative Theil indices are provided, they are weighted with EU-specific region and industry weights and refer to the EU as benchmark distribution (see above for explanations of the measures). The figures concern EU-15 for the years 1980–2003 and EU-25 for the years 1993–2003.[9] The database is provided by Cambridge Econometrics (May 2006 update) and allows for a breakdown of 246 NUTS2 regions and 15 NACE industries, including seven manufacturing and five service industries. For the sake of analysis, the industries will be aggregated to five large sectors: agriculture, manufacturing, construction, market and non-market services. Due to limited data availability, Cyprus as well as the accession countries Bulgaria and Romania had to be left out.[10]

Figure 1.1 displays the polarisation of EU-15 regions for the years 1980–2003 and of EU-25 regions for the years 1993–2003. Although reference is lacking, the general impression from the calculations is that polarisation in Europe seems not to be extraordinarily high. Moreover, polarisation seems to have decreased (according to the relative measure) or remained stable (according to the absolute measure) throughout the 1980s. Yet the calculations also reveal a trend break since the early 1990s, both in terms of the relative and absolute measure. Thus, the process of decreasing polarisation seems to have come to an end.

To get behind this evolution, Figure 1.1 also presents two decompositions of the absolute measure, to distinguish between- and within-countries components on the one hand and between- and within-sectors components of EU polarisation on the other.[11] This analysis is restricted to the years 1993–2003 to get comparable information on all EU-25 countries. The levels of the between component in both cases are not very informative: they simply reflect that not all EU countries and not all EU sectors are of similar size. More informative is the evolution over time: In the case of the decomposition between and within countries the value of the *between* component remains rather unchanged. Accordingly, the overall increase of polarisation seems to be driven primarily by the within component. In the case of the decomposition between and within large sectors the value of the *within* component remains constant. The polarisation increase seems to be driven almost exclusively by the between sectors component. Taken together, both cases show structural change to take place *within the EU countries* rather than between them, and *between the large sectors* rather than within them.

From this point of the analysis, there are two different paths to continue the investigation on the origins of EU polarisation: first, the *within-countries component* can be further dismantled to find out whether EU polarisation is rooted in the specific specialisation pattern of European countries and regions (cf. subsequent Figures 1.3 and 1.4). Second, the *within-sectors component* can be dismantled to find out whether EU polarisation is rooted in the concentration pattern of sectors and industries (cf. subsequent Figures 1.5 and 1.6). These paths end with information on country-specific indicators of regional specialisation and industrial concentration that will also be issued in the subsequent country studies albeit based on different, more detailed datasets and referring not to the EU but the respective countries as benchmarks.

Regarding the first path of investigation, the within-countries component of EU polarisation is defined as the weighted average from the polarisation values of the EU countries. Figure 1.2, therefore, displays the EU countries' polarisation values and their long-term evolutions.[12] Accordingly, average polarisation of the EU is determined by the particularly high polarisation of some countries

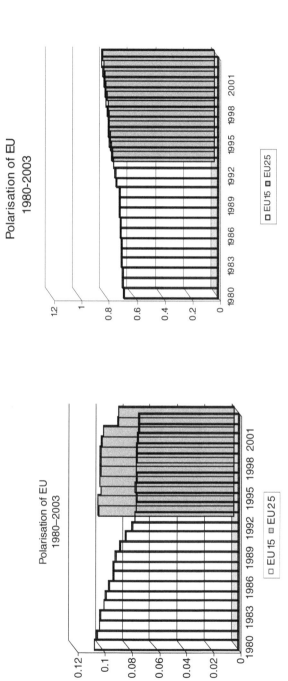

Figure 1.1 Polarisation of EU-15 and EU-25 by regions and industries: relative weighted (left-hand) and absolute (right-hand) Theil index and their decompositions within and between countries, and within and between sectors (source: Cambridge Econometrics – own calculations).

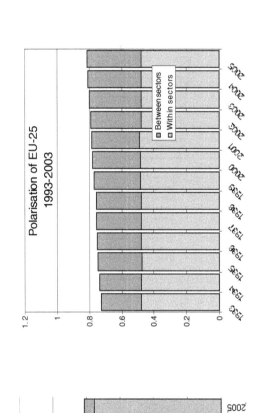

Figure 1.1 continued.

mostly from South or East Europe (highest in Greece, Poland, Portugal, Lithuania, high also in Luxemburg and Spain) and the low polarisation of most others (particularly low is the polarisation of Finland, Germany and France).

Regarding the evolution over time, polarisation decreased slightly in *all EU-25 countries* throughout the 1980s, yet the process has slowed down or has even reversed during the 1990s (this applies in the cases of the Netherlands, Luxemburg, Ireland and Portugal, if measured by the relative index as in Figure 1.2; it also applies for almost all countries if measured by the absolute index as in Figure 1.3). By contrast, polarisation remained more or less constant or decreased in most *East European countries* (with the exception of Poland).

This polarisation of each EU country can further be decomposed into between- and within-regions components (once again this is meaningful only in the case of the absolute measure: Figure 1.3).[13] Again, the analysis focuses on the years 1993–2003. The *between* and *within* components show in how far a country's polarisation is shaped by the concentration of economic activity across its regions (e.g. due to differing sizes of the regions, or due to a concentration of almost all activities in few central regions), or by the specific specialisations of these regions. Figure 1.3 shows the variation in countries' total polarisations to accrue primarily from the between-regions component. By contrast, the within-regions component appears to be fairly homogenous throughout all EU countries (takes usually a value between 0.4 and 0.6). Only, most countries from the Eastern enlargement reveal lower average specialisation degrees of their regions.

Over time, the between-regions component tends to remain more or less constant in most countries, except in the cases of Portugal and Greece. By contrast, the within-regions component increased in almost all countries. This indicates that structural change takes place almost exclusively within regions rather than between regions. Structural change thus seems to consist of a movement of

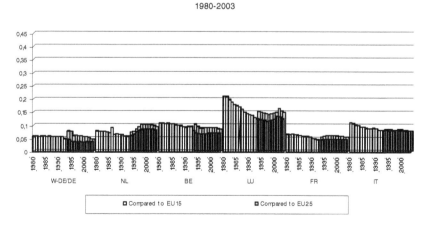

Figure 1.2 Polarisation of EU-15 and EU-25 countries, total economy by regions and industries – weighted relative Theil indices (source: Cambridge Econometrics – own calculations).

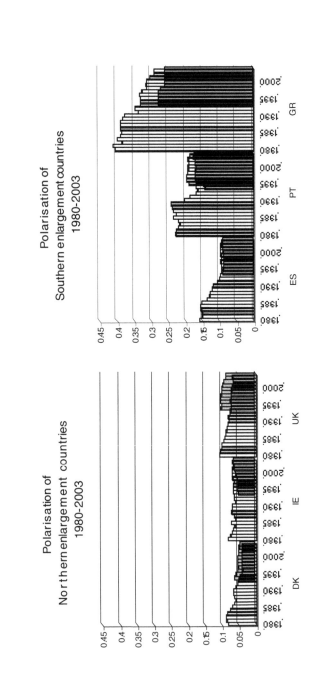

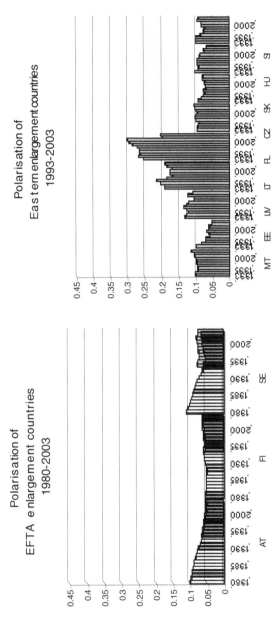

Figure 1.2 continued.

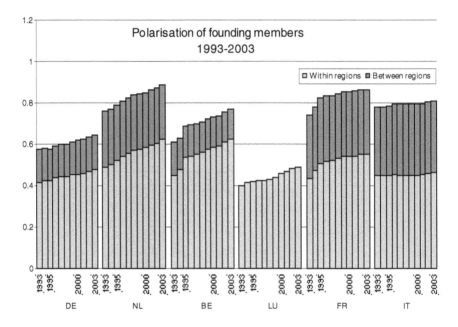

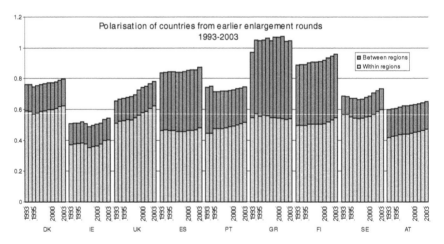

Figure 1.3 Polarisation of EU-25 countries, total economy by regions and industries: absolute Theil indices and their decomposition within and between regions (source: Cambridge Econometrics – own calculations).

workplaces *between industries within a region* rather than from one region to another. It is this changing specialisation of the regions of a country that will be further analysed in the case studies of this book.

Turning to the second path of investigation, the within-sectors component of EU polarisation is defined as the average polarisation across all large sectors in

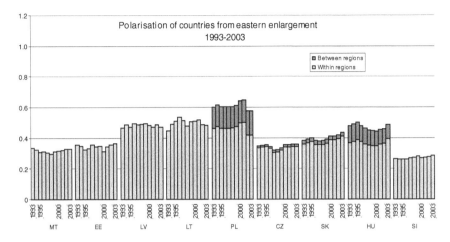

Figure 1.3 continued.

the EU. This polarisation of sectors is displayed in Figure 1.4 (cf. the columns as a whole). It shows (at least if measured by the absolute Theil index) that polarisation is particularly high for agriculture, manufacturing and market services. All these are known to exhibit a certain need for specific non-ubiquitous input resources, which may explain their higher polarisation. The index values are low

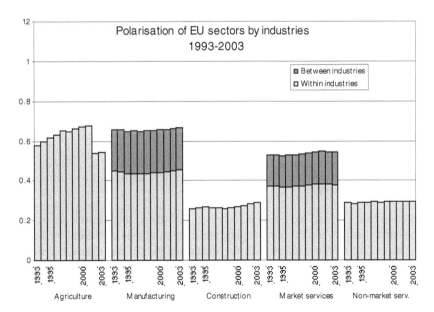

Figure 1.4 Polarisation of EU-25 sectors, by regions and industries: absolute Theil indices and their decomposition within and between industries (source: Cambridge Econometrics – own calculations).

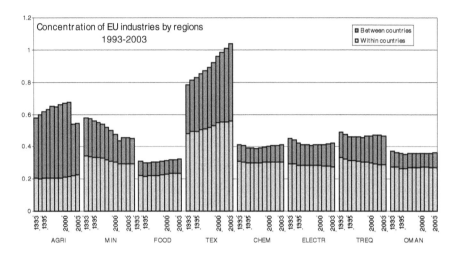

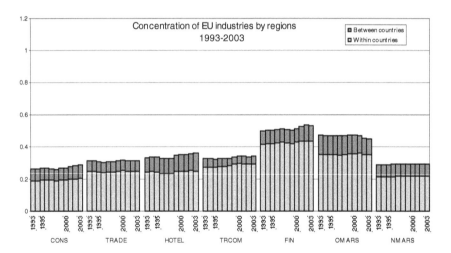

Figure 1.5 Concentration of EU-25 industries: absolute Theil indices and their decomposition within and between countries (source: Cambridge Econometrics – own
calculations).

for construction and non-market services. All these are known to be more
consumer-related, and this may explain their higher degree of dispersion. Regarding the evolution over time, Figure 1.4 shows that in line with the overall stability
of average sector polarisation, the polarisation of most sectors remains more or
less unchanged. Only the polarisation of the agricultural sector increases.[14]

The polarisation of sectors can be decomposed into a between- and within-
industries component (which is possible only for sectors with more than one industry, i.e. manufacturing and non-market services). The between and within
components show in how far a sector's polarisation is rooted in the specific special-

isation of an EU sector on its related industries (e.g. due to differing sizes of the industries as defined in the NACE industrial nomenclature), or by the specific concentrations of these industries. Figure 1.4 reveals the between-industries component, and hence the different sizes of industries, to contribute considerably to the polarisation of sectors. Still, the within-industries component rates manufacturing industries and market services higher than construction and non-market services regarding concentration degrees as is the case for total polarisation of these sectors.

Regarding the evolution over time, the between-industries component tends to remain more or less constant for the sectors. The within-industries component, too, changes very little, except in the case of agriculture. This indicates that, besides the agricultural sector, there is not much sectoral or industrial structural change at all taking place in the period under investigation. According to these calculations, *structural change seems to remain restricted to the slight concentrating of the agricultural sector.*

However, when moving one step further and dismantling the average within-industries component (Figure 1.5), some further structural change besides agriculture becomes observable: the overall stability of the manufacturing sector turns out to be the result of two opposite movements, the concentration decrease of the mining and energy sector, and the concentration increase of the textile industry. The decomposition shows these concentration processes to take place primarily from one country to the other, to a lesser degree from one region within a country to the other. Otherwise, the finding of small structural change is confirmed.

Core–periphery pattern in EU-25

We now return to the question raised by trade theories, particularly the NEG, whether integration leads to an explicit core–periphery pattern, where the core is highly specialised in modern IRS industries and the periphery is also highly specialised in few traditional backward industries, and whether this specialisation increases as integration proceeds. To answer this question, Figure 1.6 displays the specialisation degree of European regions along two longitudinal axes through the EU-25, one reaching from the utmost Northern part (Lapland) through the Scandinavian countries, North and West Germany, the Benelux countries, France and Spain to the utmost South Eastern part (Algarve), and the other reaching from the utmost Western part (Scottish Highlands and Islands) through Ireland and Great Britain, the Benelux, West and East Germany, the Czech Republic, Hungary, Austria, Slovenia, and Italy to the utmost South Eastern part (Crete). Regional specialisation is measured both by a relative and absolute Theil index (part a and part b of Figure 1.6), and the colours from yellow to red show the change of the pattern over time.

Some spatial dependency of the specialisation pattern can be observed from these graphs, particularly from the moving average (that is calculated here including seven neighbouring regions): on the one hand, specialisation seems indeed to be relatively high in the European centre around Belgium and the Netherlands (refers to both axes) and, moreover, in the English Midlands (refers to the West–East axis). Several, but not all, national centres also reveal high specialisation degrees, such as

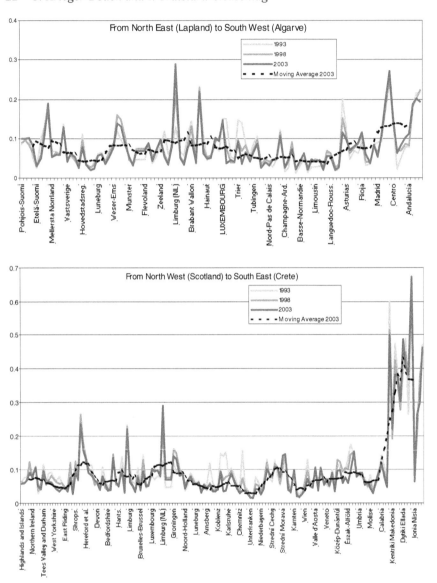

Figure 1.6a Longitudinal axes of regional specialisation in EU-25 – relative Theil
indices (source: Cambridge Econometrics – own calculations).

Copenhagen, Antwerp, Paris, Madrid and Lisbon. On the other hand, there is a
slight tendency for specialisation degrees to be higher on the two extremes of the
curve, in remote regions (more conclusive in the case of relative measures, and for
the North–South axis). Particularly high is the specialisation of Greek regions, at
least if measured with a relative index, i.e. in comparison to the European benchmark. Particularly low are the specialisation degrees of the Czech regions.

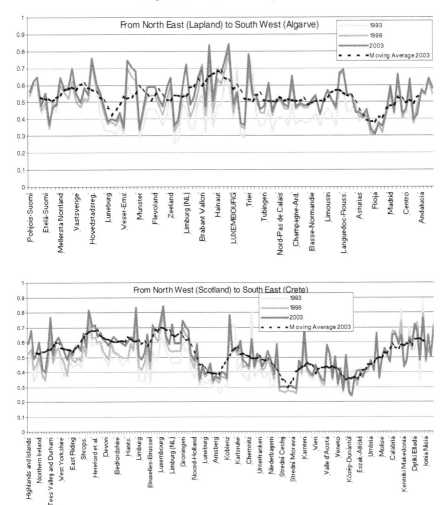

Figure 1.6b Longitudinal axes of regional specialisation in EU-25 – absolute Theil indices (source: Cambridge Econometrics – own calculations).

Over time, in line with the findings on overall polarisation in the EU-25 (Figures 1.2 and 1.3) no noticeable change is observable in terms of the relative specialisation measure, yet an explicit increase is observable in terms of the absolute specialisation measure. This latter increase concerns in particular the regions from older EU member countries, while the regions from the recently acceded countries rather reveal a decrease of specialisation.

Another conclusion from NEG would be that integration could *replace national core–periphery systems* by a unique Europe-wide core–periphery system. Yet from our calculations, no such trend can be detected, at least not for the given short observation period.

Introducing the subsequent analyses

To continue with the analysis, yet on a more detailed industrial breakdown, and based on national data, this book contains a number of country studies. The sequence of the country chapters is organised according to the length of the countries' membership in the EU. Each country chapter is put under a specific theme under the general topic of EU integration and regional structural change. Thus, the sequence starts with a chapter by Maria Giovanna Bosco on the EU founding member Italy; this chapter looks for the specific integration experience of a traditionally highly polarised country. Chapter 3 by Edgar Morgenroth analyses the particularly favourable Irish experience with the integration into the EU since 1973. Chapter 4, by Georgios Fotopoulos *et al.*, deals with the experience of Greece, which took part in the Southern EU enlargement in 1981. Chapter 5 by Christiane Krieger-Boden evaluates the experience of the Southern enlargement from 1986 on the then incumbent country France and the then acceded countries Spain and Portugal. Chapter 7 by Christian Fölzer and Bernd Brandl is dedicated to the experience of Austria, which acceded in 1995, together with Sweden and Finland, and which is characterised as a country at the interface between Western and Eastern countries. Chapter 8 by Christiane Krieger-Boden takes the German reunification (and simultaneous accession of East Germany to the EU) from 1990 as an anticipation of the Eastern enlargement. Chapters 9, 10 and 11 by Anna Wisniewski, Eva Kippenberg and Tamasz Szemler, respectively, analyse the experience of the Eastern enlargement countries Poland, Czech Republic and Hungary (accession in 2004). Chapters 12 and 13, by Anna Iara and Stoyan Totev, respectively, analyse the experience of Romania and Bulgaria that acceded in 2007. The country chapters are succeeded by a chapter by Laura Resmini on the role of FDI in the regional structural change in the European Union. In the final chapter, Edgar Morgenroth and George Petrakos conclude on the country studies and define the political challenges for the EU structural policy.

Conclusions

Trade theories predict that economic integration changes the international and interregional division of labour and increases specialisation. More specifically, the new economic geography (NEG) gives rise to expectations that integration might amplify agglomeration, support the emergence of an explicit core–periphery pattern, and lead to increasing disparities between regions. This could challenge the EU objective of regional cohesion.

Yet, the results of our empirical analysis on the EU presented in this chapter reveal only moderate structural changes:

- We find that polarisation in the EU has declined during the 1980s and has remained largely constant or has slightly increased during the 1990s.
- Polarisation often seems to be relatively high before a country accedes to the Union, and appears to decrease in these countries rapidly thereafter. By

contrast, polarisation seems to be a bit lower in the older member states and seems to increase in some of them during the 1990s.

- Structural change seems to take place *within the EU countries* and even *within the regions* rather than between them, and *between the large sectors* rather than within them. Structural change seems to consist mainly of an increasing concentration of agriculture.
- On the one hand, specialisation seems indeed to be relatively high in the European centre (particularly around Belgium and the Netherlands). Several, but not all, national centres also reveal high specialisation degrees. On the other hand, there is a slight tendency for specialisation degrees to be higher in remote regions.
- No evidence could be found that integration would *replace national core–periphery systems* by a unique Europe-wide core–periphery system.

In the country studies these issues will be analysed in more detail to confirm or contradict the overall results discussed in this chapter.

Notes

1 This research project entitled "The impact of European integration and enlargement on regional structural change and cohesion" (EURECO) was undertaken with financial support from the European Community's 5th Research and Technological Development Framework Programme, which is gratefully acknowledged.

2 Substantial contributions by Frank Bickenbach and Eckhardt Bode to this part are gratefully acknowledged. The usual disclaimer applies.

3 The characteristics may, in principle, be continuous rather than discrete, similar to the continuous measures of spatial concentration discussed in Duranton and Overman (2002), or Marcon and Puech (2003a, 2003b).

4 Thus, all measures take their minimum values if the sectoral distributions of the region in question and the reference are identical.

5 In their taxonomy of discrete regional specialisation (and industry concentration) measures, Bickenbach and Bode (2006) further distinguish between "unweighted" and "weighted" relative measures. Since unweighted relative measures are not used in the present volume this distinction will not be discussed in detail here.

6 In what follows, uppercase letters indicate absolute employment figures, lowercase letters employment shares. Moreover, 1 denotes an industry's share in total employment of a region. Likewise, 1 denotes a region's share in total national or EU employment of an industry. The corresponding CS for the industry concentration is consequently defined as $CS_i = \sum_{r=1}^{R} |\lambda_{ir} - \lambda_r|$, $0 \leq CSi \leq 2(1 - \lambda r^*)$. λr^* denotes the share of the smallest region in total national or EU employment.

7 See Cowell and Flachaire (2002) and Bickenbach and Bode (2006) for a more detailed analysis of the projection functions of various measures.

8 We are not aware of a study investigating national specialization patterns across sectors.

9 No data earlier than 1993 are available for the countries of the Eastern enlargement, and hence for EU-25.

10 Some separate calculations not presented here show Romania to be much more specialised than any other accession country compared to EU-27, and Bulgaria to be similarly specialised as Poland (which is quite high, too).

11 Such decomposition exercise is not informative in the case of the relative measure, as the between countries component equals zero: the between-countries component can be shown to be the concentration of the EU total economy across all countries, and this, by construction, equals exactly the reference distribution.

12 Noticeably, there are several obvious and substantial breaks in the data, for instance, in NL in 1986, in PL between 2001 and 2002 (this latter break even prevails to the figures on EU total polarisation, cf. the left-hand graph in Figure 1.1), and in DE and PT from 1994 to 1995. These breaks are most likely due to deficiencies in the data; as we have no further information we will not get into this issue in this chapter.

13 And such decomposition is not possible, of course, in the case of countries consisting of just one region, like Luxemburg, Malta, Estonia, Livland, Lithuania and Slovenia.

14 Another eye-catching feature of the polarisation of agriculture is the break in the data between 2001 and 2002. This break is caused by data on agriculture in Poland, where it concerns all Polish regions simultaneously. This can be inferred from the Polish figures in Figure 1.2 and Figure 1.4.

References

Aiginger, K. and S.W. Davies (2000). Industrial Specialization and Geographic Concentration: Two Sides of the Same Coin? Not for the European Union. University of Linz - Department of Economics Working Paper 23/2000.

Aiginger, K., M. Boeheim, K. Gugler, M. Pfaffermayr and Y. Wolfmayr-Schnitzer (1999). Specialization and Geographic Concentration of European Manufacturing. EU-Commission – Enterprise DG, Working Paper 1.

Akgüngör, A. and P. Falcioğlu (2005). European Integration and Regional Specialization Patterns in Turkey's Manufacturing Industry. Dokuz Eylül University Discussion Paper Series 05/01.

Amiti, M. (1999). Specialization Patterns in Europe. *Weltwirtschaftliches Archiv* 135: 1–21.

Arbia, G. (1989). Spatial Data Configuration in Statistical Analysis of Regional Economic and Related Problems. Dordrecht.

Barrios, S. and E. Strobl (2004). Industrial Mobility and Geographic Concentration in the European Union. *Economic Letters* 82: 71–75.

Bickenbach, F. and E. Bode (2006). Disproportionality Measures of Concentration, Specialization, and Polarization. Kiel Working Paper 1276. Kiel Institute for World Economics.

Brülhart, M. (1998). Trading Places: Industrial Specialization in the European Union. *Journal of Common Market Studies* 36 (3): 319–346.

Brülhart, M. (2001). Evolving Geographical Specialisation of European Manufacturing Industries. *Weltwirtschaftliches Archiv* 137 (2): 215–243.

Brülhart, M. and J. Torstensson (1996). Regional Integration, Scale Economies and Industry Location. CEPR Discussion Paper No. 1435, London.

Brülhart, M. and R. Träger (2005). An Account of Geographic Concentration Patterns in Europe. *Regional Science and Urban Economics* 35 (6): 597–624.

Cambridge Econometrics, Data delivery.

Cowell, F.A. (1995). *Measuring Inequality*. 2nd Edition. London: Prentice Hall.

Cowell, F.A. and E. Flachaire (2002). Sensitivity of Inequality Measures to Extreme Values. Discussion Paper No. DARP 60. London: London School of Economics.

Dohse, D., C. Krieger-Boden and R. Soltwedel (2002). EMU and Regional Labor Market Disparities in Euroland. In: J.R. Cuadrado-Roura and M. Parellada (eds). *Regional Convergence in the European Union*. Berlin, Heidelberg.

Duranton, G. and H. Overman (2002). Testing for Localisation Using Micro-Geographic Data. Discussion Paper 3379. CEPR Center for Economic Policy Research. London.

Ezcurra, R., C. Gil, M. Rapún and P. Pascual (2004). Regional Productivity and Inequality in the European Union. Paper presented at the 44th Congress of the European Regional Economic Association (ERSA) in Porto.

Haaland, J.I., H.J. Kind, K.H. Midelfart-Knarvik and J. Torstensson (1998). What Determines the Economic Geography of Europe? Discussion paper 98, 19, Norwegian School of Economics and Business Administration, Bergen.

Hallet, M. (2002). Regional Specialization and Concentration in the EU. In: E. Cuadrado Roura (ed.). *Regional Conseqence in the European Union: Facts, Prospects and Policies.* Berlin: Springer.

Heckscher, E. (1919). The Effect of Foreign Trade on the Distribution of Income. *Ekonomisk Tidskrift.* Reprinted in H. Ellis and A. Metzler (eds) (1949). *AEA Readings in the Theory of International Trade.* Philadelphia: Blakiston.

Helpman, E. and P. Krugman (1985). *Market Structure and Foreign Trade: Increasing Returns, Imperfect Competition and the International Economy.* Brighton: Harvester Wheatsheaf.

Hufbauer, G.C. and J.G. Chilas (1974). Specialisation by Industrial Countries: Extent and Consequences. In: H. Giersch (ed.). *The International Division of Labour – Problems and Perspectives.* International Symposium. Tübingen.

Krieger, C., C. Thoroe and W. Weskamp (1985). Regionales Wirtschaftswachstum und sektoraler Strukturwandel in der Europäischen Gemeinschaft. Kieler Studien 194. Tübingen.

Krugman, P. (1980). Scale Economies, Product Differentiation, and the Pattern of Trade. *American Economic Review* 70 (5).

Krugman, P. (1991a). *Geography and Trade.* Cambridge: MIT Press.

Krugman, P. (1991b). Increasing Returns and Economic Geography. *Journal of Political Economy* 99 (3) 483–499.

Krugman, P. and A. Venables (1990). Integration and the Competitiveness of Peripheral Industry. In C. Bliss and J. Braga de Macedo. *Policy and Dynamics in International Trade.* Cambridge: Cambridge University Press.

Krugman, P. and A. Venables (1995). Globalisation and the Inequality of Nations. *The Quarterly Journal of Economics* 110 (4): 857–880.

Leitner, W. (2001). Regional Concentration of Manufacturing in the US and the EU: A Comparative Approach with the Background of New Economic Geography. Unpublished.

Litchfield, J.A. (1999). *Inequality Methods and Tools.* London: London School of Economics (Download: http://www1.worldbank.org/prem/poverty/inequal/methods/litchfie.pdf).

Marcon, E. and F. Puech (2003a). Evaluating the Geographic Concentration of Industries Using Distance-based Methods. *Journal of Economic Geography* 3 (4): 409–428.

Marcon, E. and F. Puech (2003b). Generalizing Ripley's K Function to Inhomogeneous Populations. Mimeo (downloadable from http://e.marcon.free.fr/publications/index.htm).

Midelfart-Knarvik, K.H., H.G. Overman, S.J. Redding and A.J. Venables (2000). The Location of European Industry. Report prepared to the Directorate General for Economic and Financial Affairs, European Commission. Economic Papers 142, ECFIN/318/00-EN.

Molle, W. (1980). *Regional Disparity and Regional Development in the European Community.* Farnborough.

Molle, W. (1995). The Regional Economic Structure of the European Union: An analysis of Long Term Developments. Unpublished.

Möller, J. (2000). Spezialisierung du räumliche Konzentration der Wirtschaft in einem Europa der Regionen. *Raumforschung und Raumordnung* 28 (5): 363–372.

Möller, J. and A. Tassinopoulos (2000). Zunehmende Spezialisierung oder Strukturkonvergenz? Eine Analyse der sektoralen Beschäftigungsentwicklung auf regionaler Ebene. *Jahrbuch für Regionalwissenschaft* 20 (1): 1–38.

Ohlin, B. (1933). *Interregional and International Trade.* Cambridge: Harvard University Press.

Ottaviano, G. and D. Puga (1998). Agglomeration in the Global Economy: A Survey of the New Economic Geography. *The World Economy* 21 (6).

Paci, R. and S. Usai (2000). Technological Enclaves and Industrial Districts: An Analysis of the Regional Distribution of the Innovative Activity in Europe. *Regional Studies* 34 (2): 97–114.

Paluzie, E., J. Poris and A. Tirado (2001). Regional Integration and Specialization Patterns in Spain. *Regional Studies* 38 (4): 285–296.

Ricardo, D. (1817). *On the Principles of Political Economy and Taxation.* London: John Murray.

Südekum, J. (2006). Concentration and Specialization Trends in Germany since Reunification. *Regional Studies* 40 (8): 861–873.

Venables, A. (1996). Equilibrium Locations of Vertically Linked Industries. *International Economic Review* 37 (2).

Waniek, R.W. (1995). Sektoraler und raumstruktureller Wandel in Europa. In: H. Karl und W. Henrichsmeyer (Hrsg.), *Regionalentwicklung im Prozeß der Europäischen Integration.* Bonner Schriften zur Integration Europas 4. Bonn.

2 Specialization and concentration in a polarized country

The case of Italian regions

Maria Giovanna Bosco

Introduction

Italy is known as a country with a deep and lasting dualism between its Northern part and its South. The increase of European and global integration could influence this dualism, could contribute to a strengthening or weakening of it, since it tends to change the European and Worldwide division of labour not only between countries but between locations. Given this background, the chapter assesses the impact of such changing conditions in the international and European framework on regional cohesion in Italy and on the patterns of convergence.

The challenges that emerged for Italy and its regions in recent years are double-faced: on the one hand, Italy pays for the structural dualism between North and South, inherited from the past and never really solved by national policies. On the other hand, Italy as a highly industrialized country takes part in the dynamic structural change from a manufacturing-based to a service-based economy and in increased competition for those (traditional) manufacturing industries that historically represented the success of the Italian economy. The various stages of European economic integration that involved a growing number of partners for Italy inside the EU had initially the effect to strengthen the specialization of Italy on those sectors where relative comparative advantages could be exploited; but this held true only as long as countries with similar economic, population and demand characteristics entered the Union. Once the EU started opening her borders to East European countries, a growing competition forced many firms either to change their specialization, to re-orient their exports, or even to relocate to those new entrants where typically production costs were sufficiently lower. While this process characterized the 1990s, into the new century Italian production is now challenged particularly by East Asian countries (mostly China). The progressive reduction of international trade barriers exposed Italian firms to a sharp competition that affected in particular those regions in Italy's North-East and Centre that relied stronger than others on traditional manufacturing sectors. In contrast, the North-West and the South found some way out of the situation by turning to a more flexible production, further specialization and search for quality.

Evidently, increased cost competition from new entrants and price competition in international markets will continue to require a deep restructuring of the Italian economy that may slow the pace of growth. In response, this will justify policies that at a regional level try to promote innovation and technology transfer, as these are recognized as key issues for future growth of all European nations.

This chapter is organized as follows: it will start with some description of the dualism in the Italian economy and its evolution over time, it will then turn to a short overview on important policy measures, it will then analyse in some detail the evolution of the specialization of regions and the concentration of industries under the conditions of increasing integration, and it will end with some conclusions.

Stylized facts on value added, employment and openness

Value added

The typical North–South gap between Italian regions has remained evident through time in many respects. Per capita value added in the North has always been sufficiently higher than in the Centre and especially than in the South – this becomes obvious already from the graph below about the three typically used groups of Italian regions (Figure 2.1).[1]

Italy's economic structure is comparable to that of most other advanced OECD economies, with a diminishing primary sector and growing services, which contribute to more than two-thirds of gross value added. It is not, however, internationally very competitive in high-tech industries and in most service sectors, apart from tourism and design. Despite some progress in certain areas of the South, the North-South gap is still huge. The main dividing line is reflected by a historically high, relative specialization on industry in a narrow sense in the North and on agriculture in the South. High-tech industries tend to concentrate in the North of the country, while traditional sectors are relatively spread; the South of Italy has been historically more dependent on agriculture. Even in the underground economy, the North–South gap is evident: according to the most recent estimates by Istat (Istituto Nazionale di Statistica), it accounts for about 17 per cent of GDP in Italy as a whole, ranging from 30 per cent in the

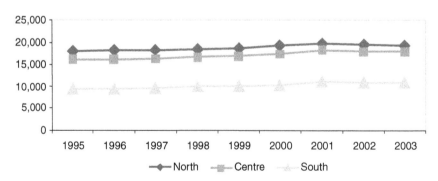

Figure 2.1 Value added per capita by groups of regions, constant 1995 prices (source: elaboration of ISTAT data).

Southern region Calabria to 8 per cent in the North. Underground businesses are widespread particularly in agriculture, construction and services.

Notwithstanding a few very large and quite dominant private companies, the strongest assets of the Italian economy are the clusters of small- and medium-sized, family-owned companies (SMEs) specialized in products of high-quality design and engineering. They are to be found in so-called industrial districts, mostly in the North-East and the Centre of the country. Average Italian firm size is the smallest among EU countries, but, with the exception of the machine tool industry, most SMEs produce high-quality consumer goods, including clothing, furniture, kitchen equipment and white goods. However, more recently, the global economic integration, particularly the low price competition from South-East Asia has challenged seriously not only the large enterprises of the automotive industry – and the regions relying on it – but also the traditional, export-oriented SMEs (particularly in the fields of textiles, garments, leather and shoes), and has made them vulnerable to acquisition by larger foreign firms seeking to obtain established Italian brands. Accordingly, Italian exports fell in all sectors in the last decade, even while world trade recovered globally. Italy's export share in world exports dropped from 4.5 per cent to 3.6 per cent between 1995 and 2002. In 2002, the contribution of net exports to GDP growth was −0.7 per cent. Still, sales abroad performed well in the metallic products branch, this effect being strongest in the North-Western regions. Low-technology industries continued to realize high export shares, particularly in Central and North-Eastern regions. The South benefited significantly from exporting oil derivatives, due to high world market prices.

Not surprisingly, productivity and the rate of employment were lower in the South than in the North. According to regional accounts for 2000–2001, within manufacturing (in a narrow sense), the value added for a standard unit of labour in the South was 86 per cent of the corresponding figure for the North–Central regions. Moreover, between 1995 and 2001, the productivity growth has been slower in the South than elsewhere.

What can be inferred about productivity cohesion among Italian regions? The available data allows for computing the standard deviation of GDP at regional level per unit of labour in 1995–2003. The results are shown in Figure 2.2.

The estimated trend reveals a growth path of 5 per cent in 1995–2003. A t-test of the average of the 1995 data against the 2003 data rejects the null hypothesis of equal means. Accordingly, the variance of regional GDP per unit of labour seems to have grown, so, as a first approximation, no sign of growing cohesion emerges.

Employment

The marked and persistent differences between regions are also reflected in the evolution of employment and unemployment.

Since the beginning of the 1990s, the number of people employed in manufacturing has fallen rapidly as a result of a process of industrial restructuring that is

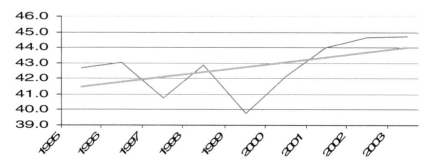

Figure 2.2 Standard deviations of regional GDP per capita and estimated trend, 1995–2003 (source: elaboration of ISTAT data, 2004).

still under way. In 2002, manufacturing employment was down to 31.8 per cent of the labour force. By contrast, as in most developed countries, the number of workers employed in the services sector increased continually, accounting for 63.2 per cent of the total workforce in 2002 and, as a result, the total number of persons employed increased, too. This trend has been particularly noticeable for the Centre (2.5 per cent), due not only to the role of services but also to the construction sector. Accordingly, the rate of unemployment in 2004 was 8.0 per cent, 0.4 percentage points less than 2003. The fall of unemployment involved all parts of the country including the South regions, and concerned only the Central regions to a somewhat lesser extent (Figure 2.3). This positive trend is largely attributable to employment growth, helped by a gradual labour market reform since 1998, particularly the introduction of measures favoring the use of part-time, fixed-term and other forms of flexible contracts. The observed patterns in valued added and employment suggest that, notwithstanding the poor performance

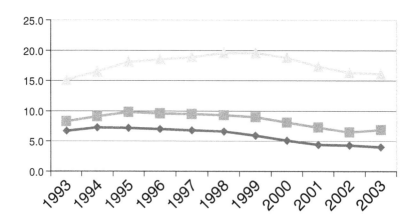

Figure 2.3 Unemployment rates by groups of regions, 1995–2003 (source: elaboration of ISTAT data).

of the economy as a whole, structural reforms undertaken by the national governments, particularly in the labour market, contributed decisively in decreasing the
unemployment rate.

Internationalization

The spatial division of labour, and thus the specialization of regions and the concentration of industries, is highly interrelated with the state of integration of
regions and industries into world markets. Italy is traditionally an open country,
whose growth in the 1980s was mainly driven by exports. When looking at
export orientation of regions and sectors, we find that openness varies significantly both with respect to regions and industries.

To measure the trade openness of Italian regions, export shares are displayed
in Figure 2.4. Once again, the North-South dualism stands out most remarkably:
Southern (and poor) regions like Calabria, Sicilia, Puglia and Campania reveal
particularly low openness. By contrast, Northern (and rich) regions like Veneto,
Piemonte, Lombardia, Friuli-Venezia Giulia and Emilia Romagna reveal quite
high openness, around 30 per cent of GDP. Yet, there are also some Northern
(and wealthy) regions like Lazio, Valle d'Aosta and Liguria, with very low
openness. These low export quotas may perhaps be due to the high significance
of the services sector.

To assess the sectoral foci of regional exports Balassa indices of specialization are calculated and displayed in Figure 2.5.[2] From these indices, one may
conclude on the relative competitiveness of the respective manufacturing industries in each area and, hence, on comparative advantages of regions.

According to this index, first, Northern regions appear less specialized than
Central and Southern regions, as the indices are close to one for all industries.
Second, Central regions are highly specialized in leather and footwear, and in

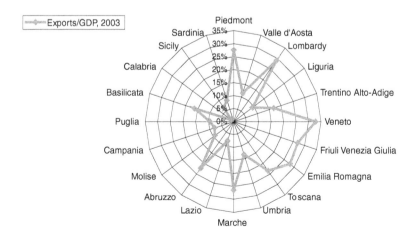

Figure 2.4 Index of trade openness, 2003 (source: elaboration of ICE–ISTAT data).

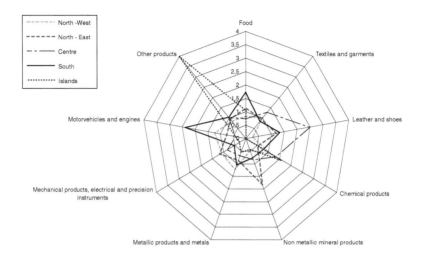

Figure 2.5 Exports index of specialization: macro-regions and manufacturing sectors, 2004 (source: elaboration of Banca d'Italia data).

textiles and clothing, taking advantage of the fact that these exports grew in value while declining in quantity. Third, the exports of mechanical products (including high-tech products), are slightly higher than average only in the North-East and North-West, while they are almost zero for the South. Fourth, the export pattern of the South, by contrast, seem to be more specialized in traditional industries (food, textile and garments) and in the automotive sector.

Turning to the development of the export pattern in recent years, almost half of the export growth in 2004 could be attributed to the mechanical and metallurgic sector, while the export of consumer goods decreased. A sharp increase in the prices of traditional sector exports was observed, perhaps due to quality gains. This development favoured in particular the North-East (except Veneto) and the South, where exports grew most rapidly in 2004. From the above-mentioned so-called industrial districts, formed by family-owned SMEs mostly in the North-East and the Centre, the best results were obtained by those specialized in machinery at the base of the value added chain, while traditionally specialized districts were hit heavily by the intensified competition from East Europe and Asia.

Italy does not have a good record regarding attractiveness for foreign investors. Inward FDI decreased steadily in the past years, making Italy drop from the seventh to the eighth position in Europe as a recipient of investment from abroad. Moreover, the sectors preferred by foreign investors are still the traditional sectors and the public utilities (in the course of privatizations). This trend strengthens the maintenance of a traditional production structure in the country. In turn, the persistence of small-sized firms and fragmented markets may be a possible reason for the disappointing performance of inward FDI in Italy. Another implication follows straight: investment in innovation and R&D

are often financed by large multinational companies from abroad via FDI, and accordingly, a lack of inward FDI implies a lack of inward technology transfers, leaving the country in a position of backwardness compared to main EU partners.

These general trends regarding the openness and competitiveness of Italy also provide some insight into the reasons for regional differences in Italy's production structure, particularly because of the historical gap between North and South, as evidenced by a broad literature (e.g. Bollino and Signorelli, 2003; Marrocu *et al.*, 2000; Istituto Tagliacarne, 2001). Some empirical studies assess differences in the production functions across different geographic areas. These differences interact adversely with an inadequate and centralized institutional framework worsening regional differences in economic competitiveness and employment performance. While until the 1970s a certain degree of convergence was observable, from the 1980s onward divergence has become the rule. Favourable initial conditions and closer international linkages led to a relocation of productive facilities and a concentration of investment, output and human capital particularly in the North–West (Dunford, 2001).[3] Moreover, Southern regions were affected by a negative impact of agglomeration economies that led many large industrial firms to relocate towards Central Europe to serve an integrated market that has also been expanding towards Eastern Europe.

Selected policies affecting the industrial performance

Privatization policies

As the scope for state activity has tightened over the past decade due to increasing deficits and due to growing competences of the EU institutions, consequently, the role of the Italian state in the economy had to be reduced. Accordingly, a wave of privatizations was initiated: the Istituto di Ricostruzione Industriale (IRI), the ENI, the Istituto Nazionale delle Assicurazioni (INA) and the Ente Nazionale per l'Energia Elettrica (ENEL) were transformed into joint stock companies; the two major IRI-owned commercial banks were floated on the stock exchange: Credito Italiano in 1993 and Banca Commerciale Italiana in 1994.

Subsequently, also Telecom Italia and Società Autostrade,[4] the motorway operator, were partially privatized. Since 2000, the privatization programme has slowed; still, the government sold its controlling stakes in Finmeccanica, the Rome airport services company, Aeroporti di Roma and residual stakes in several banks, including the Banco di Napoli. In February 2001, the Treasury sold further tranches of ENI, of Telecom Italia and of Ente Tabacchi Italiano (ETI), which controls about 25 per cent of the domestic cigarette market.

All these privatizations served theoretically to increase competition and enable market access to new entrants; they were supposed to guarantee better market conditions for the consumers. Unfortunately, this was not always the case. The lack of transparency in the way that many new entrants offered their services in the formerly state regulated markets did not always increase efficiency but led to higher prices and much confusion for the final consumers.[5] Therefore, the final outcome of the privatizations is not yet totally clear.

R&D policy

It is widely agreed upon in the recent debates about stagnation and competitiveness that innovation and technological transfer are key issues to future growth and development. Innovation has become a priority for all EU governments, not only at a national but also at a regional level. Digital technologies and ICT require more and more investments by enterprises in research activities and in the training of the workforce. According to the European Innovation Scoreboard,[6] Italy ranks below the average of EU countries regarding the main indicators of innovative capacity.

The calculation of a "Regional Summary Innovation Index" (RSII)[7] shows that in most European countries less than one-third of the regions perform above the country mean with respect to innovation activities. This confirms that national innovative capabilities tend to be concentrated in a few regions. In Italy, the percentage of innovating regions is low. Also, the percentage of innovating firms (with at least ten employees) has barely reached 38 per cent on average in 1998–2000, the lowest figure after Spain among those European countries. The same figure is 60 per cent in Germany and about 50 per cent in Finland, the United Kingdom and Portugal. Once again, the North-South dualism of the Italian economy becomes manifest: the percentage of industrial innovating firms is 41 per cent in Northern Italy, while it is 36.5 per cent in the Centre and 25 per cent in the South.

Innovating ability grows with a firm's size. According to the Banca d'Italia's survey on industrial firms, the percentage of innovating firms reaches 78 per cent for firms with at least 200 employees and 65 per cent for those with 50–199 employees. The SME-based, fragmented structure of the Italian economy, particularly in its Southern parts, seems to be detrimental to innovative activities.

However, the weak presence of high-tech industries in Italy and the sluggish innovative process are also due to a lack of resources, public and private, devoted to research and development. According to Istat information, in 2000, R&D expenditure in Italy has been slightly below 12.5 billion €, and 1.1 per cent of GDP (compared to 1.9 per cent on average of EU countries, according to OECD estimates). In North-Western countries and in the Centre, the expenditure as a percentage of GDP has been 1.3 per cent and 1.4 per cent, in North-East and in the South 0.8 per cent, respectively.

Lombardy is the Italian region that performs best in terms of R&D expenditure and share of patents at the European Patent Office. Moreover, Lombardy's recent regional policy has made a dramatic change in its innovation and technology policies. Together with Baden-Wurttemberg, Generalitat de Catalunya and Rhone-Alpes, Lombardy has formed a workgroup called "Four Engines for Europe", whose aim it is to propose themselves as examples of excellence in economic performance and institutional evolution in the EU. This initiative is built on the presumption that economic and political progress depends on local policies to a considerable degree.

More generally, there has traditionally been a divide regarding regional innovation policies: while in the South the first move had to be initiated by national interventions, in the North private firms and universities took the lead due to own initiatives. In any case, there was, in the 1990s, much scope to increase efficiency in the innovation and technology diffusion process by improving the networking among stakeholders of innovation and knowledge creation: actually, the Northern regions progressed more rapidly into this direction than the Southern ones. The technological gap between both will increase further unless the Southern and Central regions do not adopt new, more coherent innovation policies. A broader convergence in innovation policies is necessary to make all regions achieve a competitiveness similar to their most competitive European neighbours.

Regional policy

Turning to regional policy, the most problematic issue in the Italian economy has always been the North–South gap. The large and persistent gap in productivity, employment and infrastructure seemed to call for continuous interventions for the Southern regions, while the other regions received only marginal funding according to regional policy programmes by the central government. However, the interventions targeting the South actually did neither contribute to closing the gap to the Central and Northern regions, nor did they help improving significantly the economic structure of the South.

A main criticism addressed to the policy-makers concerned the type of aids and grants applied: to a large extent, they were awarded as unconditional transfers (also dubbed as "rain interventions") to local administrations rather than as project-specific funds, and the whole process completely lacked monitoring on the results. Another typical instrument of intervention took the form of exemptions from fiscal or social security contributions.

In 1994 the European Commission banned the traditional Italian system of government subsidies via social security exemptions to firms in the South, as it was regarded a breach of EU competition law. In January 1995, Italy agreed to a gradual phasing out of these exemptions, potentially increasing labour costs in the South by an estimated 20 per cent and highlighting the need for wage differentiation with the North. However, the South is eligible for investment incentives from the EU Regional Development Fund and the Italian government, and in 1998 the European Commission agreed to ease restrictions on tax and social security exemptions.

Specialization and concentration analysis

Specialization of regions: indexes and interpretation

In order to assess in which way Italian regions are embedded into the international and interregional division of labour during times of increasing integration, indicators of regional specialization are applied, as measured by employment. These measures indicate whether a region depends on a small number of major industries or rather possesses a wide diversification of different industries. The indicators can be defined either as absolute or relative measures, where the former compares the specialization of a region to a zero- or equal-shares distribution, and the latter to a given reference distribution. In the following, separate statistics both for absolute specialization and relative specialization (referring to the national average) for Italian regions are provided, allowing for further comments to the previous statements about the production structure and regional gap.

A commonly used index of absolute specialization is the Herfindahl index of regional specialization. It sums up the squares of industry shares in the total activity in the region. It takes values between zero and one and is positively related to regional specialization. Given its reference to a zero-shares distribution, the sum of the squares of shares is biased towards larger regions. It is defined as[8]:

$$H_j^s = \sum_i (s_{ij}^s)^2 \quad s = \text{shares}, j = \text{region}, i = \text{industry (sector, branch)}$$

where s_{ij}^s represents the share of employment in industry i in region j in total employment of region j. Figure 2.6 shows the Herfindahl index of absolute specialization for Italian regions in 2002.

By and large, one may infer from Figure 2.6 a certain confirmation of the dualism between North and South, and this result is in line both with the above

Figure 2.6 Herfindahl index of absolute specialization, 2002 (source: elaboration on ISTAT data).
Note: Lighter grades of shading stand for lower specialization.

results on the different levels of regional development and with the above results on the different export dynamics. Southern regions like Calabria, Sicilia, Sardegna and Puglia appear to be heavily specialized, while Northern regions like Emilia Romagna, Veneto, Marche, Abruzzi and Umbria seem to have a more balanced industrial structure. However, there are also highly specialized regions to be found in the Centre (Lazio) and in the North (Liguria). Southern regions are much more tied to specific industries that might have been less successful in recent years.

Calabria is the region with the highest degree of absolute specialization. Calabria relies heavily on agriculture compared to other Italian regions. Moreover, Gioia Tauro, near Reggio Calabria, is an important and booming port of the Mediterranean Sea that also attracts specific associated commercial activities. Lazio ranks second: this can be explained by the massive presence of public administration activities that concern the national government and related institutions. Liguria ranks third, probably because of the Genova maritime commercial traffic; Sicily, Sardinia and Puglia are traditionally specialized in tourism and agriculture.

Information on the change of this industrial panorama can be drawn from Figure 2.7, where the Herfindahl index is plotted for 1995 and 2002. In eight years, the index has remained almost stable. However, a certain trend towards convergence of regional specialization may be observed, as lowly specialized regions tended to become more specialized, and highly specialized regions tended to become less specialized. This trend does not apply to the highly and increasingly specialized regions of Lazio and Liguria.

A relative specialization indicator is provided by the so-called Krugman specialization index (see for example Hallet, 2000) that sums up the absolute

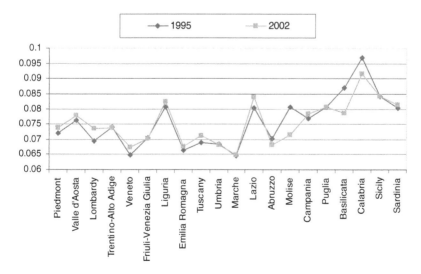

Figure 2.7 Herfindahl index of absolute specialization, 1995 and 2002 (source: elaboration on ISTAT data).

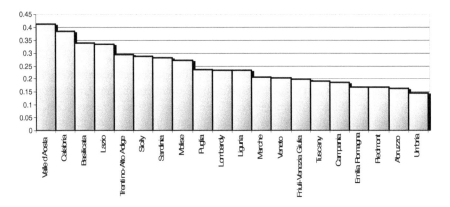

Figure 2.8 Krugman index of relative specialization, 2002 (source: elaboration on ISTAT data).

difference of the industrial structure of an observation region k and a benchmark region l:

$$K_{jl} = \frac{1}{2} \sum_i \left| s_{ik} - s_{il} \right|$$

The index is zero if the two regions compared have the same industrial structure. Its maximum value is 1 if the two regions do not have common industries. In this case each region's economic structure is compared to Italy's economic structure; that is, each region is compared to the structure of the economy as a whole. Results are reported in Figure 2.8.

An intuitive way to interpret this index is to think of a distance: the higher the values in the histogram, the more a region's industrial structure differs from the average structure. In comparing these results to those found for the Herfindahl absolute index, some qualifications apply: the results do not so much confirm the dualism between North and South than rather a certain dualism between relatively smaller regions (some of them with a specific status of autonomy) that are more specialized and relatively larger regions that are less specialized. One interpretation is that smaller regions are simply less likely to reveal the same degree of variation than large regions. Another interpretation is that relatively large regions like Umbria and Abruzzo are much closer to the average Italian specialization measure than smaller regions. Besides these more technical interpretations, it appears that the regions with the largest physical distance from a theoretical "centre" seem to be most specialized. These are apart from Valle d'Aosta (which is one of the richest regions with a very small population) the regions in the South and the Islands (Figure 2.9).

Comparing the index values for 1995 with those for 2002 (Figure 2.10) confirms the basic stability of the specialization pattern. For the Southern regions, however, displayed on the right–hand side of the graph, relative specialization has slightly decreased between 1995 and 2002. Although some differences

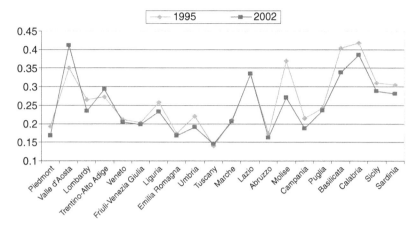

Figure 2.9 Krugman index of relative specialization, 1995 and 2002 (source: elaboration on ISTAT data).

remain between the regions in the North and the Centre on the one hand, and the South on the other, this general trend, may be interpreted as the South's production pattern approaching towards the Italian average during these years. As for the other regions the index is almost stable, a certain convergence of specialization degrees among Italian regions seems to have taken place.

Concentration of industries: indexes and interpretation

Concentration indices provide some information on the spatial distribution of industries across regions. They thus indicate whether industries tend to cluster together in certain areas or whether they tend to locate genuinely dispersed across space. As in the case of specialization, two different indexes are calculated: an absolute and a relative index of concentration. The analysis was carried at the maximum level of disaggregation available for the employment data in 2002.

A commonly adopted measure of absolute concentration is the Herfindahl Concentration Index; it takes into account the absolute number of employees per region and per country and is calculated as the sum of the regions' shares in national employment in a particular industry:

$$H_i^C = \sum_j (s_{ij}^C)^2 \quad s = \text{shares}, j = \text{region}, i = \text{industry (sector, branch)}$$

Being computed as the square of a share, it ranges between zero and one (Figure 2.10).

The general outcome of Figure 2.10 is that industry as a whole and manufacturing in particular appear more concentrated than services and agriculture. The index reaches almost 20 per cent of its maximum value for the most concentrated sector, that is the set of oil-related activities. This industry,

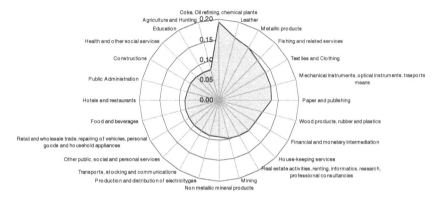

Figure 2.10 Herfindahl index of absolute concentration, 2002 (source: elaboration on ISTAT data).

being characterized by considerable scale economies, is quite obviously at the top of the ranking. On the other hand, employment in agriculture is highly dispersed, as it is bound to the availability of soil. Within the relatively highly concentrated sector of industry, construction is the one to be least concentrated. This may be accounted to the fact that the typical firm size in this branch in Italy is quite small, often consisting of a single entrepreneur. There are few large construction companies, but it seems that this activity is still very embedded in the territory, and proximity and trust still play a role in determining the related demand.

By contrast, within the typically quite dispersed services sector, the financial intermediation branch is the one to be most concentrated. These last years in Europe have been characterized by an increasing degree of concentration among banks and financial institutions, both at national and international level, as required by the rules of international competition. If the process of the acquisition of East European banks by West European financial institutions is also considered, the process becomes even more evident.

Comparing the indices for 1995 and 2002, a high degree of stability emerges, as already observed for the specialization pattern (Figure 2.11). This stability may indicate, on the one hand, that each industry is concentrated adequately and there is little need for change in spite of increasing integration and globalization. Yet, on the other hand, the general impression of slow structural change may also reflect low intersectoral mobility of workers due to severe labour market barriers, and a general policy attitude towards the preservation of existing structures.

As a measure of relative concentration of industries, the Dissimilarity Index of Geographical Concentration (DCR) is applied, which sums up the absolute differences between the regional and the national shares in total employment in a particular industry, thereby taking the national share of an industry in total employment as a benchmark to which regional shares are related. As seen above

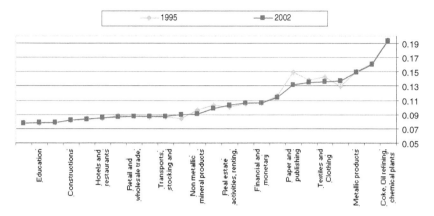

Figure 2.11 Herfindahl index of absolute concentration, 1995 and 2002 (source: elaboration on ISTAT data).

with respect to the Krugman measure of specialization, this index can be interpreted as a distance measure.

$$DCR_i = \sum_j \left| s_{ij}^C - s_j \right|$$

where s_{ij}^C represents the share of employment in industry i in region j in total employment of industry i.

The index is zero in case of equal distribution of the particular industry across regions and increases up to a maximum value of two the more the respective industry is concentrated in a few regions. Results for the DCR are shown in Figure 2.12. This index should be interpreted as follows: the longer the segment, the less concentrated is the sector, in that the share of employment in a given sector is quite far from the national average.

The results show the real estate and trade branches to be the relatively least concentrated industries, while the leather manufacturing branch appears to be the relatively most concentrated industry. While for trade, which is spread across the country in different forms and organizations, a low concentration level is quite intuitive, the high concentration of the leather manufacturers is to be seen in relation to the requirement of huge quantities of water that are needed to treat leather. That is, the leather-manufacturing branch is an industry with high economies of scale, and it is therefore highly concentrated in water-abundant districts (e.g. around Florence or near Lake Garda). A similar reasoning applies for the oil derivatives branch, which, too, is an industry with high economies of scale, as has been observed already from the absolute concentration index. More generally, in line with the observations from the absolute concentration index, manufacturing industries prove to be more concentrated and services prove to be less concentrated. Agriculture, however, quite different to the absolute concentration measure, is rated to be highly concentrated by this relative concentration measure. As agriculture is bound to soil, it tends to be particularly

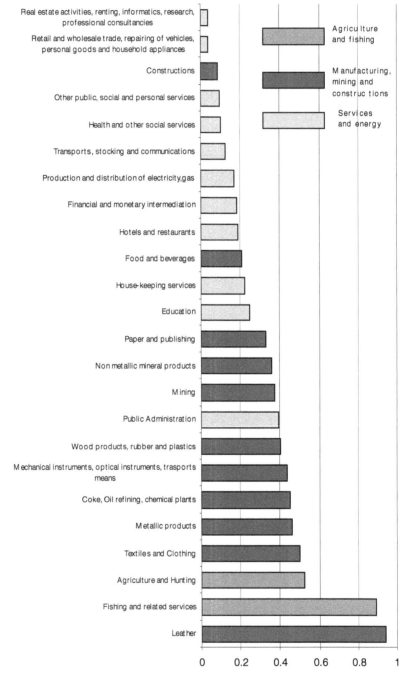

Figure 2.12 Dissimilarity Concentration Index (DCR), 2002 (source: elaboration on ISTAT data).

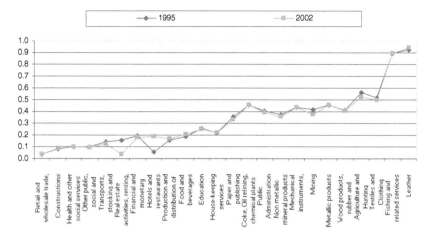

Figure 2.13 DCR relative concentration index, 1995 and 2002 (source: elaboration on ISTAT data).

significant where there is no other economic activity around, and particularly insignificant in the presence of lots of other economic activities.

In an intertemporal perspective, the DCR index in 1995 and 2002 is reported in Figure 2.13. The index remains quite stable in the period considered; the only noticeable change concerns the service sector, where the trade industry becomes less concentrated and the hotels and restaurants industry becomes instead more concentrated. This last movement can be explained by the increasing interest shown by multinational companies during the last years in managing whole sets and chains of hotels and resorts in those countries for which tourism is a comparative advantage.

Considering the analysis on openness, specialization and concentration together allows us to draw some general conclusions. First, the most open regions are not necessarily the most specialized. Indeed, openness seems related to the valued added per capita rather than to specialization. Just consider that in absolute terms Calabria is one of the most specialized regions, but its international position in terms of exports is quite below the other regions in the North. Second, high specialization seems to coincide to some extent with high relative concentration in some industries: for instance, Liguria and Lazio turn out to be absolutely very specialized and this relates to the high concentration of administrative and port activities of these areas. For some regions only, relative specialization (in services sectors, in this case) and concentration are positively correlated.

Conclusions

The objective of this chapter was to give a picture of Italy's broad economic and structural characteristics in the framework of increasing European integration and worldwide globalization, and to provide an insight of the specialization of regions and the concentration of sectors within this setting.

Similar to most other OECD and EU countries, the Italian economy is characterized by a growing tertiary sector and by a retrenching secondary sector, while the primary sector's share in GDP has remained more or less stable. The particular strength of the Italian economy has traditionally been in manufacturing, especially thanks to small- and medium-sized firms specializing in products that require high-quality design and engineering. However, despite being traditionally export-oriented, these SMEs now face the serious challenge of global economic integration and increased competition.

Regarding the spatial structure of the Italian economy, the traditional and well-known dualism between the Italian North and Centre and the South still exists, in terms of productivity, employment and wealth. This dualism concerns also the main findings from the analysis of regional specialization. The Southern regions Calabria, Sicily and Lazio prove to be the most specialized in absolute terms. In terms of relative specialization (in terms of "distance" from a national average), some Southern regions like Calabria and Basilicata appear highly specialized, but also the particularly small region of Valle d'Aosta, situated at the Northern periphery. The analysis of industrial concentration shows services to be relatively less concentrated than manufacturing, except for some service branches like financial intermediation, that are going through a progressive phase of aggregation of companies. Those manufacturing sectors whose processes are characterized by high economies of scale (as the leather industry) are relatively highly concentrated.

Apart from a slight convergence of the degrees of regional specialization, the pattern of specialization and concentration did not change much during the recent years of the observation period.

Moreover, the process of EU integration seems to have had no particularly favourable impact on the cohesion of Italian regions. On the contrary, while the pattern of specialization and concentration remained largely unchanged, exports fell, and employment rose only thanks to the creative accounting of the "employed" population by new definitions of part-time and innovative contracts. As a consequence, cohesion in terms of convergence to similar levels of GDP per capita does not seem to increase, but to decrease. Yet, those Southern regions that still lag behind in terms of economic development turn out to be dynamic in responding to the new challenges of international competition, occasionally beating the performance of Northern regions in terms of exports records.

To conclude, for a polarized country such as Italy, the recent trend did not bring any significant structural change (relative weight of employment by sector) or higher cohesion. The economic structure has been subject to some change in recent years, probably more as an answer to the tertiarization process under way all over the world than as a reaction to EU enlargement. Regional convergence of GDP per capita seems to have decreased, but again, it is difficult to attribute this trend to EU integration alone or to a higher global competition.

The permanence of a deep divide among groups of regions through time indicates that subsequent phases of European integration, at least in the considered decade, did not have strong influences on the performance of regions. Only slight changes in the type of production structure in different regions can be attributed to higher international competitive pressure and new EU standards and codes, and to some extent to a delocalization effect of firms that moved from costly Italian production sites to countries with lower production costs.

Notes

1 North regions are: Piemonte, Valle d'Aosta, Lombardia, Liguria, Veneto, Trentino-Alto Adige and Friuli-Venezia Giulia. Centre regions are: Emilia Romagna, Toscana, Umbria, Marche, Lazio and Abruzzo. South regions are: Molise, Campania, Basilicata, Puglia, Calabria, Sicilia and Sardegna. Another common nomenclature divides North-West (Piemonte, Valle d'Aosta, Liguria, Lombardia) from North-East (Veneto, Trentino-Alto Adige, Friuli-Venezia Giulia).
2 See the Rapporto ICE 2004–2005 for methodology.
3 Bagnasco (1977) proposed the hypothesis of the "Three Italies" because of the stunning cultural and economic different conditions between North-West and North-East.
4 Società Autostrade is the company that holds and manages the majority of Italy's highways.
5 See for example, the case for the liberalization of the telephone information services.
6 The European Innovation Scoreboard is an annual assessment of innovation performance in the individual member states of the European Union. It was an explicit request of the European Council meeting in Lisbon in March 2000.
7 The Revealed Regional Summary Innovation Index tries to take into account both a region's innovative performance relative to the EU mean and a region's relative performance within the country. The RRSII is thus calculated as the average of the following two indexes (using rescaled values of the two composite indicators:

    1   The average of the re-scaled indicator values using only regions within each particular country (RNSII: regional national summary innovation index).
    2   The average of the re-scaled indicator values using all regions within the EU (REUSII: regional European summary innovation index). (cf. Technical Paper No 3).

8 See Traistaru and Iara (2003) for a compendium of indexes definition and sources.

References

Bagnasco, A. (1977). *Tre Italie. La problematica territoriale dello sviluppo Italiano.* Milan: Feltrinelli.
Banca d'Italia (2003). "Sintesi delle note sull'andamento dell'economia delle regioni italiane nel 2002". Official website: www.bancaditalia.it.
Bollino, C.A. and Signorelli, M. (2003). "Evolution of Production Structure in the Italian Regions", in Di Matteo and Piacentini (eds), *The Italian Economy at the Dawn of the 21st century*, Aldershot: Ashgate.
Confindustria official website: www.confindustria.it.
Dunford, M. (2001). "Italian Regional Evolutions", Working Paper 5–01, School of European Studies, University of Sussex.
European Commission, European Trend Chart on Innovation, 2003. "2003 European

Innovation Scoreboard: Technical Paper No 3 - Regional innovation performances". 28 November, 2003.

Hallet, Martin (2000). "Regional Specialisation and Concentration in the EU", Economic Papers, European Commission Directorate-General for Economic and Financial Affairs, No. 141.

ICE – Istituto per il Commercio Estero official website: www.ice.it.

ISTAT official website: www.istat.it.

Istituto Tagliacarne 2001 – Centenario dell'Unione Italiana delle Camere di Commercio – Spunti per una lettura di cento anni dello sviluppo territoriale italiano. Official website: www.tagliacarne.it.

Marrocu, M., Paci, R. and Pala, R. (2000). "Estimation of Total Factor Productivity for Regions and Sectors in Italy. A Panel Cointegration Approach", CRENOS Working Papers 00/16.

Traistaru, I. and Iara, T. (2003) "European Integration, Regional Specialization and Location of Industrial Activity: Data and Measurement", with Anna Iara, in Iulia Traistaru, Peter Nijkamp, Laura Resmini (eds), *The Economic Geography in EU Accession Countries*, Aldershot: Ashgate.

3 Economic integration and structural change

The case of Irish regions

Edgar Morgenroth

Introduction

Following a prolonged period of relative economic isolation Ireland opened up its trade to international competition during the 1960s and became a member of the European Economic Community (EEC) in 1973. This meant that the indigenous firms that grew up under the protection of tariff barriers were exposed to international competition. Subsequent initiatives by the European Union, such as the Single European Market (SEM) and European Monetary Union (EMU) have further contributed to the economic integration of Ireland into Europe. Ireland is now one of the most open economies in the world with the sum of imports and exports accounting for about 150 per cent of GDP, although it should be noted that Ireland has particularly strong trading links with non-EU countries and especially the US. In addition to the opening of trade, from the 1960s Ireland pursued an industrial policy focused on attracting foreign direct investment (FDI).

While the change in economic policy during the 1960s brought only limited success in terms of convergence of living standards until the late 1980s, Ireland has experienced rapid economic growth during the 1990s during which convergence to the average EU living standards was achieved. The reasons for this recent rapid convergence are multiple and complex. The contributory factors, other than EU membership and a successful industrial policy could only have had their positive impact in the context of a favourable general economic environment, which contrasts with the preceding period. Thus, stable and credible government policies, a highly educated young workforce and a favourable tax regime all contributed to this impressive economic performance (for more details see Barry, 1999).

Apart from the national trends and their underlying causes, which clearly serve as a good example of successful policy reforms, it is also important to consider the degree to which the national turnaround in economic fortunes has been mirrored at the regional level. While the national trends are well known, the regional trends are often ignored for lack of data. However, as with the national case the regional development trends serve as an important case study of the trends that occur in periods of slow and fast growth.

It is particularly interesting to study the impact of the integration process on regional economic activity in Ireland, since the experience of the Irish regions may serve as a useful case study for the new EU member states which are all lagging in development, and have been subject to substantial trade opening and reorientation. Furthermore, the recent Irish growth experience seems to contradict the recent New Economic Geography literature, which predicts strong specialization of core regions in the high returns to scale activities.

This chapter is organized as follows. In the next section we summarize the evolution of some key regional variables over time and we review the major regional policy initiative. We then analyse the evolution of regional specialization and industrial concentration and outline more robust econometric evidence. Finally, we summarize our findings and draw some conclusions.

The regional structure of the country and its change

Before we deal with the degree of regional specialization and industrial concentration, which is the subject of the next section, we concentrate on the key variables that describe the development of the NUTS 3 regions, in Ireland. There are eight NUTS 3 region, and these make up two NUTS 2 regions, namely the Border, Midlands and West region, and the Southern and Eastern region. While these regions do not constitute functional regions in the economic sense, they are the administrative regions for which data is available. It would be possible to further disaggregate to the county level but this would result in a serious reduction in the number of variables available for analysis.

Table 3.1 shows the key variables in each case for two years, one being the most recent year for which the data is available and one chosen close to the starting point of the analysis of specialization and concentration in 1972. Data availability means that particularly for the labour market variables the most recent year is 1983.[1] The first two rows show an index of per capita Gross Value Added (GVA), which is expressed as a percentage of the national average. Thus, in 1981 the Border region had a per capita GVA, which was 17 per cent lower than the national average. This gap had grown to almost 30 per cent by 2002. Overall, looking at these figures, it is clear that there has been a process of divergence among the Irish regions. What the table does not show is that there was very slight convergence over the period up to the late 1980s after which divergence became an increasing phenomenon (this is also supported by a number of studies such as Boyle et al., 1999; O'Connor, 1999 and O'Leary, 1999, 2001). This trend occurred despite the fact that all regions have recorded very substantial annual average GVA growth rates of over 5 per cent so that in EU terms all Irish regions have been converging to the EU average. Particularly pronounced are the growth rates for the Mid-East and the South West which both have a high proportion of multinational firms especially in manufacturing.

As output variables are susceptible to biases due to commuting patterns and transfer pricing by multinational firms, it is also useful to consider an indicator

Table 3.1 Summary statistics on key variables on regional development

	Border	Midlands	West	Dublin	Mid-East	Mid-West	South-East	South-West	State
Per capita gross value added (% of national 1981)	83.2	84.4	79.7	129.7*	61.8*	95.3	96.8	101.1	100.0
Per capita gross value added (% of national, 2002)	71.3	63.4	71.4	128.3	80.4	82.8	89.4	131.4	100.0
Avg. annual growth in real gross value added 1981–2002 (%)	6.7	5.2	7.2	8.4	12.6	6.8	7.5	12.5	9.8
Per capita income (% of national, 1973)	84.4	83.6	82.6	122.9	94.8	95.7	91.2	99.0	100.0
Per capita income (% of national, 2002)	89.2	90.9	90.3	115.9	102.6	97.3	89.5	94.5	100.0
Avg. annual growth in real per capita income 1973–(%)	5.4	5.4	5.8	4.7	5.7	4.8	5.2	4.8	4.6
Unemployment rate (1983 Q2) PES (%)	16.9	12.0	10.3	14.6	13.6	14.5	14.8	13.3	14.0
Unemployment rate (2004 Q2) PES (%)	7.9	6.0	5.3	6.1	4.8	6.6	5.8	5.4	6.0
Persons at work (1983 Q2) / Persons at work (2004 Q2)	121,600 / 183,200	63,200 / 101,000	114,800 / 169,400	351,100 / 526,900	90,300 / 198,000	95,600 / 151,200	117,700 / 186,900	170,900 / 253,600	1,125,200 / 1,770,200
Avg. annual employment growth 1983–2004 (%)	1.6	1.8	1.5	1.6	2.6	1.8	1.8	1.6	1.7
Population (1971) / Population (2004)	360,790 / 448,100	178,908 / 236,800	312,267 / 394,300	852,219 / 1,144,400	210,001 / 437,300	269,804 / 345,400	328,604 / 440,400	465,655 / 597,100	2,978,200 / 4,043,800
Avg. annual population growth 1971–2004 (%)	0.6	0.7	0.6	0.8	1.6	0.7	0.8	0.7	0.8

Source: CSO Census of Population; CSO Labour Force Survey; CSO Quarterly National Household Survey.

Note
* These figures are own estimates.

of personal income, which is shown in the table for 1973 and 2002. Immediately apparent is the smaller gap between the "richest" and "poorest" region, which was approximately 40 per cent in 1973 and was 17 per cent in 2002, which suggests that the regions have converged over that period. This is also confirmed by the growth rates, which for the "poorer" regions exceed that of the richer regions. Notable too is the fact that the average annual growth rates are substantially lower for income than for output, which confirms the impact of foreign firms, which through transfer pricing artificially inflate the GVA figures. In summary we find that output, that is economic activity, appears to be diverging and thus concentrating while income is converging.

The extent to which the strong growth in both output and income is mirrored in the labour market statistics is also shown in the table. This shows that the unemployment rate, defined on the Principle Economic Status definition, has declined from 14 per cent to 6 per cent nationally and the highest rate of unemployment which is recorded for the Border regions standing at less than 8 per cent. However, the relative dispersion has increased slightly. Apart from the drastic reduction in the unemployment rate the strong growth in the numbers employed is apparent. Nationally employment increased by about 650,000 over the period 1983 to 2004, which is an increase of over 60 per cent. Indeed, employment growth exceeded 60 per cent in all regions except the Mid-East where employment more than doubled.

Finally, turning to the evolution of the population this has grown strongly over the period, although there was strong emigration and slight population decline during the 1980s. While all regions increased their population by about one-quarter compared to 1971, one region, namely the Mid-East, stands out having doubled its population over the period. Of course, this region is the one that surrounds Dublin, the only city in Ireland with an international role, and this population growth reflects on the one hand rural-urban migration flows and development constraints in Dublin.

An important aspect of the regional divergence among Irish regions is the contribution of the broad sectors to this. Data limitations mean that the regional gross value added can only be disaggregated into three broad sectors namely:

1   agriculture, forestry and fishing;
2   manufacturing, building and construction;
3   market and non-market services, for a relatively short period of time.

Table 3.2 shows the recent evolution of the sectoral shares. Most noticeable is the decline of the primary sector in all regions. Furthermore, the secondary sector has increased its importance, while overall the tertiary sector has maintained its share. However, the table also indicates that the tertiary sector has increased in importance in some regions such as the Midlands region.

Decomposing the sectoral contributions to overall growth in the regions yields some interesting results. Here we follow Morgenroth and O'Malley

Table 3.2 Sectoral shares in Gross Value Added (GVA) by region for 1991 and 2002

	Agriculture, forestry and fishing (%)	Manufacturing, building and construction (%)	Market and non-market services (%)	Total (%)
1991				
Border	13.1	42.4	44.5	100
Midlands	15.5	35.6	48.9	100
West	13.4	33.9	52.6	100
Dublin	0.5	28.8	70.7	100
Mid-East	12.2	36.9	50.9	100
Mid-West	11.3	41.3	47.4	100
South-East	16.4	39.1	44.6	100
South-West	12.7	42.0	45.3	100
State	8.2	35.2	56.6	100
2002				
Border	6.3	41.3	55.1	100
Midlands	5.5	39.1	61.9	100
West	5.0	42.0	59.0	100
Dublin	0.3	28.6	71.1	100
Mid-East	3.1	53.0	43.9	100
Mid-West	4.2	40.6	55.2	100
South-East	4.7	50.5	44.7	100
South-West	2.8	61.1	36.1	100
State	2.7	41.4	55.9	100

Source: own calculations using CSO Regional Accounts.

(2003) by first showing the absolute growth rates of each sector in each region in Table 3.3, which also shows the relative contributions of the sectors to the overall growth performance. The latter is calculated by weighting the absolute growth rate by the sectoral share in GVA. Thus, while the overall performance of the primary sector is very poor, given the relatively small share of the primary sector this has a relatively small contribution to the overall growth rate. The tertiary sector has on average the largest contribution to overall growth, but in the case of two regions, namely the Mid-East and the South-West, the secondary sector has grown particularly strongly.

Given the findings above it is also useful to consider how the sectoral performance has contributed to convergence or divergence, that is faster or slower growth relative to the national average. This is shown in Table 3.4 where the national average growth rate for each sector is subtracted from the regional sector growth rates. This shows that the deviations from the national growth rate of the primary sector are very small. However, these deviations are larger and very heterogeneous across regions for the secondary sector, and small but heterogeneous for the tertiary sector. Thus, one can conclude that the performance of the secondary sector has the largest bearing on the convergence/divergence performance of the regions, and it is therefore particularly relevant to further analyse the secondary sector.

Table 3.3 Average annual growth rates of total real regional Gross Value Added (GVA) for the period 1991–2002 and sectoral decomposition, and weighted sectoral contributions to total growth

	Agriculture, forestry and fishing	Manufacturing, building and construction	Market and non-market services	Total	Agriculture, forestry and fishing	Manufacturing, building and construction	Market and non-market services	Total
Border	-1.2	6.6	12.6	8.2	-0.2	2.8	5.6	8.2
Midlands	-3.3	7.1	13.6	8.7	-0.5	2.5	6.7	8.7
West	-2.4	11.5	12.8	10.3	-0.3	3.9	6.7	10.3
Dublin	0.7	10.3	10.5	10.4	0.0	3.0	7.5	10.4
Mid-East	-2.2	33.7	16.2	20.4	-0.3	12.4	8.2	20.4
Mid-West	-2.9	8.9	12.4	9.2	-0.3	3.7	5.9	9.2
South-East	-3.3	20.3	13.5	13.4	-0.5	7.9	6.0	13.4
South-West	-3.6	31.6	12.8	18.6	-0.5	13.3	5.8	18.6
State	-2.7	16.1	11.9	12.2	-0.2	5.7	6.7	12.2

Source: own calculations using CSO Regional Accounts.

Table 3.4 Relative GVA growth rates and sectoral contributions to convergence/divergence

	Agriculture, forestry and fishing	Manufacturing, building and construction	Market and non-market services	Total
Border	0.1	−2.9	−1.1	−3.9
Midlands	−0.3	−3.1	−0.1	−3.5
West	−0.1	−1.7	0.0	−1.8
Dublin	0.2	−2.7	0.7	−1.7
Mid-East	0.0	6.8	1.5	8.2
Mid-West	−0.1	−2.0	−0.9	−2.9
South-East	−0.3	2.3	−0.7	1.2
South-West	−0.2	7.6	−0.9	6.5

Source: own calculations using CSO Regional Accounts.

Policy background

As was shown above, as in all countries, Irish economic activity is not evenly spread throughout the country and indeed over the recent periods regional disparities have increased. As a consequence of the uneven spread of economic activity a range of policies has been pursued.

Post-war Irish regional policy started with the Underdeveloped Areas Act in 1952, which remained in place until 1969. The key feature of this legislation was to allow a differential in industrial development grants across regions, favouring the less developed regions. Towards the end of the 1950s the regional dimension of the act was increasingly neglected in favour of national growth, a trend which was reinforced by subsequent acts such as the Industrial Grants Acts of 1956 and 1959. These acts reduced the grant differential between the designated regions and the rest of the country.

During the 1960s the idea of growth centres was promoted although no specific policies to promote growth centres were enacted. The concept of developing growth centres derived from the assumption that growth will only be self-sustaining in centres above a critical size. The debate about this policy was extensive and the government finally decided upon a policy of more dispersed development through the Regional Industrial Plans, which were published by the Industrial Development Agency (IDA) in 1972. These were aimed at dispersing industrial development rather than concentrating it in a few growth centres. In general the IDA managed to generate substantial numbers of manufacturing jobs. During the 1980s regional issues lost in importance as unemployment soared, and job creation at any location became the national priority.

The EU Structural Funds are also an important regional development policy for Ireland. However, since Ireland as a whole constituted on Objective 1 region and Ireland had not been split up into distinct regions for Structural Funds purposes, no serious economic evaluation of the regional impact of the Structural

Funds has been carried out (see FitzGerald *et al.*, 2003). While the economic impact of the Structural Funds was not assessed at the regional level, various evaluations have shown a strong economic return (e.g. Honohan, 1997; Bradley *et al.*, 2003).

Following on from the first two Structural Funds programmes, 1989–1994 and 1995–1999, the Irish government published the National Development Plan (NDP) for the period 2000–2006, in 1999, which included the objective to achieve a more balanced regional development, reducing the disparities between and within the two NUTS 2 regions which were established in 2000. The recent mid-term evaluation of the NDP showed that on the one hand there appeared to be some evidence that the NDP is reducing disparities, but on the other hand it highlighted that much of the investment under the NDP is not allocated with regional development in mind.

In 2001 the government published the National Spatial Strategy (NSS), which is a wide ranging document in that it does not concentrate merely on enterprise development, but deals with all aspects of regional development an most importantly land use. Interestingly it returned to the centre based approach that was put forward during the 1960s and which was dismissed then in favour of a dispersal policy. Another development that started in 1989 was the programme to "decentralize" civil servants away from Dublin. In addition to the decentralization that took place during the 1990s a new programme of "decentralization" has been announced in the budget (2004). So far no evaluation of the decentralization programmes has been published.

A descriptive analysis of regional specialization and concentration

Differences regarding the manufacturing sector at the regional and county level were explored in Bradley and Morgenroth (1999). Their paper showed that with regard to a number of performance indicators the differences within the regions (at county level) are greater than those between the regions. More recently, Morgenroth (2001) carried out an analysis of the Dublin and Mid-East regions which included a detailed analysis of the manufacturing sector in these regions that focused on sectoral specialization and clustering. This research found large differences between counties regarding their concentration of employment in fast growing sectors that explain much of the differences in performance.

At the national level, the Food and Beverage sector constitutes the largest sector in terms of employment. Noticeable is also that the Chemicals and Pharmaceuticals sector is now the second largest sector and the Medical, Precision and Optical Instruments sector is the third largest sector, while Office Machinery has also grown significantly. Sectors that have declined in importance include Textiles, Wearing Apparel and Fabricated Metal products. Thus, there is a gradual shift from the traditional sectors towards more high-tech sectors.

Turning to the regional employment shares these are shown for 2003 in Table 3.5. In that table notable deviations are marked with bold text. Thus for

Table 3.5 Regional employment shares, 2003

	B (%)	M (%)	W (%)	D (%)	ME (%)	MW (%)	SE (%)	SW (%)
15 Food and beverages	28.9	25.8	**14.1**	25.2	21.0	**14.7**	24.5	24.6
16 Tobacco	0.2	1.2	0.2	0.8	0.0	0.0	0.0	0.0
17 Textiles	**4.4**	1.1	1.3	1.0	1.8	0.5	0.4	2.8
18 Wearing apparel	**2.3**	0.7	0.5	**2.6**	0.5	0.5	0.6	1.1
19 Leather and leather products	0.2	0.1	0.4	0.0	0.1	0.1	0.4	0.0
20 Wood and wood products	4.2	**6.4**	3.7	1.1	2.2	1.9	3.2	4.4
21 Paper and pulp	0.4	0.4	1.3	**5.1**	2.6	1.6	0.4	1.1
22 Publishing	2.2	2.6	2.2	**10.9**	2.2	1.5	2.0	2.2
23 Fuel	0.0	0.0	0.3	0.0	0.0	0.0	0.0	0.6
24 Chemicals, pharmaceuticals and man-made fibres	**10.4**	**1.8**	9.7	11.8	13.6	8.5	12.2	**16.0**
25 Rubber and plastics	**6.5**	**7.0**	2.3	2.8	3.0	2.5	3.0	2.9
26 Non-metallic minerals	7.3	7.7	3.4	2.3	7.9	5.8	10.6	3.6
27 Basic metals	0.5	1.5	0.1	0.3	0.2	2.3	0.7	0.1
28 Fabricated metal products	6.4	6.9	6.4	5.8	4.5	10.5	7.3	6.2
29 Machinery nec.	6.0	4.5	6.9	2.6	4.0	4.7	**10.4**	3.4
30 Office machinery	1.9	1.6	2.5	4.7	**23.1**	**14.8**	0.1	3.8
31 Electrical machinery nec.	3.3	2.0	7.3	3.5	3.0	14.9	1.7	5.6
32 Radio, television and communications	3.0	2.1	2.9	5.1	1.6	3.2	0.9	9.3
33 Medical, precision and optical instruments	4.4	**12.5**	**30.0**	3.7	3.0	9.1	12.8	7.8
34 Motor vehicles and trailers	2.0	6.5	0.5	0.9	1.3	0.2	2.0	1.5
35 Other transport equipment	0.2	1.5	0.1	4.0	0.1	0.8	3.3	1.3
36 Manufacturing nec. incl. furniture	5.5	6.1	3.8	5.6	4.4	2.0	3.4	1.8

Source: own calculations using Forfás Employment Survey data.

Notes
Column headings refer to the regions: B (Border), M (Midlands), W (West), D (Dublin), ME (Mid-East), MW (Mid-West), SE (South-East), and SW (South-West).

example the West and Mid-West regions have relatively low employment shares in the Food and Beverages sector, while the West region has a high employment share in Textiles. For both the Border and Dublin regions Wearing Apparel is more important than in the other regions. For the Midlands region Wood and Wood products and Rubber and Plastics are relatively more important while Chemicals and Pharmaceuticals play a relatively small role. Chemicals and Pharmaceuticals are more important in the South-West region and Publishing is significantly more important in the Dublin region, which is of course related to its capital city status. Finally for the West region Medical, Precision and Optical instruments is a very important sector. From this table it is immediately apparent that there are significant differences regarding the sectoral specialisation at the regional level but this simple analysis is not sufficient to fully capture the specialisation and concentration of sectors and regions. Thus, a more thorough analysis using a number of indices will be carried out below.

An important feature of Irish industrial development is the role of foreign multinational firms, which have invested heavily over a longer timespan. In order to identify the regional importance of foreign direct investment (FDI) we plot the share of manufacturing employment in foreign owned firms in Figure 3.1. Overall the importance of FDI has increased over time. Indeed in the Mid-West the share of manufacturing employment in foreign firms is over 60 per cent. However in a number of regions such as the Border and Midlands that importance has been declining recently.

Given the level of detail available it is possible to calculate the specialization and concentration indices at different levels of sectoral disaggregation. Since the two-digit level is too aggregate and the four-digit level might introduce some errors due to difficulties in coding firms into the right sector at that level, the most

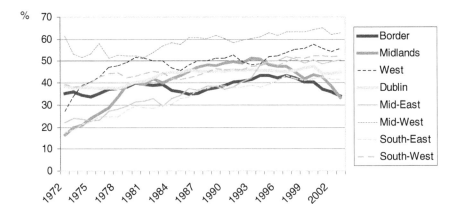

Figure 3.1 Foreign share in manufacturing employment (source: own calculations using plant level data from the Fofas Emploment Survey. Note that foreign firms are those that have at least 50 per cent foreign ownership).

useful level is the three digit NACE level. Here we concentrate on the Krugman index, which is defined relative to the national average sectoral distribution.[2] In general, the Krugman index is perhaps the more useful measure since this is less influenced by a few large observations than the Herfindahl index, which is more of a problem with three digit data as the shares are typically small except for a few large shares.

The Krugman index of relative specialization is shown in Figure 3.2. Overall, the level of specialization appears to have declined slightly for most regions but particularly for the Mid-West there has been a decline in special-ization in the 1970s. Indeed only the Midlands region has a higher level of specialization in 2003 than in 1972. If one disregards the Midlands region then there appears to be some convergence between the regions in terms of their specialization. However, if one disregards the Mid-West then the degree of specialization is diverging even though in general specialization is declin-ing. In other words the rate of change may differ significantly between the regions.

As was noted above, foreign direct investment is particularly important in Ireland, and this importance has increased over time as shown in Figure 3.1. It is therefore likely that foreign firms have influenced the degree of regional special-ization. In order to test this we disaggregate the data into foreign and indigenous and construct the specialisation indices for both and compare them with each other and the total ones outlined above. As Figure 3.3 shows, initially the index defined for the indigenous employment is most highly correlated with the one defined for all employment while that defined over foreign employment has a lower correlation coefficient. However, from the mid-1990s onwards the reverse is the case. The correlation between the foreign and indigenous index is lower but still positive. This suggests, first, that FDI plays a strong and increasing role in determining the degree of regional specialization. Second, as there is a positive

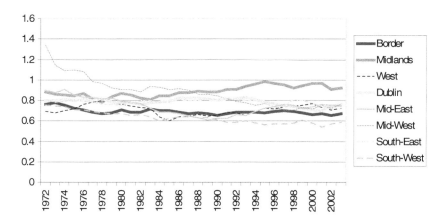

Figure 3.2 Krugman index of relative specialization (3Digit) (source: own calculations using Forfas Employment Survey data).

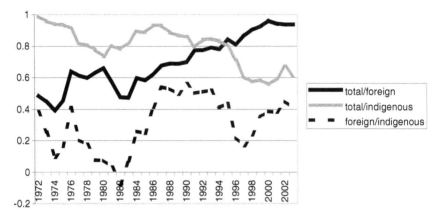

Figure 3.3 Correlation between the Krugman specialization index defined for total, indigenous and foreign employment over time (source: own calculations using Forfas Employment Survey data).

correlation between the indigenous and foreign indices, FDI and indigenous employment are not counterbalancing each other in determining the overall index. As there is a general trend towards less specialization this implies that both indigenous and foreign employment are both contributing to this trend, with FDI having a stronger influence over more recent years.

Clearly not all regions are the same and it is possible to group regions into some broad categories according to their industrial structure which allows for a comparison across these categories. First, given the importance of a core-periphery pattern in the New Economic Geography (NEG) literature, it is useful to consider central regions. These are particularly important in monocentric countries such as Ireland and these central regions tend to be more specialized in knowledge intensive industries. Second, regions proximate to these central regions may benefit from spillovers from the central regions so these are also identified. Apart from the central regions, which tend to contain accumulations of knowledge intensive industries, highly industrialized regions can often also be identified, but in the Irish case due to the late industrialization such a region does not exist. On the other hand peripheral regions tend to have more basic industry mix, focusing more on resource intensive industries, agriculture and footloose industries can also be identified. These are usually situated at the external EU borders. Of course some regions have an industry mix characteristic of both peripheral and highly industrial regions, and they may be referred to as semi-peripheral. Thus we define five types of regions: central; semi-central; highly industrialized; peripheral and semi-peripheral, but in Ireland we identify just four types. Once one groups the regions into these categories, the extreme observations are averaged out and we find that with the exception of peripheral regions, specialization declines over time. Even for peripheral regions specialization does not increase.

An important question is the degree to which regional performance is related to specialization. Because the specialization indices are defined for manufacturing sectors only it is only valid to consider the relationship of specialization with measures of manufacturing performance. First, we calculate the correlation of output per worker with the relative measure of specialization, which is shown for the period 1979 to 2002 in Figure 3.4. This shows clearly that there is a strong negative correlation between these two variables, which is becoming stronger over time. In other words, more highly specialized regions have a lower productivity. It is also useful to calculate correlation coefficients between specialization and growth rates in both output and employment. As these correlations may not be constant over time we calculate them for different periods. Furthermore, since we are also interested in the effect of changes in specialization on growth we calculate the correlations between the economic performance measures and the initial specialization and the change in specialization over the period. The results in Table 3.6 show that a higher level of initial specialization was associated with higher employment growth in all periods except the high growth 1990s. The opposite was found for the correlation between the change in specialization and employment growth, which was negatively correlated in all periods except the 1990s. On the other hand the correlations between specialization and output growth were negative in all cases, indicating that more diverse regions grow faster and indeed that an increase in specialization reduces growth.

Of course it is also interesting to consider what happened to individual sectors in terms of their concentration, that is the degree to which they are concentrated in a few regions. Again we calculate relative Krugman indices that we used above. Individual sectors have quite different levels of concentration as is shown in Table 3.7. For example the Fuel sector is extremely highly concentrated, while other sectors like Wood and Wood products is quite dispersed. As can be seen in

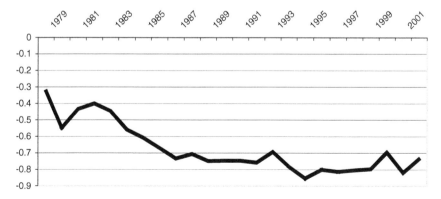

Figure 3.4 Correlation between net output per worker in manufacturing and specialization (source: own calculations using CSO Census of Industrial Production and Forfas Employment Survey data).

Table 3.6 Correlation coefficients between specialization and growth in manufacturing employment and productivity

	Initial specialization and annual average employment growth	Change in specialization and employment growth	Initial specialization and output growth	Change in specialization and output growth
1972–1980	0.58	−0.21		
1980–1990	0.13	−0.23	−0.45	−0.39
1990–2000	−0.49	0.59	−0.31	−0.44
2000–2003	0.19	−0.52	−0.09*	−0.04[a]

Source: own calculations using CSO Census of Industrial Production and Forfas Employment Survey data.

Note
a For the last period the correlations with respect to net output growth are calculated only for the period 2000–2002.

the last two rows of the table, on average the level of concentration is declining as is the dispersion between the sectors. However, as is evident in the indices many sectors are perfectly concentrated initially, but as Ireland developed this level of concentration has declined very quickly. Importantly, the more high-tech industries appear to have become less concentrated.

The table shows that the average level of concentration has declined. In particular there was rapid decline of concentration from 1973 to 1994, but there a slight increase over the more recent period. Furthermore, there is little evidence that the dispersion of the concentration has declined. Interestingly, there are sectors, which are becoming more concentrated, such as some of the food subsectors, while others such as pharmaceuticals continually disperse and other sectors concentrate after a period of dispersal (e.g. Basic Metals).

Given the large number of sectors it is useful to categorize them into different groups, identifying especially those that are subject to increasing returns to scale (IRS). This is particularly interesting since NEG models predict that those sectors that are subject to increasing returns to scale concentrate in the central regions, so that these ought to be more concentrated. Specifically, it is usual to classify industries into high increasing returns to scale industries according to the classification produced by Pratten (1988) and resource intensive industries according to the classification of the OECD. Furthermore, we classify the remaining sectors into footloose sectors that have either medium or low returns to scale. Thus, all industries were categorized into four groups: increasing returns; resource intensive; footloose medium and footloose low. The average concentration is for these groups is shown in Figure 3.5.

The most notable result is that the concentration of the high returns to scale sectors which was relatively high at the in 1973 has decreased continually so that it now is relatively low. Thus there is no evidence in favour of the catastrophic relocation of high returns to scale sectors as is predicted by the NEG literature.

Table 3.7 Krugman index of relative concentration for three-digit sectors, for selected years

	1973	1979	1987	1994	2000	2003
Food and beverages	1.73	1.69	1.67	1.30	0.91	0.79
Processing and preserving of meat	0.44	0.39	0.48	0.40	0.37	0.36
Processing and preserving of fish	0.35	0.52	0.62	0.70	0.73	0.73
Processing and preserving of fruit and vegetables	0.47	0.67	0.79	0.66	0.66	0.76
Vegetable and animal oils	1.28	1.24	1.00	0.86	1.24	1.18
Dairy products	0.43	0.46	0.52	0.57	0.66	0.64
Grain mill products	0.31	0.23	0.51	0.41	0.56	0.59
Prepared animal feeds	0.62	0.62	0.70	0.60	0.63	0.65
Other food products	0.43	0.37	0.35	0.35	0.41	0.49
Beverages	0.41	0.47	0.56	0.43	0.45	0.49
Tobacco	0.87	0.91	0.88	0.83	0.87	1.11
Spinning of textile fibres	0.96	1.07	0.98	0.91	0.98	0.94
Textile weaving	0.59	0.80	0.53	0.79	1.24	1.06
Finishing of textiles	1.24	1.20	1.10	0.88	1.31	1.35
Man-made textile articles except apparel	0.76	0.57	0.58	0.50	0.43	0.34
Other textiles	1.16	1.05	1.03	0.97	0.88	0.74
Textiles n.e.c.	–	–	–	1.69	1.74	1.76
Knitted and crocheted articles	0.88	0.93	0.97	0.97	0.88	0.82
Leather clothes	1.24	1.36	1.37	0.88	1.21	1.44
Other leather wearing apparel	0.53	0.59	0.64	0.58	0.58	0.64
Dying of fur, leather n.e.c.	0.82	0.89	1.09	1.65	–	–
Tanning and dressing of leather	1.18	1.31	0.74	1.07	1.20	1.15
Luggage, handbags and saddliery	0.96	0.73	0.76	0.82	0.54	0.80
Footwear	0.94	0.86	1.12	1.36	1.24	1.19
Sawmilling and planing of wood	0.73	0.63	0.47	0.47	0.51	0.54
Veneer, plywood and laminboard	1.57	1.44	1.37	0.91	0.87	0.83
Builders' carpentry	0.88	0.63	0.47	0.60	0.74	0.68

continued

Table 3.7 continued

	1973	1979	1987	1994	2000	2003
Wooden containers	0.89	0.65	0.68	0.68	0.74	0.82
Other woods products	0.62	0.89	0.45	0.44	0.47	0.47
Pulp, paper, paperboard	0.69	0.66	0.73	0.71	0.92	0.94
Articles of paper and paperboard	1.04	1.01	0.92	0.91	0.76	0.76
Publishing	0.56	0.61	0.73	0.71	0.60	0.52
Printing and service activities related to printing	0.62	0.73	0.76	0.95	0.88	0.86
Refined petroleum products	–	–	1.86	1.46	1.35	1.40
Basic chemicals	1.59	1.56	1.42	1.41	1.38	1.45
Pesticides and agrochemicals	0.79	0.98	0.86	0.83	0.72	0.69
Paints, varnishes and coatings	1.59	1.52	1.32	0.71	0.68	0.81
Pharmaceuticals, medical chemicals and botanical products	0.86	0.80	0.73	0.55	0.51	0.43
Soap and detergents	0.57	0.38	0.33	0.21	0.24	0.31
Other chemical products	0.98	0.62	0.65	0.56	0.75	0.74
Man-made fibres	0.62	0.61	0.78	0.75	0.55	0.59
Rubber and plastics	1.43	1.54	1.56	1.53	1.75	1.76
Rubber products	1.24	1.20	1.26	1.02	1.03	1.06
Plastic products	0.52	0.38	0.42	0.66	0.60	0.62
Non-metallic mineral products	0.54	0.26	0.28	0.18	0.24	0.28
Glass and glass products	–	1.85	1.81	1.75	1.56	1.52
Non-refractory ceramics	0.91	0.89	0.98	0.87	0.82	1.01
Ceramic tiles	1.24	1.15	0.85	0.66	0.55	0.62
Bricks and tiles made from clay	–	–	1.53	1.69	1.30	1.27
Cement, lime and plaster	0.78	0.93	0.80	1.09	1.04	1.04
Concrete articles	1.20	1.21	1.22	1.14	1.18	1.26
Cutting, shaping and finishing of stone	0.24	0.25	0.43	0.37	0.32	0.34
Other non-metallic minerals	0.86	0.72	0.71	0.75	0.72	0.70
Basic iron and steel	1.54	1.31	0.92	0.85	0.79	0.83

Cast iron tubes	1.32	1.13	1.59	1.57	0.70	1.04
Basic precious and non-ferrous metals	1.24	1.52	1.44	1.24	1.24	1.22
Casting of metals	–	–	–	1.90	1.41	–
Fabricated metal products	1.29	0.87	1.16	1.06	1.03	1.06
Structural metal products	1.54	1.08	0.93	0.87	0.83	1.20
Tanks, reservoirs and other metal containers	1.53	1.28	0.68	0.61	0.83	0.33
Steam generators	0.62	0.43	0.22	0.19	0.28	0.31
Forging, processing and stamping of metal	0.76	0.79	0.66	0.49	0.48	0.41
Metal coating	1.69	1.69	1.55	1.50	1.46	1.76
Cutlery, tools and general hardware	1.90	1.71	1.68	1.05	0.99	0.99
Other fabricated metal products	0.52	0.52	0.51	0.57	0.40	0.48
Machinery and equipment n.e.c.	0.93	0.94	0.85	0.76	0.62	0.64
Machinery for mechanical power	0.31	0.15	0.24	0.36	0.38	0.43
Other general purpose machinery	–	1.69	1.31	1.27	0.99	0.96
Agricultural and forestry machinery	0.91	0.94	0.73	0.85	0.89	0.71
Machine tools	0.70	0.61	0.49	0.41	0.41	0.45
Other special purpose machinery	0.90	0.82	0.44	0.76	0.68	0.65
Domestic appliance n.e.c.	1.69	1.08	0.99	0.78	0.81	0.99
Office machinery and computers	0.61	0.48	0.46	0.56	0.52	0.52
Electric motors, generators and transformers	1.61	1.34	1.19	1.12	1.18	1.32
Electricity distribution and control equipment	1.40	0.59	0.44	0.62	0.80	0.93
Insulated wire and cable	–	–	1.83	1.37	1.17	1.25
Accumulators, primary cells and primary batteries	1.08	0.85	0.50	0.72	0.67	0.54
Lighting equipment and electric lamps	1.71	1.60	1.15	1.04	0.81	0.79
Electrical equipment n.e.c.	0.84	0.95	0.71	0.69	0.69	0.67
Electronic valves, tubes and other components	1.24	1.36	1.45	1.33	1.54	1.57
Televisions and radio transmitters and telephone equipment	1.07	0.99	0.76	0.71	0.62	0.58
Televisions and radio receivers, sound and Video recording equipment	1.23	1.00	0.82	0.60	0.38	0.70
Medical and surgical equipment	1.90	1.30	1.05	0.95	0.80	0.75
Instruments and appliances for measuring, checking and navigation	1.10	0.63	0.89	0.62	0.58	0.85

continued

Table 3.7 continued

	1973	1979	1987	1994	2000	2003
Industrial process equipment	1.20	1.01	0.61	1.06	1.00	1.33
Optical instruments and photographic equipment	0.73	1.00	0.74	0.83	0.84	0.77
Motor vehicles, trailers and semi-trailers	1.16	0.71	0.66	0.48	0.40	0.44
Coachwork for motor vehicles, trailers and semi-trailers	1.90	1.86	1.27	0.84	0.70	0.83
Parts and accessories for motor vehicles	0.93	0.92	1.23	1.41	1.29	1.31
Building and repairing of ships	–	–	1.90	1.43	1.54	0.00
Railway and tramway rolling stock	0.83	0.88	1.07	0.85	0.84	1.02
Aircraft and spacecraft	0.40	0.82	0.43	0.68	0.91	0.93
Motorcycles and bicycles	1.01	0.64	0.60	0.76	0.80	0.71
Other transport equipment n.e.c.	0.91	1.05	0.73	1.01	0.83	0.70
Furniture	1.93	1.90	1.90	1.81	1.89	1.88
Jewellery	1.25	1.31	1.26	1.13	0.96	0.99
Musical instruments	1.24	1.36	–	–	1.77	1.76
Sports goods	–	1.90	1.90	1.33	1.43	1.48
Games and toys	0.52	0.47	0.47	0.51	0.48	0.44
Miscellaneous manufacturing n.e.c.	0.57	0.68	0.58	0.83	0.89	0.96
Average	1.55	1.19	0.84	0.69	0.77	0.75
Standard deviation	1.31	1.58	1.37	1.35	1.34	1.35

Source: own calculations using Forfás Employment Survey data.

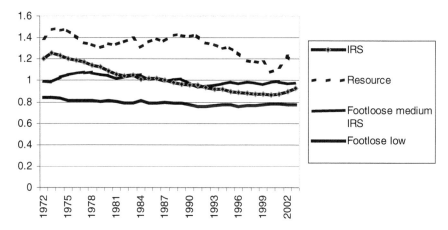

Figure 3.5 Average concentration indices for manufacturing industry groups (source: own calculations using CSO Census of Industrial Production and Forfas Employment Survey data).

In general there is decreasing concentration, but resource intensive industries have concentrated sharply over recent year. However, it should be noted that resource intensive industries have only a small share in total employment and the closure of one plant can have a significant impact.

Finally, since foreign multinationals are more prominent in some sectors than other it is also important to check the degree to which they determine the overall concentration levels. Again, this can be done through the calculation of correlation coefficients, which show a strong positive correlation across the sectors between the concentration indices defined over total employment and those defined for foreign employment only. Furthermore, if one calculates these correlations for each sector across time then the majority, 52 out of 64 sectors, show a positive correlation, so that on average the degree of sectoral concentration of foreign owned plants corresponds to that of indigenous plants.

Specialization, structural change and regional growth

The above analysis is largely descriptive, in that it focuses on the indices and simple correlations. However, the significance of the relationships can only be established once one conditions in other variables since these may dominate. It is thus necessary to conduct econometric analysis.

Some related econometric analysis has already been carried out by other authors. For example Barrios *et al.* (2003a) compare the spatial distribution of manufacturing activity for Belgium, Ireland and Portugal for one year, 1998 using the Ellison and Glaeser (1997) index. Thus, in contrast to our study they are not analysing the change in industrial concentration over time. Overall they find that the EG index is significantly different from zero in about 25 per cent of the sectors. In general it appears that the degree and pattern of concentration in Ireland differs from that in Belgium and Portugal.

Their paper also aims to explain the determinants of agglomeration using regression analysis, where the EG index is the dependent variable and the data is pooled across the three countries. The degree of economic integration of the country or region is not taken into account in this analysis. Of the explanatory variables, input purchases, wages and salaries, purchase of energy inputs, average plant size, are the only statistically significant explanatory variables. Overall the authors conclude that agglomeration forces are stronger at a more disaggregated spatial level which of course, supports the focus on NUTS 3 regions in this paper as compared to the common use of NUTS 2 level or even country level data. Furthermore, they conclude that forward and backward linkages increase agglomeration while wages decrease agglomeration. However, given that the variables used in the analysis do not identify where purchases take place this conclusion should be interpreted cautiously.

Another paper which utilises the Ellison and Glaeser index in the Irish context is that by Barrios *et al.* (2003b), which aims at analysing the impact of the agglomeration of foreign firms on local firms. They analysis covers the period 1972 to 1999 and they find that there is significant co-agglomeration of foreign and local firms in a many of sectors, which supports the findings above. They further investigate how the extent of co-agglomeration impacts on employment growth in indigenous firms they estimate plant level employment growth equations where the regressors include, lagged employment growth, output, wage growth, growth in the sector, lagged foreign share in the sector, lagged foreign density in the sector. They find that output, wage growth, sectoral growth and lagged foreign share are significant determinants of firm level employment growth. The latter indeed suggests the positive spillover of foreign firms on the indigenous firms. However, with regard to the other coefficients, endogeneity issues are not taken into account, which may bias the results.

A different approach is taken in Morgenroth (2005). He first attempts to explain the impact of integration on specialization, by regressing the specialization index on a measure of foreign direct investment, the degree of trade openness and the degree of urbanization. This relationship is estimated for the regions using seemingly unrelated regression (SUR). All three variables have significant impact on specialization. While, urbanization reduces specialization, presumably because it allows for more diversification through scale, trade openness seems to increase specialization. On the other hand a higher foreign employment share reduces specialization, which supports the findings of the descriptive analysis above.

This paper also seeks to explain the impact of specialization on productivity. A production functions for the manufacturing sector are estimated at the county level, for the period 1979 to 2002. The data used is from the annual Census of Industrial Production (CIP) with the specialization indices, namely the Herfindahl and the Krugman index, are added to the standard log-linearized Cobb-Douglas function as additional variables. The results yield a negative coefficient for the specialization indices, which in the case of the Krugman and a lagged Krugman index are statistically significant at the 99 per cent level. These results are robust to the inclusion of further explanatory variables to capture agglomeration, high-tech and FDI effects. However, the results throw up a peculiar finding that once fixed effects are taken account of, and all variables are included then the coefficients for population density and the percentage of employment in high-tech firms is negative and significant while that for the percentage of employment for foreign firms is positive and significant. In other words indigenous high-tech firms have not performed as well and firms in the more urbanized counties have also been performing less well.

Conclusions

Ireland has been one of the fastest growing economies in the Western world over the last decade and a half. While this national performance is impressive, less is known about the regional distribution of this growth. In terms of per capita Gross Value Added there has been divergence during the so-called Celtic Tiger era, despite (or perhaps in spite) of the fact that Irish regions have all grown faster than the EU average so that they have been converging (and in some cases surpassing) the EU average. A decomposition of regional growth suggests that the differences in the manufacturing growth rates between regions are primarily responsible for the divergence. Thus, the focus on manufacturing in this chapter is warranted.

A prominent feature of Irish economic development has been the dramatic increase in economic openness as measured by trade volumes relative to output and in terms of FDI. While it is difficult to identify precisely what role integration has played in the change of specialization and concentration, the analysis presented here shows that FDI and indigenous development have worked in the same direction, namely to reduce specialization and to reduce by and large average concentration of industries. However, the evidence provided by Morgenroth (2005), suggests that trade openness works to increase specialization while FDI reduces specialization.

The results of our analysis suggests that a high level of specialization is not conducive to growth, so that specialization inhibits convergence. While the degree of specialization is declining in most regions this is not the case in the peripheral regions. Given the negative relationship between specialization and growth this divergence of the degree of specialization appears to be a factor that can explain the divergence in terms of GVA that was outlined above.

To the extent that there was convergence during the 1980s one might be given to think that Irish regional policy was successful, but while regional policy was of high importance during the 1950s, 1960s and 1970s, less importance was attached to regional issues as there were important national issues to be dealt with first. Similarly, the fact that there was divergence over the 1990s is in itself not enough to conclude that the regional policy initiatives including the Structural Funds were a failure, since it is not clear what the counterfactual development would have been without these. Clearly, this is an area that requires further work, including research on the more recent policy initiatives, such as the National Spatial Strategy and the Decentralization Plan.

Finally, the New Economic Geography literature has received much attention. Initially, this was largely a theoretical literature, the results of which were largely untested. Here we were able to analyse on prediction from this literature, namely, that increasing returns to scale industries agglomerate in the economic centre once transport costs are positive but not prohibitive. For Ireland we found these increasing returns to scale sectors to be declining in concentration rather than increasing in concentration. Indeed these sectors have increased their overall share in manufacturing employment from 13 per cent in 1972 to 30 per cent in 2003.

Notes

1 It would be possible to use Census data for 1971 or 1981 but this is likely to suffer from consistency problems with the annual data that is collected specifically for labour market analysis. As the labour market indicators chosen here are those that are used by the statistics office for regional comparisons we utilize this data.
2 Additional detail using the two digit level and the Herfindahl and Theil index is available in Morgenroth (2004).

References

Barrios, S., Bertinelli, L., Strobl, E. and Teixeira, A.C. (2003a) "Agglomeration and the Location of Industries: A Comparison of three Small Countries", CORE Discussion Paper, 2003/67.

Barrios, S., Bertinelli, L. and Strobl, E. (2003b) "Coagglomeration and Growth", Centre for Economic Policy Research (CEPR) Discussion Paper. No. 3969.

Barry, F. (ed.) (1999) *Understanding Ireland's Economic Growth*, London: Macmillan Press Ltd.

Boyle, G.E., McCarthy, T. and Walsh, J.A. (1999) "Regional Income Differentials and the Issue of Regional Equalisation in Ireland", *Journal of the Statistical and Social Inquiry Society of Ireland*, Vol. 152, pp. 155–199.

Bradley, J. and Morgenroth, E. (1999) "Celtic Cubs? Regional Manufacturing in Ireland", in D. Duffy, J. FitzGerald, I. Kearney and D. Smyth (eds), *Medium-Term Review 1999–2005,* Medium Term Review Series No. 7, Dublin: Economic and Social Research Institute.

Bradley, J., Morgenroth, E. and Untiedt, G. (2003) "Macro-regional evaluation of the Structural Funds using the HERMIN modelling framework", *Italian Journal of Regional Science*, Vol. 3, No. 3, pp. 5–28.

Ellison, G. and Glaeser, E. (1997) "Geographic Concentration in U.S. Manufacturing Industries: A Dartboard Approach", *Journal of Political Economy*, Vol. 105(5), pp. 889–927.

FitzGerald, J., McCarthy, C., Morgenroth, E. and O'Connell, P. (2003), "The Mid-Term Evaluation of the National Development Plan (NDP) and Community Support Framework (CSF) for Ireland, 2000–2006", Policy Research Series, No. 50, Dublin: Economic and Social Research Institute.

Honohan, P. (ed.) (1997) *EU Structural Funds in Ireland: A Mid-Term Evaluation of the CSF 1994–99*, Policy Research Series, Paper No. 31.

Morgenroth, E. (2001) "Analysis of the Economic, Employment and Social Profile of the Greater Dublin Region", ESRI Books and Monographs Series Paper No. 161, Dublin: Economic and Social Research Institute.

Morgenroth, E. (2004) *European Integration, Regional Structural Change and Cohesion in Ireland*, EURECO Project Country Study (available at http://www.zei.de/eurec/WP2_Ireland.pdf).

Morgenroth, E. (2005) "The Impact of Regional Specialisation, Urbanisation and Agglomeration on Economic Activity in Ireland: An Empirical Analysis", mimeo.

Morgenroth, E. and O'Malley, E. (2003) "Regional Development and SMEs in Ireland", in B. Fingleton, A. Eraydin and R. Paci (eds), *Regional Economic Growth, SMEs and the Wider Europe*, London: Ashgate.

O'Connor, F. (1999) "Regional Variation in Economic Activity: Irish Regions", ESRI Seminar Paper presented at the Economic and Social Research Institute, Dublin, 4 April 1999.

O'Leary, E. (1999) "Regional Income Estimates for Ireland, 1995", *Regional Studies*, Vol. 33(9), pp. 805–814.

O'Leary, E. (2001) "Convergence in Living Standards among Irish Regions: The Roles of Productivity, Profit Outflows and Demography", *Regional Studies*, Vol. 35(3), pp. 197–206.

Pratten, C. (1988) "A Survey of Economics of Scale", in CEC (ed.), *Research on the Cost of Non-Europe*, Vol. 2, Luxembourg: CEC.

4 A Southern perspective on economic integration and structural change

The case of Greek regions

George Petrakos, Georgios Fotopoulos and Dimitris Kallioras

Introduction

The aim of this chapter is to draw a basic picture of the Greek experience within the European Union (EU), describing the country's spatial and structural patterns of development. In doing so, Greece and its economy are put within a European perspective in the next section. The third section gives an account of the regional outlook of the Greek economy and its time evolution along with a discussion of the empirical evidence existing about regional inequalities and economic conver-gence (divergence) of the Greek regions. This is supplemented with some basic analysis. An account of the regional dimension of Greek industrial policy is given in the fourth section. The time evolution of regional specialization and sectoral geographic concentration are the subject matter of the penultimate section. There, the analysis rests in using information-theory derived entropy measures of specialization and concentration along with some indices of structural change. Some concluding remarks are offered in the last section.

Greece in the European Union

Greece is a small open-market economy of almost 132,000 km² and 11,000,000 inhabitants, located in Europe's Southern-most tip. Following the end of the Second World War and the Greek Civil War, Greece experienced its highest levels of economic growth at the start of the 1950s. The Greek post-war economy recorded an annual growth rate of 6.5 per cent – the second highest in Europe after the respective rate of West Germany – until the first oil crisis of 1973 (Kazakos, 2001). Greece joined the (then called) European Economic Community (EEC) in 1981, after a long pre-accession period, in conditions of increasing economic depression. The EEC membership was a highly debated political decision, mostly on the part of the socialist and the communist parties, since it determined, to a great extent, the future of the country. This fierce debate is now a memory of the past. However, some scepticism concerning the impact of the EU membership on the Greek economy remains. Even though Greece is considered to be one the developed economies of the world – 27th in GDP terms, 41st in per capita GDP terms and 24th in Human Development Index terms (Kollias *et al.*, 2005) – its ability to compete successfully in the Single European Market environment is limited. Low growth rates, high public debt, industrial decline and unemployment are the symptoms of this inability. If significant assistance had not been provided to the less advanced Greek regions, in the context of the Community Support Frameworks, the debate regarding the Greek membership would have been more intense.

The structure of the Greek economy is sketched in Figure 4.1 where the shares of the three basic economic sectors (primary, secondary, tertiary), in Gross Value Added (GVA) terms, are provided in comparison to the respective of the EU-15 average economy. It becomes immediately apparent that the country experienced a significant de-industrialization from 1980 onwards but more pronouncedly so from the second half of the 1990s and even more dramatically in the dawn of the new millennium. This decreasing share of manufacturing industries in GVA was coun-terbalanced by the increasing share of services sectors. On the other hand, agricul-tural share in GVA demonstrates a rather steady decline, remaining, however, larger when compared to the respective EU-15 average. What is striking in the data concerning 2005 is that a reversal of the previous trends can be observed. This is because, for the first time, the manufacturing share in Greece's GVA becomes

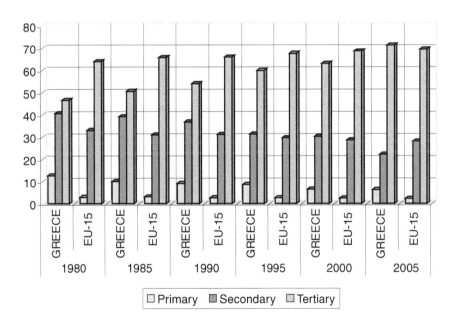

Figure 4.1 Comparison of the Greek and the EU-15 economic structures: GVA shares (%) of the basic economic sectors, 1980–2005 (source: data from AMECO Database (ECOFIN) and European Regional Database (Cambridge Econometrics) elaborated by the authors).

smaller than the corresponding one in EU-15, whereas the share of the services sector in the Greek GVA becomes larger than the corresponding one in EU-15.

The annual percentage real changes of GDP per capita, labour productivity and industrial production (constant 1995 prices) are provided for the Greek and the EU-15 economy, for the period 1961–2005, in Figures 4.2, 4.3 and 4.4, respectively. It becomes evident that these indicators were higher for the Greek economy for most of the 1960s and the 1970s (a notable exception is 1974 when the fall of the military junta, the Turkish invasion of Cyprus and the oil crisis had a major negative impact). Real GDP per capita has been growing in Greece with an average annual rate of 8.5 per cent in the 1960s and 4.6 per cent in the 1970s, while the corresponding EU-15 figures were 4.9 per cent and 3.0 per cent, respectively. This changed during the 1980s when the annual percentage growth rate was only

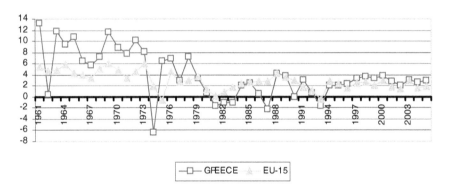

Figure 4.2 GDP per capita (1995 constant prices) annual growth (%): Greece vs. EU-15, 1961–2005 (source: data from New Cronos Database (EUROSTAT) elaborated by the authors).

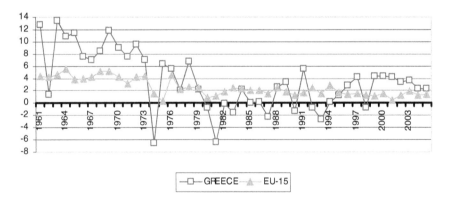

Figure 4.3 Labour productivity (1995 constant prices) annual growth (%): Greece vs. EU-15, 1961–2005 (source: data from New Cronos Database (EUROSTAT) elaborated by the authors).

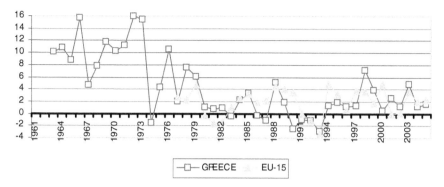

Figure 4.4 Industrial production (1995 constant prices) annual growth (%): Greece vs. EU-15, 1961–2005 (source: data from New Cronos Database (EUROSTAT) elaborated by the authors).

0.7 per cent for Greece, significantly lower than the 2.4 per cent of the EU-15. The situation continued until 1995 when the Greek governments began efforts to achieve the country's entry to the Economic and Monetary Union (EMU). Similar are the patterns discerned in terms of labour productivity and industrial production real growth.

Trade activity between Greece and the EU-15 average economy, captured by the exports to imports ratio, was lower in the 1960s compared to the corresponding activity with the rest of the world. A reverse trend emerged in the 1970s and persisted for most of the 1980s, demonstrating that trade conditions had been more favorable for intra-EU trade. A new reversal emerged at the beginning of the 1990s in favour of extra-EU trade, as it is presented in Figure 4.5. During this period, two opposite forces are at work with respect to the Greek trade performance in the international markets (Petrakos and Pitelis, 2001). On the one hand, there is a deterioration of the Greek exports to the EU-15 markets and, on the other hand, there is an amelioration of trade with the rest of the world. This evolution is highly correlated with the collapse of the former Eastern bloc and the new political and economic conditions shaped in Greece's neighbouring Balkan countries (Petrakos and Christodoulakis, 1997 and 2000).

The level of the integration of the Greek economy within the respective EU-15 can be assessed by using the Index of Economic Integration (IEI) proposed by Petrakos *et al.* (2005). The index has been calculated under the formula:

$$IEI = \frac{TRADE_{EU\text{-}15}}{TRADE_{WORLD}}$$

where $TRADE_{EU\text{-}15}$ and $TRADE_{WORLD}$ is the trade activity (imports and exports, in value terms) of Greece with the EU-15 and the world, respectively. The IEI takes values within the interval [0, 1], ranging from no to complete economic integration

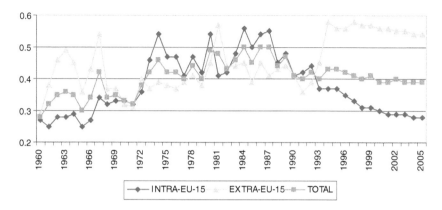

Figure 4.5 Intra-EU-15, extra-EU-15 and total trade activity (% GDP) of Greece, 1960–2005 (source: data from New Cronos Database (EUROSTAT) elaborated by the authors).

with the average EU-15 economy.[1] The IEI present an extremely interesting trend, shown in Figure 4.6, drawn together with the level of the country's per capita GDP. Between 1984 and 1987, Greece's relative GDP per capita was falling while, at the same time, the IEI was increasing. Since then, while the IEI has been fluctuating in time more than the relative GDP per capita, it is also apparent that progressively relative GDP per capita has been increasing while at the same time the IEI was decreasing (this becomes more pronounced during the period 1995–2000). Though a lot of speculation can be made on the causes of this pattern, it seems less disputable to argue that in the years after Greece's accession to the EEC, the Greek economy experienced a significant shock. This shock

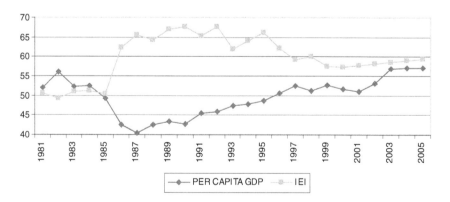

Figure 4.6 Greece per capita GDP (% of the EU-15 average) and IEI (multiplied by 100): a comparative parathesis, 1981–2005 (sources: data from New Cronos Database (EUROSTAT) and COMEXT Database (EUROSTAT) elaborated by the authors).

appeared not immediately after the accession but with a time lag and lasted for few years. Possibly this shock can be attributed to the entrance of Spain and Portugal (Greece's close competitors to European markets) to the EEC, in 1985.

Regional structure of Greece and changes over time

Spatial distributions of population and economic activity are characterized by unevenness among the 51 NUTS 3 regions of Greece.

Map 4.1 presents the population of the Greek regions for the year 2000 as well as the respective population growth for the period 1981–2000. The most populated regions are those of Attiki – the greater Athens area – and Thessaloniki that both account for about half of the population in Greece. The other most populated regions are Achaia, Irakleio, Larissa and Magnesia that contain

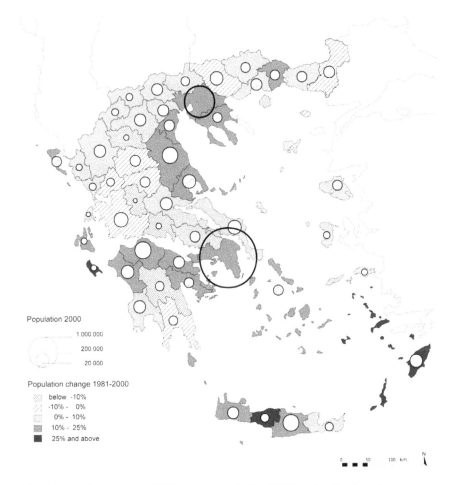

Map 4.1 Population level (2000) and growth (1981–2000) in the Greek regions (source: data from Regio Database (EUROSTAT) elaborated by the authors).

the urban areas (medium-sized cities) of Patras, Irakleio, Larissa and Volos respectively. Taking into account the population change that took place in the period 1981–2000, it becomes evident that all major urban areas recorded large percentage increases. This indicates that a rural-urban shift holds strong over this period. Besides the high percentage increments in the population of major urban areas, there is a complementary tendency related to the considerable percentage gains in the population of areas situated close to Greece's major cities, Athens and Thessaloniki. Thus, Korinthia, Voiotia and Evoia, situated close to Athens, and Pieria, Chalkidiki and Imathia, situated close to Thessaloniki, recorded considerable population percentage gains. There are, however, some island regions belonging to the complexes of Ionian Islands, South Aegean Islands and Crete, that also record high percentage population gains. In contrast, there are rural areas situated all over continental Greece such as Evrytania, Grevena, Fokida and Arcadia that exhibit high percentage population loses.

Map 4.2 presents simultaneously the real per capita GDP (1995 constant prices) of the Greek regions for the year 2000 and the respective real per capita GDP growth for the period 1981–2000. The prosperous Greek regions are concentrated in the Greek mainland, along the Patras-Athens-Thessaloniki corridor, where the metropolitan cities of Athens and Thessaloniki and the medium-sized cities of Patras, Larissa and Volos are situated. Exceptions to this general rule are the economies of Crete and some of the Aegean and Ionian islands economies that are mainly specialized in the tourism sector.

Recent scientific literature contains a number of studies that have tried to evaluate the level of regional disparities among the Greek regions. The results found are in favour of both convergence (Giannias *et al.*, 1997; Konsolas *et al.*, 2002; Liargovas *et al.*, 2003) and divergence (Siriopoulos and Asteriou, 1998; Fotopoulos *et al.*, 2002; Tsionas, 2002). This contradiction can be mainly attributed to differences regarding the methods employed and the time periods analysed. The most conciliatory finding provided from Petrakos and Saratsis (2000) who supported that regional inequalities in Greece have a pro-cyclical character, increasing in periods of economic expansion and decreasing in periods of economic recession. This evidence can be attributed to the existence of strong spatial imbalances in Greece due to its dualistic economic base, with the prevalence of Athens and Thessaloniki urban systems (Petrakos and Tsoukalas, 1999; Ioannides and Petrakos, 2000).

Providing evidence that poorer Greek regions, in per capita GDP terms, grow faster may not be unproblematic since both Greece's largest regions, Attiki and Thessaloniki, have "exported" a significant part of their industrial activity to their neighbouring satellite regions (Petrakos and Psycharis, 2004). This is in order to avoid congestion costs and negative externalities and to exploit the incentives provided from the Greek governments for the decentralization of industrial activity. Though interesting, this might distort the picture obtained. Having no data for the regional counterpart of Gross National Product (GNP) and, as yet, no data on cross-regional commuting makes it difficult to account for this caveat.

Recognizing these deficiencies and seeking for a more encompassing index of

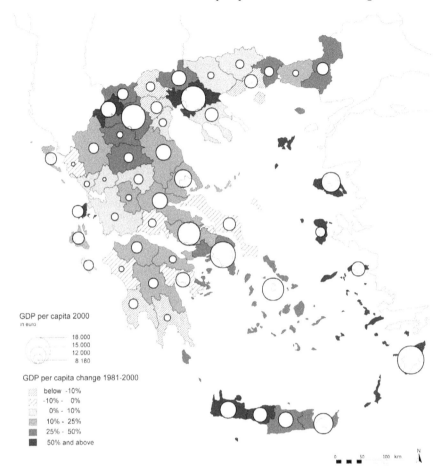

GDP per capita 2000
in euro

18.000
15.000
12.000
8.180

GDP per capita change 1981-2000

below -10%
-10% - 0%
0% - 10%
10% - 25%
25% - 50%
50% and above

0   50   100 km

Map 4.2 Per capita GDP level (2000) and real growth (1981–2000; constant 1995 prices) in the Greek regions (source: data from Regio Database (EUROSTAT) elaborated by the authors).

regional development, Petrakos and Psycharis (2004) introduced the Composite Index of Welfare and Development (CIWD) that summarizes information from 21 standardized economic, demographic and geographic variables (see Table 4.A1 in Appendix 1 for details). Figure 4.7 presents the time evolution path of regional inequalities in Greece in both per capita GDP and CIWD terms using the σ-convergence concept. That is the coefficient of variation (Barro and Sala-i-Martin, 1991) weighted by the population of each region i under the formula:

$$CV_W = \frac{\sum_i ((X_i - \overline{X})^2 * \sqrt{(P_i / P)})}{\overline{X}}$$

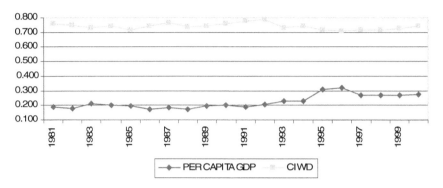

Figure 4.7 Regional inequalities in Greece in GDP per capita and CIWD terms, 1981–2000 (source: data from Regio Database (EUROSTAT) and Petrakos and Psycharis (2004) elaborated by the authors).

where X_i is the variable under consideration at the regional level, $\bar{X}$ is its average value, P_i is the population at the regional level and P is the national population. The CVw takes values greater than 0, ranging from lower to higher inequality. The CVw of the CIWD is always higher than the corresponding figure for the GDP per capita. This may suggest that inequalities are larger when a measure that is more informed than GDP per capita is used. Moreover, both indices move over time within a narrow band indicating persistence of inequalities for most of the time period covered. It is also worth noting that in the middle of the 1990s regional inequalities in GDP per capita terms, rose and then stabilized in a somewhat higher level than that prior to 1993.

The regional dimension of the Greek industrial policy

Given the restrictions imposed on trade of agricultural products and the non-tradable character of most services, the analysis of the spatial and structural impact of economic integration is far more interesting when it focuses on the sector of industry. This sector constitutes the main diffusion channel of the economic integration dynamics, presenting strong linkages with the other productive sectors as producer and consumer of final and intermediate goods.

Greek industrial policy aims at reducing regional inequalities through the enhancement of industrial activity for specific sectors, in specific areas. Development Laws, together with the Community Support Framework (CSF) funds, constitute the basic policy instruments for the fulfilment of the two components of this objective, following the gradual abolition of protective measures. The first component – the enhancement of industrial activity – is pursued through the provision of economic and financial incentives (subsidies and tax reductions), while the second component – the reduction of regional inequalities – is pursued through the division of the country into discrete geographic zones (according to the levels of economic development) that correspond to specific incentive categories.

The First Development Law under the EEC membership (Law 1262/1982) divided the country into four incentive zones and required that the potential entrepreneur participates in the overall project funding. This law can be considered successful since, in a depressive and unstable economic environment, it succeeded in attracting a significant amount of capital, although the majority of this amount was directed to labour-intensive investments. The Second Development Law (Law 1892/1990 supplemented by Law 2234/1994), managed to improve the country's investment climate since it improved the regulations of the previous one. Subsidies were given to enterprises that submitted a business plan, situated in Industrial Areas or Industrial Decline Areas and set up in technology-driven sectors, amongst others. The Third Development Law (Law 2601/1998) attempted to change the overall investment philosophy of the country in order to be more compatible with the EU directives. Enterprises existing for over five years (and wishing to expand their activities) are not entitled to subsidies whereas new start-ups have the right to choose between subsidies and tax reductions. This law attempted to make enterprises less state-dependent, forcing them to enhance their competitiveness. Under this law, the majority of the Greek medium-sized enterprises (SMEs) have no access to direct subsidization; they regain this potential, however, if they choose to operate in joint ventures with other SMEs. The current Development Law (Law 3299/2004), further improved the regulations of the previous one, offering ten-year fixed tax rates for sizeable investments (over 30 million), decreased tax rates for the large enterprises (earnings higher than 50,000) and higher subsidies for the creation of new job positions.

Greek industrial policy, trying to harmonize the enterprises investment priorities with the free-market demands, can be evaluated positively in respect to the enhancement of industrial activity (Papadoulis *et al.*, 2004). In terms of reducing regional inequalities, a weakening of the regional dimension can be observed over time in the regulations of the Development Laws (Papadoulis *et al.*, 2004). Laws 2601/1998 and 3229/2004, when compared to the previous Development Laws, present smaller regional diversity in relation to the provided levels of subsidies and tax reductions. This deterioration of the regional component is mainly based on the Greek regional GDP statistics that take into account neither the metropolitan regions industrial activity spillover to the neighbouring areas (Petrakos and Psycharis, 2004) nor the existence of regional multipliers (Polyzos and Petrakos, 2005). Moreover, the regional component of the Greek industrial policy is distorted from the a-spatial financing potentials (Regional Operational Programmes and SMEs Community Initiatives) that emerged under the CSF context. The objective of the CSF funds is to mobilize locally available sources-factors and not to direct them towards less advanced areas (Papadoulis *et al.*, 2004). The prevalence of the Attiki region in attracting new business plants is unavoidable under these conditions. The fact that in the period 1995–1999, half of the new industrial enterprises were situated in the capital region (Stratos, 2000) is quite characteristic.

The gradual deterioration of the regional dimension of the Greek industrial policy relies neither on Greek reality nor on international experience. The emerging dynamics in the European space necessitate the existence of the industrial incentives under a regional perspective since many Greek regions are in danger of creating a state of economic isolation (Papadoulis *et al.*, 2004). Balancing these two components in industrial policy, however, is not an easy task.

Regional-industrial employment patterns in Greece: sectoral dispersion and regional diversity

The analysis of regional-industrial employment patterns in Greece faces some data-related difficulties (see Appendix 4.2 for details).

Having this caveat in mind, the recent-past time evolution of the basic economic structure for each of the 13 Greek NUTS 2 regions is provided in Table 4.1. What becomes evident is that the de-industrialization pattern that was earlier diagnosed for the country as a whole also holds true for the majority of regions. The most pronounced exceptions are the region of Central Greece where the share of manufacturing in GVA rose by 8.95 percentage points during the period 1988–1995 and the region of Peloponnesus where the respective share rose by 5.40 percentage points during the period 1995–2002. These regions constitute the major industrial hubs of the capital region of Attiki.

As far as the regional distribution of manufacturing employment is concerned this is provided in Table 4.2 where a classification of sectors, proposed by Jackson and Petrakos (2001), in labour-intensive (LINT = food, textiles, leather, wood, paper, miscellaneous), intermediate (IINT = fuel, chemicals, rubber and plastic, non-metallic products, fabricated metals) and capital-intensive sectors (CINT = machinery, electrical machinery and optical equipment, transport equipment) is used. The interesting, overall, pattern that emerges is that over time the employment share of CINT sectors has been declining in most of the regions at the benefit of the employment in the other two industrial groups. Some exceptions to this general pattern appear to be the cases of Western Greece and Peloponnesus where the employment share of CINT sectors had, by 2000, been increased, and Central Macedonia and Attiki where the corresponding shares could be characterized (despite small fluctuations) as relatively stable. The regions of West Macedonia and South Aegean Islands have experienced the highest increases in LINT sector employment-share by 2000. In all other regions there has been considerable fluctuation over time in relation to reallocation of employment among industry groups.

The information conveyed so far brings about the question of structural changes taking place in the regional economies and thus a more detailed analysis of regional economic structure is called for. As a measure of regional-structural change, the difference in the Coefficient of Regional Specialization (CRS)[2] between two periods could be calculated. Such a measure, however, would be partially determined by shifts over time in sectoral employment shares defined at the national level $\left(\dfrac{E_i}{E}\right)$. A measure that does not depend on

Table 4.1 Structure of the Greek economy: GVA shares (%) of the basic economic sectors (primary, secondary, tertiary) at the NUTS 2 spatial level, selected years

	1988			1995			2002		
	Primary	Secondary	Tertiary	Primary	Secondary	Tertiary	Primary	Secondary	Tertiary
Eastern Macedonia and Thrace (GR11)	23.71	27.35	48.94	20.76	27.23	52.02	16.37	24.83	58.80
Central Macedonia (GR12)	12.25	29.95	57.80	10.90	24.82	64.28	7.35	22.21	70.44
Western Macedonia (GR13)	14.10	44.47	41.43	11.95	33.83	54.22	14.52	25.55	59.93
Thessaly (GR14)	22.68	26.57	50.75	21.35	23.92	54.74	15.81	21.68	62.51
Ipeiros (GR21)	18.07	23.46	58.47	16.57	14.74	68.69	9.30	15.56	75.15
Ionian Islands (GR22)	15.67	20.35	63.98	13.21	8.70	78.09	8.59	8.35	83.06
Western Greece (GR23)	22.76	25.29	51.95	17.39	21.70	60.91	12.58	17.03	70.39
Central Greece (GR24)	18.56	39.29	42.15	10.56	48.23	41.20	9.49	43.34	47.17
Peloponnesus (GR25)	29.08	23.98	46.94	21.27	24.76	53.96	14.08	30.17	55.75
Attiki (GR3)	1.24	26.59	72.17	1.26	17.66	81.08	0.49	17.99	81.52
North Aegean Islands (GR41)	14.12	20.14	65.74	12.36	22.94	64.70	12.34	23.92	63.74
South Aegean Islands (GR42)	9.53	28.46	62.01	7.29	10.78	81.93	7.55	7.54	84.91
Crete (GR43)	23.06	16.64	60.30	21.45	11.20	67.35	10.83	11.12	78.06

Source: data from NSSG elaborated by the authors.

Table 4.2 Regional manufacturing employment shares (%): labour (LINT), intermediate (IINT) and capital-intensive sectors (CINT), selected years

	1980			1990			2000		
	LINT	*IINT*	*CINT*	*LINT*	*IINT*	*CINT*	*LINT*	*IINT*	*CINT*
Eastern Macedonia and Thrace	79.75	17.93	2.32	81.79	15.92	2.29	78.84	20.56	0.60
Central Macedonia	71.51	17.55	10.94	75.51	16.86	7.63	67.18	23.03	9.79
Western Macedonia	47.15	51.06	1.79	26.27	65.89	7.84	83.83	16.17	0.00
Thessaly	61.50	30.94	7.56	64.65	24.24	11.11	56.75	36.96	6.29
Ipeiros	83.48	16.52	0.00	81.79	18.21	0.00	79.19	20.81	0.00
Ionian Islands	95.28	4.72	0.00	68.71	31.29	0.00	100.00	0.00	0.00
Western Greece	80.92	16.05	3.03	72.58	22.86	4.56	62.72	18.30	18.98
Central Greece	36.93	42.58	20.49	33.91	42.44	23.65	31.64	48.22	20.14
Peloponnesus	66.79	20.45	12.76	65.49	24.19	10.32	62.55	23.36	14.09
Attiki	47.89	30.27	21.84	48.30	31.03	20.67	51.40	28.71	19.89
North Aegean Islands	87.82	12.18	0.00	93.68	6.32	0.00	80.83	19.17	0.00
South Aegean Islands	49.39	46.24	4.37	41.14	57.54	1.32	75.13	24.87	0.00
Crete	79.22	14.85	5.93	69.39	28.09	2.52	69.80	28.21	1.99

Source: data from NSSG elaborated by the authors.

the latter would be to compute the Coefficient of Regional Redistribution (CRR) defined as:

$$CRR_r = \tfrac{1}{2} \sum_i \left| \left(\frac{E_{ir}}{E_r} \right)_t - \left(\frac{E_{ir}}{E_r} \right)_{t-1} \right|$$

where *i* stands for the industrial sector, *r* for the region and *E* for employment (Isard, 1960: 275; Dixon and Thirlwall, 1975: 19). This coefficient ranges between zero (no change in the distribution of regional employment over the period) and unity (complete reallocation of resources). In Table 4.3 the results of calculating the CRR for selected periods are presented.

In the first of the periods considered (1980–1985) most of the regions present considerable inertia with the exception of Ionian Islands and West Macedonia and, to a much lesser extent, the regions of Peloponnesus and Ipeiros. During the second half of the 1980s, West Macedonia and Ionian Islands continue to experience considerable structural change. However, the regions of North and South Aegean Islands appear to have been experiencing even more structural change primarily due to their further de-industrialization. During most of the 1990s, some of the earlier tendencies continue (Ionian Islands, West Macedonia), while more continental Greek regions (Thessaly, Ipeiros), as well as the

Table 4.3 Regional structural change, in industrial employment terms, based on the estimation of the CRR

	1980–1985	*1985–1990*	*1993–1998*
Eastern Macedonia and Thrace	0.0671	0.0981	0.1167
Central Macedonia	0.0514	0.0429	0.0714
Western Macedonia	0.2356	0.3061	0.1940
Thessaly	0.0386	0.0902	0.1622
Ipeiros	0.1043	0.1210	0.1713
Ionian Islands	0.3156	0.3361	0.1966
Western Greece	0.0467	0.0733	0.1698
Central Greece	0.0970	0.0653	0.0794
Peloponnesus	0.1127	0.0860	0.1093
Attiki	0.0567	0.0562	0.0560
North Aegean Islands	0.0671	0.3761	0.1115
South Aegean Islands	0.0708	0.5464	0.4450
Crete	0.0802	0.1224	0.1583

Source: data from NSSG elaborated by the authors.

island economy of Crete, also appear to experience some sizeable structural change.

Turning tables the other way around, a measure of locational change may also be computed for each industry. Such a measure can be the Coefficient of Industrial Redistribution (*CIR*) defined as:

$$CIR_r = \tfrac{1}{2} \sum_r \left| \left(\frac{E_{ir}}{E_r} \right)_t - \left(\frac{E_{ir}}{E_r} \right)_{t-1} \right|$$

where *i* stands for the industrial sector, *r* for the region and *E* for employment (Isard, 1960: 254; Dixon and Thirlwall, 1975: 20). This coefficient ranges between zero (no change in the distribution of sectoral employment across regions over the period considered) and one (complete reallocation of the sectoral employment across regions). In Table 4.4 below the results of calculating the CIR for a number of selected periods are detailed.

During the 1980s the sectors experiencing locational reorganization across regions were primarily those of leather products (DC), non-metallic minerals (DI), machinery (DK), other manufactured products (DN) and rubber and plastic products (DH). Between 1993 and 1998 the sectoral redistribution across Greek regions appears to be lower and primarily takes place in the sectors of machinery (DK) and transport equipment (DM).

Between the sectoral and regional dimensions analysed above, a considerable amount of information may be lost in respect to sector specific results of regional specialization and how the latter changes over time. Ideally this information could be retrieved using the employment location quotient (*ELQ*) at various points in time. However, even in relatively small designs as the ones

Table 4.4 Sectoral structural change, in industrial employment terms, based on the estimation of the CIR

	1980–1985	*1985–1990*	*1993–1998*
Food, beverages and tobacco (DA)	0.0433	0.0374	0.0298
Textiles and wearing apparel (DB)	0.0499	0.0872	0.0774
Leather products (DC)	0.3796	0.2598	0.0658
Wood products (DD)	0.0292	0.0800	0.0992
Paper, publishing and printing (DE)	0.0482	0.0325	0.0312
Fuel products (DF)	0.0433	0.0322	0.0688
Chemical products (DG)	0.0385	0.0611	0.0238
Rubber and plastic products (DH)	0.1148	0.1587	0.0777
Non-metallic mineral products (DI)	0.1257	0.1211	0.0240
Fabricated metal products (DJ)	0.0762	0.0486	0.0540
Machinery (excl. electrical) (DK)	0.1145	0.2016	0.1352
Electrical machinery and optical equipment (DL)	0.0743	0.0647	0.0523
Transport equipment (DM)	0.0666	0.0532	0.1032
Other manufactured products (DN)	0.0929	0.1614	0.0428

Source: data from NSSG elaborated by the authors.

used here (13 NUTS 2 regions and 14 NACE 2-digit sectors) this would require a considerable amount of space. Instead, the top three industrial sectors, in terms of *ELQ* being larger than one, for each region at various points in time will only be presented. This is done in Table 4.5 that follows. The employment location quotient is defined as:

$$ELQ_{ir} = \frac{E_{ir}}{E_i} \Big/ \frac{E_r}{E} = \frac{E_{ir}}{E_r} \Big/ \frac{E_i}{E}$$

where *i* stands for the industrial sector, *r* for the region and *E* for employment. If $ELQ_{ir} > 1$, the region is considered to be specialized in the particular industry relative to all other regions. It appears that in most regions two out of three industrial sectors with $ELQ_{ir} > 1$ remained the same in both of the first five-year periods considered. Such stability also exists in the 1990s (1993–1998). However, there are differences between the 1980s and the 1990s in most of the regions.

The extent of structural change presented above has not been necessarily unidirectional for all Greek regions in the sense that their structure approaches that of a European representative (average) regional economy. The time evolution of similarity or dissimilarity of regional structures when compared to a representative EU regional economy was explored using the Index of Dissimilarity in Industrial Structures, proposed by Jackson and Petrakos (2001). This is defined as:

$$IDIS = \sum_i ((a_{it} - b_{it})^2)$$

Table 4.5 Top-three industrial sectors in each NUTS 2 region ($ELQ_{ir} > 1$), selected years

	1980	1985	1990	1993	1998
Eastern Macedonia and Thrace	DI	DC	DB	DC	DC
	DB	DE	DE	DI	DD
	DA	DB	DI	DD	DI
Central Macedonia	DA	DK	DA	DC	DB
	DD	DA	DB	DB	DC
	DB	DB	DK	DD	DA
Western Macedonia	DC	DC	DC	DL	DL
	DG	DG	DG	DD	DD
	DF	DH	DI	DC	DC
Thessaly	DJ	DJ	DK	DB	DI
	DI	DI	DI	DI	DJ
	DB	DB	DB	DJ	DB
Ipeiros	DI	DD	DA	DB	DA
	DD	DA	DJ	DD	DD
	DA	DN	DB	DA	DB
Ionian Islands	DN	DN	DN	DI	DI
	DA	DB	DI	DN	DG
	DB	–	DA	DA	DA
Western Greece	DC	DC	DC	DI	DK
	DA	DB	DB	DA	DI
	DB	DA	DA	DC	DA
Central Greece	DJ	DI	DJ	DJ	DJ
	DI	DJ	DL	DD	DD
	DL	DL	DI	DM	DM
Peloponnesus	DF	DF	DF	DF	DF
	DA	DL	DL	DL	DL
	DL	DA	DA	DD	DD
Attiki	DM	DE	DG	DG	DG
	DG	DG	DM	DE	DE
	DF	DM	DE	DM	DF
North Aegean Islands	DC	DC	DC	DA	DA
	DA	DA	DA	DB	DB
	DI	DI	DB	DN	DN
South Aegean Islands	DM	DM	DH	DI	DM
	DB	–	DN	DN	DI
	–	–	DB	DC	DD
Crete	DA	DA	DI	DF	DI
	DK	DI	DH	DI	DA
	DI	DK	DA	DA	DH

Source: data from NSSG elaborated by the authors.

where *a* and *b* are the economies under comparison in the year *t* for the industrial sectors *i*. The IDIS, comparing the sectoral distributions of industrial employment between two economies over time (with one of them being the benchmark), reveals negative (defensive) structural change if it presents increasing trends and positive (offensive) structural change if it presents decreasing trends. The negative structural change can be associated with the higher presence of inter-industry type of trade activity whereas the positive structural change can be associated with the higher presence of intra-industry type of trade activity.[3] The results of this exercise, not presented here due to space restrictions, indicate that regions containing the country's metropolitan and urban centers (Attiki, Central Macedonia, Central Greece, Thessaly and Western Greece) present low or decreasing values of the IDIS. It seems that the Greek urban regions are primarily those that approach, in structural terms, the representative EU regional economy. In contrast, island economies (Ionian Islands, North and South Aegean Islands) present extremely high and increasing values of dissimilarity and indicate widening structural differences with the EU-15 economy and the rest of the country. To these island economies, the behaviour of the region of Peloponnesus in the second half of the 1990s may also be added as it is characterized by increasing dissimilarity.

Sectoral dispersion across space and regional diversity in economic activity are analysed using information-theory based (entropy) measures, introduced to economics by Theil (1967, 1972) in his seminal works (see Appendix 4.3 for details). The results following the application of the Theil Index for NUTS 2 regions[4] are presented in Table 4.6 that follows. These results pertain to 14 manufacturing industries. The analysis of the regional specialization patterns in the Greek economy reveals that the more diversified (less specialized) regions are those containing the largest urban areas in Greece: Attiki (Athens), Central Macedonia (Thessaloniki), Western Greece (Patras) and Thessaly (Larissa and Volos). Less diversified are most of the island economies (Crete could be regarded as an exception) and the Greek mainland regions of Ipeiros and West Macedonia. In contrast East Macedonia and Thrace remains a relatively diversified region, most probably as the result of regional policy which for decades aimed to attract firms and stimulate indigenous firm formation in this part of the country.

Table 4.6 Theil index of industrial diversity, selected years

	1980	*1985*	*1990*	*1995*	*2000*
Eastern Macedonia and Thrace	1.6714	1.7099	1.5917	1.9577	1.7158
Central Macedonia	1.8849	1.8670	1.8210	2.1771	2.1797
Western Macedonia	1.6337	1.6792	1.6824	1.8272	0.9686
Thessaly	1.9074	1.8801	1.9465	2.2075	2.0293
Ipeiros	1.2427	1.3267	1.3311	1.5728	1.1842
Ionian Islands	1.2364	0.8249	1.2639	1.1703	0.000
Western Greece	1.6708	1.6614	1.7612	1.9792	1.9029
Central Greece	2.1687	2.1441	2.1786	2.2376	2.1724
Peloponnesus	1.7789	1.8224	1.8524	2.1594	1.8070
Attiki	2.2520	2.2727	2.2844	2.4431	2.4332
North Aegean Islands	1.3742	1.3864	1.0274	1.3757	0.4887
South Aegean Islands	1.2118	1.1967	1.3498	1.7234	0.8433
Crete	1.4135	1.3947	1.5565	1.7558	1.6255

Source: data from NSSG elaborated by the authors.

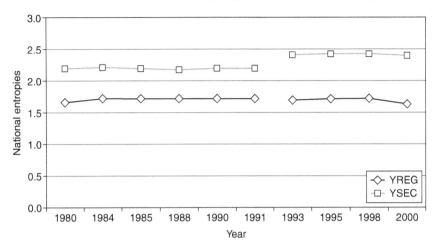

Figure 4.8 National entropies calculated over regions (YREG) and over sectors (YSEC) (source: data from NSSG elaborated by the authors).

Using information over the regional and sectoral dimensions of the data, the time evolution of the corresponding entropies at the national level may be explored further. These national level entropies, presented in Figure 4.8, are meant to capture the extent of the overall spatial unevenness and sectoral specialization. The gap that exists between 1991 and 1993 denotes that the analysis after 1993 is not comparable with that of the earlier period because of the data problems explained earlier. The national entropies calculated when each of the dimensions of the data (regional, sectoral) is taken in isolation present considerable stability as they move over time within a rather narrow band. However, there is some indication for a slight decrease in regional specialization between 1990 and 2000.

Conclusions and policy implications

It seems that the Greek experience within the EU has been one of early divergence (1981–1995) and later convergence to the European average. As far as manufacturing employment is concerned, some existing evidence suggests that in the first years after the Greek accession to the EU the Greek industry suffered a shock. In this context, regional specialization was working against rather than for regional employment growth (at least in manufacturing). As far as overall regional economic convergence is concerned, the existing evidence does not offer clearcut answers. However, independently of the convergence concept employed and the technique used, the evidence seems to suggest that convergence (if it exists) is slow and significant regional disparities persist. In addition, regional inequalities are more pronounced when more informed indices of welfare and development are used instead of merely GDP per capita figures.

To this background, the evidence produced in this chapter suggests that there is a weak tendency overall for larger regional specialization and sectoral concentration but only from 1998 onwards. For the period considered as a whole, there has been considerable stability in the processes of regional-industrial diversity and industrial-spatial concentration. Despite the overall de-industrialization of the country and the rather unfavorable intra-EU trade conditions, it seems that, within manufacturing, structural change across Greek regions has been a rather slow process. This may attributed to considerable sectoral inertia in manufacturing activity.

Production remains largely concentrated in labour-intensive sectors producing rather undifferentiated products. At the spatial level, capital-intensive sectors appear to be concentrated in more urbanized and more developed regions. This raises concerns about rising regional inequalities in the future.

These tendencies are accompanied by a gradual deterioration of the regional dimension of the Greek industrial policy. This may be unfortunate since the already more developed regions are those that are more diversified and thereby better equipped to deal with shocks.

Appendix 4.1: Indices included in the CIWD

Table 4.A1 Indices included in the CIWD

GDP per capita (€/inhabitant)
Stated income per capita (€/inhabitant)
Savings per capita (€/inhabitant)
Use of electrical power for household purposes (MWh/100 inhabitants)
Private cars (Cars/100 inhabitants)
Telephone connections (Connections/100 inhabitants)
GDP of secondary sector (% of total GDP)
GDP of tertiary sector (% of total GDP)
Population density (inhabitants/km²)
Population change from 1961 (% of population 1961)
Urban population (% of total population)
Economically active population (% of total population)
Employed population (% of labour force)
Graduates of tertiary education (% of total population)
Area of new buildings (km²/10,000 inhabitants)
Hotel beds (Beds/1,000 inhabitants)
Tickets in museums (Tickets/1,000 inhabitants)
Gravity index (Distances from all regions weighted by their populations)
Schools (Number/10,000 students)
Hospital beds (Beds/10,000 inhabitants)
Use of electrical power for industrial purposes (MWh/100 inhabitants)

Source: Petrakos and Psycharis (2004).

Appendix 4.2: Data-related difficulties

These primarily have to do with the abolishment of the Census of Manufactures (the last one conducted was in 1988). Data from this source had the advantage of covering the total population of firms operating in Greece, independently of their size. An alternative data source is the Annual Industrial Survey conducted by the National Statistical Service of Greece (NSSG). Here, the advantage lies in the fact that the data becomes available on annual basis. This, however, comes at the expense of data coverage since establishments employing less than ten employees are excluded from the survey. Furthermore, firms employing from 10–19 employees have only been sampled for the survey years up until 1992. When it comes to the spatial dimension of the survey data, however, these become available for firms employing 20 or more employees. This data-coverage problem is further accentuated by NSSG policy (based on confidentiality) whereby data in cases where there are two of less establishments in a region (NUTS 2 or NUTS 3) cannot be provided. Since approximately 85 per cent of Greek enterprises employ less than five people (Gekas, 2005), the case in which information is withheld arises often. This, in effect, results in missing observations and, to some extent, distorts the perceived regional distribution of manufacturing establishments. From 1993 onwards, firms employing less than ten employees continue to be excluded from the surveys; however the population of all remaining firm-size strata (in employment terms) is being surveyed. Data at the regional level that become available from 1993 onwards relate to establishments employing ten or more employees. This creates some additional problems as far as a direct comparison of surveys before and after 1993 is concerned.

Appendix 4.3: A brief description of the Theil index

Theil (1972: 23–32) was interested in applying entropy (expected information) measures for analysing industrial diversity in Standard Metropolitan Statistical Areas (SMSAs) in the USA. Despite this original application to the problem matter by Theil, interest in applying entropy measures for analysing industrial specialization of regional economies (inverse regional diversity) and geographical concentration of industries (inverse sectoral dispersion) was only recently renewed by Aiginger and Davies (2004) and Aiginger and Pfaffermayr (2004). A brief description of the method drawn from Theil (1972: 26–27) is given in order to facilitate interpretation. Let $empl_{ri}$ be the employment in region r and industrial sector i and define $p_{ri} = \dfrac{empl_{ri}}{\sum_r \sum_i empl_{ri}}$, having the property that $\sum_r \sum_i p_{ri} = 1$.

The Theil regional-diversity entropy-measure is Hthen: $H_r = \sum_i \dfrac{p_{ri}}{p_r} \log \dfrac{p_r}{p_{ri}}$,

where p_r is defined as $\sum_i p_{ri}$. This measure takes the value of 0 when only one sector is present in region r and the value ln(n) where all n industrial sectors employ the same number of persons in the region in question. In order to establish correspondence with the work of Aiginger and Davies (2004) and avoid possible misunderstandings note that $\dfrac{p_{ri}}{p_r} = \dfrac{\dfrac{empl_{ri}}{\sum_r \sum_i empl_{ri}}}{\dfrac{\sum_i empl_{ri}}{\sum_r \sum_i empl_{ri}}} = \dfrac{empl_{ri}}{\sum_i empl_{ri}}$. Since the right

hand side of the previous formulation is bounded in the interval [0, 1] and Aiginger and Davies (2004) essentially define their specialization measure as

$\sum_i \dfrac{p_{ri}}{p_r} \log \dfrac{p_{ri}}{p_r}$, multiplying their measure by -1 is needed to make their

measure positive.[5] That is $Spec_r = -\sum_i \dfrac{p_{ri}}{p_r} \log \dfrac{p_{ri}}{p_r}$. Thus, the measure used in this

study is equivalent to that used in the recent literature and has the same properties and interpretation (Aiginger and Davies 2004: 235). A national-level entropy can be derived using information in the regional dimension of the data using the

relationship $\bar{H}_r = \sum_r p_r \log$ (Theil 1967: 296). An entropy measure for the

spatial dispersion at the sectoral level (notion inversely related to concentration)

can be calculated using: $H_i = \sum_r \dfrac{p_{ri}}{p_i} \log \dfrac{p_i}{p_{ri}}$, where $p_i = \sum_r p_{ri}$. This measure

takes the value of 0 if the sector in question is met in only one region and the maximum value of $\ln(v)$ (where v is the number of regions) if all v regions employ the same number of people in this sector. Equivalence to the corresponding index for geographic concentration used in Aiginger and Davies (2004) can also be established. A national-level entropy can also be constructed from the

sectoral dimension of the data using the formula: $\bar{H}_i = \sum_i p_i \log \dfrac{1}{p_i}$. The Theil

index has the advantage that it is a decomposable inverse index of absolute regional specialization.

Appendix 4.4: The influence of the level of spatial aggregation on the estimation of Greek regional-industrial patterns

Before presenting results of applying the Theil index to Greek data, a decision must be reached regarding the level of spatial aggregation to be used in the analysis. It appears that the regional-industrial patterns of the Greek economy are not significantly influenced by the spatial level of analysis, as it is revealed from an indirect comparison of the values of the Theil index for the NUTS 2 and NUTS 3 regions (a direct comparison is not possible due to the different number of regions

Table 4.A4 Intertemporal Spearman rank correlation coefficients of Theil indices, selected periods

Period	Regional diversification (NUTS 2)	Regional diversification (NUTS 3)	Sectoral dispersion (NUTS 2)	Sectoral dispersion (NUTS 3)
1980–1985	0.989	0.910	0.952	0.978
1980–1990	0.929	0.807	0.921	0.912
1980–1995	0.956	0.786	0.969	0.974
1980–2000	0.909	0.654	0.934	0.929
1985–1990	0.934	0.866	0.903	0.925
1985–1995	0.962	0.851	0.982	0.943
1985–2000	0.874	0.762	0.940	0.912
1990–1995	0.984	0.918	0.868	0.881
1990–2000	0.888	0.789	0.890	0.907
1995–2000	0.937	0.843	0.951	0.940

Source: data from NSSG elaborated by the authors.

that each spatial level contains). The relative positions of each region and each sector are correlated for discrete time periods, separately for each spatial level, using the Spearman correlation coefficient. The five-year and the ten-year Spearman averages, presented in Table 4.A4, reveal a great deal of intertemporal persistence of the regional diversification and sectoral dispersion patterns between the two spatial levels of analysis.[6] As is to be expected, this persistence is higher over five-year than ten-year intervals and over NUTS 2 rather than NUTS 3 levels of spatial aggregation. However, as a general pattern, it appears that persistence in both regional and sectoral dimensions was higher in the 1980s than in the 1990s.

Notes

1 It is possible for the IEI to take high (low) values for sectors that have minimal (intense) trade activity both with the EU-15 and the world. Perceiving economic integration as a relation of interdependence among the members of an economic union, this "paradox" does not invalidate the IEI.

2 $CRS_r = \frac{1}{2} \sum_i \left| \frac{E_{ir}}{E_r} - \frac{E_i}{E} \right|$

where E denotes for employment, i for industrial sectors and r for regions. The value of the coefficient is within the interval $[0, 1]$, ranging from complete similarity to complete dissimilarity between the regional and the national distribution of employment across industrial sectors.

3 Intra-industry trade is considered to be more beneficial to economic performance since it favours the exploitation of scale economies and stimulates innovation; moreover it is less disruptive since production factors remain within the same industry. On the other hand, inter-industry trade, though positive in some cases, cannot produce long-term convergence.

4 Regional-industrial patterns of the Greek economy are not significantly influenced by the spatial level of analysis (see Table 4.A4 in Appendix 4.4).

5 Alternatively it can be shown that:

$$\sum_i \frac{p_{ri}}{p_r} \log \frac{p_{ri}}{p_r} = \sum_i \frac{p_{ri}}{p_r} \log\left(\frac{1}{\frac{p_r}{p_{ri}}}\right) = \sum_i \frac{p_{ri}}{p_r}\left[\log(1) - \log \frac{p_r}{p_{ri}}\right] = -\sum_i \frac{p_{ri}}{p_r} \log \frac{p_r}{p_{ri}}$$

6 The respective comparison between the European Regional (Cambridge Econometrics) data for the NUTS 2 spatial level and the NSSG data for the NUTS 3 spatial level reveals the same intertemporal persistence concerning the regional diversification patterns.

References

Aiginger, K. and Davies, S.W. (2004), Industrial Specialization and Geographic Concentration: Two Sides of the Same Coin? Not for the European Union, *Journal of Applied Economics*, vol. 7, n. 2, pp. 231–248.

Aiginger, K. and Pfaffermayr, M. (2004), The Single Market and Geographic Concentration in Europe, *Review of International Economics*, vol. 12, n. 1, pp. 1–11.

Barro, R.J. and Sala–i–Martin, X.X. (1991), Convergence across States and Regions, *Brookings Papers on Economic Activity*, vol. 1, pp. 107–179.

Dixon, R.J. and Thirlwall, A.P. (1975), *Regional Growth and Unemployment in the United Kingdom,* London: Macmillan.

Fotopoulos, G., Giannias, D. and Liargovas, D. (2002), Economic Development and Convergence in Greek regions, 1970–1994, *Aichoros*, vol. 1, n. 1, pp. 60–91 (in Greek).

Gekas, R. (2005), Sectors of the Greek Economy: Structural Problems and Prospects, in Kollias, C., Naxakis, H. and Chletsos, M. (eds): *Contemporary Approaches of the Greek Economy*, Athens: Patakis, pp. 139–184 (in Greek).

Giannias, D., Liargovas, P. and Manolas, G. (1997), Regional Disparities in Greece, 1961–1991, *Topos*, n. 13/97, pp. 47–61 (in Greek).

Ioannides, Y. and Petrakos, G. (2000), Regional Disparities in Greece: The Performance of Crete, Peloponnese and Thessaly, *European Investment Bank Papers*, vol. 5, n. 1, pp. 31–58.

Isard, W. (1960), *Methods of Regional Analysis*, Cambridge: MIT Press.

Jackson, M. and Petrakos, G. (2001), Industrial Performance under Transition, in Petrakos, G. and Totev, S. (eds) *The Development of the Balkan Region*, Aldershot: Ashgate, pp. 141–174.

Kazakos, P. (2001), *Between the State and the Market*, Athens: Patakis.

Kollias, C., Manolas, G. and Palaiologou, S.M. (2005), The Greek Economy: Comparative Position and Evolution of Basic Figures, in Kollias, C., Naxakis, H. and Chletsos, M. (eds) *Contemporary Approaches of the Greek Economy*, Athens: Patakis, pp. 67–100 (in Greek).

Konsolas, N., Papadaskalopoulos, A. and Plaskovitis, I. (2002), *Regional Development in Greece*, Berlin: Springer.

Liargovas, P., Giannias, D. and Fotopoulos, G. (2003), Convergence and Divergence in the Quality of Life in Greece, 1960–2000, *Aichoros*, vol. 2, n. 1, pp. 114–128 (in Greek).

Papadoulis, A., Petrakos, G. and Psycharis, Y. (2004), Investment Incentives Policies and Regional Development: Survey and First Assessment, *Review of Economic Sciences*, vol. 5, pp. 5–40 (in Greek).

Petrakos, G. and Christodoulakis, N. (1997), Economic Development in the Balkan Countries and the Role of Greece: From Bilateral Relations to the Challenge of Integration, *CEPR Discussion Paper Series*, n. 1620.

Petrakos, G. and Christodoulakis, N. (2000), Greece and the Balkans: The Challenge of Integration, in Petrakos, G., Maier, G. and Gorzelak, G. (eds.) *Integration and Transition in Europe: The Economic Geography of Interaction*, London: Routledge, pp. 269–294.

Petrakos, G. and Pitelis, C. (2001), Peripherality and Integration: The Experience of Greece and its Implications for the Balkan Economies in Transition, in Petrakos, G. and Totev, S. (eds) *The Development of the Balkan Region*, Aldershot: Ashgate, pp. 283–316.

Petrakos, G. and Psycharis, Y. (2004), *Regional Development in Greece*, Athens: Kritiki (in Greek).

Petrakos, G. and Saratsis, Y. (2000), Regional Inequalities in Greece, *Papers in Regional Science*, vol. 79, pp. 57–74.

Petrakos, G. and Tsoukalas, D. (1999), Metropolitan Concentration in Greece: An Empiric Survey, in Economou, D. and Petrakos, G. (eds) *The Development of Greek Cities: Interdisciplinary Approaches of Urban Analysis and Policy*, Volos: University of Thessaly Press, pp. 247–266 (in Greek).

Petrakos, G, Rodriguez-Pose, A. and Rovolis, A. (2005), Growth, Integration and Regional Disparities in the European Union, *Environment and Planning A*, vol. 37, n. 10, pp. 1837–1855.

Polyzos, S. and Petrakos, G. (2005), Evaluation of the Greek Regional Policy with the Use of Regional Multipliers, in Kollias, C., Naxakis, H. and Chletsos, M. (eds) *Contemporary Approaches of the Greek Economy*, Athens: Patakis, pp. 269–303 (in Greek).

Siriopoulos, C. and Asteriou, D. (1998), Testing the Convergence Hypothesis for Greece, *Managerial and Decision Economics*, vol. 18, pp. 1–8.

Stratos, I. (2000), Manufacturing: Guarantee of the Economy's Development, *Economikos Tahidromos*, Special Issue 16/03/2000, pp. 40–41 (in Greek).

Tsionas, E. (2002), Another Look at Regional Convergence in Greece, *Regional Studies*, vol. 36, pp. 603–609.

Theil, H. (1967), *Economics and Information Theory*, Amsterdam: North-Holland.

Theil, H. (1972), *Statistical Decomposition Analysis: with Applications in the Social and Administrative Sciences*, Amsterdam: North-Holland.

5 Southern enlargement and structural change

Case studies of Spain, Portugal and France

Christiane Krieger-Boden[1]

Introduction

The Southern enlargement of the European Union in 1981 (accession of Greece) and 1986 (accession of Spain and Portugal), respectively, marks an event with many analogies to the current process of Eastern enlargement, particularly regarding the economic heterogeneity between accession and incumbent countries. Therefore, it seems worthwhile to examine the experience of the Southern enlargement in order to apply the results to the current enlargement process. In this chapter, we analyse the experience of the then accession countries Spain and Portugal, and of the then incumbent country France that is most adjacent to the former two.

France was among the founding members of the European Union and participated in all subsequent integration steps, i.e. since the 1980s, in the Southern enlargement in 1981/1986, the completion of the Single Market in 1992, the Northern enlargement in 1995, and the creation of the European Monetary Union in 1999/2002 (which, however, is too recent to be covered by the present analysis). By contrast, Spain and Portugal kept on experimenting with autarkic and corporative economic regimes for some time after the war. Both countries relied on external protection via high customs tariffs, and on internal dirigisme, and they thus were isolated from external markets. In the late 1950s, however, they gradually opened up to world markets. In 1960, Portugal joined the EFTA. In the early 1970s, both countries concluded trade agreements with the then EEC stipulating gradual and mutual reductions of customs tariffs (Schrader and, Laaser, 1994). In 1974 and 1975, respectively, the authoritarian Portuguese and Spanish regimes were vanquished and transformed into modern democratic societies. Subsequently in 1977, negotiations with the EU started and succeeded in the accession of the two countries in 1986, and it was only then that the countries completely broke with their protectionist tradition. The respective transition periods after the accession ended in 1993 (Portugal) and 1996 (Spain).

The three countries represent specific cases with peculiarities that might affect their specialization pattern:

- All three of them are shaped in a rather monocentric way – rooted in the centralistic tradition of the former monarchies. This pattern persists to this day, notwithstanding major efforts in all countries to decentralize administrative responsibilities (major devolution steps in France since 1982, transformation into a federal state in Spain in 1992), and notwithstanding the vigorous and sometimes even violent movements for autonomy in various regions.

- France and Spain are relatively large countries covering an area of 550 and 500 thousand square kilometres, respectively, with populations of about 55 and 38 million people, respectively. Portugal, by contrast, covers only 92 thousand square kilometres and has a population of about 8.5 million people. All three are much more sparsely populated than most countries in Central Europe.
- France represents a country with a relatively high development level. By contrast, Spain and even more so Portugal revealed a low development level at least before their accession to the EU. This initial situation was very much comparable to that of the present enlargement process.

Moreover, all three countries represent a political tradition inclined towards a very active role for governments in economic policy (cf. Dormois, 1999 for France), and this, again, might affect their specialization pattern. In all three countries, the state protected and supported domestic firms and branches regarded as important for the country, though with different intentions. The French "planification" after the war was aimed at reducing the extent of uncertainty and risk of entrepreneurs by dispersing as much exante information as possible between all economic actors (Foucauld, 1994). By contrast, the economic policies of the authoritarian Salazár and Franco regimes were mainly aimed at rapidly industrializing the countries while protecting the corporative structure and the existing oligopolies (Balbín, 1999; Confraria, 1999). All three countries radically and rapidly liberalized and modernized their respective economies after their accession to the EU (OECD, 2000), with the major difference that this accession was in 1957 in the case of France, and in 1986 in the cases of Spain and Portugal.

More specifically, the structural policies in all three countries were by far not neutral to industrial and regional structures. The industrial policies relied heavily on state-owned enterprises (SOEs). All three countries saw massive waves of nationalizations of private enterprises: Portugal started socialist nationalizations after the revolution of 1974. Spain, after 1976, transformed the Franco-created state-owned holding company INI (Instituto National de Industria) into an "enterprise hospital" that acquired several large private firms in trouble. France in 1982 engaged in a number of nationalizations after the socialist party came into power. But in the 1990s, all three countries performed a complete turnaround and embarked onto a policy of privatizing SOEs. However, governments still quite readily bail out failing formerly SOEs, and the bulk of subsidies seems also be directed towards these enterprises. More generally, subsidies tended to be directed towards:

1   industries that used to be regarded as being important for a strong and self-sufficient economy, and that are now ailing, like agriculture, iron and steel and shipbuilding (e.g. Salmon, 1995 for Spain);

2   industries regarded as being modern and growth-promoting like aeronautics, nuclear industries and telecommunications.

Also, subsidies tended to favour large firms. Portugal also embarked on a special programme to support its large amounts of small and medium sized enterprises (Amaral, 2003). Regarding regional policies, the three countries used all kinds of policy instruments at hand (regional incentive schemes, SOEs, indicative planning, installation and support of high-technology parks) in trying to decentralize the economy, and to counterbalance at least partially the rather centripetal stance of their industrial policies (Balchin and Sýkora, 1999). It is against this background that the structural change during the integration process must be seen.

The remainder of the chapter is organized as follows: the next starts with describing the degree and nature of regional specialization and its change, and compares it to the regional structure of the countries with respect to population density. We then compare the structural change between South European regions to their performance with respect to income and growth as well as to employment. The chapter concludes by discussing what can be learnt from the specific Southern enlargement experiences for the overall regional consequences of integration and Eastern enlargement on regional structural change.

The regional specialization in Southwest Europe and its change during integration

The changing position of regions in a changing division of labour can be highlighted by the specialization pattern of regions: regions that reveal a high degree of specialization compared to others play a specific role in the division of labour, and it depends on the specific nature of this specialization, i.e. on the specific industry mix in the region, what this role is like. Accordingly, a change of specialization indicates a structural change of this role that may impact on the employment and income opportunities of the region. In the following, it will be shown that there is a characteristic spatial division of labour in the three countries under investigation, and that their specialization decreased after their accession.

The *degree* of regional specialization in Southwest Europe was found, in Chapter 1 of this volume, to be relatively lowly for French regions and relatively high for Spanish and Portuguese regions, particularly before their accession to the EU. In this chapter, the regional specialization is analyzed in more detail on the ground of national and much more disaggregated databases.[2] It has to be kept in mind that these databases differ substantially from one country to the other, and that the levels of specialization cannot be compared between the regions of any two countries, but only within one country. In Figure 5.1, absolute and relative specialization degrees of French, Spanish and Portuguese regions are provided, where the regions have been arranged according to their approximate geographic situation and adjacency from North to South. French regions appear to be specialized relatively homogenously, with the Southern regions tending to be a bit more specialized than the Northern, and with a few regions standing

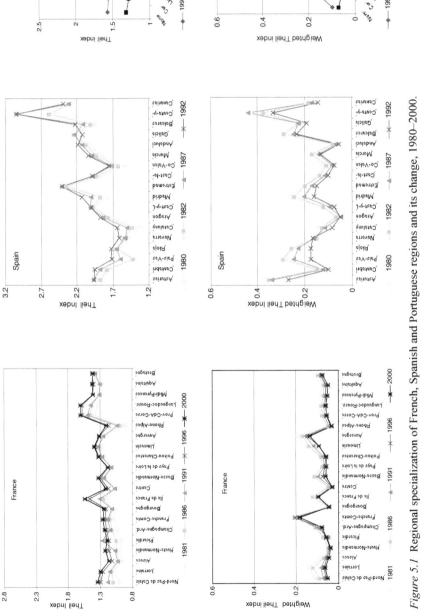

Figure 5.1 Regional specialization of French, Spanish and Portuguese regions and its change, 1980–2000.

out: Île de France, Limousin, Languedoc-Roussillon and Provence-Alpes-Côte d'Azur seem to divert from their surroundings in terms of absolute special-ization, Franche-Comté, Limousin and Auvergne in terms of relative special-ization. Spanish and Portuguese regions seem to be more heterogeneous, with a certain tendency towards higher specialization at the borders and in Southern regions.[3] Moreover, as compared to their surrounding regions, Extremadura stands out in terms of absolute specialization, and Madrid stands out in terms of relative specialization. In Portugal, the region of the capital city Lisboa e Vale de Tejo is characterized by a particularly low specialization, which is in contrast to the results for the French and Spanish capital cities.

Over time, the data allow for an insight on the evolution of specialization during the southern enlargement, as they cover most parts of the accession period at least in the case of France and Spain (see above; unfortunately, for Portugal, no figures for a comparable period were available). During this period, both, French and Spanish regions underwent a process of increasing absolute and decreasing relative specialization (Figure 5.1):[4] They became at the same time more similar to the average specialization of their respective home country, more similar also to the average EU specialization (cf. Chapter 1), but less similar to the absolute, equal-shares distribution. Portugal experienced decreas-ing specialization during the 1990s. All regions within a country also became more similar to each other, as there was a negative correlation between initial specialization and the subsequent change of specialization (Table 5.1). Taken together, these results seem to indicate a structural convergence of the regions towards a moving target: a changing national and perhaps even changing European industry mix. The results also underline the finding from Chapter 1

Table 5.1 Initial specialization and subsequent specialization change

	Theil index		Weighted Theil index	
	Pearson correlation coefficient	Error probability	Pearson correlation coefficient	Error probability
French regions 1981–2000	**−0.461***	**0.04**	**−0.704***	**0.00**
Spanish regions 1980–1992	−0.122	0.63	**−0.730***	**0.00**
Portuguese regions 1991–2001	−0.488	0.27	**−0.762***	**0.05**

Source: SESSI, Enquête annuelle d'entreprise; INE Spain, EIG data; INE Portugal, Census data; CE, data.

Notes
* Significant at the 5% level.
** Significant at the 1% level.
*** Significant at the 0.1% level.

that the change of specialization seems to be more pronounced for countries during their respective accession period, which may be due to their initially higher specialization degree.

This analysis of the degree of specialization opens up to a more in-depth analysis of the *nature* of regional specialization. A highly specialized region could be specialized on quite different kinds of industries, and this could entail much different perspectives regarding the income and employment performance of the region. In order to condense the information on regional specialization from a breakdown of up to 244 industries (cf. note 1), groups of industries are identified with similar (exogenous) characteristics related to trade and location theories. Trade theories predict certain concentration and dispersion adjustments from integration, and these differ for different industries: the new trade theories and new economic geography (NEG), for instance, expect an extreme concentration of industries with scale economies at only one location, accompanied by a monopolistic competition that allows such industries and their locations to achieve a higher income than others. Ricardian trade theories state a concentration or dispersion pattern according to the availability of resources for resource dependent industries. Heckscher-Ohlin trade theories, by contrast, state a concentration and dispersion behaviour along the lines of comparative advantage for industries that neither contain scale economies nor require very specific resource inputs, and that are often referred to as being footloose. Industries of these various types are expected to impact differently on the regions in which they are located.

The following groups of industries are distinguished assessing also their actual concentration pattern (Figure 5.2):[5] *Agricultural activities* such as plant growing, livestock production, forestry and fisheries need land as a resource, and they are believed to bear little economies of scale. In line with this expectation, usually, they are indeed highly dispersed across the territory. Within manufacturing, *resource intensive industries* are identified according to their dependence on highly localized resources, such as coal mining and coke ovens, iron and steel works, mining, production and transformation of metals and non-metals, petroleum refining, and, in fact, these industries are found to be concentrated where the respective resources are accessible (at their deposits or at specific harbors).[6] From the other manufacturing industries, some are characterized particularly by *high internal IRS*, such as the aircraft industry, some branches of the chemical and machinery industries, automobile industry, office and computing machinery and electronic material industries, optical and professional instruments industries, some food industries.[7] These are predicted by NEG theory to be highly concentrated, too. Actually, most of these industries are found to be highly concentrated, with some exceptions though, that reduce the average concentration degree of the whole group. The remaining manufacturing industries may be labelled *footloose industries,* as they require no specific locational characteristics and, therefore, can be expected to be dispersed. Still, some of them are found to be quite *concentrated*, i.e. some food industries, footwear, while most are indeed found to be fairly *dispersed*, like branches

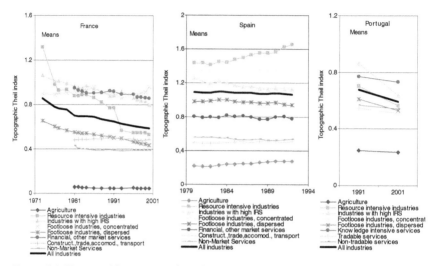

Figure 5.2 Topographic concentration of French, Spanish and Portuguese industries and its change over time (source: SESSI, Enquête annuelle d'entreprise; INE Spain, EIG data; INE Portugal, Census data; CE, data; own estimates).

of the textiles industry, automotive industry, chemical industry and several consumption industries.

The large group of services is roughly divided into three groups that can also be expected to follow different spatial pattern. *Knowledge intensive services* (i.e. financial and other market services in the case of France and Spain) require a high knowledge input to be found primarily in agglomerations and indeed they appear to be the most concentrated among all services.[8] All other *tradable services* (i.e. construction, trade, accommodation and transport services in the case of France and Spain) require no specific locations, and in line with this, they are actually among the lowest concentrated industries. Finally, non-tradable services (i.e. non-market services in the case of France and Spain) offer consumer-related services and can thus be expected to be located where the people are, and indeed they come out to be lowly concentrated.

Figure 5.2 displays not only the initial concentration/dispersion pattern of these industry groups in France, Spain and Portugal, but also its evolution over time, during the period of Southern enlargement. On average, the concentration of all industries seems to have decreased, more explicitly in the case of France (and Portugal in the 1990s), less explicitly in the case of Spain. This overall trend applies in particular to industries with scale economies, and to footloose industries that were already dispersed. It also applies to resource intensive industries, except in Spain where these industries became even more concentrated.

These industry groups with their characteristic concentration behaviour are used as an input to classify French, Spanish and Portuguese regions according to

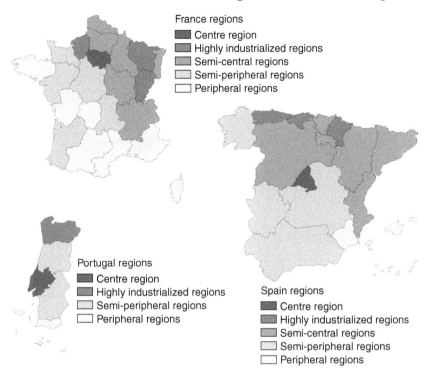

Figure 5.3 French, Spanish and Portuguese region classes based on industrial structures (source: SESSI, Enquête annuelle d'entreprise; INE Spain, EIG data; INE Portugal, census data; CE, data).

the nature of their initial specialization.[9] Five classes of regions with different industry mixes are distinguished (Figure 5.3). Their different industry mixes are presented in Figure 5.4 that displays the location coefficients for the industry groups described before, in the various region classes, for different selected years.[10] Although the region classes are classified solely according to their structural decomposition, they are found to share further characteristics with respect to population density and geographic situation (cf. Table 5.2).

- One region class, labelled *highly industrialized regions*, contains regions with relatively high shares of manufacturing industries, and (except in the case of Portugal) with a focus on resource dependent industries. In France, this class includes the three regions Haute Normandie, Lorraine and Franche-Comté, in Spain the regions Asturias, Cantabria and Navarra, and in Portugal the region Norte. The French regions are also characterized by a focus on some footloose industries. These regions are situated at the Northern borders of their respective countries (that is, as closely as possible to the central parts of Europe), and they are often densely populated (Table 5.2).

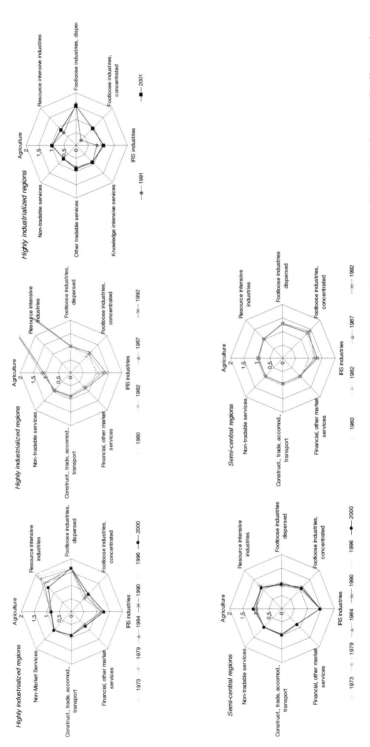

Figure 5.4 Industry mix of French, Spanish and Portuguese regions, 1973–2000 (location coefficients) (source: SESSI, Enquête annuelle d'entreprise; INE Spain, EIG data; INE Portugal, census data; CE, data).

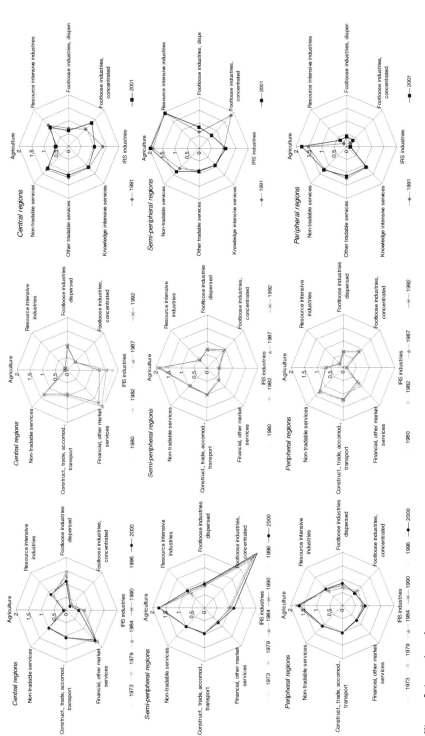

Figure 5.4 continued.

Table 5.2 Population density of region classes (persons/sqkm)

France	(Total 108.0)	Spain	(Total 79.5)	Portugal	Total 112
Highly industrialized regions					
Haute Normandie	145.1	Asturias	99.6	Norte	171
Lorraine	98.2	Cantabria	99.9		
Franche-Comté	69.1	Navarra	51.7		
Semi-central regions					
Picardie	52.4	País Vasco	284.7		
Champagne-Ardennes	96.0	Rioja	52.9		
Bourgogne	51.0	Aragón	24.5		
Nord-Pas de Calais	322.6	Castilla y Leon	26.2		
Alsace	211.0	Cataluña	194.1		
Rhône-Alpes	129.9	Communidad Valenciana	174.6		
Central regions					
Île de France	914.0	Madrid	649.1	Lisboa e Vale de Tejo	289
Semi-peripheral regions					
Centre	62.6	Galicia	92.5	Centro	75
Basse Normandie	81.1	Castilla la Mancha	21.7	Alentejo	20
Pays de la Loire	101.1	Extremadura	25.9		
Auvergne	70.8	Andalucía	83.3		
Aquitaine	50.4				
Peripheral regions					
Bretagne	107.3	Murcia	159.1	Algarve	78
Poitou-Charentes	63.8	Baleares	100.1	Açores	102
Limousin	56.6	Ceuta y Melilla	4545.2	Madeira	312
Midi-Pyrénées	42.0	Canarias	236.9		
Languedoc-Roussillon	84.5				
Provence-Alpes-Côte d'Azur-Corse	140.0				

Source: Eurostat, REGIO Database.

- Another region class is labelled *semi-central regions* (to qualify them as relatively similar to the group of central regions defined hereafter), and is characterized by a certain focus on industries with high IRS, and by location coefficients close to one for most other sectors (i.e. the respective industrial shares are close to average). In France, this class contains the regions Nord-Pas de Calais, Picardie, Champagne-Ardennes, Alsace, Bourgogne and Rhône-Alpes, in Spain Pais Vasco, Rioja, Castilla y Leon, Aragon, Cataluña and Communidad Valenciana. No Portuguese regions fit into this class. The regions happen to be situated between the classes of highly industrialized and central regions, in a belt stretching from Northwest to Southeast of each respective country.
- The class of *central regions* contains the capitals of the three countries, the regions Île de France, Madrid and Lisboa e Vale de Tejo. The regions are characterized by a focus on knowledge intensive (or financial and other market) services, yet they differ with respect to other foci: Île de France is specialized on dispersed footloose industries, Madrid and Lisboa on IRS industries. All three regions reveal to be very densely populated, and to be situated at the centre of their respective countries.
- A region class labelled s*emi-peripheral regions* (to distinguish it from further, more remote regions) is characterized by a focus on agriculture, moreover, in the case of France, on concentrated footloose industries. This class contains the French regions Basse Normandie, Pays de la Loire, Centre, Auvergne and Aquitaine, the Spanish regions Galicia, Extremadura, Castilla la Mancha and Andalucía, and the Portuguese regions Centro and Alentejo. These regions are often sparsely populated. They happen to be situated between centre and peripheral regions in the Southwestern part of each country.
- The last group, *peripheral regions*, differs between the countries: the French and Portuguese regions are characterized by a focus on agriculture, the Spanish and Portuguese regions are characterized by relatively high shares of tradable services (or construction, trade, accommodation and transport services in the case of Spain) due to their focus on tourism activities, or even on non-tradable services. In France, the group consists of Bretagne, Poitou-Charentes, Limousin, Midi-Pyrénées, Languedoc-Roussillon and Provence-Alpes-Côte d'Azur-Corse, in Spain of Murcia, Baleares, Ceuta y Melilla and Canarias, and in Portugal of Algarve, Madeira and Açores. Particularly in the case of Spain and Portugal, the regions are rather remote (some even offshore).

All in all, these specialization patterns seem to imply that the spatial structure of all three countries is still significantly shaped from the industrialization process that spread from central Europe from the Northeast to the Southwest of France, crossed the Spanish and Portuguese borders and proceeded stepwise further southwestwards (cf. Rosés, 2003).

Over time, during the period of accession to the EU, the specific special-ization pattern of the region classes got more reinforced in most Spanish cases, less reinforced in most French cases (also in most Portuguese cases during the 1990s), as Figure 5.4 also demonstrates: in various Spanish region classes, the specific foci became more pronounced, with the exception of the central region Madrid. In France, by contrast, the foci of most region classes weakened or remained more or less unchanged, while only the focus of the semi-peripheral region class strengthened. Accordingly, Spanish regions seemed to have become more directed towards their specific comparative advantage. French regions seemed to have diversified their structural mix.

Specialization, structural change and regional performance

Trade theories, particularly NEG, hold that a specific industry mix may determine the performance of a region. Accordingly, the region classes identified according to their industry mix should share common characteristics regarding their performance both in terms of income and employment.

In fact, some relations between region classes and their income and growth performance can be detected. Figure 5.5 shows the static and dynamic dimension of income performance for the regions of the five region classes. To begin with, French regions realized higher income levels (French average: € 23,740, Spanish average: € 15,333, Portuguese average € 11,500 in 2000) while Spanish and Portuguese regions developed more dynamically (French average: 4.0 per cent GDP growth, Spanish average: 4.4 per cent GDP growth, Portuguese average: 7 per cent GDP growth, in the 1990s; for a more meaningful comparison, however, inflation rates would have to be considered).

Beyond these characteristics that are common to all regions of the same country, there are also characteristics that are common to the regions of the same region class, both within each country and also compared to the respective regions of the other countries: highly industrialized regions tended to grow relatively slowly, compared to the respective national average, and to reveal per-capita incomes below the national average, mostly in France, less often in Spain (and not in Portugal). The central regions (except Lisboa e Vale de Tejo) grew faster than their national average and realized above-average income levels. Several peripheral regions tended to grow rapidly in all countries but still realized only below-average income levels. Semi-peripheral and semi-central regions, however, behaved differently in the different countries: in the case of France and Portugal, semi-peripheral regions tended to grow faster than average, and semi-central showed no obvious trend. In the case of Spain, they appeared to develop less dynamically than other regions, and the two groups seemed to be separated by their different income levels (higher for semi-central regions, lower for semi-peripheral regions).

Turning to the employment performance of the regions, there could be expected an even closer relationship to the industrial structure of regions, given that these structures are expressed as employment shares. Yet, some stylized facts on this relationship do not exactly support this expectation. Figure 5.6 displays the static and dynamic dimension of the employment performance: the recent unemployment record, and the preceding employment change in the regions. To start with, it shows the average unemployment to be worse in the former accession country Spain than in the always-incumbent country France (13 per cent compared to 8.5 per cent on average in 2000), yet it is lowest in Portugal (4 per cent on average in 2000). There was not much difference regarding the ability of France and Spain to create new jobs (employment increase around 0.4 per cent in both countries), yet again, Portugal was more successful (1.2 per cent).

The evidence for region classes and their regions in all countries is rather mixed: some regions reveal high rates of unemployment in spite of marked employment increases, others reveal low unemployment rates in spite of severe employment decreases. No unambiguous trends for region classes with their

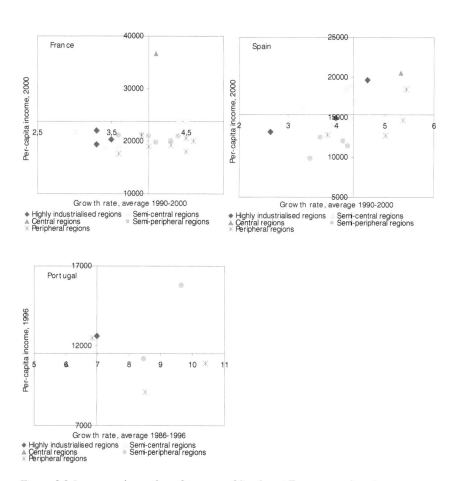

Figure 5.5 Income and growth performance of Southwest European regions (source: eurostat).

Note
The point of origin marks the respective average values of each country.

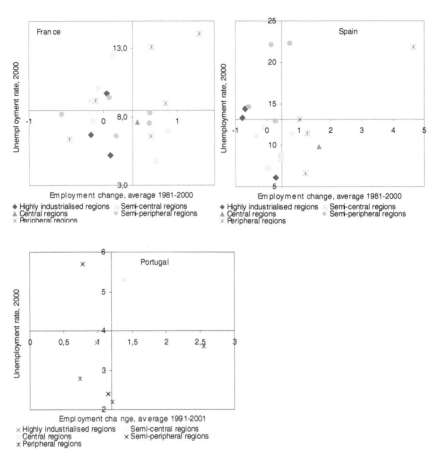

Figure 5.6 Employment performance of Southwest European regions (source: Eurostat).

Note
The point of origin marks the respective average values of each country.

different industry mixes can be detected: only highly industrialized regions were concordant in that they all developed relatively badly with respect to employment. By contrast, in the case of France and Portugal, semi-central, semi-peripheral and peripheral regions exhibited scattered results with respect to their employment performance. In the case of Spain, a bit more conformance is observed: semi-central regions showed little employment change while unemployment was relatively low. Semi-peripheral regions seemed to be worst off with high unemployment and below-average employment development. By contrast, peripheral regions performed relatively well with high employment increases and mostly moderate unemployment levels.

To analyse the relationship between structural change and employment performance in more detail, correlations between both the degree and the nature

Table 5.3 Specialization and employment change

	Initial specialization ↔ subsequent employment change		Specialization change ↔ simultaneous employment change	
	Pearson correlation coefficient	Error probability	Pearson correlation coefficient	Error probability
Theil index				
French regions 1981–2000	−0.228	0.32	0.202	0.38
Spanish regions 1980–1992	0.419	0.08	**0.753*****	**0.00**
Portug. regions 1991–2001	−0.106	0.82	0.377	0.40
Weighted Theil index				
French regions 1981–2000	−0.416	0.06	0.364	0.10
Spanish regions 1980–1992	0.433	0.07	−0.262	0.29
Portug. regions 1991–2001	0.195	0.67	−0.178	0.70

Source: SESSI, Enquête annuelle d'entreprise; INE Spain, EIG data; INE Portugal, Census data; CE, data.

Notes
* Significant at the 5% level.
** Significant at the 1% level.
*** Significant at the 0.1% level.

of regional specialization and the regional employment performance are provided. First, these calculations show that the *degree* of specialization and the employment performance were hardly related. Table 5.3 provides correlation coefficients between the initial specialization of a region and its subsequent employment change, and these coefficients are not significant. Also, there seems to be no very explicit relationship between the change of regional specialization and the simultaneous employment change. Only for Spanish regions, the probability for regional job gains was significantly higher the faster the specialization degree of the respective region increased.

Second, by contrast, the specific *nature of regional specialization*, i.e. the specific industry mix of the regions, seems to coincide more directly with regional employment performance. Table 5.4 looks for the relationship between the initial localization of industry groups in regions (as displayed in Figure 5.4 for region classes) and the subsequent change of employment in this industry group and this region, and of total employment in the region. Accordingly, regional localization seems to be highly and negatively correlated to the subsequent regional employment performance of the respective industry group in the cases of agriculture, resource intensive industries, IRS industries and footloose industries (column 1): the more these specific industry groups were already localized in a specific region, the more they tended to experience job losses in the region. This backlash trend was most pronounced for agriculture and resource intensive industries, confirming widespread expectations on the decline of these industries particularly at their specific

Table 5.4 Regional localization of industry groups and employment change

| | Initial regional location coefficient of industry group ↔ change of… | | Change of regional location coefficient of industry group ↔ change of… | |
	…respective industry group employment in the region	…total regional employment	…respective industry group employment in the region	…total regional employment
	Pearson correlation coefficients (Error probabilities in parentheses)			
Agriculture				
French regions 1981–2000	**-0.939** (**0.00**)	-0.144 (0.53)	**0.582** (**0.01**)	-0.063 (0.79)
Spanish regions 1980–1992	**-0.931** (**0.00**)	**-0.578** (**0.01**)	-0.061 (0.76)	-0.077 (0.76)
Portug. regions 1991–2001	**-0.857** (**0.01**)	-0.309 (0.50)	-0.072 (0.88)	-0.308 (0.50)
Resource intensive industries				
French regions 1981–2000	**-0.972** (**0.00**)	-0.105 (0.65)	**0.980** (**0.00**)	0.125 (0.59)
Spanish regions 1980–1992	**-0.973** (**0.00**)	-0.380 (0.12)	**-0.684** (**0.00**)	-0.225 (0.37)
Portug. regions 1991–2001	**-0.986** (**0.00**)	-0.262 (0.57)	0.427 (0.34)	-0.151 (0.75)
Industries with high IRS				
French regions 1981–2000	**-0.859** (**0.00**)	-0.092 (0.69)	**0.851** (**0.00**)	0.198 (0.39)
Spanish regions 1980–1992	-0.411 (0.09)	-0.273 (0.27)	**0.863** (**0.00**)	-0.176 (0.48)
Portug. regions 1991–2001	0.507 (0.25)	-0.199 (0.67)	0.665 (0.10)	-0.267 (0.56)
Concentrated footloose industries				
French regions 1981–2000	**-0.904** (**0.00**)	-0.366 (0.10)	-0.369 (0.10)	**-0.570** (**0.01**)
Spanish regions 1980–1992	**-0.754** (**0.00**)	-0.094 (0.71)	**0.468** (**0.05**)	**-0.602** (**0.01**)
Portug. regions 1991–2001	**-0.983** (**0.00**)	-0.092 (0.84)	**0.985** (**0.00**)	0.096 (0.84)
Dispersed footloose industries				
French regions 1981–2000	**-0.537** (**0.01**)	-0.349 (0.12)	**0.814** (**0.00**)	-0.224 (0.33)

Spanish regions 1980–1992	**-0.774**	**(0.00)**	-0.299	(0.23)	0.438	(0.07)	**-0.694**	**(0.00)**
Portug. regions 1991–2001	-0.292	(0.52)	-0.374	(0.41)	**0.973**	**(0.00)**	0.089	(0.85)
Knowledge intensive services								
French regions 1981–2000	**0.676**	**(0.00)**	0.395	(0.08)	-0.231	(0.31)	-0.334	(0.14)
Spanish regions 1980–1992	**0.809**	**(0.00)**	0.119	(0.64)	**-0.465**	**(0.05)**	**-0.618**	**(0.01)**
Portug. regions 1991–2001	0.736	(0.06)	0.403	(0.37)	-0.240	(0.60)	-0.720	(0.07)
Tradable services								
French regions 1981–2000	**0.462**	**(0.03)**	**0.583**	**(0.01)**	0.098	(0.67)	-0.169	(0.46)
Spanish regions 1980–1992	**0.814**	**(0.00)**	**0.726**	**(0.00)**	**-0.651**	**(0.00)**	**-0.931**	**(0.00)**
Portug. regions 1991–2001	0.740	(0.06)	**0.805**	**(0.03)**	-0.391	(0.39)	-0.711	(0.07)
Non-tradable services								
French regions 1981–2000	0.162	(0.48)	0.372	(0.09)	0.235	(0.30)	-0.397	(0.08)
Spanish regions 1980–1992	**0.769**	**(0.00)**	**0.829**	**(0.00)**	-0.078	(0.76)	-0.219	(0.38)
Portug. regions 1991–2001	0.063	(0.89)	-0.287	(0.53)	**0.841**	**(0.02)**	-0.026	(0.96)

Source: SESSI, Enquête annuelle d'entreprise; INE Spain, EIG data; INE Portugal, Census data; CE, data.

Note
Bold figures indicate significance at least at the 5%-level.

locations. However, a negative correlation is also observed for the group of industries with high IRS, contradicting familiar NEG perceptions that such industries would get increasingly localized. Also, a negative correlation is observed for concentrated footloose industries. By contrast, the employment changes of services were usually positively correlated to the initial degree of localization of these industries.

In most cases, however, such backlash trends from localized industries seemed not to be strong enough to also determine the overall employment performance of the regions concerned. This is indicated by the mostly insignificant correlations in the second column of Table 5.4. That is to say, the initial localization of an industry group in a certain region is not followed by a systematic increase or decrease of total regional employment and, accordingly, the

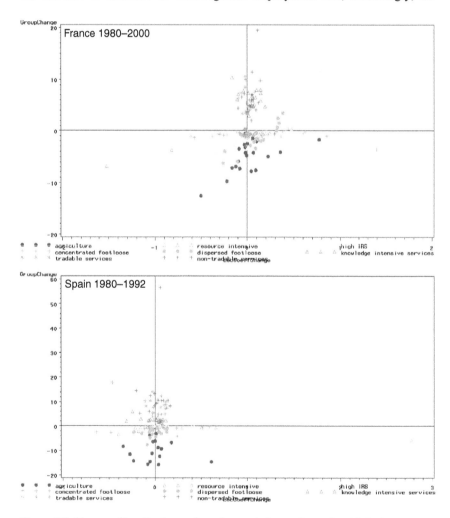

Figure 5.7 Change of localization and employment change, by regional industry groups.

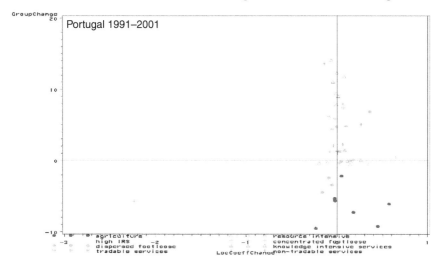

Figure 5.7 continued.

regions concerned by job losses in highly localized industries seem to have found some compensation by job creation in other industries.

Finally, the data offer information on how the restructuring process between industry groups at their various locations takes place. Table 5.4 and, in confirmation of it, Figure 5.7, provide correlations between the change of the localization of an industry group in a region and the simultaneous change of employment in this very industry group in the respective region. These correlations prove to be positive and significant in several cases. Accordingly, an industry group that got less localized in a certain region, like agriculture (dark spots in Figure 5.7), resource intensive industries (light triangles), high IRS industries (light asterisks) or dispersed footloose industries (light spots), did so by retreating from this region, not by expanding in other regions.[11] For the services sectors with increasing localization, however, the correlations between localization change and employment change are usually insignificant. Accordingly, in these cases, the restructuring process seems to have taken place both via the generation of new jobs in the regions with increased location coefficients as well as via employment reduction in all other regions.

Conclusions

The Southern enlargement of the European Union provides a useful example of an enlargement with very heterogeneous partners and hence with analogies to the current eastern Enlargement. The major results of this enlargement round with respect to the then-incumbent country France and the then-accession countries Spain and Portugal are discussed below.

Regarding the *degree of specialization*, its level was low in France, but relatively high in the accession countries Spain and Portugal, particularly before their accession. This high specialization of the then accession countries declined rapidly during the accession period (cf. Chapter 1). Within the countries, specialization degrees tended to rise from the centre to the peripheries, where the French centre Île de France itself was relatively highly specialized, too, in contrast to the Spanish and Portuguese centers. Over time, French, Spanish and Portuguese regions became at the same time more similar to the average specialization of their respective home country, more similar also to the average EU specialization, and more similar to each other, yet less similar to the absolute equal-shares distribution. They seemed to have converged towards a changing national and perhaps even changing European industry mix.

Regarding the *nature of their specialization*, a certain weak core-periphery pattern is detected, as region classes with similar industry mix seem to be situated in characteristic succession across space, with a characteristic central region in the middle, with a highly industrialized periphery situated at the borders towards Central Europe, with a remote and backward periphery and with some in-between regions. The specific specialization pattern of the region classes got more reinforced in most Spanish cases, less reinforced in most French cases. Accordingly, Spanish regions seemed to have become more directed towards their specific comparative advantage, while French regions seemed to have diversified their structural mix.

The *income and growth performance* of the regions differed markedly, but regions belonging to the same region classes with a similar industrial mix seemed to share some stylized characteristics, distinct from other region classes, both within each country and also compared to the respective regions of the other countries: the highly industrialized regions thus appear as falling-back regions, performing low growth and ending up with below-average per-capita incomes. The central regions realised above-average income levels and grew fast in France and Spain, not in Portugal. The remote peripheral regions appear as catching-up regions; they tended to reveal medium to high growth rates but still realized only below-average income levels. Semi-peripheral and semi-central regions, however, did not show a very obvious uniform performance behaviour.

The relationship of the *regional employment performance* to the regional industrial structure is weak. A high initial specialization of a region onto a specific industry had a negative effect on subsequent employment growth in that specific industry (which is consistent with a general tendency towards decreasing specialization). This negative relationship can be observed, in particular, in regions specialized in resource dependent and IRS industries. The significantly negative industry-specific specialization-growth nexus did, however, generally not translate into a negative aggregate specialization-growth nexus: there is little evidence of a high initial specialization onto single industries, or a comparatively high aggregate specialization generally shaping aggregate regional employment growth to a notable extent.

Notes

1 I like to thank Florian Siedenburg for substantial and valuable research assistance, and Eckhardt Bode and Rüdiger Soltwedel for useful comments and suggestions to earlier versions. Remaining errors are mine.
2 In the case of France and Spain, data are from annual enterprise surveys in the manufacturing sector (SESSI, various years, and INE Spain, various years), supplemented by data from Cambridge Econometrics to cover the remaining sectors (agriculture, construction and services). In the case of Portugal, data are from the decennial census (INE Portugal, various years). The data sets thus contain data for 21 French NUTS2 regions in a sectoral breakdown of 43 industries and for years between 1980 to 2000, for 18 Spanish NUTS2 regions in a sectoral breakdown of 96 industries and for the years 1980–1992, and for five Portuguese NUTS2 regions in a sectoral breakdown of 244 industries and for the years 1991 and 2001. The degree of specialization is measured by an absolute Theil index and a weighted relative Theil index as presented in Chapter 1 of this volume.
3 Notice that the calculated specialization figures are not directly comparable between the regions of different countries, as the underlying data vary considerably regarding the depth of the sectoral breakdown, the classification scheme for industries, and the comprehensiveness of the surveys. The Spanish region Ceuta y Melilla is an outlier, as it is formed by the two small exclave cities, Ceuta and Melilla, situated on African territory beyond the street of Gibraltar.
4 Cf. Paluzie *et al.* (2001) for a similar result for Spanish regions in terms of the relative measure.
5 The concentration is measured by a Brülhart-Träger-Theil index with the topographic space as a benchmark. It compares the actual distribution of industries across regions to the distribution of space across regions. See Brülhart and Träger, 2004, and the explanations in Chapter 1 of this book. Cf. also the analysis on the concentration of French industries by Maurel and Sédillot, 1999.
6 The classification of the respective industries draws on an OECD, 1987, classification of resource intensive industries, yet applying it only to those industries where resources are localized and not ubiquous.
7 The classification of the respective industries draws on Pratten, 1988, who identified industries with different levels of technical IRS (low, medium, high). It is here referred to industries with a high level of IRS – as far as they are not dependent on localized resources.
8 A classification of services into the groups of knowledge intensive services, other tradable services and non-tradable services is to be found in Grupp *et. al.*, 2000.
9 Applying Ward's minimum cluster analysis, separately for each country, for the initial years 1973, 1978 and 1991, respectively.
10 Location coefficients are here calculated as an industry's share in a region's total economy, compared to the same industry's share in the country's economy.
11 Exception: resource intensive industries in Spain. The correlation for this industry group is biased by an extreme outlier (Asturias).

References

Amaral, L.M. (2003). "Finance for SMEs: The Portuguese Experience: from PEDIP to EURO", Rome.
Balbín, P.F. (1999). "Spain: Industrial Policy under Authoritarian Politics". In: J. Foreman-Peck, and G. Federico (eds), *European Industrial Policy: The Twentieth Century*. Oxford: Oxford University Press.
Balchin, P.N. and Sýkora, L. (1999). *Regional Policy and Planning in Europe*. London: Routledge.

Brülhart, M. and Träger, R. (2004). "An Account of Geographic Concentration Patterns in Europe", mimeo (forthcoming in *Regional Science and Urban Economics*; downloadable from http://www.hec.unil.ch/mbrulhar/-Research.

Confraria, J. (1999). "Portugal: Industrialization and Backwardness". In: J. Foreman-Peck and G. Federico (eds), *European Industrial Policy*. Oxford: Oxford University Press.

Dormois, J.-P. (1999). "France: the Idiosyncrasis of Voluntarisme". In: J. Foreman-Peck and G. Federico (eds), *European Industrial Policy: The Twentieth Century*. Oxford: Oxford University Press.

Foucauld, J.B. de (1994). "Strategic Planning in a Market Economy: The Case of the 11th French Plan". In: R. Delorme and K. Dopfer (eds), *The Political Economy of Diversity*. Aldelshot: Edward Elgar.

Grupp, H., Legler, H., Jungmittag, A., and Schmoch, U. (2000). Hochtechnologie 2000. Neudefinition der Hochtechnologie für die Berichterstattung zur technologischen Leistungsfähigkeit Deutschlands Bericht des FhG-ISI und des NIW im Auftrag des Bundesministeriums für Bildung und Forschung.

Instituto Nacional des Estadística (INE), Spain, Online data, "Encuesta Industríal EIG".

Instituto Nacional des Estatística (INE), Portugal, Census data.

Maurel, F. and Sédillot, B. (1999). "A Measure of the Geographic Concentration in French Manufacturing Industries". *Regional Science and Urban Economics* 29: 575–604.

Organisation for Economic Co-operation and Development (OECD) (1987). *Structural Adjustment and Economic Performance*. Paris.

Organisation for Economic Co-operation and Development (OECD) (2000). *Regulatory Reform in Spain*. Paris.

Paluzie, E., Pons, J. and Tirado, D.A. (2001). "Regional Integration and Specialization Patterns in Spain". *Regional Studies* 34 (4): 285–296.

Pratten, C. (1988). A Survey of the Economies of Scale. In: Commission of the European Communities, *Research on the "Cost of Non-Europe"*. Volume 2: *Studies on the Economics of Integration*. Luxemburg.

Rosés, J.R. (2003). "Why Isn't the Whole of Spain Industrialized? New Economic Geography and Early Industrialization, 1797–1919". *The Journal of Economic History* 63 (4): 995–1022.

Salmon, K. (1995). *The Modern Spanish Economy: Transformation and Integration into Europe*. 2nd. ed. London Pinter.

Schrader, K. and Laaser, C.-F. (1994). Die baltischen Staaten auf dem Weg nach Europa: Lehren aus der Süderweiterung der EG. Kieler Studien, 264. Tübingen: Mohr.

Services des Statistiques Industrielle (SESSI). *Enquête Annuelle d' Entreprises*. Various years. Paris.

6 Regional structural change at the interface between old and new member states

The case of Austrian regions

Bernd Brandl and Christian Fölzer

Introduction

The aim of this work is to take a closer look at the industrial structure of the Austrian economy with a special focus on regional and industrial structural change. Since Austria joined the European Union in the mid 1990s, one might have expected a certain tendency towards increasing specialisation of regions and concentration of industries due to increased competition in the larger European market. Any such Austrian experience with integration would be of special interest to the new accession countries, as Austria's accession to the European Union is still fairly recent and most of the new entrants are of similar size. Moreover, Austria is a close neighbour to several of the new entrants, and it shares a common history with them that may also affect economic structures, trade relations and general attitudes to a certain degree up to today. Accordingly, a vast literature has already analysed integration-induced changes in the Austrian industrial structure. In supplementing this literature, this work analyses the industrial structure and the shifts within it not only in a sectoral but as well in a regional breakdown. To this behalf, quantitative measures on a regional basis will be applied.

The chapter is organised as follows: to present the background of structural change in Austria, the first part of the chapter will be devoted to an overview of some stylised facts about the Austrian economy. Thereafter, the Austrian economic policy, which is dominated by the so-called "Social Partnership", will be described. We will then evaluate the specialisation pattern of Austrian regions and the spatial concentration of industries across these regions at the background of regional growth performance. A final section will conclude.

Stylised facts

Compared to most of the members of the European Union (EU-15), Austria is a very small country with an area of 83,870.66 km² (Table 6.2). Austria is divided into nine so-called Länder (provinces). These Länder are: Burgenland, Kärnten, Niederösterreich, Oberösterreich, Salzburg, Steiermark, Tirol, Vorarlberg and Wien, the latter being also the capital of Austria. On NUTS 3 level there are 35 units. 26 of these are the so-called Bezirke (districts), all others are so-called Gerichtsbezirke (circuits). Wien is not further divided.

The overall population in Austria is increasing (Table 6.1): if the figures for the year 1995 are set equal to 100, the index for Austria as a whole reaches 100.49 in 2003; Vorarlberg on top of the scale reaches 103.05 and Steiermark at the bottom of the scale reaches 99.19.

Austria has established a reputation as a well-performing economy in recent years. Among all OECD members, Austria is one of the richest countries in terms of GDP per capita. Moreover, between 1990 and 2002, Austria outperformed most EU countries with an average annual GDP growth rate of 2.3 per cent while the average annual GDP growth rate of the European Union as a whole was only 2.0 per cent. In the same period productivity increased by 1.9 per cent in Austria compared to only 1.4 per cent in the EU. In particular, Austria performed better than its main trading partner Germany with a GDP growth of merely 1.4 per cent and a productivity growth of 1.3 per cent. Especially in the manufacturing sector, which is traditionally a very important sector in Austria, productivity increased more rapidly than in Germany: 4.2 per cent, compared to 2.8 per cent.

Table 6.1 Population[1]

	1995	2000	2001	2002	2003
Burgenland	274,334	276,707	275,913	275,076	274,191
Kärnten	560,994	564,150	564,035	563,771	563,375
Niederösterreich	1,518,254	1,537,375	1,535,672	1,533,688	1,531,437
Oberösterreich	1,385,769	1,377,694	1,379,059	1,380,083	1,380,813
Salzburg	506,850	516,086	517,353	518,497	519,509
Steiermark	1,206,317	1,201,743	1,200,221	1,198,525	1,196,586
Tirol	658,312	669,245	671,313	673,152	674,804
Vorarlberg	343,109	349,317	350,810	352,249	353,607
Wien	1,592,596	1,598,661	1,596,437	1,594,157	1,591,848
Austria	8,046,535	8,090,978	8,090,813	8,089,198	8,086,170

Table 6.2 Area[2]

	km²	*Population/km²*
Burgenland	3,965.46	68
Kärnten	9,535.97	57
Niederösterreich	19,177.78	77
Oberösterreich	11,981.74	111
Salzburg	7,154.22	67
Steiermark	16,391.93	72
Tirol	12,647.93	50
Vorarlberg	2,601.48	127
Wien	414.66	3,711
Austria	83,870.66	93

This productivity growth helped Austria gaining better competitiveness. Austria's industry underwent some changes as to its unit labour costs position during the 1990s. In the first half of the decade, it deteriorated by 5.0 per cent, although at the same time the currency position improved and wage gains became more moderate. Since the mid 1990s, the competitive position of Austria strengthened as unit labour costs dropped substantially. This was made possible by a combination of increased productivity and a cut in unit wage costs relative to the average Austrian trading partners by 2.25 per cent p.a., in manufacturing as well as in the overall economy. Accordingly, the Austrian economy's position in terms of price competition also improved by 15 per cent since 1995.

Also, since 1995, Austria has experienced an exceptional growth of inward direct investment. By contrast, Austrian outward foreign direct investment (FDI) followed international trends closely until 2000. Thereafter, Austrian FDI flows remained strong, whereas global FDI flows decreased because of the upcoming recession and the burst of the "new economy" bubble. All in all, at the beginning of the new century, net FDI inflows into Austria had increased tremendously, putting Austria at the forefront of FDI recipients in the EU although it was a latecomer (Table 6.3). Still, inward as well as outward investment flows remain below the OECD average. The bulk of all FDI originated from EU members: in 1995, their share was 57.6 per cent; in 2000, their share had risen to 90.0 per cent (Aussenwirtschaft, 2003).

The most important target industry for inward FDI in 1995 was trading (€3,311 m). Other important targets were: the electricity sector, the information, technology and optics industry, the fabrication of machinery and chemicals, the automotive industry, and real estate and business services. This is a typical pattern for an industrialised country where foreign direct investment goes primarily to more sophisticated branches whereas low-technology industries are left behind.[3] As a result of FDI, the overall numbers of people employed in firms with high participation of foreign capital increased from 207,684 in 1995 to 245,559 in 2001. A remarkable case is real estate and business services, where FDI rose from €3,196 m in 1995 to €13,690 m in 2001, and accordingly, employment exploded from 10,518 workers in 1995 to 21,603 workers in 2001. The share of this industry in total employment increased from 5.06 to 8.80 per cent.

Table 6.3 Austrian foreign direct investment (inflows net of outflows, millions €)

	Net FDI
1995	1,395
1996	3,405
1997	2,354
1998	4,078
1999	2,792
2000	9,595
2001	6,603

Regarding the regional dimension of FDI inflows, data is largely missing. The emergence of an automotive cluster in the province of Steiermark with considerable foreign participation may indicate that some amount of foreign direct investment went to Steiermark. Also, in recent years, several multinational enterprises set up their new regional headquarters in the urban area of Wien. These headquarters play an important role as a centre not only for Austria but for the transition countries in the East as well.

In spite of this FDI-related progress, the transition of the Austrian economy into a modern knowledge economy has not yet been completed. For centuries, the Austrian economy was dominated by the steel and iron industry. Some regions were and still are specialised in iron and steel. These regions are Linz-Wels-Steyr in Oberösterreich and Obersteiermark in Steiermark due to natural resources in iron. Another industry, which dominated whole regions is the textiles industry in Vorarlberg and Niederösterreich, even though specialisation on this industry is declining.

Since the 1980s and until at least the mid 1990s, the structure of the Austrian economy was always reported to be focused on traditional industries and medium technology segments, rather then on high technology branches.[4] One possible reason at the roots of this industrial structure may be seen in the particularly low expenditure on research and development (R&D): in 1995 Austria spent only 1.59 per cent of GDP on R&D. As a result, the Austrian economy faces a considerable technology gap.

This technology gap may be seen as a key element of the Austrian economy, responsible for the deficits in the overall structure and the lack of more dynamic branches. It stands in obvious contrast to the high level of income, employment and growth in Austria. But when since the mid 1990s growth rates slowed down in Austria (like in most parts of the world though less strongly than in most parts of the world), technology policy gained increasing attention. Accordingly, the expenditure on R&D rose to 1.95 per cent of GDP or €4,217 m in 2002, and to 2.09 per cent in 2003 (Forschungsbericht, 2003).

The increasing attention towards R&D can also be observed at the regional level (NUTS 2). Yet, the contribution of the provinces to overall R&D is rather small and increased only slightly over time. Before joining the EU, Austria's provinces financed 5.63 per cent of all R&D, which is 0.08 per cent of GDP. In the year of EU accession, this figure was 5.69 per cent or 0.09 per cent of GDP. In 2003, the Austrian provinces financed 6.70 per cent of all R&D activities, which equals 0.13 per cent of GDP (Forschungsbericht, 2002, own calculations). On the side of expenditure, in 1998, an amount of €1,650 m was spent on R&D in Wien, making the Austrian capital the most important location of R&D activities among Austrian provinces. Another amount of €599.6 m was spent in Steiermark. Both Wien and Steiermark host extensive clusters of universities, research institutes and multinational enterprises. Out of 2,743 research institutions in Austria, 968 are situated in Wien and 483 in Steiermark. As a consequence of the presence of the large state universities in these provinces, the share of public R&D within total R&D was immense compared to all other provinces. Only 30.3 and 31.6 per cent of all R&D expenditure came from private enterprises. However, the R&D contributions from foreign countries were relatively large (27.5 per cent in Steiermark and 26.4 per cent in Wien, compared to the Austrian average of 20.1 per cent). In 1998, an amount of €44,308 m R&D investments originated from various EU countries. Most of these investments, again, went to Wien and Steiermark (€19,990 m and €10,153 m, respectively).

R&D employment in Austria accounted for about 31,307.6 persons in 1998.[5] About 46.0 per cent of these researchers work in the capital of Austria (14,386.6 researchers). The second most important province is Steiermark with 18.7 per cent of all researchers (5,851.5). Once again, these two provinces prove to be most important for R&D activities. In the case of Steiermark, it is particularly the link from universities, firms and public offices to the above-mentioned automotive cluster that favoured the development of R&D activities in this region.

Within Austria's private sector, there were a number of 1,317 research institutions in 1998. Of these, 201 institutions worked in the machinery industry, 120 in business services and 108 in the metal goods industry. Not surprisingly, these sectors were among the frontrunners of economic development. All in all, Austrian R&D activities seem to comply with the specialties of the Austrian economy, being closely related to the manufacturing sector, more particularly to the fabrication of metal goods and machinery and to the regions in which these are prevalent, and being less related to the services sector (STAT.AT, 2002). Although this could be taken as an indication of prolonged backwardness of the Austrian economy, it could also be interpreted as an effort to strengthen its specific virtues regarding medium technology and traditional industries in Austria. And it could even be regarded as a successful strategy, given the favourable performance of the Austrian economy.

All recent advances of the Austrian economy most likely can be attributed to the European integration and the increase in competition it entailed. But the increased competition had not only favourable consequences: people were made redundant, the rate of unemployment and the number of early retirements rose considerably. Between 1980 and 1990, the workforce in industry was reduced at an average rate of 1.4 per cent p.a., between 1990 and 1995, this figure increased to 3.1 per cent p.a., and this loss of industrial employment was only partially offset by the creation of new employment in services.

Economic policy

A characteristic feature of Austrian economic policy is that not only political parties but also socially relevant groups are involved that together form the so-called "Social Partnership". Such groups are: the Austrian Trade Union Federation, the Federal Chamber of Labour, the Economic Chamber of Austria and the Standing Committee of Residence of the Chambers of Agriculture[6] (Nowotny, 1997). The Social Partnership is a means to coordinate the economic and social policy of the government as well as the collective agreements of employees' and employers' associations concerning wage levels, and to consolidate the different interests related to it (Guger *et al.*, 2001).

One of the key issues of economic policy since Austria joined the European Union was the privatisation of state-owned companies. State-owned companies are in the hands of the so-called Österreichische Industrieholding AG (ÖIAG), owned by the Federal Ministry of Finance. As a start, as early as 1987, a 15 per cent trench of the then ÖMV AG[7] was floated on the stock exchange. All in all, stocks equalling an amount of 5.5 per cent of GDP have been sold since this start. This seems to be quite large by international standards. Privatisations seem to have contributed to the considerable productivity growth of the manufacturing sector in Austria (OECD, 2003).

Competition and its regulation is another essential policy issue of Austria as a member of the European Union. In response to respective EU regulations, Austria established a Federal Competition Authority (Bundeswettbewerbsbehörde), a Competition Commission (Wettbewerbskommission) and regulatory bodies in the telecommunication, electricity and railroads industries, and launched a new cartel law in 2002 (Böheim, 2002).

This led to more openness and transparency of the Austrian economy, and hence to more competition, which is among the main benefits from EU membership. For consumers, a wider range of products became available. Inefficient firms were driven out of the market or had to increase their productivity. Markets grew more international and more concentrated, and mergers and acquisitions became more common. As these reorganisations of the markets also seem to have contributed to recent Austrian productivity growth, competition policy is widely accepted in Austria (Pfaffermayr, 2003).

Another EU benefit widely acknowledged in Austria is the abolishment of exchange rate risks and the reduction of transaction costs due to the introduction of the EURO (Pfaffermayr, 2003). Moreover, the tight monetary policy of the ECB kept the currency stable and the inflation rate low, thus accommodating the respective preferences of the inflation-averse Austrian people.

Since Austria has joined the European Union, regional policy is an important element of the economic policy. To encourage the development of peripheral regions, for instance in Burgenland, in some Southern parts of Steiermark or in some Northern parts of Niederösterreich, there are several programmes initiated and co-financed by the EU.

Regional performance, specialisation of regions and concentration of industries

One of the forces driving structural change in Austria since the accession to the EU has been the increasing integration between Austrian regions and nearby foreign countries. It can be argued that the increased openness of Austrian economy changes the interregional division of labour thereby increasing regional specialisation and concentration of industries. According to different strands of economic trade theory, specialisation and concentration could increase as a result of integration either by adjustment to comparative advantages (refers to the traditional Heckscher-Ohlin-Samuelson model, HOS) or by exploitation of externalities (refers to new trade theories and new economic geography, NEG). Such externalities are the so-called Marshall-Arrow-Romer (MAR) externalities (or localisation economies) such as labour market pooling, availability of specialist suppliers and technological spillovers that are relevant within a certain branch, as well as the so-called Jacobian externalities (or urbanisation economies) such as a broad and diversified supply of various intermediates and an overall innovative spirit. These externalities act as centripetal forces in that they favour the clustering of activities at few locations. Within the emerging core-periphery system, considerable regional disparities may evolve. However, some NEG models hold that at a very high degree of integration the thereby induced increase of competition may act as centrifugal force and lead to a (re-)dispersion of industries, a diversification of regional industry portfolios, and receding regional disparities. Data will show which direction can be observed for Austria. The considered time period is 1998 to 2003.

To give an impression on the evolution of regional performance, Table 6.4 and Figure 6.1 show the change of regional employment from 1998 to 2003. Total employment in Austria rose by 3.57 per cent. Burgenland, Tirol and Oberösterreich denoted a particularly high increase in employment. By contrast, Wien was confronted with a remarkable decline of employment by about 1 per cent. Besides Wien, also Niederösterreich and Kärnten recorded an employment change significantly below Austrian average. All in all, comparing Table 6.4 and Figure 6.1 with Table 6.1 and 6.2 shows that large regions tended to lose, and small regions tended to gain employment opportunities, and it thus seems to indicate a (very slight) convergence of employment opportunities between regions. Next will be to look how this coincides with an increase or decrease of regional specialisation.

Specialisation of regions

Specialisation of regions is analysed using the Herfindahl and Krugman (dissimilarity) indices. While the Herfindahl index is a measure of absolute, the

Table 6.4 Regional employment and its change[8]

Region	1998	2003	Share 1998 (%)	Share 2003 (%)	Change (%)
Burgenland	79,829	86,448	2.58	2.69	8.29
Niederösterreich	515,938	530,545	16.65	16.53	2.83
Wien	770,314	763,295	24.86	23.78	−0.91
Kärnten	195,335	200,543	6.30	6.25	2.67
Steiermark	422,959	441,809	13.65	13.77	4.46
Oberösterreich	521,438	558,003	16.83	17.39	7.01
Salzburg	210,909	219,427	6.81	6.84	4.04
Tirol	253,649	273,634	8.19	8.53	7.88
Vorarlberg	128,320	135,638	4.14	4.23	5.70
Austria total	3,098,691	3,209,342	100.00	100.00	3.57

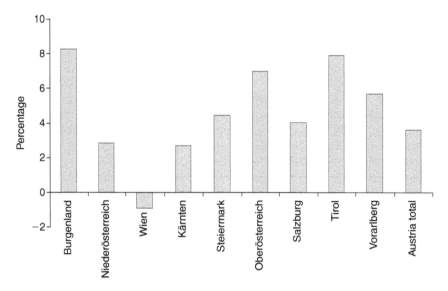

Figure 6.1 Regional change in employment (1998–2003).

Krugman index is one of relative specialisation, i.e. relative to a benchmark, the national specialisation. The empirical results are shown in Table 6.5 and Table 6.6. Different to other studies for Austria (see for example Badinger and Breuss, 2004) we use all industries, i.e. also sectors that are not exposed to international competition, in our analysis.[9]

As can be seen from Table 6.5 and Figure 6.2, the degree of specialisation was highest initially in Wien and Burgenland, and lowest in Vorarlberg and Oberösterreich. During the observation period, on average, specialisation degrees decreased from 0.0584 in 1998 to 0.057 in 2003. Yet, in highly specialised Burgenland specialisation fell most substantially by about 7 per cent, while in most other regions specialisation remained on the same level. On

Table 6.5 Herfindahl index: specialisation of region

	1998	1999	2000	2001	2002	2003
Burgenland	0.0706	0.0705	0.0693	0.0678	0.0660	0.0653
Kärnten	0.0544	0.0542	0.0540	0.0532	0.0536	0.0544
Niederösterreich	0.0546	0.0547	0.0547	0.0542	0.0539	0.0540
Oberösterreich	0.0494	0.0495	0.0495	0.0489	0.0488	0.0493
Salzburg	0.0592	0.0594	0.0589	0.0587	0.0580	0.0577
Steiermark	0.0555	0.0563	0.0559	0.0559	0.0557	0.0562
Tirol	0.0549	0.0553	0.0545	0.0539	0.0540	0.0546
Vorarlberg	0.0500	0.0497	0.0493	0.0489	0.0485	0.0482
Wien	0.0768	0.0754	0.0733	0.0729	0.0717	0.0733
Average	0.0584	0.0583	0.0577	0.0572	0.0567	0.0570

average we observe no substantial shifts over time and Austrian regions sustain their structure in terms of their specialisation degrees.

At the background of such evolution of regional specialisation degrees is the evolution of certain industries within the regions. Among the more interesting branches (because of its key role in the process of economic growth) with larger changes in the interregional structure is research and development. In this sector, Wien witnessed the largest number of new jobs adding to its already relatively large amount in this field. Yet, other regions caught up, e.g. Steiermark, Oberösterreich (with an increase of 81 per cent) and Tirol (with an increase of 55 per cent) due to the foundation of several universities of applied sciences. Nevertheless, Wien still dominates this industry with a share of 55 per cent in 1998 and 53 per cent in 2003.

After discussing the Herfindahl index we take a look at the Krugman index. The empirical results are shown in Table 6.6 and illustrated in Figure 6.3. As this index is a relative measure, the specialisation pattern of Austria as a whole serves as benchmark. Results are similar to the Herfindahl index in that once again changes of specialisation over time are small and seem to tend towards a slight increase in specialisation. Yet there are also some differences. Notable is that the specialisation in Burgenland did not fall as dramatically as described by

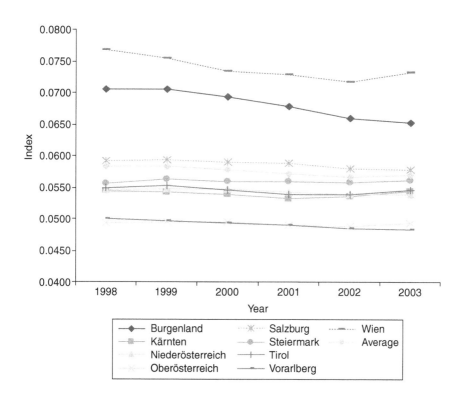

Figure 6.2 Herfindahl Index: specialisation of regions.

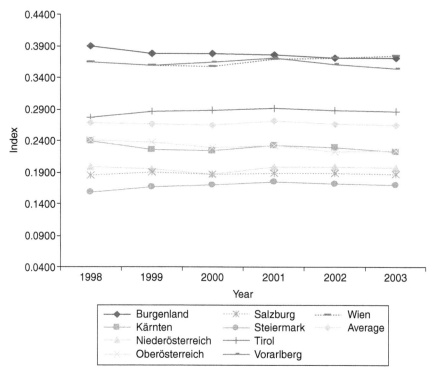

Figure 6.3 Krugman Index: specialisation of regions.

the Herfindahl index. Burgenland and – different to the Herfindahl index – also Wien appear to be highly specialised (compared to other regions) and Kärnten, Niederösterreich, Steiermark and Salzburg are specialized on a moderate level. Moreover, since Wien, due to its large size, seems to have driven the benchmark specialisation of Austria as a whole, as a result, the convergence of regional specialisation degrees over time is less explicit.

Table 6.6 Krugman index: specialisation of regions

	1998	*1999*	*2000*	*2001*	*2002*	*2003*
Burgenland	0.3900	0.3772	0.3777	0.3757	0.3705	0.3709
Kärnten	0.2396	0.2258	0.2237	0.2331	0.2288	0.2225
Niederösterreich	0.1987	0.1957	0.1874	0.1989	0.1990	0.1973
Oberösterreich	0.2411	0.2376	0.2286	0.2317	0.2222	0.2247
Salzburg	0.1850	0.1899	0.1860	0.1880	0.1880	0.1864
Steiermark	0.1583	0.1664	0.1697	0.1756	0.1721	0.1706
Tirol	0.2757	0.2860	0.2887	0.2918	0.2881	0.2864
Vorarlberg	0.3642	0.3591	0.3637	0.3706	0.3604	0.3532
Wien	0.3642	0.3584	0.3575	0.3699	0.3703	0.3740
Average	0.2685	0.2662	0.2648	0.2706	0.2666	0.2651

Spatial concentration of industries

We now discuss the spatial concentration of industries. As with the special-isation of regions, the Herfindahl and the Krugman indices are used to measure concentration. Industries which are most concentrated are the mining of coal and lignite (10), mining of crude oil and gas (11), mining of metal ores (13), manu-facture of coke, refined petroleum products and nuclear fuel (23), manufacture of radio, television and communication equipment and apparatus (32), water transport (61), air transport (62), real estates activities (70), computer and related activities (72) and research and development (73). The fact that these mining industries are heavily concentrated is due to the highly localised availability of the related resource deposits. However, the absolute number of employees in these highly concentrated industries is low.

The spatial concentration of all other industries is relatively homogeneous with a mean (over all industries and over time) of 0.25 and a standard deviation of 0.16 with regard to the Herfindahl index and a mean of 0.55 with a standard deviation of 0.36 regarding the Krugman index. These results support the find-ings by Janger and Wagner (2004) who analyse the concentration pattern of value-added production instead of employment. Industries with lowest concen-tration level are fishing, operation of fish hatcheries and fish farms (5), electric-ity, gas, steam and water supply (40), construction (45), sale, maintenance and repair of motor vehicles and motorcycles (50) and hotels and restaurants. The first of those industries, fishing, is very small. However, there are also some of the largest (in terms of the number of employees) industries in this group of industries: construction industry, energy and water supply and hotels and restaurants. The former industries are highly dispersed in accordance with the spread of population because they are consumer related industries. The latter, hotels and restaurants industry is highly dispersed because nearly all Austrian regions are heavily engaged in tourism.

Regarding the evolution of industrial concentration over time, Figure 6.4 shows the development of the weighted (by the number of employees) spatial concentration of industries for the Herfindahl index and for the Krugman index. It shows the Herfindahl index to decrease and the Krugman index to increase slightly over time, however, the more general message is, once again, that there is not much movement at all. By looking at the evolution of standard deviation (over all industries) a remarkable increase can be found. The stan-dard deviation of the Herfindal index in 1998 is 0.0043 and increased monoto-nically to 0.0045 in 2003. The same can be seen for the Krugman index with a standard deviation of 0.0053 in 1998 and a standard deviation of 0.0062 in 2003. This result of the evolution of the standard deviation indicates rising heterogeneity among sectors. Yet, even though no substantial overall change of concentration can be observed still there are some sectors with a consider-able change like post and telecommunication (64) with an increase in con-centration of 64 per cent and manufacture of medical, precision and optical instruments, watches and clocks (33) with an increase of 58 per cent.

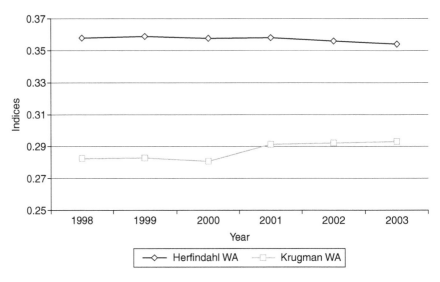

Figure 6.4 Spatial concentration indices (weighted averages according to the number of employees) over time.

In contrast, there are sectors with remarkable decreases in concentration such as activities auxiliary to financial intermediation (67) with a decrease of 28 per cent and electricity, gas, steam and hot water supply (40) with a decrease of 23 per cent. Industries such as mining of uranium and thorium ores (12) and manufacture of fabricated metal products, except machinery and equipment (28) faced no change over time. Again, these results support those by Janger and Wagner (2004).

Conclusions

The aim of this work was to take a closer look at the industrial and regional change in Austria and its changes in the years after Austria's accession to the EU. Stylised facts and characteristics of Austrian regions and of Austria in general have been discussed. This has revealed that Austria, when entering the EU, was perhaps a bit insulated from international competition and stricken with a considerable technological gap, yet managed quite rapidly and success-fully to adjust to the new conditions. We analysed whether the specialisation of Austrian regions and the concentration of Austrian industries increased or not since Austria joined the European Union, and we found no substantial changes of either specialisation or concentration on a general (overall) level. As regards regional specialisation, it appears to be higher in urban regions (Wien) and lower in other (rural) regions thus exhibiting a certain core-periphery pattern of specialisation. Moreover, this pattern became more pronounced as Wien, differ-ent to other regions, experienced an increase in specialisation. More generally, however, specialisation degrees seem to increase only very slightly and they seem to converge to become more similar among Austrian regions. The disparity between Wien and all other regions of Austria seems to diffuse as Wien loses overall employment while all other regions and Austria as a whole gain employment. Accordingly, there is not much support for the hypothesis that increased competition would force an increased specialisation of regions and aggravate the polarisation of regional disparities. The reason for the slow structural change can be found in the stickiness of employment. Fundamental changes take decades rather than years. This refers, for instance, to the change of the Austrian economy from the secondary to the tertiary sector. This refers also to the ongoing specialisation of the Austrian economy as a whole on hotels and restaurants, on education and business activities. All in all, intra-industrial and intra-regional structural changes after the EU-accession of Austria were small and they can not be attributed without ambiguity to the accession alone. Rather they need also be explained by general trends from globalisation or even by specific Austrian characteristics.

Notes

1 Source: Statistik Austria.
2 Source: Statistik Austria.
3 Source: Oesterreichische Nationalbank.
4 For more details see: Felderer *et al.*, 2000.
5 Full time equivalent.
6 Österreichischer Gewerkschaftsbund, Kammer für Arbeiter und Angestellte, Wirtschaftskammern Österreich und Präsidentenkonferenz der Österreichischen Landwirtschaftskammern.
7 Now OMV AG, a company dealing with gasoline, chemicals and fertilisers.
8 Note that all industries are included.
9 See Badinger and Breuss, 2004 for pro and cons and details on the exclusion of specific industries such as for example public administration (75), education (80), health and social work (85), sewage and refuse disposal, sanitation and similar activities (90), activities of membership organisations (91), recreational, cultural and sporting activities (92), other service activities (93), activities of households as employers of domestic staff (95), extra-territorial organisations and bodies (99). Numbers in parenthesis indicate the subsections of NACE Rev. 1.1 industries as defined in the Commission Regulation (EC) No 29/2002 of 19 December 2001. Not included in the NACE Rev. 1.1 are the conscript army and people on maternity leave (data was available, but not included in this analysis).

References

AK (2003). Fusionen und Übernehmen, Teil 1 – Wettbewerbsbericht der AK 2002, Beiträge zur Wirtschaftspolitik Nr. 12, Vienna.
Aussenwirtschaft (2003). Österreichs Aussenwirtschaft 2002/2003, edited by Bundesministerium für Wirtschaft und Arbeit, Vienna.
Badinger, H. and Breuss, F. (2004). Has Austria's Accession to the EU Triggered an Increase in Competition? A Sectoral Markup Study, WIFO Working Paper 220.
Bellak, C., Clement, W. and Hofer, R. (1997). "Wettbewerbs- und Strukturpolitik". In

Grundzüge der Wirtschaftspolitik Österreichs, edited by Nowotny, E. and Winckler, G. 2nd ed. Manz, Vienna, 127–165.

Böheim, M. (2002). "The Future of Austrian Competition Policy". In *Competition and Competitiveness in a New Economy*, edited by Handler, H. and Burger, C. Austrian Federal Ministry of Economic Affairs and Labour, Vienna, 51–63.

Breuss, F. (2000). "An Evaluation of the Economic Effects of Austria's EU Membership", *Austrian Economic Quarterly*, 4, 171–196.

Felderer, B., Fölzer, C. and Helmenstein, C., Pippan, H. and Talkner, C. (2000). "Public Private Ownership", Institute for Advanced Studies, Vienna.

Forschungsbericht (2002). "Österreichischer Forschungs- und Technologiebericht 2002. Lagebericht gem. § 8 FOG über die aus Bundesmitteln geförderte Forschung, Technologie und Innovation in Österreich", edited by Bundesministerium für Bildung, Wissenschaft und Kultur, Bundesministerium für Verkehr, Innovation und Technologie, Wien.

Forschungsbericht (2003). "Österreichischer Forschungs- und Technologiebericht 2003. Bericht der Bundesregierung an den Nationalrat gem. § 8 (2) FOG über die Lage und Bedürfnisse von Forschung, Technologie und Innovation in Österreich", edited by Bundesministerium für Bildung, Wissenschaft und Kultur, Bundesministerium für Verkehr, Innovation und Technologie, Wien.

Guger, A. (2003). "Internationale Lohnstückkostenposition 2002 geringfügig verbessert", *WIFO-Monatsbericht*, 9, 683–691.

Guger, A. (2004). "Internationale Lohnstückkostenposition 2003 wechselkursbedingt verschlechtert", *WIFO-Monatsbericht*, 9, 679–687.

Guger, A., Runggaldier, U. and Traxler, F. (2001). Lexikon der Arbeitsbeziehungen, Beschäftigung und sozialen Sicherung Österreich Manz, Vienna.

Janger, J. and Wagner, K. (2004). "Sektorale Spezialisierung in Österreich und in den EU-15-Ländern". In *Geldpolitik und Wirtschaft Q2/04*, edited by Österreichische Nationalbank, Wien.

Keuschnigg, C. and Kohler, W. (1996). "Austria in the European Union: Dynamic Gains from Integration and Distributional Implications", *Economic Policy*, 22, 155–211.

Marshall, A. (1966). *Principles of Economics*, Macmillan, London (8. ed., repr.).

Nowotny, E. (1997). "Grundlagen und Institutionen der Wirtschaftspolitik". In *Grundzüge der Wirtschaftspolitik Österreichs*, edited by Nowotny, E. and Winckler, G. 2nd ed. Manz, Vienna, 11–48.

OECD (1997). "OECD Economic Surveys 1996–1997 Austria", Organisation for Economic Co-operation and Development, Paris.

OECD (2003). "OECD Economic Surveys 2002–2003 Austria", Organisation for Economic Co-operation and Development, Paris.

Pfaffermayr, M. (2003). "Austria's Performance within an Integrating European Economy". In *Österreich in der Europäischen Union. Bilanz seiner Mitgliedschaft Austria in the European Union. Assessment of her Membership*, edited by Gehler, M., Pelinka, A. and Bischof, G. Böhlau, Vienna, 201–218.

STAT.AT (2002). "Forschung und experimentelle Entwicklung in Österreich 1993–2002", *Statistische Nachrichten*, 8, 567–587.

STAT.AT (2003). "Finanzierung der Ausgaben für Forschung und experimentelle Entwicklung in Österreich", *Statistische Nachrichten*, 6, 430–438.

7 Eastern enlargement in a nutshell

Case study of Germany

Christiane Krieger-Boden[1]

Introduction: the background to specialization and integration

The German reunification process marks a very special case in the context of integration experiences, as it encompasses the many facets of the integration of former socialist countries into the Western world at a smaller scale within one country. Since this integration process is already going on for some while, it may provide useful insights for the current process of Eastern enlargement that has just started. This chapter analyses the experience of the incumbent country West Germany with various EU integration steps since the 1980s, and the experience of both West and East Germany after the reunification in 1990 regarding the specialization of the regions concerned.

West Germany was one of the founding members of the European Union and participated in all subsequent integration steps. During the observation period since 1980, these steps included in particular the Southern enlargement in 1981/1986, the completion of the Single Market in 1992, and the EFTA enlargement in 1995. In 1990, with the reunification, East Germany acceded to West Germany and to the EU at the same time.

Among the countries analysed in this volume, Germany also represents the specific experience of a relatively large country, with a traditionally polycentric structure, with a traditionally high development level, particularly in the case of West Germany, and with East Germany's experience of the transition from a socialist to a market economy:

- Germany covers an area of about 350 thousand square kilometres and inhibits a population of about 82 million people, i.e. 8.8 per cent of the total area and 17.8 per cent of total population of the EU-25.
- In line with a long tradition, when Germany existed only as a union of lots of small autonomous principalities, the administrative structure of present Germany is that of a federal republic. An increasing system of mutual controls between the federal states ("Bundesländer") and federal government overlaid the original responsibilities and led to deadlocks in necessitating reforms.

- For long, West Germany was among the countries with highest GDP per capita in Europe, and East Germany had the highest standard of living in socialist East Europe. Germany lost its top position gradually, beginning with the 1970s, when several other West European countries quickly made up the leeway, and continuing in the 1990s, when Germany experienced a period of lasting stagnation. This relative decline was accompanied by a stepwise increase of unemployment.
- The East German economy suffered a tremendous transition shock from reunification, particularly from the depression of East Germany's traditional East European and Russian markets, and from a sharp increase of East German real wage levels. This shock eroded East Germany's industrial base dramatically (Sinn and Sinn, 1992). An enormous divide between the Western and the Eastern part of the enlarged country became evident, and the East German unemployment rate rose up to 16 per cent in 1993. To be sure, the transition process started more smoothly than in the neighbouring Eastern countries, thanks to the transmission of a functioning legal and welfare system and huge financial transfers from the West, and the initial shock was followed by a few years of recovery and catching up. Yet, in contrast to other East European economies, this process slowed down in the mid 1990s (Burda, 1994; Bode, 2002) and, since then, the East German economy seems to be caught in a number of almost inevitable poverty traps (Snower and Merkl, 2006).

More generally, in the first decade after German unification, German regions revealed a trend towards a club convergence of GDP, where a few top regions (Hamburg, München, Frankfurt), on the one hand, and the large group of remaining regions, on the other, converged each within these specific "clubs", while the clubs themselves tended to fall apart. Empirical evidence substantiated the emergence of two to three such clubs at different per capita income levels (Bode, 2002; Colavecchio *et al.*, 2005).

(West) Germany is also often looked at as a case of relatively undisturbed market processes and thus also of rather undisturbed structural change, since it has been known traditionally for a general orientation towards a non-interventionist, free trade and framework-oriented economic policy. Yet, the actual degree of governmental interventionism varied significantly throughout the last five decades (Koopmann *et al.*, 1997). Particularly after the first oil-price shock, during the 1970s, the subsequent governments resorted to more interventionist structural conservation programmes and programmes for the promotion of expected future sectors. The 1980s saw a gradual return to a more reserved role for the state, reflected in commitments towards deregulation and the cutback of subsidies. After the reunification, in the 1990s, interventionism exploded with huge financial transfers being directed towards the East German regions combined, however, with a quick privatization (and often close-down) of East German state-owned enterprises.

More specifically, the orientation of German structural policies cannot be regarded as neutral towards industrial and regional structures. West German industrial policy traditionally focuses on subsidies for private enterprises rather than on public ownership as main instruments. The majority of the subsidies are dedicated to traditional sectors like agriculture, mining, the transportation and the residential industry (these four together receive 68 per cent of all subsidies; Boss and Rosenschon, 2006), thus giving industrial policy a rather structural conserving touch. Small- and medium-sized enterprises (SMEs) are regarded as being important for the success of the German economy, giving rise to numerous assistance programmes, although the actual amount of subsidies to SMEs may not mirror the official rhetoric (Krakowski, 1993). In spite of a relatively high regional homogeneity in West Germany, as compared to other European countries, much emphasis has always been placed on regional policies. The main instruments are a financial equalization scheme between the "Bundesländer" and an investment grant scheme for lagging regions. The latter is granted both to infrastructure projects for communities as well as to investment projects for private enterprises, usually from the manufacturing sector. The socialist East German government used to direct the investments for its state-owned enterprises particularly towards heavy industries, these being regarded as key industries for industrial countries. These industries were concentrated in large vertical combines. By contrast, investment in consumer goods industries and in services was largely neglected. The socialist government at the same time aimed at equipping all parts of the country with at least one large combine, even rather remote areas. In its late days, however, the socialist system was mainly characterized by general under-investment and depletion. All in all, both West German and East German structural policies acted towards the maintenance of a high share of manufacturing industry in the economy, and towards a high degree of regional homogeneity within each respective part of the country, and this influenced the industrial and regional structure of the country. After the reunification, transfers from West to East Germany favoured the non-tradable sector, particularly the construction industry, the boom of which was, however, followed by a severe decline as soon as the immediate reconstruction requirements were satisfied.

Against this background, regional specialization and its change in West and East Germany is analysed in this chapter. The remainder of the chapter is organized as follows: the next section describes the degree and nature of regional specialization and its change, and compares it to the regional structure of the country, with respect to population density as well as with respect to income and growth. The following section compares the structural change between German regions to the regional performance regarding, income, growth and employment. The chapter on discussing concludes what can be learnt from the specific German experiences for the overall regional consequences of integration and Eastern enlargement.

The regional specialization of Germany and its change during integration

The processes of European integration and of reunification can both be expected to increase trade, factor mobility and competition among German and towards European regions thereby affecting the interregional division of labour and the role of each region within this division. In particular, regions that are highly specialized are likely to play a very specific role in this division of labour as compared to diversified regions, and this role may depend on the nature of their specialization, i.e. on their specific industry mix. Accordingly, the regional structural change required to adjust to the changing division of labour may depend both on the degree and the nature of regional specialization.

Therefore, the analysis starts with an evaluation of the *specialization degree* of German regions. Compared to other European countries and measured relative to a European benchmark, the degree of regional specialization in (West) Germany has always been relatively low and relatively homogeneous across regions (see Chapter 1). This general impression is confirmed when analysing regional specialization in more detail on the ground of a national database.[2] Figure 7.1 displays the absolute and relative specialization of German regions that have been arranged according to their approximate geographic situation and their adjacency from North to South. From this, a somewhat elevated level of specialization may be observed only for regions like Hamburg, Bremen and West Berlin, and like Braunschweig (seat of "Volkswagen") and Saarland (a traditional coal, iron and steel producing location). The data allow for an insight on the change of regional specialization in West Germany during the 1980s and 1990s, that is, during times of increasing integration among West European countries (see above), and during the integration of East Germany: for the whole period, the specialization degrees remained more or less unchanged in terms of the absolute indicator and decreased gradually in terms of the relative indicator. This gradual decrease seems to have been a bit stronger in the early 1990s (immediately following reunification). In East Germany, specialization degrees were markedly higher, and particularly high was the specialization degree of East Berlin. These specialization degrees declined significantly in the aftermath of the reunification. As in West Germany, they declined particularly strongly in the immediate post-reunification period (early 1990s). Both in West and East Germany, the higher specialization degrees were initially, the move they declined (Table 7.1). East German specialization thus came down to similar levels as West German specialization.

More details on what drives regional structural change can be expected from a more in-depth evaluation of the *nature of regional specialization*, i.e. the specific industry mixes realized in the regions. Different regional specializations on different industries may imply quite different regional perspectives for income, growth and employment. In order to structure and condense the information from a breakdown of 294 industries in each region, groups of industries are identified, with similar (exogenous) characteristics. Such characteristics are derived from trade theories that expect different concentration and dispersion behaviour for different industries: the new trade theories and new economic geography, for instance, expect an extreme concentration of industries with scale

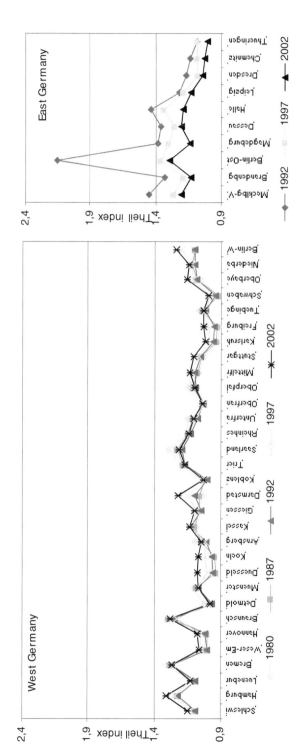

Figure 7.1 Regional specialization of West and East German regions and its change, absolute and relative measures, 1980–2002 (source: BA(Bundesagertur für Arbeit), Sozialversicherungspflichtig Beschäftigte).

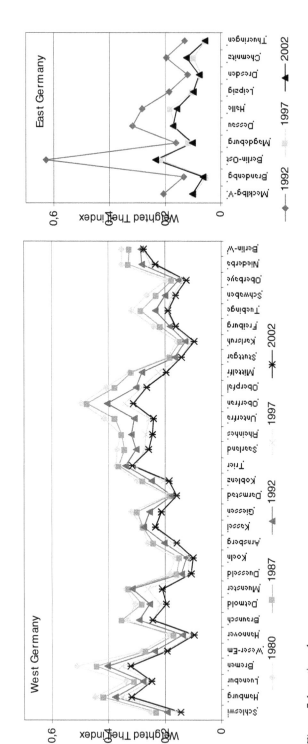

Figure 7.1 continued.

Table 7.1 Initial specialization and subsequent specialization change

	Theil index		Weighted Theil index	
	Pearson correlation coefficient	Error probability	Pearson correlation coefficient	Error probability
West German regions 1980–1992	−0.529***	0.00	−0.665***	0.00
West German regions 1992–2002	−0.263	0.15	−0.599***	0.00
East German regions 1992–2002	−0.980***	0.00	−0.985***	0.00

Source: BAA Sozialversicherungspflichtig Beschäftigte.

Notes
* Significant at the 5% level.
** Significant at the 1% level.
*** Significant at the 0.1% level.

economies at only one location and in a monopolistic market environment that allows such industries and their locations to achieve a higher income than others. Ricardo trade theories state a concentration and dispersion pattern according to the availability of resources for resource dependent industries. Heckscher-Ohlin theories, by contrast, state a concentration and dispersion behaviour along the lines of comparative advantage for industries that neither contain scale economies nor require very specific resource inputs, and that are often referred to as being footloose. Industries of these various types can thus be expected to be located in different regions and to impact differently on the regions in which they are located.

Along these lines, the following type groups of industries are distinguished (Figure 7.2 displays their concentration pattern) whose actual concentration pattern largely complies with respective theories:[3] *agricultural activities* need land as a resource, and they bear little economies of scale. As Ricardian industries with a highly ubiquitous resource base, they are actually found to be highly dispersed across the territory. Within manufacturing, *resource intensive industries* depending on highly localized resources, such as coal mining and coke ovens, iron and steel works, mining, production and transformation of non-ferrous metals and non-metal minerals, petroleum refining, are found to be concentrated where the respective resources are accessible (at their deposits or at specific harbours).[4] From the other manufacturing industries, some are characterized by *high internal IRS*, such as the aircraft industry, some branches of the chemical and machinery industries, automobile industry, office and computing machinery and electronic material industries, optical and professional instruments industries, some food industries.[5] These are expected by NEG theory to be highly concentrated, too, and indeed most of these industries are found to be highly concentrated in Germany, with several exceptions

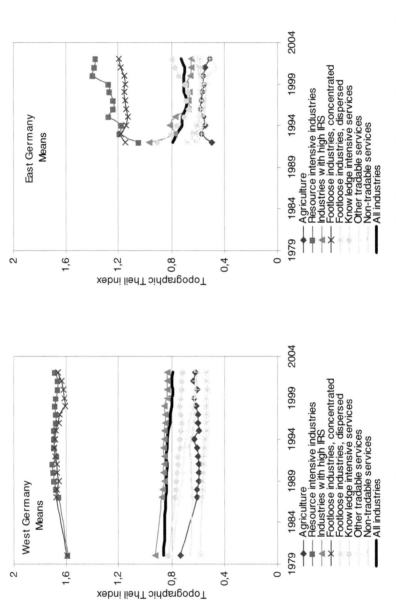

Figure 7.2 Topographic concentration of German industries and its change over time (source: BA, Sozialversicherungspflichtig Beschäftigte).

though, that reduce the average concentration degree of the whole group. The remaining manufacturing industries may be labelled *footloose industries* as they require no specific locational characteristics. As Heckscher-Ohlin industries, they can be expected to locate according to comparative advantages. Actually, some of them are found to be quite *concentrated*, i.e. some food industries, footwear industry, shipbuilding, the pharmaceutical industry, while others are found to be fairly *dispersed*, like branches of the textiles industry, automotive industry, chemical industry, and several consumption industries.

The large group of services is roughly divided into three groups that can also be expected to exert different spatial effects. Within the services sector, *knowledge intensive services*, such as engineering and consulting services, air traffic, credit, financing and insurance services, education and cultural services, require a high knowledge input to be found primarily in agglomerations and, accordingly, they appear to be highest concentrated among all services.[6] All other *tradable services*, such as construction activities, trading, catering, accommodating and transporting services, and commercial care, require no specific locations, and accordingly, they are among the lowest concentrated industries. Finally, *non-tradable services*, such as administration, non-market services, can be expected to be located where the people are, and they come out to be lowly concentrated across the territory.

Besides the initial concentration/dispersion pattern of these industry groups in Germany, Figure 7.2 also displays the evolution during increasing integration in the 1980s and 1990s and, more particularly, during the reunification process in the 1990s. In the case of West Germany, a very slight trend towards decreasing concentration may be observed, particularly during the 1980s, yet at the same time the industries with highest concentration seem to get even more concentrated. Similar trends may be observed for East Germany, with much higher intensity, however. Strikingly, the initial concentration degrees seemed to be quite homogeneous across industries, which may be due to the policy of directed investment in the centrally planned East German economy. This changed dramatically in the immediate post-reunification period, as the concentration of resource intensive and some footloose industries increased and the concentration of all other industries decreased. Subsequently, the concentration pattern of East German industries became more similar to that of West German industries. Since the mid 1990s, the pace of the diverging process in the East German concentration pattern slowed down.

The industry groups with their characteristic concentration behaviour are then used as an input to classify German regions according to the nature of their initial specialization.[7] We arrive at five type classes of German regions (Figure 7.3). For these region classes, Figure 7.4 displays the location coefficients of the industry groups, for different selected years, and thus offers an impression of the industrial foci that were relevant for their classification.[8] Moreover, although classified solely according to their structural decomposition, these region classes

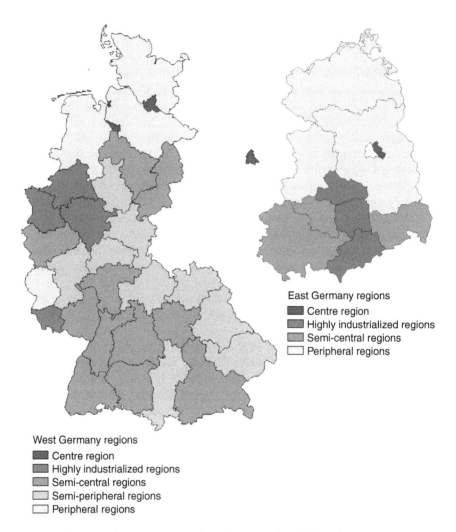

Figure 7.3 West and East German region classes based on industrial structures, 1980 and
1991, respectively.

share further characteristics with respect to population density and geographical
situation. All in all, they can thus be described as follows:

- One region class, labelled *highly industrialized regions*, is made up of
  regions with relatively high shares of manufacturing, and with a focus on
  resource dependent industries. In West Germany, this class includes the three
  regions forming the Ruhr area and the Saarland, in East Germany the regions
  Dessau, Leipzig, Chemnitz (which are moreover characterized by a focus on
  some footloose industries). These regions are usually densely populated.

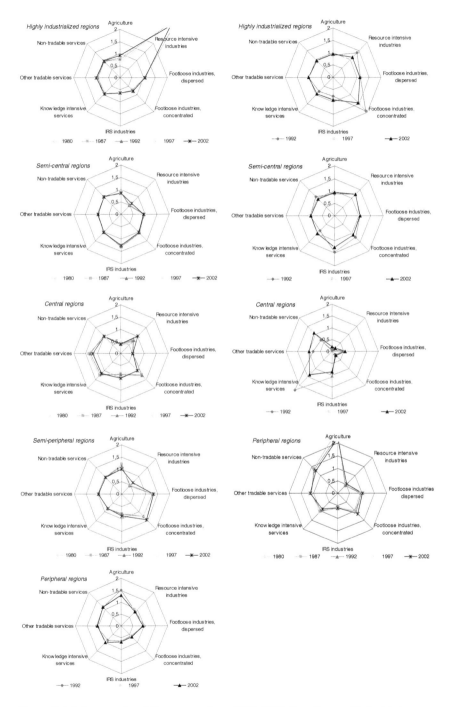

Figure 7.4 Industry mix of German regions 1980–2002 (location coefficients) (source: BA, Sozialversicherungspflichtig Beschäftigte).

- Another region class, labelled *semi-central regions* (to qualify them as relatively similar to purely central regions), consists of regions with a certain focus on industries with high IRS, and with industrial shares close to average for most other sectors (i.e. the respective location coefficients are close to one). They are situated predominantly in the South-Western/Southern part of the country.[9] In West Germany, this class contains the quite densely populated urban areas of West Berlin, Oberbayern (München), Stuttgart, Darmstadt (Frankfurt), Köln, Hannover, in East Germany, the regions Thüringen, Halle and Dresden.

- A further region class contains the West German urban centres Hamburg and Bremen, and the East German part of Berlin and is therefore labelled *central regions*. Both West and East regions of this class are characterized by a focus on knowledge intensive services, yet they differ with respect to other foci: West German regions are specialized on some footloose industries, the East German regions reveal relatively low shares of most manufacturing industries.

- A fourth region class consists of regions with a focus on agriculture and concentrated footloose industries and is labelled s*emi-peripheral regions* (to distinguish it from further, more remote regions). In West Germany, this class is situated usually in central parts of the country and contains the regions Detmold, Giessen, Kassel, Freiburg, Tübingen, Ober-, Unter- and Mittelfranken, Schwaben, Niederbayern and Oberpfalz, regions that are mostly less densely populated. No East German region fits into this class.

- Finally, a fifth class of regions with relatively high shares of agriculture, tradable and non-tradable services is labelled *peripheral regions*. In West and East Germany, these regions are to be found primarily in the northern parts of the country and include rather remote or sparsely populated regions: Schleswig-Holstein, Lüneburg, Weser-Ems, Trier and Koblenz in

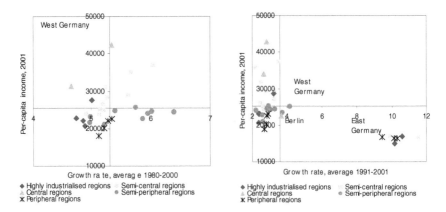

Figure 7.5 Income and growth performance of German regions (source: Eurostat. The point of origin marks the respective average values for the whole country).

the one case, Mecklenburg-Vorpommern, Magdeburg and Brandenburg in the other.

Over time, the specific specialization pattern of these region classes tended to get levelled, as Figure 7.4 also demonstrates. Both West and East German regions envisaged a downsizing of their specific foci, and an upsizing of their underrepresented sectors (location coefficients approaching 1 from above and below). Only, in the case of East German regions, this process proceeded most rapidly immediately after the reunification, whereas West German regions, e.g. semi-central and semi-peripheral regions, underwent a particularly slow restructuring process. As a result of all these movements, the nature of regional specialization, the industrial structure of all region classes, tended to converge towards an average state with less explicit foci. The maintenance or decrease of regional specialization degrees in West and East German regions, respectively, stated at the start of this chapter, thus coincides with concentrated industries losing significance particularly in their specific locations (even services losing relative significance in regions with a focus on these services).

Specialization, structural change and employment

The analysis now turns to the question of whether the degree and nature of regional specialization also affects the performance of the regions regarding GDP and growth, and regarding employment and unemployment.

In fact, the regions of each class seem to share stylized characteristics of economic success, as measured by income per capita and income growth, at least in the case of West Germany. Figure 7.6 presents recent GDP per capita

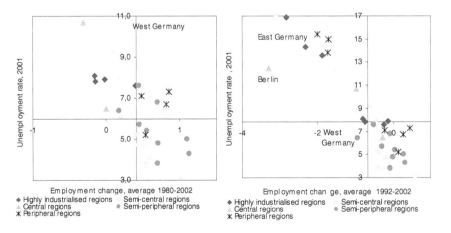

Figure 7.6 Employment performance of German regions (source: Eurostat. The point of origin marks the respective average values for the whole country).

(in current prices) and growth rates of GDP for West and East German regions and for the 1980s and 1990s, respectively. Accordingly, the highly industrialized regions appear to be falling back during the observation period of the 1980s and 1990s, performing low growth and ending up with quite low income (with Düsseldorf as an outlier). The central regions revealed only low to medium growth rates; they maintained a still elevated income level only due to a start from quite high levels. The peripheral regions were not able to catch up markedly from their backwardness due to only medium growth rates. By contrast, semi-peripheral and semi-central regions usually realized quite high growth rates during the 1980s and 1990s. They reached medium to high income levels, and these levels were higher, the higher the preceding growth was.

For East German regions in the 1990s, the most obvious feature was their much higher GDP growth and still much lower level of per capita income. Yet, a clear relation between belonging to a certain region class and performing better or worse than the East German average is not noticeable: in the aftermath of the immediate breakdown of 1990 to 1991, all regions experienced high growth

Table 7.2 Specialization and employment change

	Initial specialization ↔ subsequent employment change		Specialization change ↔ simultaneous employment change	
	Pearson correlation coefficient	*Error probability*	*Pearson correlation coefficient*	*Error probability*
Theil index				
West German regions 1980–1992	**−0.392***	**0.03**	0.272	0.14
West German regions 1992–2002	−0.176	0.34	−0.157	0.40
East German regions 1992–2002	**−0.910*****	**0.00**	**0.880*****	**0.00**
Weighted Theil index				
West German regions 1980–1992	−0.074	0.69	−0.097	0.60
West German regions 1992–2002	−0.235	0.20	0.125	0.50
East German regions 1992–2002	**−0.978*****	**0.00**	**0.950*****	**0.00**

Source: BAA Sozialversicherungspflichtig Beschäftigte.

Notes
* Significant at the 5% level.
** Significant at the 1% level.
*** Significant at the 0.1% level.

Table 7.3 Regional localization of industry groups and employment change

	Initial regional location coefficient of industry group ↔ change of …		Change of regional location coefficient of industry group ↔ change of …	
	… respective industry group employment in the region	… total regional employment	… respective industry group employment in the region	… total regional employment
	Pearson correlation coefficients (Error probabilities in parentheses)			
Agriculture				
West regions 1980–1992	**−0.575** (0.00)	**0.403** (0.02)	**0.979** (0.00)	−0.336 (0.06)
West regions 1992–2002	**−0.465** (0.01)	**0.466** (0.01)	**0.961** (0.00)	−0.261 (0.16)
East regions 1992–2002	**−0.984** (0.00)	**0.692** (0.03)	**0.915** (0.00)	−0.476 (0.16)
Resource intensive industries				
West regions 1980–1992	**−0.935** (0.00)	**−0.570** (0.00)	**0.584** (0.00)	0.048 (0.80)
West regions 1992–2002	**−0.953** (0.00)	−0.137 (0.46)	**0.763** (0.00)	0.049 (0.79)
East regions 1992–2002	**−0.940** (0.00)	0.222 (0.54)	**0.955** (0.00)	0.077 (0.83)
Industries with high IRS				
West regions 1980–1992	0.100 (0.59)	0.172 (0.36)	**0.912** (0.00)	−0.099 (0.60)
West regions 1992–2002	**−0.632** (0.00)	−0.037 (0.84)	**0.753** (0.00)	0.109 (0.56)
East regions 1992–2002	**−0.687** (0.03)	−0.101 (0.78)	**0.939** (0.00)	0.477 (0.16)
Concentrated footloose industries				
West regions 1980–1992	**−0.770** (0.00)	0.061 (0.75)	**0.789** (0.00)	−0.010 (0.96)
West regions 1992–2002	**−0.749** (0.00)	−0.149 (0.42)	**0.639** (0.00)	0.176 (0.34)
East regions 1992–2002	**−0.952** (0.00)	0.177 (0.63)	**0.834** (0.00)	0.275 (0.44)

continued

Table 7.3 continued

	Initial regional location coefficient of industry group ↔ change of ...		Change of regional location coefficient of industry group ↔ change of ...	
	... respective industry group employment in the region	... total regional employment	... respective industry group employment in the region	... total regional employment
	Pearson correlation coefficients (Error probabilities in parentheses)			
Dispersed footloose industries				
West regions 1980–1992	**0.533** (**0.00**)	**0.439** (**0.01**)	**0.672** (**0.00**)	−0.030 (0.87)
West regions 1992–2002	−0.323 (0.08)	0.227 (0.22)	**0.616** (**0.00**)	0.343 (0.06)
East regions 1992–2002	−0.575 (0.08)	**0.757** (**0.01**)	**0.886** (**0.00**)	−0.304 (0.39)
Knowledge intensive industries				
West regions 1980–1992	−0.007 (0.97)	−0.297 (0.10)	**0.619** (**0.00**)	0.206 (0.27)
West regions 1992–2002	**0.362** (**0.05**)	−0.099 (0.60)	**0.410** (**0.02**)	**−0.524** (**0.00**)
East regions 1992–2002	**−0.972** (**0.00**)	**−0.857** (**0.00**)	**0.992** (**0.00**)	**0.860** (**0.00**)
Tradable services				
West regions 1980–1992	−0.322 (0.08)	−0.219 (0.24)	**0.543** (**0.00**)	0.031 (0.87)
West regions 1992–2002	**−0.436** (**0.01**)	−0.135 (0.47)	**0.816** (**0.00**)	0.308 (0.09)
East regions 1992–2002	−0.080 (0.83)	**0.684** (**0.03**)	0.028 (0.94)	**−0.822** (**0.00**)
Non-tradable services				
West regions 1980–1992	**0.410** (**0.02**)	0.150 (0.42)	0.266 (0.15)	**−0.604** (**0.00**)
West regions 1992–2002	**−0.648** (**0.00**)	−0.049 (0.79)	**0.476** (**0.01**)	**−0.557** (**0.00**)
East regions 1992–2002	**−0.901** (**0.00**)	**0.676** (**0.03**)	**0.853** (**0.00**)	**−0.851** (**0.00**)

Source: BAA, Sozialversicherungspflichtig Beschäftigte.

Note
Bold figures indicate significance at least at the 5% level.

rates and almost equal per capita income levels, except for the very special case of Berlin (includes East and West Berlin).

Turning to the employment performance of the regions, one might expect an even closer relation to the industrial structures of regions, as this structure is measured in terms of employment shares. Yet the stylized facts on this relation do not support this expectation. Figure 7.7 displays the recent unemployment record as well as the preceding employment change in the regions. While the graphs show quite clearly the obvious negative relation between both (regions that had the worst employment decline suffer from the highest unemployment thereafter, and vice versa), they are less clear regarding the relative position of the regions of a region class with respect to employment performance. To be sure, the highly industrialized regions tended to experience massive employment decrease and high unemployment; and the peripheral regions tended to experience relatively high employment increase, yet (still?) relatively high unemployment. But for all other classes the evidence is rather mixed. This observation holds also for East Germany.

Yet, when getting into more detail, some relations between structural change and employment performance can well be fixed. To this end, correlations between both the degree and the nature of regional specialization and the regional employment performance are provided.

First, there seems to be a negative relation between the *degree* of specialization and the employment performance. Table 7.2 provides correlation coefficients between the initial specialization of a region and its subsequent employment change, and shows that such a negative relation may exist: it is, however, usually not significant for West German regions. Even less coincidence seems to exist between the change of regional specialization and the simultaneous employment change according to Table 7.2. By contrast, for East German regions, the probability for regional job losses was significantly higher both the more specialized the respective region was initially, and the faster its specialization degree declined.

Second, the specific *nature of regional specialization*, i.e. the specific industry mix of the regions, seems to coincide more directly with regional employment performance than the degree of specialization. Table 7.3 presents the relation between the initial localization of industry groups in regions (as displayed in Figure 7.4 for region classes) and the subsequent employment performance of:

1 this industry group within the region;
2 the region in total.
   Also, the change of the location coefficient is related to the performance of:
3 the industry group;
4 the region.

According to these calculations, the degree of regional localization seems to be highly and usually negatively correlated to the subsequent regional employment performance of the respective industry group (column 1): the more a specific industry group is already localized in a specific region, the more it tends to experience job losses in the very region. This backlash trend is most pronounced for resource intensive industries, confirming widespread expectations on the decline of these industries particularly at their specific locations. However, a negative correlation is also observed for the industry group of perceived high-IRS industries, contradicting familiar NEG perceptions that such industries would get increasingly localized. Also, a negative correlation is observed for concentrated footloose industries.

Such backlash trends from localized industries usually seem not to be strong enough to also determine the overall employment performance of the regions concerned. This is indicated by the mostly insignificant correlations in the second column of Table 7.3: the initial localization of an industry group in a certain region is not followed by a systematic increase or decrease of total regional employment, and accordingly, the regions concerned by job losses in highly localized industries seem to have found some compensation by job creation in other industries.

Finally, Table 7.3 and, in confirmation of it, Figure 7.7, show significant correlations between the change of the localization of an industry group in a region and the simultaneous change of employment in this very industry group in the respective region: an industry group that gets less localized in a certain region, like agriculture (dark spots in Figure 7.7), resource intensive industries (light triangles) or dispersed footloose industries (light spots), does so by setting off its employees in this very region, not by increasing employment in other regions. By the same token, an industry group that gets more localized in a certain region, like knowledge intensive services (open triangles), does so by generating new jobs in this region, not by destroying jobs in other regions. This observation holds both for West and East Germany.

Conclusions

Among the countries analysed in this book, Germany may be taken as a case study for Eastern enlargement in a nutshell, due to the unique reunification process that encompasses the many facets of the integration of former socialist countries into the Western world at a smaller scale within one country. The German case may thus provide useful insights for the influence of current integration process on regional structural change in East European countries. The major findings are as follows.

Both the initial specialization pattern as well as the subsequent evolution differed substantially between West and East German regions. While West German regions were quite moderately specialized and did not change much to this respect over a period of 20 years of increasing EU integration and the reunification process, East German regions were highly specialized, particularly directly after the reunification, and experienced a dramatic structural change bringing down

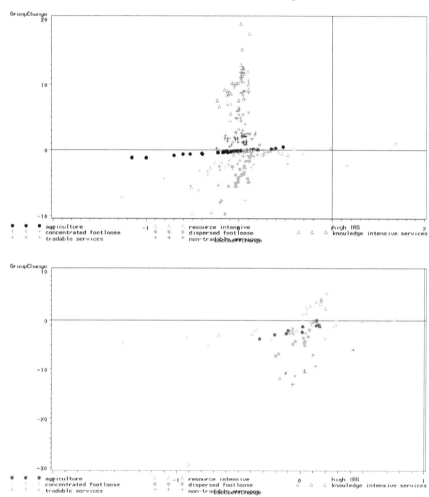

Figure 7.7 Employment change and change of localization, by industry groups and regions (source: BA, Sozialversicherungspflichtig Beschäftigte).

specialization to West German levels. Thus, it seems to be not so much the normal process of EU integration that exerts a substantial influence on regional structural change, but rather the extraordinary event of the transition from a socialist to a free-market economy.

In contrast to other European regions, the German regions do not underlie an obvious core-periphery pattern due to their polycentric tradition, but rather a South–North divide, where the regions corresponding closest to a periphery-type industry mix are situated in the Northern parts, and the regions with a more core-type industry mix are situated in the Southern parts of the country – both in West and East Germany. This divide, however, seems to get levelled over time, as the industrial structures of the regions tend to converge and specialization degrees to decrease.

Concerning the relation between regional industry mix and regional GDP and growth performance, the West German results suggest there might be some interdependence, with highly industrialized and at the same time highly specialized regions falling back, and peripheral regions catching up slowly. No such relation can be observed for East German regions.

Relations between the regional industry mix and regional employment performance seem to be more complex: while a high initial specialization of a region onto a specific industry had a negative effect on the subsequent employment growth of the very industry group in this region, this negative industry-specific specialization-growth nexus did not translate into a negative aggregate specialization-growth nexus. In the case of West German regions, at least, there is little evidence of a high initial specialization generally shaping aggregate regional employment growth. By contrast, the transformation regions from East Germany seemed to have suffered the more the higher they were specialized initially.

Notes

1　I like to thank Florian Siedenburg for substantial and valuable research assistance, and Eckhardt Bode and Rüdiger Soltwedel for useful comments and suggestions to earlier versions. Remaining errors are mine.
2　I use data from the Bundesagentur (former Bundesanstalt) für Arbeit on persons employed that are subject to social insurance contributions. The dataset contains data for 31 NUTS 2 regions ("Regierungsbezirke") in a sectoral breakdown of 294 branches, and for the years 1980, 1987–2002 in the case of West Germany, for the years 1992–2002 in the case of East Germany. The degree of specialization of German regions is measured by a Theil index and a weighted Theil index as presented in Chapter 2 of this volume.
3　The concentration is measured by a Brülhart–Träger–Theil index with the topographic space as a benchmark. It compares the actual distribution of industries across regions to the distribution of space across regions.
4　The classification of the respective industries draws on an OECD (1987) classification of resource intensive industries, yet applying it only to those industries where resources are localized and not ubiquitous.
5　The classification of the respective industries draws on Pratten (1988) who identified industries with different levels of technical IRS. It is here referred to industries with a high level of IRS – as far as they are not dependent on localized resources.
6　The classification of the respective industries draws on a classification by Grupp *et al.* (2000).
7　Applying Ward's minimum cluster analysis, separately for West and East Germany, for the initial years 1980 and 1991, respectively.
8　Location coefficients are defined as regional employment shares of an industry, compared to the respective national employment share of the very industry.
9　In other, more monocentric countries like France and Spain, these type of regions tend to form a belt between highly industrialized and central regions.

References

Bade, F.-J., C.-F. Laaser and R. Soltwedel (2004). "Urban Specialization in the Internet Age: Empirical Findings for Germany". Kiel Working Paper 1215.

Balchin, and P.N.L. Sýkora (1999). *Regional Policy and Planning in Europe*. London: Routledge.

Bode, E. (2002) "Räumliches Muster des Aufholprozesses". In: Institut für Wirtschafts forschung Halle (ed.) Fortschrittsbericht wirtschaftswissenschaftlicher Institute über die wirtschaftliche Entwicklung in Ostdeutschland, Halle, 31–90.

Boss, A. and A. Rosenschon (2006). Der Kieler Subventionsbericht: Grundlagen, Ergebnisse, Schlussfolgerungen. Kieler Diskussionsbeiträge 423, Institut für Weltwirtschaft Kiel.

Bundesanstalt für Arbeit (today: Bundesagentur für Arbeit), Sozialversicherungspflichtig Beschäftigte. Datenlieferung.

Bundesregierung der Bundesrepublik Deutschland (2003). 19. Subventionsbericht.

Burda, M. (1994). "Ist das Maß halb leer, halb voll oder einfach voll? Die volkswirtschaftlichen Perspektiven der neuen Bundesländer". Antrittsvorlesung, Humboldt Universität zu Berlin, 26 Oktober 1994.

Colavecchio, R., D. Curran and M. Funke (2005). "Drifting Together or Falling apart? The Empirics of Regional Economic Growth in Post-Unification Germany". CESIFO Working Paper 1533.

Feldenkirchen, W. (1999). "Germany: The Intervention of Interventionism". In: J.S. Foreman-Peck and G. Federico (eds) *European Industrial Policy*. Oxford: Oxford University Press, 98–117.

Grupp, H., H. Legler, A. Jungmittag and U. Schmoch (2000). Hochtechnologie 2000. Neudefinition der Hochtechnologie für die Berichterstattung zur technologischen Leistungsfähigkeit Deutschlands Bericht des FhG-ISI und des NIW im Auftrag des Bundesministeriums für Bildung und Forschung.

Hallet, M. (2000). "Regional Specialization and Concentration in the EU". European Commission Economic Papers 131. Brussels.

Koopmann, G., C. Kreienbaum and C. Borrmann (1997) *Industrial and Trade Policy in Germany*. Baden-Baden: Nomos-Verl-Ges.

Krakowski, M. (1993): "The Globalization of Economic Activities and the Development of Small and Medium Sized Enterprises in Germany". HWWA-Report 132. Hamburg.

Organisation for Economic Co-operation and Development (OECD) (1987). "Structural Adjustment and Economic Performance". Paris.

Pratten, C. (1988). "A Survey of the Economies of Scale". In: Commission of the European Communities, *Research on the "Cost of Non-Europe"*. Volume 2: *Studies on the Economics of Integration*. Luxemburg: CEC.

Sinn, H.W. and Sinn G. (1992). *Jumpstart. The Economic Unification of Germany*. Cambridge: MIT Press.

Snower, D.J. and C. Merkl (2006). "The Caring Hand that Cripples: The East German Labour Market after Reunification (Detailed Version)". Kiel Working Paper 1263.

8 European integration, regional structural change and cohesion in Poland

Anna Wisniewski

Introduction

Transformation and integration have brought about important and visible changes in the production structure in Poland both on a national and a regional level. Though the transformation process has been exemplary for other countries, even in Central and Eastern Europe, the quick macroeconomic changes aiming at financial stability, however, were not followed by equal measures in the micro-spheres. The unbalanced political situation in the beginning of the 1990s made it impossible to carry out a comprehensive privatisation and restructuring process, which had a long lasting effect on the competitiveness of the Polish economy and also had implications for its spatial structure. The country study provides a first assessment of the major country characteristics, concentrating in the first part on the development patterns in the Polish economy. The second part describes the spatial differences of the economy, and gives some methodological notes important to understand regional data on Poland. This section analyses Polish regional characteristics on the basis of population, employment and production statistics. The next part describes specialisation and concentration measures and changes in these variables and finally we make some conclusions on our findings.

Stylised country characteristics

Poland became a member state of the European Union on 1 May 2004, with 38,000,000 inhabitants and a total area of 322,000 km^2. The first year spent in the Community was evaluated as a great success both to the economy and the society. The relatively high growth rates (5.4 per cent in 2004 and the 4.0 per cent and 4.8 per cent expected in the following two years), the improving export and investment performance, as well as the slightly diminishing unemployment rates all prove that. The new impetus caused by EU-accession has been of highest importance to the country, which despite the above-average growth rate recorded over the past 15 years, has still a development level much lower than the European average (Table 8.1).

Table 8.1 GDP per capita (PPS) and GDP growth (%), 1995–2004

		1995	1996	1997	1998	1999	2000	2001	2002	2003	2004
GDP/capita in PPS, EU-25 = 100	EU-15	110.8	110.5	110.2	110.1	110.0	109.8	109.7	109.5	109.2	108.9
	Poland	40.5	42.2	43.9	44.8	45.4	45.9	45.4	45.3	45.6	46.7
GDP growth %, constant prices (1995)	EU-15	2.6	1.7	2.7	2.9	2.9	3.7	1.8	1.1	0.9	2.2
	Poland	2.7	6.0	6.8	4.8	4.1	4.0	1.0	1.4	3.8	5.3

Source: Eurostat.

Table 8.2 Development of key macroeconomic figures

	Unemployment (%)		Employment rate (%)		Productivity (EU-25=100)		Inflation rate (%)		Unit labour cost growth (%)	
	1998	2004	1998	2004	1995	2004	1998	2004	1998	2004
EU-25	9.5	9.0	61.2	63.3	100.0	100	2.1	2.1	−1.0	–
EU-15	9.3	8.0	61.4	64.8	110.1	106.4	1.3	2.0	−0.8	−0.9
Czech Republic	6.4	8.3	67.3	64.2	57.5	63.7	9.7	2.6	−3.1	−2.5
Poland	**8.4**	**18.8**	**59.0**	**51.7**	**43.9**	**60.2**	**11.8**	**3.6**	**−1.3**	**−3.6**
Hungary	10.2	5.9	53.7	56.8	58.2	69.4	14.2	6.8	−1.8	1.4
Slovakia	16.7	18.0	62.9	57.0	46.6	61.4	6.7	7.4	2.8	0.1

Source: Eurostat.

The structure of the economy has gone through deep changes in the past 15 years, with the trade and services sectors gradually gaining importance, the share of industry and especially agriculture in Poland's Gross Domestic Product (GDP) has been steadily falling over the last few years. Along with a diminishing share of industry in the Polish economy, the transformation brought on progressive modernisation, reflected for example in growing exports and productivity. Today the share of agriculture in GDP is 3.8 per cent (after 13.1 per cent in 1988), the share of industry (excluding construction) decreased to 24.1 per cent from 41.7 per cent and its structure has changed significantly, manufacturing gaining importance. The most important change, however, took place in services, the share of which increased from 34.5 per cent to 64.8 per cent by 2002.

The transformation process brought about huge drops in employment at the beginning of the 1990s, due to this, the employment rate fell from around 70 per cent at the end of the 1980s to 51.7 per cent in 2004, which is significantly lower than the EU average and also less than the similar rate of the neighbouring countries. The structure of employment changed radically as far as the whole territory of Poland is concerned. Employment decreased in agriculture and industry and increased in the service sector. Compared to the European average, however, agricultural employment is still very high, according to European statistics still reaching 18 per cent. Unemployment reached double-digit figures in the mid-1990s and since 1998 it has shown a tendency towards fast growth. It went up from 6.1 per cent in 1989 to 10.4 per cent in 1998 reaching 18.8 per cent at the end of 2004. Underlying unemployment trends, we find the impact of transformation (restructuring of loss-making enterprises), the economic slow-down in 1998 because of the Russian crisis, and also demographic trends, appearance of a young workforce on the labour market. Poland is a relatively young country, 53 per cent of the population is between the age of 25 and 65, while only 13 per cent belongs to the age group over 65. Compared to 1995, however, the share of the population in pre-working age decreased significantly, from 25 per cent to 17 per cent, a trend characteristic of more developed countries.

External trade was vital to the transformation of the Polish economy. Increased access to competitive imports following trade liberalisation has facilitated Poland's export-led growth. The share of merchandise trade (exports and imports) to GDP increased from 38 per cent in 1994 to 49 per cent in 1997, before falling to 44 per cent in 1999. The trade structure changed as well, manufactured products accounting for over three-quarters of Polish trade; export shares of these goods increased from 59 per cent in 1992 to 77 per cent in 1998.

During the transformation period, Poland's external trade turnover increased more than three times. Total exports almost doubled, external balance, however, remains problematic, as imports increased nearly five times over the past period. Trade balance has been in deficit for a long time, in 2002 reaching $10.3 million, which is, however, less than in 2000 and 2001. Since 2000 exports have been growing at a faster rate than imports due to slower growth in domestic consumption and improved competitiveness of Polish goods. The steady increase of the country's share in world trade is indicated by statistical figures; her share in exports went up from 0.43 per cent in 1989 to 0.6 per cent in 2001, while the imports went from 0.34 per cent to 0.8 per cent respectively. The opening up of the Polish economy to the world, however, was not as large as that of her neighbours. Despite steady growth throughout the 1990s, Poland's export to GDP ratio reached 22 per cent in 2002, while in the Czech Republic this ratio was 55 per cent, in Hungary 65 per cent. The export per inhabitant value also remains at a low level, reaching only $1,062 in 2002 (in Hungary $3,400, in the Czech Republic $3,700).

Over the past decade, geographic patterns of Poland's external trade have changed significantly. After signing the European Agreement, the European Community market has started to become more and more important in Poland's external relations. Presently, the share of the EU in exports is 69 per cent. The countries of the EU are the main suppliers for the Polish economy (about 61 per cent share in total import) in terms of investment and intermediate goods. This market has also a very significant influence on foreign trade deficit (41.3 per cent of the total deficit is attributed to countries of the European Union).[1] Even before the second World War, Germany used to be Poland's main trading partner. The fall of the USSR in this respect restored the previous structure; presently Poland's most important trade partner is Germany, accounting for a 47 per cent share in

Table 8.3 Trade with EU-15 in % of GDP

	Imports				Exports				Imports and exports			
	1999	*2000*	*2001*	*2002*	*1999*	*2000*	*2001*	*2002*	*1999*	*2000*	*2001*	*2002*
Czech Republic	32.8	38.7	39.4	35.2	33.0	38.7	40.3	37.7	65.8	77.4	79.7	72.9
Hungary	37.6	40.2	37.6	29.8	39.7	45.3	43.7	36.7	77.3	85.5	81.3	66.1
Poland	**19.2**	**18.3**	**16.9**	**18.0**	**12.5**	**13.5**	**13.7**	**14.9**	**31.7**	**31.8**	**30.5**	**32.8**
EU-15	14.6	15.8	15.5	14.7	15.5	16.9	16.8	16.1	30.2	12.7	32.3	30.8

Source: EUROSTAT.

Table 8.4 Trade with EU-15 in % of total trade

	Imports				Exports				Imports and exports			
	1999	*2000*	*2001*	*2002*	*1999*	*2000*	*2001*	*2002*	*1999*	*2000*	*2001*	*2002*
Czech Republic	64.2	62.1	61.8	60.1	69.2	68.7	68.9	68.1	68.2	68.6	62.1	62.0
Hungary	64.4	58.5	57.8	56.3	76.2	75.2	74.3	75.1	57.5	57.0	55.7	55.6
Poland	**65.0**	**61.2**	**61.4**	**61.7**	**70.5**	**70.0**	**69.2**	**68.7**	**62.8**	**59.8**	**61.8**	**62.2**
EU-15	59.4	56.4	56.6	57.0	62.2	60.8	60.7	60.5	60.8	58.6	58.7	58.7

Source: EUROSTAT.

exports and nearly 40 per cent in imports. The share of the former Soviet Union countries had decreased below 10 per cent, although dependence on the oil and gas supply from this geographical direction still determines Eastern trade relations. Commercial relations with the neighbouring countries went through a deep decline in the beginning of the 1990s, recovering smoothly following the creation of the CEFTA free trade agreement. The share of this group of countries, however, is still not very significant; it even declined to less than 5 per cent in 2002 exports, but slightly increased in imports. The structure of foreign trade has also changed in the past years, the commodity composition of both the exports and imports moved towards manufactured goods and machinery. The comparative advantage of Polish exports, however, is still stronger in labour-intensive industries, such as paper and wood products, the textile industry, and also transport equipment, than in the high-tech sectors.

The level of Poland's integration to the European Union can be measured by the trade with the EU-15 in per cent of GDP ratio. In terms of trade, Poland is highly integrated into the European market. The respective figures for the country resemble the large and less opened markets, such as Germany or France. The ratio of Poland's trade with EU-15 in total trade shows a similarly high correlation.

Trade liberalisation and the high level of integration in terms of trade to EU market caused the intra-industry trade to increase as well. Calculations[2] with regard to changes in the level of intra-industry trade show that its share has grown from 32 per cent to 55.1 per cent between 1993 and 2000.

Regional characteristics of Poland

Poland's historical heritage had an impact not only on the territorial division, but also on regional development differences in the country. It was, however not the centralisation efforts during the socialist era, or the shifting of the country's territory to the West after the Second World War that had the greatest influence. The boundaries of Poland's partition in the nineteenth century between Russia (Central-East), Prussia (North-West) and Austria (South-East) determine even today the pattern of regional development. Present-day Poland still consists of a better-off West and South, and a less developed, rural, Eastern part. Apart from these two, the central part of Poland (e.g. the capital and its surroundings) is the most developed region in the country. The transformation and integration process has not diminished; it rather reinforced old regional disparities. Some regions have been able to take advantage of the changes over the past decade; the winners of the integration and transformation process are regions with the biggest agglomerations: Warsaw (Mazowieckie voivodship), Poznań (Wielkopolskie), Wrocław (Dolnośląskie) and Cracow (Małopolskie). These are economic, cultural and scientific centres, and are also favoured by foreign capital. The position of the centrally located Mazowieckie region and the capital of Warsaw clearly play a dominant role in regional development. The least developed Eastern regions (Podlaskie, Lubelskie, Podkarpackie, Świętokrzyskie) are sparsely populated;

the share of agriculture is very high both in employment and in gross value added, while regional development level is relatively low. In the transformation process, there are specific problems linked to the old industrial regions, such as the textile-oriented region of Łódź or coal mining in Śląsk. The problem of these regions can only be solved with the consistent implementation of regional development policy plans.

Methodological notes

Analysis of regional disparities and cohesion in Poland requires certain methodological comments as far as database is concerned. First of all, one has to be aware of the constant changes in the territorial division of the country. Polish regional structure has been altered several times in the past few decades: up until 1975 the country territory was divided into 17 regions – traditionally called voivodships. This system was reshaped into a 49-voivodship regional structure, which was part of a two-tier system. As the integration aspirations of Poland to the European Union came closer to reality, this system of 49 voivodships seemed too small and weak to function as effective partners of the EU regions. The need to "harmonise" the regional divisions in Poland was generally accepted, the number and shape of the new regions, however, stirred up a lot of controversy. The decentralisation reform in 1999[3] finally created 16 regions that correspond to the EU NUTS 2 level.

However, disparities arising from the changing of the boundaries in the transition from the old to the new territorial units have created an obstacle to objective comparison of data over the long term. The study therefore focuses on regional development dynamics after 1998; only in cases where recalculated data are

Map 8.1 New territorial division of the state-voivodships (source: GUS. *Statistical Yearbook of the Regions*, Warszawa, 1999).

Table 8.5 The nomenclature of territorial units for statistics in Poland and in EU-15

Poland
NUTS 1 – the whole of Poland NUTS 2 – 16 regions called voivodships NUTS 3 – 44 subregions called podregiony NUTS 4 – 380 poviats NUTS 5 – 2489 communas called gminas

Source: Regions. Nomenclature of territorial units for statistics, Eurostat, 1999.

available (e.g. for gross domestic product or gross value added) was it possible to provide longer-time analysis.

The Regional Data Bank has been compiled since 1995 in Poland with regional data on the socioeconomic situation of gminas (NUTS 5), poviats (NUTS 4) and voivodships (NUTS 2). Data on NUTS 3 level (e.g. subregions – podregiony), however, was created only in 2000 and has been expanded since.

Major economic indicators at a regional level

The regional population pattern in Poland is a decentralised one, the primacy of Warsaw is quite low – it contains only some 5 per cent of the population of the country, while the Mazowieckie region has only 13.4 per cent. The combined number of population of the six regional capitals (Cracow, Poznań, Wrocław, Poznań, Gdańsk, Łódź and Katowice) is over twice of that of the capital. The Silesian region has only slightly less than the share of the Mazowieckie region in population and it is, as far as density is concerned, the most densely populated region of Poland. The other most densely populated region is the urbanised Małopolskie, with the cultural and academic centre of Cracow. Owing to the lack of large cities in the Eastern part of the country, (the biggest ones are Białystok with only 17 per cent of the population of Warsaw and Lublin with 22 per cent) Warsaw performs many functions of a regional capital for most of the Eastern part of Poland.

Spatial population mobility has been decreasing since the late 1970s, while interregional migration reached 964,000 in 1978, this number decreased to 640,000 by 1988 and by mid-1998 it was down to 425,000. This trend has continued since, with the number of people changing their place of residence at only 403,000 in 2002. The drop in migration also shows a tendency for rural-to-urban migration to drop. This tendency is attributable to the fall in demand for labour in certain industries and industrial regions. Apart from this characteristic of transformation, certain other regional centres have been successful in re-orienting their economic base from the previous dependent industry to a dominance of the service sector. This kind of transformation process can also be detected in regional migration trends, where the Mazowieckie, Małopolskie and Wielkopolskie regions attract the largest number of people.

Table 8.6 Population distribution in Poland in the period 1995–2002

Region	Total area in km²	Population per 1 km²			
		1995	*2000*	*2001*	*2002*
Dolnośląskie	19,948	150	149	149	146
Kujawsko-Pomorskie	17,970	116	117	117	115
Lubelskie	25,114	89	89	89	87
Łubuskie	13,984	73	73	73	72
Lódzkie	18,219	148	145	145	143
Małopolskie	15,107	211	214	214	214
Mazowieckie	35,579	142	143	143	144
Opolskie	9,412	116	115	115	113
Podkarpackie	17,926	117	119	119	117
Podlaskie	20,180	61	61	60	60
Pomorskie	18,293	118	120	121	119
Śląskie	12,331	399	394	393	384
Świetokrzyskie	11,691	114	113	113	111
Warmińsko-Mazurskie	24,203	60	61	61	59
Wielkopolskie	29,826	112	113	113	112
Zachodniopomorskie	22,902	75	76	76	74
POLAND	**312,685**	**123**	**124**	**124**	**122**

Source: GUS, *Statistical Yearbooks of the Regions*, Warszawa, 2000–2002.

Despite the above-average growth rate recorded in Poland over the past decade, the development level of the country measured by GDP is still low compared to the European average although the gross domestic product on current prices has nearly doubled. In 1995 in Poland the gap is still large; only ten regions have a higher GDP level than 40 per cent of EU average. On a regional level, development differences do not seem to be larger than the European average (it does not exceed the 1:2 ratio), but data for subregions show high and ever-growing disparities.

The most developed regions in GDP terms are Mazowieckie (the subregion around Warsaw), Wielkopolskie (the subregion of Poznań), Silesia (the subregion of Katowice), Pomorskie (the subregion of Gdańsk) and Dolnośląskie (the subregion of Wrocław). The least developed ones are the rural Eastern territories, the Lubelskie, Warminsko-Mazurskie and Podkarpackie voivodships. It is important to note that the Malopolskie region is also one of the least developed voivodships with a dynamically growing regional capital of Cracow (the differences, however, remain at 1:2.5). The widest gap both on a regional, but more visibly on a subregional level can be noted between Warsaw and the rest of the country. (The difference between the most developed Warsaw and the least developed Elckie subregion is 1:5.)

The transformation process brought about huge drops in employment at the beginning of the 1990s and, due to this, the employment rate fell from around 70 per cent at the end of the 1980s to 55.2 per cent in 2001, which is lower than the EU average. The highest rate, however, cannot be attributed to the best

Map 8.2 Gross domestic product per capita in Poland according to NUTS 2 regions in 2003 (EU average = 100) (source: GUS, *Statistical Yearbook of the Regions*, 2006).

developed regions – apart from the Mazowieckie voivodship. All the other best performing regions from this point of view are rural ones, in the Eastern part of the country, like Lubelskie or Podlaskie. The Western part of the country, on the other hand, shows lower employment rate and very high unemployment ratios. The most severely affected regions of transformation were Northern ones,

Table 8.7 Employment rate (%) according to regions (1995–2001)

Region	1995	1996	1997	1998	1999	2000	2001
Dolnośląskie	56.3	56.4	55.7	57.5	56.8	51.1	49.0
Kujawsko-Pomorskie	56.9	58.2	58.7	59.2	56.9	53.0	52.8
Lubelskie	70.2	67.1	65.6	67.6	61.9	63.5	60.7
Lubuskie	53.6	53.1	54.9	59.9	52.4	50.2	50.8
Łódzkie	62.8	63.4	63.8	62.3	61.4	57.5	54.8
Małopolskie	65.2	64.4	63.5	64.8	63.1	60.8	62.2
Mazowieckie	64.0	64.0	65.1	65.6	63.5	63.6	61.0
Opolskie	59.3	59.2	60.8	60.8	55.7	57.3	54.9
Podkarpackie	66.5	65.2	65.6	64.3	60.1	59.6	58.8
Podlaskie	66.2	70.4	69.3	63.1	61.2	60.9	62.1
Pomorskie	57.8	55.5	56.3	57.4	57.9	53.2	54.2
Śląskie	57.2	56.2	57.2	56.3	55.4	49.4	49.2
Świętokrzyskie	67.0	68.6	66.3	63.6	61.7	55.9	51.2
Warmińsko-Mazurskie	52.4	50.2	53.2	55.7	52.4	50.8	49.7
Wielkopolskie	58.3	58.4	59.2	60.8	60.5	57.5	54.9
Zachodniopomorskie	56.8	55.2	55.9	56.9	54.8	52.3	51.1
POLAND	**60.8**	**60.4**	**60.8**	**61.1**	**59.2**	**56.6**	**55.2**

Source: Central Statistical Office (GUS) regional database, 2003.

dominated previously by state-owned farms, or single-industry regions, such as the textile oriented Łódź.[4]

The structure of employment changed significantly as far as the whole territory of Poland is concerned. Employment decreased in agriculture and industry and increased significantly in the service sector. The quality of the changes, however, varies significantly from region to region. The Eastern voivodships have not been able to restructure their economies and re-orientate their workforce to new activities; people continue to cultivate their land or draw unemployment benefits. The success story on the other hand is again the Mazowieckie voivodship, where the market service sectors (especially financing and insurance) have been able to replace traditional activities. The Silesian region has been a success story on two counts – on one hand, it has been able to develop a well-functioning market service sector, which employs large numbers of people, on the other hand the industrial regions have been reshaped and the old industries have been compensated for by the automobile industry. Not all the industrial regions can tell such success stories. Upper Silesia, on the other hand, still bears the burden of the declining mining and coal industries – industries which still have the restructuring and privatisation process before them.

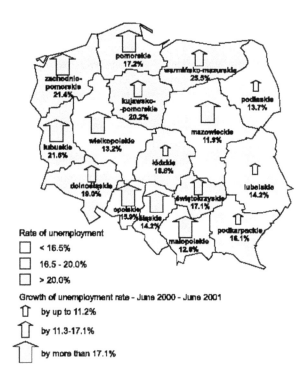

Map 8.3 Registered unemployed persons in 2001 (source: Information on socioeconomic situation of voivodships, GUS, 2/2001).

Unemployment trends do not always follow the employment and development figures; there are cases where employment is high and unemployment falls as a result. In some cases, however, even with high employment the unemployment rate remains at a high level.

Unemployment reached double-digit figures in the mid-1990s and since 1998 it has shown a tendency towards fast growth. It went up from 6.1 per cent in 1989 to 10.4 per cent in 1998, reaching 18 per cent at the end of 2002. The dramatic unemployment situation varies significantly across voivodships, and the differences are even more striking when looking at subregional statistics. The disparities resemble the European average when comparing the lowest rate of Mazowieckie and the highest rate of the Warminsko-Mazurskie voivodship (1:2). When comparing the unemployment rate of Warsaw (6.2 per cent in 2002) with that of Koszalin (31.1 per cent) or Slupsk (30.4 per cent), the ratio is already much higher (1:5). Although a large proportion of the unemployed are under 25 in Poland (around 30 per cent); even so migration to better possibilities as far as job offers are concerned are quite low. This can be attributed to three factors:

1   very high housing prices and underdeveloped renting market;
2   skills mismatch, as the educational profiles of the unemployed do not match the categories sought (e.g. in the market service activities new and tertiary education is needed, while most of the unemployed have only vocational education);
3   finally, there are still incentives for people in rural areas to stay, one of them is of course the low land prices, and the other is the significant difference between the contribution for farmers (KRUS) and the regular Social Security Fund (ZUS).

The transformation process in Poland and private sector development was accompanied by a buoyant investment trend until the end of the century. This is understandable, as investment is the key to modernisation and competitiveness of enterprises. In a regional dimension, the largest shares of investments concentrate on three voivodships: the central Mazowieckie region is well ahead of any other part of Poland, followed by the Silesian and the Wielkopolskie voivodships. More precisely, it is Warsaw, Katowice and Poznan where the most investment has been made and this pattern can be followed back to as early as the beginning of the 1990s. Differences in investment are enormous both on a regional (1:16 when comparing the Mazowieckie voivodship with Podlaskie) and subregional level (1:60 when comparing Warsaw again with the least developed Elck). While in the Mazowieckie region most of the investment (70 per cent) goes to market services, in Śląsk and Wielkopolska it is industry that dominates investment.

The structure of regional GVA shows significant changes over the past decade. The share of agriculture has decreased in all regions, its importance, however, is still considerable in the Eastern part of the country – in the Podlaskie, Lubelskie and Warminsko-Mazurskie voivodships. Industry still dominates in the Slaskie (mining and automobile), the Lodzkie (textile industry) and the

Table 8.8 Gross value added by kinds of activities and regions, 1995 and 2001

Regions	Agriculture		Industry		Manufacturing		Construction		Market services	
	1995	2001	1995	2001	1995	2001	1995	2001	1995	2001
Dolnośląskie	6.0	2.7	33.0	26.5	22.8	19.7	8.3	7.3	38.8	46.3
Kujawsko-Pomorskie	8.2	4.6	31.2	25.5	28.1	23.6	7.1	6.9	40.1	45.9
Lubelskie	13.6	7.0	24.1	19.2	21.1	16.0	6.3	6.4	38.6	45.7
Lubuskie	6.5	4.0	24.4	24.3	21.2	20.1	6.5	6.4	44.2	46.8
Łódzkie	7.3	3.9	31.6	27.4	23.4	20.6	5.6	5.6	41.2	46.1
Małopolskie	4.9	2.3	30.3	23.4	24.7	19.1	8.5	7.8	40.7	48.2
Mazowieckie	6.4	3.5	24.7	19.2	21.1	14.1	7.2	6.2	47.9	57.8
Opolskie	10.2	5.0	32.3	28.3	28.3	20.8	8.5	7.5	36.3	41.4
Podkarpackie	8.2	3.0	32.1	26.9	28.2	23.8	7.5	6.9	36.3	42.8
Podlaskie	13.8	7.1	21.8	19.4	19.4	17.3	5.9	6.8	39.6	45.6
Pomorskie	5.0	2.4	28.8	23.8	25.6	21.3	7.2	8.0	44.4	48.9
Śląskie	2.0	1.2	41.6	32.7	21.1	18.1	8.5	7.2	38.7	45.8
Świętokrzyskie	10.5	5.0	28.0	23.9	23.7	18.8	7.4	8.9	41.4	43.1
Warmińsko-Mazurskie	12.2	6.3	26.0	22.1	23.0	19.9	7.2	6.6	38.2	44.1
Wielkopolskie	11.3	6.7	30.6	25.9	25.9	22.7	8.4	7.3	37.2	45.7
Zachodniopom	7.4	4.3	24.6	20.5	20.9	16.5	7.0	6.8	46.0	51.1
POLAND	**7.1**	**3.8**	**30.5**	**24.5**	**23.3**	**18.7**	**7.5**	**6.9**	**41.2**	**48.6**

Source: *Statistical Yearbook of the Regions*, 2003 and regional dataset of Central Statistical Office.

Table 8.9 Share (%) of regions in industrial production

	1998	1999	2000	2001	2002
Dolnośląskie	6.4	6.7	7.3	7.2	7.3
Kujawsko-Pomorskie	5.2	5.3	5.0	5.1	4.8
Lubelskie	3.0	2.8	2.9	2.7	2.7
Lubuskie	2.1	2.2	2.2	2.1	2.1
Łódzkie	6.1	6.1	5.7	6.3	6.2
Małopolskie	7.4	7.0	7.0	6.8	7.1
Mazowieckie	18.9	19.7	20.3	20.5	20.6
Opolskie	2.4	2.6	2.5	2.5	2.4
Podkarpackie	3.7	3.7	3.9	3.9	3.8
Podlaskie	1.8	1.7	1.7	1.8	1.8
Pomorskie	5.6	5.6	6.0	5.9	6.1
Śląskie	18.4	17.4	17.4	16.8	16.9
Świętokrzyskie	2.2	2.2	2.3	2.2	2.2
Warmińsko-Mazurskie	2.6	2.5	2.4	2.6	2.6
Wielkopolskie	10.4	10.6	10.0	10.3	10.3
Zachodniopomorskie	4.0	3.7	3.5	3.4	3.0
POLAND	**100.0**	**100.0**	**100.0**	**100.0**	**100.0**

Source: *Statistical Yearbook of the Regions*, 1999–2003.

Opolskie voivodships. The share of the market services prevail the GVA structure of the Mazowieckie, Malopolskie and the Zachodniopomorskie region.

Sold industrial output has grown steadily over the transformation period of Poland, reaching 511 billion zlotys by 2002. Regional trends differed significantly in this respect; six of the regions recorded decline in industrial output by 2002. The largest decreases were found in the Zachodniopomorskie (92.0 per cent), Kujawsko-Pomorskie (93.8 per cent) and Warminsko-Mazurskie (95.4 per cent) voivodships. The best performing regions from this respect are the Pomorskie and the Malopolskie. The highest value of industrial output was achieved by those regions, where the level of GDP is the highest: in the Mazowieckie, Slaskie and Wielkopolskie voivodships. These three provinces have achieved 48.9 per cent of the total value of sold industrial output. The Lubuskie, Swietokrzyskie and Podlaskie voivodships have had the smallest share in the value, generating only 6.0 per cent of the production.

Industrial production concentration is visible in Poland at the regional level; industry concentrates on the agglomeration of the capital – Mazowieckie voivodship, the old industrial region of Silesia, which could restructure its production profile with the help of foreign capital inflow to the automobile industry. Finally, the Wielkopolskie voivodship is also one of the favourite target places of foreign investments, the region is mainly specialised on manufacturing.

Regional policy in Poland

Regional policy in Poland was introduced in the mid-1990s and its development was determined by the integration process of the country. The first step towards "harmonisation" was the rearrangement of Poland's territorial structure; the act on regional self-government adopted in 1998 divided the country into 16 regions (called voivodships), 380 poviats (administrative districts) and 2,489 gminas (communes). The reform reshaped the structure of competencies as well, decentralising many of the public tasks. At the regional level the Sejmik, a regional parliament headed by the chairman, deals with programming of regional policies. The Voivodship Board (Zarząd Województwa) is an executive body, headed by the Marshal (Marszalek), whose duties are connected with making development policies and control their implementation.

The devolution of expenditure responsibilities from the centre within the 1999 reform concerned mostly the areas of education, roads and healthcare. *Voivodship* self-governments are responsible for regional development policies, higher vocational schools, larger cultural facilities and specialised regional hospitals. Moreover, they participate in the supervision of autonomous health funds. The *poviats*, as the lower-middle level of sub-national governments, are responsible for special lower secondary schools and high schools, police and fire protection, the operation of larger social assistance facilities and nursing homes, county-level roads and general hospitals. The *gminas'* main responsibilities include primary and lower secondary education; waste disposal; provision of electricity, heat and gas; operation of social assistance facilities; the disbursement of various allowances; maintenance of *gminas'* own housing stocks; primary healthcare clinics and local transport service among others.

The successful implementation of the decentralisation reform lied mainly in its financial feasibility; the competencies had to be supported by resources sufficient to handle them. Within the regional policy framework, poviats and voivodships get their revenue mostly from the state budget in the form of subsidies and grants. Poviats are entitled to the share of 1 per cent of the Personal Income Tax (PIT), which is a state tax. Voivodships are entitled to 1.5 per cent of PIT and to 0.5 per cent of the Corporate Income Tax. Other sources of revenue for these two tiers are the income from own property, user fees and loans. As the per capita revenue of administrative units is still very low in Poland, further decentralisation would be inevitable. On the other hand, state budget consolidation has not yet been implemented, and almost 40 per cent of total public money is still under the control of unconsolidated agencies and funds (7 per cent within the healthcare system), and the territorial government (voivodships, poviats and gminas) have slightly over 10 per cent of the public funds.[5] Fiscal consolidation is one of the priorities of the present Polish economic policy.

The Polish regional policy has been shaped by the National Regional Development Strategy for the years 2000–2006 and by the regional strategies prepared by the regional government, that are basically with the former.[6] According to the document, therefore, Polish regional policy focuses on the creation of conditions for an increase in the regions' competitiveness and preventing the decline of certain areas to ensure a long-term development of the country; economic, social and territorial cohesion and integration with European Union. The Regional Development Strategy specifies the five main goals of the regional policy:

* *Infrastructural development* to strengthen competitiveness of the regions;
* *Economic restructuring* in the regions, creating conditions for its diversification;
* *Human resources development;*
* *Assistance* to least developed areas threatened by marginalisation;[7]
* *Enhancing inter-regional cooperation.*

The experience of regional policy in Poland proved to be successful in creating viable territorial units and a functioning legislative framework. On the other hand, decentralisation is not a completed process so far. The financial decentralisation must continue to ensure proper functioning of the territorial units. Without a comprehensive reform of the public finances, however, no successful regional policy can be implemented.

A very important achievement of the reform is, on the other hand, that the previously centrally defined development tasks have been transferred to regional level, which shows a clear change in approach to regional policy. Furthermore, the framework of regional policy also marks a beginning of integrating sectoral and regional policies; very often funds previously assigned to institutions dealing with sectoral issues appear on the regional level. The administrative reform brought important benefits through creating a body able to perform long-term strategic planning of regional development. The new structure enables the regions to conduct an active innovation policy and to individually shape the investment environment. Furthermore, foreign cooperation of voivodships, the better implementation of everyday tasks at the poviat level, all seem to prove the larger efficiency of the new regional structure.

Specialisation and concentration measures for Polish regions

Assessment of regional specialisation and concentration patterns was carried out on the basis of two indices: the Herfindahl on absolute specialisation and concentration and the Krugman index on relative specialisation and concentration.[8] The analysis of specialisation and concentration characteristics of Polish regions have been prepared on the basis of employment statistics of the Central Statistical Office of Poland (GUS) for the years 1998–2002. Long-term analysis was not possible because of recalculated data shortage for earlier years according to the new territorial division of the country. The borders of old and new regions have been reshaped, the continuity of statistical data, therefore, is not ensured by the aggregation of earlier regional data. The regional employment data for Poland in NUTS 2 and NUTS 3[9] division could be found only for NACE1 sectors. Due to lack of sufficiently detailed data deeper analysis, e.g. for the manufacturing branches, could not be made for the Polish regions.

Certain observation is possible on the other hand, on the basis of empirical analysis.

Absolute specialisation of regions

The absolute specialisation measure for Polish regions range between 0.13 and 0.31. Differences between absolute specialisation levels have not changed significantly over the examined period of time which was due to the slow modernisation process in agriculture, the relatively slow pace of privatisation and the reluctance of governments to restructure heavy industry. The regional pattern therefore still shows the old distribution of sectors, which is also the result of investor decisions to locate industry to regions with industrial past. The regions with the highest absolute specialisation values are the Eastern, mostly rural, voivodships: the Lubelskie, Podkarpackie and Swietokrzyskie. Lowest absolute specialisation indices are characteristic for the Zachodniopomorskie, Dolnoslaskie region and the Mazowieckie where, due to the capital, the service sector, besides various other industries, has become significant.

The same calculations have been made for the NUTS 3 territorial units, the data set, however, is based on slightly different figures. The result gives a picture with more differences in absolute specialisation indices. The rural subregions are still the ones with the highest values, the towns, e.g. the capital Warsaw or Posnan, seem to be the most specialised units, which is in the first case based on the services sector, mostly finances and administration, while in the second case of industry.

Table 8.10 Absolute specialisation of Polish regions on the basis of the Herfindahl index

Absolute specialisation	1998 HSj	1999 HSj	2000 HSj	2001 HSj	2002 HSj
Dolnośląskie	0.14	0.14	0.13	0.13	0.13
Kujawsko-Pomorskie	0.16	0.16	0.16	0.16	0.16
Lubelskie	0.29	0.29	0.30	0.31	0.31
Lubuskie	0.14	0.14	0.14	0.14	0.13
Łódzkie	0.19	0.18	0.19	0.19	0.19
Małopolskie	0.19	0.18	0.19	0.19	0.19
Mazowieckie	0.14	0.14	0.14	0.14	0.14
Opolskie	0.17	0.16	0.16	0.17	0.16
Podkarpackie	0.26	0.26	0.27	0.28	0.28
Podlaskie	0.25	0.25	0.26	0.26	0.26
Pomorskie	0.13	0.13	0.13	0.13	0.13
Śląskie	0.17	0.16	0.16	0.15	0.15
Świętokrzyskie	0.27	0.27	0.28	0.29	0.29
Warmińsko-Mazurskie	0.15	0.15	0.15	0.15	0.15
Wielkopolskie	0.17	0.16	0.16	0.17	0.16
Zachodniopomorskie	0.12	0.12	0.12	0.12	0.12

Source: own calculation on the basis of data from the Statistical Office.

Table 8.11 Relative specialisation of Polish regions on the basis of the Krugman index

Relative specialisation	1998 DSRj	1999 DSRj	2000 DSRj	2001 DSRj	2002 DSRj
Dolnośląskie	0.24	0.26	0.26	0.27	0.27
Kujawsko-Pomorskie	0.07	0.07	0.08	0.08	0.07
Lubelskie	0.48	0.49	0.49	0.50	0.50
Lubuskie	0.23	0.22	0.21	0.22	0.22
Lódzkie	0.13	0.12	0.12	0.13	0.12
Malopolskie	0.16	0.15	0.17	0.18	0.17
Mażowieckie	0.19	0.18	0.20	0.20	0.20
Opolskie	0.07	0.07	0.07	0.07	0.07
Podkarpackie	0.38	0.38	0.39	0.39	0.39
Podlaskie	0.36	0.36	0.37	0.37	0.37
Pomorskie	0.26	0.27	0.27	0.29	0.29
Śląskie	0.39	0.38	0.38	0.38	0.39
Świętokrzyskie	0.40	0.41	0.42	0.42	0.42
Warmińsko-Mazurskie	0.09	0.08	0.07	0.08	0.08
Wielkopolskie	0.08	0.10	0.11	0.11	0.12
Zachodniopomorskie	0.25	0.26	0.27	0.27	0.27

Source: own calculation on the basis of data from the Statistical Office.

Relative specialisation of regions

Measuring the average difference of the employment share of a sector to the average share of other sectors, we get the relative specialisation values, which vary more visibly from region to region in Poland. It is the highest in the Lubelskie, Swietokrzyskie, Podlaskie and Podkarpackie voivodships. The lowest relative specialisation can be detected in the Kujawsko-Pomorskie, Opolskie and Warminsko-Mazurskie regions. Over the examined period it is hard to examine dramatic changes in the relative specialisation levels in Polish regions.

Absolute concentration of industries

Absolute concentration values measured by the Herfindahl index show high concentration of all sectors in the Polish regions, the highest level, however, marks financial services and real estate. Generally those indices show growth, that show the most dynamic role of certain regions in the transformation process. An example can be the Mazowieckie voivodship, which is mostly specialised on financial services. Industry dominates in the Slaskie and Wielkopolskie regions, in the latter, however, this is mainly attributable to manufacturing industry. Industry concentrates furthermore to the Dolnoslaskie and the Lodzkie regions. Agricultural concentration is the highest, besides the Mazowieckie voivodship, in the Eastern part of Poland, e.g. in the Lubelskie, Malopolskie and Podkarapckie voivodships.

Table 8.12 Absolute concentration of Polish industries (1998, 2002)

Absolute concentration	1998 Hci	1999 Hci	2000 Hci	2001 Hci	2002 Hci
Agriculture, hunting, forestry and fishing (A)	0.08	0.09	0.09	0.09	0.09
Industry (mining, manufacturing, electricity) (C+D+E)	0.09	0.09	0.09	0.09	0.09
Construction (F)	0.09	0.09	0.09	0.09	0.09
Trade and repair (G)	0.09	0.09	0.09	0.09	0.09
Hotels and restaurants (H)	0.09	0.09	0.09	0.09	0.09
Transport, storage and communication (I)	0.08	0.08	0.09	0.09	0.09
Financial intermediation (J)	0.10	0.10	0.12	0.12	0.12
Real estate, renting and b. act. (K)	0.12	0.12	0.11	0.11	0.11
Public administration (L)	0.08	0.08	0.08	0.08	0.08
Education (M)	0.08	0.08	0.08	0.08	0.08
Health and social work (N)	0.08	0.08	0.08	0.08	0.08

Source: own calculation on the basis of data from the Statistical Office.

Table 8.13 Relative concentration of industry according to the Krugman index

Relative concentration	1998 DCRi	1999 DCRi	2000 DCRi	2001 DCRi	2002 DCRi
Agriculture, hunting, forestry and fishing (A)	0.48	0.48	0.50	0.49	0.50
Industry (mining, manufacturing, electricity) (C+D+E)	0.27	0.27	0.28	0.28	0.28
Construction (F)	0.20	0.19	0.19	0.19	0.20
Trade and repair (G)	0.16	0.16	0.19	0.18	0.18
Hotels and restaurants (H)	0.25	0.28	0.28	0.29	0.28
Transport, storage and communication (I)	0.16	0.17	0.18	0.20	0.20
Financial intermediation (J)	0.21	0.20	0.28	0.28	0.28
Real estate, renting and b. act. (K)	0.34	0.33	0.30	0.30	0.28
Public administration (L)	0.18	0.17	0.14	0.14	0.16
Education (M)	0.09	0.08	0.09	0.10	0.09
Health and social work (N)	0.12	0.11	0.12	0.12	0.12

Source: own calculation on the basis of data from the Statistical Office.

Relative concentration of industries

Relative concentration values show the concentration of certain sectors across regions with regard to other sectors. The Polish relative concentration index is very high for agriculture, which shows the concentrated territorial setting of this sector in the country. This relative concentration has grown over the years parallel to the increasing role of manufacturing and certain services in other regions. A high concentration of industry is seen in case of Slask, of construction and services in Mazowieckie and a very high concentration of agriculture in the Eastern regions, like Podkarpackie voivodship.

Conclusions

Transformation and integration have brought about important and visible changes in the production structure of the country on a national level. This sectoral change could not be transformed into a change in the regional specialisation pattern. The old division of labour with industrial production concentration is visible in Poland at the regional level; industry concentrates on the agglomeration of the capital – Mazowieckie voivodship, the old industrial region of Silesia, which could restructure production profile with the help of foreign capital inflow to the automobile industry. Finally, the Wielkopolskie voivodship is also one of the favourite target places of foreign investments, the region is mainly specialised on manufacturing. The structure of foreign trade has also changed in the past years, the commodity composition of both the exports and imports moved towards manufactured goods and machinery. The comparative advantage of Polish exports, however, is still stronger in labour-intensive industries, such as paper and wood products, the textile industry, and also transport equipment, than in the high-tech sectors. To sum up, on a national level the upgrading of the production structure either with the help of endogenous development (restructuring old industries), or with exogenous tools (foreign capital) through privatisation or green-field investment had a very visible impact on the production structure in certain industries (such as the auto industry) but could not yet change at a national level the specialisation on labour-intensive industries.

The foreign capital inflow and also the restructuring and reorientation of foreign trade had a very clear and visible regional concentration in Poland. The previously more developed regions, with traditional services and industrial specialisation, were favoured by both domestic and foreign investors. These regions were able to restructure and upgrade their economies and develop more quickly and in accordance with the needs of more developed export markets. The analysed data show that more successful regions with higher export-orientation and high FDI levels show higher relative specialisation (the highest level is achieved by the capital and main industrial towns). Although we do not have detailed data on the distribution of industrial branches in Polish regions, empirical analysis shows that the technologically more intensive industrial branches (electronics industry, machinery, auto-parts manufacturing) have a very high concentration in Poland, basically in the most developed three regions. On a NACE1 digit level absolute specialisation indices are very high for Eastern regions due to the slow restructuring in the agricultural sector.

The regional specialisation pattern in Poland is based basically on the historical development of the country (more industrialised regions are in the Western parts, which used to belong to Prussia for a period of time). This basic pattern was reinforced by the socialist period when the traditional industries were favoured and supported by the governments. The integration process has achieved changes in certain regions but the Western border as such has not really had an impact on the specialisation. Although German capital preferred regions that are more to the West, the primary criterion was still the regional level of development, the size of agglomeration and not the geographical setting. It is not surprising that the Southern-Central regions have high regional specialisation in more developed industries. The modernisation of production structure was easier in regions with an industrial tradition than in those places where a complete bottom-up process was needed.

Regional disparities have not disappeared, they even got more apparent with the transformation process; while some regions have been able to modernise their economic structures there are some that still lag behind. The industrial and agricultural restructuring processes have not been finished in many voivodships, which is visible in the still high level of employment in these sectors. These structural problems entail considerable threats. Large proportions of the agricultural sector, as well as traditional branches of industry that have not undergone restructuring, are sources of further prospective social problems and a burden on the public sector as well. This is all the more threatening and noticeable in single-industry areas and in regions where non-modernised small farming prevails. Areas of former state-owned farms (Northern regions) are characterised by structural unemployment and the entailed aggravation of social problems. The most developed regions (such as the Mazowieckie and the Wielkopolskie) could transform their economic profile with the help of investments by the domestic private enterprises and thanks to the inflow of foreign capital. The relative specialisation of these regions is high; the concentration of industry is more apparent here, which helped the production to become more competitive in external terms as well.

Assessment of regional specialisation and concentration patterns shows a rather unchanging level of absolute specialisation but a more visible differentiation of sector concentration. Disparities in absolute specialisation levels have not changed significantly over the examined period which was due to the slow modernisation process in agriculture, the relatively slow privatisation and the reluctance of governments to restructure heavy industry. Relative specialisation of regions changed more visibly in the past years, espscially on the subregional level. Agriculture still dominates in the Eastern part of the country, employing a large proportion of the population. In most dynamic forerunner regions, mostly main towns, manufacturing and market-services started to concentrate.

Notes

1 Ministry of Economy, Labour and Social Policy, 2003.
2 Gabrisch-Segnana, 2003.

3 The act on regional self-government was adopted on 5 July 1998 and came in to force on 1 January 1999.
4 Przybyla and Rutkowski, 2001.
5 Gorzelak, 2002.
6 National Regional Development Strategy, Kancelaria Prezesa Rady Ministrow, 2000.
7 80 per cent of the governmental assistance to the regions is assigned according to the size of their population. Some 10 per cent each of allocations are calculated on the basis of two indicators:

- GDP per capita – preferences will be given to the areas (NUTS 3) in which GDP per capita level does not exceed 80 per cent of the national average;
- rate of unemployment – preferences will be given to the areas (poviats, NUTS 4) in which the level of unemployment in each of the last three years exceeded 150 per cent of the national average.

In regional allocations preferences are given to areas where the share of employment in agriculture exceeds 150 per cent of the national average; the share of population employed in industry exceeds 125 per cent and the unemployment level exceeds 150 per cent of the national average; or such urban areas (cities), where the rate of long-term unemployment exceeds 150 per cent of the national average, besides there is high level of poverty, low level of education and high level of crime (Gorzelak, 2002).

8 THE HERFINDAHL INDEX – ABSOLUTE SPECIALISATION/ CONCENTRATION MEASURE

Specialisation of region j $\qquad H_j^s = \sum_i (s_{ij})^2 \qquad 0 \le H_j^s \le 1$

Spatial concentration of industry i $\quad H_i^c = \sum_j (c_{ij})^2 \qquad 0 \le H_i^c \le 1$

The index is increasing with specialisation of regions/concentration of industries (the higher the index the higher the specialisation of regions/concentration of industries).

KRUGMAN SPECIALISATION INDEX – RELATIVE SPECIALISATION/ CONCENTRATION MEASURE

Specialisation of region j $\quad K_j = \sum_i \left| s_{ij} - \bar{s}_{il} \right|$ with $\bar{s}_{il} = \dfrac{\sum_{l \ne j} E_{il}}{\sum_i \sum_{l \ne j} E_{il}}$

$\bar{s}_{il}$ is the average employment share in industry i in all other regions except region j

Spatial concentration of industry i $\quad K_i = \sum_j \left| c_{ij} - \bar{c}_{kj} \right|$ with $\bar{c}_{kj} = \dfrac{\sum_{k \ne i} E_{kj}}{\sum_j \sum_{k \ne i} E_{kj}}$

$\bar{c}_{kj}$ is the average regional share of the other industries except industry i

$0 \le K_i,\ K_j \le 2$. The higher the index the higher the specialisation of regions/concentration of industries. K_j (K_i) = 0 indicates that that the production (spatial) structure of region j (industry i) is identical to the average production structure of the other regions (spatial structure of the other industries); Kj (Ki) = 2 indicates that the production structure of region j has no industries in common with the other regions (that industry i, is located in a single region).

Notation: E – employment; i,k – industries; j,l – regions; E_{ij} – employment in industry i in region j; s_{ij} – share of employment in industry i in region j in total employment of region j; c_{ij} – share of employment in industry i in region j in total national employment in industry i.

9 The NUTS 3 employment database received from the Central Statistical Office (GUS) differs from the NUTS 2 sums and divided for other NACE sections.

References

Bakács, A. and Wisniewski, A. (2002), A hazai nagyvállalatok helyzete és a gazdaság-politika Lengyelországban (Situation of domestic enterprises and economic policy in Poland), *IWE HAS Working paper*, Budapest, August 2002.

Deichmann, U. and Hendersson, V. (1998), Urban and Regional Dynamics in Poland, *Development Research Group of the World Bank*, Washington, 1998.

Gabrisch, H. and Segnana, M.L. (2003), *Vertical and horizontal patterns of intra-industry trade between EU and candidate countries*, Halle, April 2003.

Gorzelak, G. (2002), *New Model of Polish Regional Policy in a Decentralized State*, EUROREG, Warsaw University, 2002.

Gross Domestic Product by Voivodships in the Years 1995–1998, General Statistical Office, Katowice, 2000.

Gross Domestic Product by Voivodships in 1999, Central Statistical Office, Katowice, 2001.

GUS. *Statistical Yearbook of the Regions – Poland, Warsaw*, 1999.

GUS. *Statistical Yearbook of the Regions – Poland, Warsaw*, 2000.

GUS. *Statistical Yearbook of the Regions – Poland, Warsaw*, 2001.

GUS. *Statistical Yearbook of the Regions – Poland, Warsaw*, 2002.

GUS. *Statistical Yearbook of the Regions – Poland, Warsaw*, 2003.

Hausner, J. (1997), The Polish Industry in: *The Future of Industry in Central and Eastern Europe*, Institut Arbeit und Technik.

Information on the Socio-economic Situation of Voivodships – Central Statistical Office, 2/2001.

Kosarczyn, H. (2001), *Regional Development in Poland – An Overview*, Polska Agencja Rozwoju Regionalnego, Warszawa.

National Development Plan, Ministry of Economy, Labour and Social Policy. www.mpips.gov.pl/english/index.php.

National Regional Development Strategy, Kancelaria Prezesa Rady Ministrow, Warsaw, 2000.

OECD Economic Surveys: Poland, OECD 2002.

Poland-Report 2003, Ministry of Economy, Labour and Social Policy, Warsaw.

Polska, Raport o stanie gospodarki, Ministerstwo Gospodarki, Warszawa, 2001.

Przybyla, M. and Rutkowski, J. (2001), *Poland-Regional Dimensions of Unemployment*, World Bank–Bertelsmann project.

Report on the Condition of the Small and Medium-Size Enterprise Sector in Poland for the Years 1998–1999, Polish Agency for Enterprise Development, Warszawa, 2001.

9 Economic integration and structural change

The case of Hungarian regions

Tamás Szemlér

Introduction

Since 1989, Hungary has gone through a phase of fundamental economic and social transformation from a centrally planned economy into a functioning market economy. This change was not as sudden as in some other countries of the former Soviet bloc, as reform attempts have been present in Hungary since 1968; however, it was a systemic change bringing new issues and problems into the foreground.

After the first phase of economic transition, GDP (in real terms) began to rise again in Hungary in the mid-1990s. Economic growth – especially strong from 1997 – led to the decline of the unemployment rate, and the decline of the consumer price index, as well as of the gross public debt/GDP ratio also showed the stabilisation of the Hungarian economy.

The integration of the country into the EU has become an outstanding priority; the steps towards integration (including the Association Agreement signed as soon as December 1991) also determined the changes to a great extent. Hungary began its negotiations on EU accession in March 1998 and concluded them in December 2002 and, as a result, became a member of the EU on 1 May 2004.

Integration prospects (EU requirements) played an important role in re-designing domestic policies in the new member states. This is especially true for regional policy in Hungary. In order to understand the regional development in Hungary after 1990, it is necessary to know the situation before the beginning of transformation. The territorial changes of the country during the twentieth century have influenced the regional development considerably: these changes (after the First World War, then reconfirmed after the Second World War) meant the end of their organic links for several territories near the new borders of Hungary. As a result, these territories have become peripheral, and the centre–periphery problem has emerged: due to its population and its importance as an economic centre, Budapest has become the only outstanding centre of the country.

During the time of the centrally planned economy, the economic policy (concentrating on industrialisation, especially on heavy industry), could not find solutions to the regional problems in the long run. Regional development based on centralised direct methods and often on reasons of political nature, not leaving space for local initiatives, proved to be unsuccessful in the long run, as it was clearly shown by the economic problems already before the beginning of the transformation process. This kind of development policy was not able to cope with the double challenge of fighting overall underdevelopment and regional inequalities.

Regional economic inequalities remained (and in some cases have become even more accentuated) in the 1990s. For the beginning of the 2000s, in terms of GDP/head, the data characterising the most developed region (Central Hungary) was more than the double of that of the least developed regions (Northern Hungary and Northern Great Plain). The centre–periphery problem has been aggravated in the first years of market economy: the poorer territories (generally also with less developed infrastructure) were not able to compete with the economic possibilities offered by Budapest.

Foreign direct investment, playing a key role in the economic modernisation of Hungary, looking for the best investment possibilities, also contributed to the increase of regional inequalities. Beyond the centre–periphery problem, East–West differences have become stronger. Especially territories lying along the Vienna–Budapest axis or near the Austrian border have experienced a rapid development, partly due to the interest of foreign capital. Among other factors – relatively well-developed or rapidly developing infrastructure, availability of qualified and cheap labour force – the neighbourhood of the EU market was an important motivation.

Under market economy circumstances new problems (unknown in the previous decades of centrally planned economy) have surged as well. The most important one is unemployment, where – according to difference in regional development – regional inequalities are considerable. Most of the territories severely hit by unemployment are in Northern Hungary and in the Northern Great Plain region. The problem is aggravated there by the fact that the activity rate of the population is much lower than the already very low national average. Labour market inequalities are reflected in the regional differences in wages as well.

Beyond persisting or even increasing regional inequalities, (relative) overall underdevelopment has also remained a major problem, especially in the light of the prospects of EU accession. National and regional development policy (as in most countries in Central and Eastern Europe) has to deal with both problems.

The changes since the beginning of the 1990s pushed regional policy to the foreground in Hungary. This is reflected by several changes, which, especially after 1996, with the adoption of the Law on Regional Development and Land-use Planning (Law XXI/1996), meant important steps in the direction of being compatible with EU requirements. Despite the considerable development acknowledged by the EU itself, in a number of aspects – way of financing, scales of direct financing, dominant element of the implementation, dominant favoured sectors – the degree of EU-compatibility remained low. Beyond this, some practical questions – concerning especially the (re-)definition of the borders, competencies and resources of the NUTS 2 units – are to be solved as well.

The above developments contributed considerably to the change of the geographical distribution of production in Hungary, which is the main topic of this chapter. The structure of the chapter is the following: the next section is divided into three sub-sections; the first describes territorial demographic changes, the second deals with regional differences of economic development, while the third presents the main results of statistical analysis of specialisation and concentration. The final section summarises the main findings and conclusions of the chapter.

The regional structure of the country and its change

Population: evolution and distribution in space

The population of Hungary (10.1 million) puts the country into the group of the Czech Republic, Greece, Belgium and Portugal (EU member states with similar populations). If we take only the evolution of the population of the country, Hungary has belonged to the developed world for decades: its population shows a decline every year.

The decline of population is quite evenly distributed; it is due to the fact that internal migration is in most cases low. The clear exceptions are the capital (with the strongest negative internal migration balance) and county Pest (with the strongest positive one); a considerable part of the internal migration takes place between these two units. Outside Central Hungary, county Győr-Moson-Sopron had the strongest positive relative migration balance in 2002, while counties Borsod-Abaúj-Zemplén and Szabolcs-Szatmár-Bereg were at the other

Figure 9.1 Counties (NUTS 3 units) and regions (NUTS 2 units) in Hungary (source: Kóvári Jósef, Márton Mátyás, Zentai László).

end. At the level of NUTS 2 units, Central Hungary, Central Transdanubia and Western Transdanubia showed a positive balance in 2002, while the other regions (Southern Transdanubia and all the regions entirely east to the Danube) experienced a negative internal migration balance.

The distribution of the population of Hungary is very uneven. Budapest, the capital of the country still represents about 17 per cent of the total population of the country, while the second city by population (Debrecen) only 2 per cent.[1] In the last decade, with the decrease of the population of Budapest, the concentration of the population seems to diminish, but there is no real tendency behind the figures: in fact, most of the people leaving the capital move to its agglomeration. As a consequence, the role of the capital does not diminish, and even new problems occur (concerning e.g. transport relations between Budapest and its agglomeration).

If one looks at the question of the distribution of population among NUTS 3 or NUTS 2 regions, once again, the role of Budapest distorts it at both levels. Not taking into account the capital, population density varies between 56 and 173 persons per sq. km (counties Somogy and Pest, respectively) on the NUTS 3 level, and between 70 and 100 (not taking into account Central Hungary; Southern Transdanubia and Central Transdanubia, respectively) on the NUTS 2 level. In this latter case, it is interesting that only Central Hungary is above the country average.

There are important differences in the settlement structure in different parts of the country: while some parts of Hungary are characterised by a dense net of small settlements, in other parts of the country the structure of settlements is not so dense, and the settlements themselves are bigger on average. However, an important overall characteristic of the settlement structure in Hungary is that the net of settlements consists of a high number of small municipalities (3,200 municipalities for a country of 10 million people).

Regional differences can be observed not only in the size, but also in the administrative status of settlements. While Central Hungary has the biggest share of towns, on the other end, Western Transdanubia, Southern Transdanubia and Northern Hungary are characterised by an especially large number of villages (these three regions giving approximately two-thirds of the villages of he country). Looking at the NUTS 3 level, Budapest is again an exception; outside Budapest, the biggest shares of towns can be observed in Békés and Hajdú-Bihar, while Borsod-Abaúj-Zemplén is richest in villages.

Economic activities: overall evolution and distribution in space

After the first phase of the economic transition, GDP (in real terms) began to rise again in Hungary in the mid-1990s. Economic growth – especially strong from 1997 – led to the decline of the unemployment rate. The consumer price index went down from nearly 30 per cent to 5 per cent, and the decline of the gross public debt/GDP ratio also showed the stabilisation of the Hungarian economy (see Table 9.1).

Table 9.1 Hungary: some basic macroeconomic indicators, 1995–2004

	1995	1996	1997	1998	1999	2000	2001	2002	2003	2004
Real GDP growth (%)	1.5	1.3	4.6	4.9	4.2	5.2	3.7	3.5	3.0	4.0
Unemployment rate (%)	10.2	9.9	8.7	7.8	7.0	6.4	5.7	5.8	5.8	5.9
Consumer price index (%)	28.2	23.6	18.3	14.3	10.0	9.8	9.2	5.3	4.7	6.8
Gross public debt/GDP (%)	85.2	71.9	62.9	61.1	60.4	55.3	52.1	55.2	56.9	57.6

Source: Central Statistical Office of Hungary, National Bank of Hungary.

Economic growth, however, was not evenly distributed among counties and regions. The clear winners of the 1990s are Central Hungary, Western Transdanubia and Central Transdanubia. These three NUTS 2 regions gave in 2001 64 per cent of the Hungarian GDP. The share of Central Hungary alone was 44 per cent and that of Budapest 35 per cent – these figures illustrate clearly the economic weight of the capital (but also county Pest alone had a weight similar to the average NUTS 2 regions not taking into account Central Hungary).

Territorial imbalances can be seen much more clearly in GDP per capita data. The development concentrated to Central Hungary and the North-Western part of the country (Northern Transdanubia and Central Transdanubia) led to the increase of the – in most cases traditional – differences. This development is strongly related to the geographical position of the regions: outside the economic centre of the country, regions closer to the Western borders – it means also closer to new markets and closer for potential foreign investors – took most advantage of the changes, while the relative situation of the Eastern part of the country (even if not without differences in itself) worsened.

It is no wonder that in the ranking of the NUTS 2 regions on the basis of the GDP per capita in 2001 Central Hungary had the first place. It is, however, interesting to see, how heterogeneous this region is: while the capital was at 108 per cent of the average of the EU-15 (on PPP), county Pest (including the agglomeration of Budapest) stood only by 44 per cent of it; with this result, this county had only the ninth position in the ranking of counties (NUTS 3 units). The second biggest difference between counties of a same NUTS 2 region could be found in Western Transdanubia (Győr-Moson-Sopron with 63 per cent and Zala with 44 per cent). Besides the special role of Central Hungary, the overall East–West division of the country is reflected in the data (only one county entirely East to the Danube can be found in the first half of the counties in the ranking by GDP per capita – Csongrád at tenth position).

Considering employment figures, the importance of Central Hungary is clear again, although the concentration is a bit less strong. Central Hungary had about 35 per cent of all the employees – this is about 25 per cent (or seven percentage points) more than its share in the population of the country. Even if the statistics do not include all the employees (see the methodological remark under the table), the picture can be taken as representative.

Territorial differences are clearly expressed in the differences of earnings. On NUTS 3 level, average gross earnings in 2002 in Budapest were 77 per cent higher than in Szabolcs-Szatmár-Bereg. Looking at net earnings, the difference between the top and the bottom ends is in the range of 60 per cent. On NUTS 2 level, the differences were smaller (64 per cent in gross earnings, 50 per cent in net earnings), but while on NUTS 3 level, a very slow convergence can be observed, it is hardly remarkable on NUTS 2 level.

Data on employed and inactive population make the picture of territorial inequalities even clearer. In four of the seven NUTS 2 regions, economically inactive population is bigger than the number of employed (this aggravates the problem of overall low economic activity of the population). Looking at the NUTS 3 level, this problem is most serious in Borsod-Abaúj-Zemplén and Szabolcs-Szatmár-Bereg. On the other end, the share of economically inactive population is the smallest in county Vas.

Unemployment rate showed a constant decline since 1995 (until 2003). Regional differences in unemployment, however, persist. Once again the East-West divide of the country (again with the exception of Southern Transdanubia) is very clear on the NUTS 2 level: while in Central Hungary, Central Transdanubia and Western Transdanubia the unemployment rate did not exceed 5 per cent in 2002, NUTS 2 regions East of the Danube had unemployment rates between 6.2 per cent and 8.8 per cent. It means that Central Hungary and the biggest part of Transdanubia were well under the average, while the Eastern part of the country and Southern Transdanubia were well above it. In the latter four regions we can find in 2002 only one county (Csongrád) where the unemployment rate was under the country average (in 1999–2000, there were three such counties).

Structural changes: specialisation and concentration

Specialisation and concentration – sectors and measures

The data available made possible to analyse specialisation and concentration pattern based on the number of employees, the volume of output and exports in the industry. The sectors are aggregated on NACE level according to the following codes (Table 9.2).

The applied indices are the following (where: E – employment; i,k – industries, j,l – regions; E_{ij} – employment in industry i in region j; s_{ij} – share of employment in industry i in region j in total employment of region j; c_{ij} – share of employment in industry i in region j in total national employment in industry i; $\bar{s}_{il}$ is the average employment share in industry i in all other regions except region j; $\bar{c}_{kj}$ is the average regional share of the other industries except industry l):

Table 9.2 NACE aggregation codes for sectors

Sector	NACE code
Mining	C
Food, beverages, tobacco	15, 16
Textiles, wearing, leather	17–19
Wood, paper	20–22
Chemical	23–25
Non metallic mineral	26
Basic metal	27, 28
Machinery and equipment	29–35
Manufacturing n.e.c.	36, 37
Manufacturing	**D**
Electricity, gas, water	E
Industry	**C, D, E**

THE HERFINDAHL INDEX – ABSOLUTE SPECIALISATION/
CONCENTRATION MEASURE

Specialisation of region j $$H_j^s = \sum_i (s_{ij})^2 \qquad 0 \le H_j^s \le 1$$

Spatial concentration of industry i $$H_i^c = \sum_j (c_{ij})^2 \qquad 0 \le H_i^c \le 1$$

The index is increasing with specialisation of regions/concentration of industries (the higher the index the higher the specialisation of regions/concentration of industries).

KRUGMAN SPECIALISATION INDEX – RELATIVE SPECIALISATION/
CONCENTRATION MEASURE

Specialisation of region j $$K_j = \sum_i \left| s_{ij} - \bar{s}_{il} \right| \quad \text{with} \quad \bar{s}_{il} = \frac{\sum_{l \ne j} E_{il}}{\sum_i \sum_{l \ne j} E_{il}}$$

Spatial concentration of industry i $$K_i = \sum_j \left| c_{ij} - \bar{c}_{kj} \right| \quad \text{with} \quad \bar{c}_{kj} = \frac{\sum_{k \ne i} E_{kj}}{\sum_j \sum_{k \ne i} E_{kj}}$$

$0 \le K_i, K_j \le 2$. The higher the index the higher the specialisation of regions/ concentration of industries. K_j (K_i) = 0 indicates that that the production (spatial) structure of region j (industry i) is identical to the average production structure of the other regions (spatial structure of the other industries); K_j (K_i) = 2 indicates that the production structure of region *j* has no industries in common with the other regions (that industry *i*, is located in a single region).

Research results

The 1990s have brought a fundamental change in the life of the Hungarian economy. As a result of the processes summarized above, the specialisation and concentration pattern of the counties and industries has also changed significantly. Rédei *et al.* (2002) have calculated absolute and relative specialisation and concentration indices for the Hungarian counties in the 1990s. Their main findings can be summarised in the following:

- In the 1990s, the absolute specialisation of the counties have been increasing in Hungary, but the absolute concentration of industries (both measured by the Herfindahl index) declined. Changes were most important in export sales, less important in total sales, and least important in industrial employment.
- The main factor behind increasing absolute specialisation was the growing importance of machinery; as a result, this sector became most important in several counties (especially in Transdanubia), while the earlier dominance of food industry declined. The main reason of the decline of absolute concentration was the increasing importance of services in Budapest; this process led to a smaller share of the industry in the capital, lowering the level of absolute concentration.
- Relative specialisation and concentration values (measured by the DCR index) showed a different picture. Relative specialisation was declining, relative concentration growing on average. Behind the decline of relative specialisation, the main reason was the increasing importance of machinery in several counties, which made the industrial structure of the counties more similar to each other. Increasing relative concentration was mainly due to the fact that in the new industrial structure – dominated by machinery – the geographical distribution of most industrial branches has much less influence on the geographical distribution of the industry as a whole, and thus differs from it much more than before.
- Increase of specialisation can be the result of the increasing weight of an industrial branch; increase of concentration can be the result of the increasing weight of a county. However, the increase of the value of these indices can also be the consequence of the decrease of the importance of the formerly dominant industry/county, or the consequence of the rapid increase of the importance of a formerly negligible industry/county. The reasons can be detected by the simultaneous analysis of the real changes (in export sales, total sales and employment) and the specialisation and concentration indices.
- According to this analysis, increasing regional specialisation was mainly due to the increasing importance of dominant industries (first of all,

machinery). In the case of relative specialisation, however, the situation is more complex: in the case of total sales and export sales, correlation between indices and real changes had a negative sign. This means that those counties which behaved most similar to the overall tendencies – mainly due to the strengthening of machinery – produced highest growth, while counties following alternative paths of development had lower growth rates.

- Between absolute concentration and growth of industries, correlation is generally negative. This is also due to the rapid increase of the weight of machinery: this industry was the most rapidly growing one, it spread to most parts of the country, therefore its concentration decreased. The only exception is export sales, due to the high share of export sales of electric energy, concentrated increasingly in Budapest.

In the present chapter, we extended the analysis in time and space. In time, data for employment cover a longer period: latest data are available for 2002; unfortunately, for output and export, data are available only until 1999. In space, we calculated the measures both for counties (NUTS 3 units) and regions (NUTS 2 units). Finally, the definition for relative specialisation/concentration measures differs from those used by Rédei *et al.* (2002). Our most interesting results can be summarised as follows.[2]

- Absolute specialisation generally increased on NUTS 3 level. This trend is most expressed in export, relatively clear in output, and least sensible in employment data. It is important to note that there have been numerous exceptions of this general trend. The same trends can be seen on NUTS 2 level, and the number of exceptions is much smaller; in fact, there is only one exception: Southern Great Plain shows a slightly decreasing absolute specialisation in exports (see Tables 9.3, 9.7 and 9.11).
- Relative specialisation measures show a mixed picture on NUTS 3 level. In the case of employment data, the trend is the decrease of relative specialisation. In the case of output and export data, there is no clear trend: in 60 per cent of the units there is a considerable increase of the measure, while the other 40 per cent show a decrease of relative specialisation. On NUTS 2 level, the same mixed trends can be observed; the differences, however, are smaller than in the case of the NUTS 3 units (for details, see Tables 9.4, 9.8 and 9.12).
- Absolute concentration of industries on NUTS 3 level is generally decreasing in the case of employment and output data, but increasing in the case of export data. The differences between the values of the first and last years of observation are, however, relatively small. On NUTS 2 level, the decreasing trend dominates the calculations from all the three data sets (see Tables 9.5, 9.9 and 9.13 for details).
- Relative concentration of industries on NUTS 3 level is generally decreasing in the case of employment data, while generally increasing in the case of

Table 9.3 Absolute specialisation, NUTS 2 units, employment data

Absolute specialisation (2 digit)	1992 HSj (2 digit)	1993 HSj (2 digit)	1994 HSj (2 digit)	1995 HSj (2 digit)	1996 HSj (2 digit)	1997 HSj (2 digit)	1998 HSj (2 digit)	1999 HSj (2 digit)	2000 HSj (2 digit)	2001 HSj (2digit)	2002 HSj (2 digit)
Central Hungary	0.17	0.16	0.15	0.15	0.15	0.16	0.17	0.16	0.16	0.16	0.19
Central Transdanubia	0.10	0.09	0.10	0.11	0.12	0.15	0.14	0.16	0.17	0.19	0.24
Western Transdanubia	0.16	0.16	0.16	0.16	0.16	0.17	0.18	0.18	0.21	0.21	0.23
Southern Transdanubia	0.11	0.11	0.10	0.11	0.11	0.12	0.13	0.14	0.15	0.15	0.20
Northern Hungary	0.10	0.11	0.10	0.10	0.10	0.10	0.10	0.11	0.12	0.12	0.17
Northern Great Plain	0.15	0.14	0.14	0.13	0.14	0.14	0.16	0.16	0.17	0.18	0.20
Southern Great Plain	0.18	0.17	0.17	0.16	0.16	0.17	0.16	0.15	0.15	0.15	0.18

Table 9.4 Relative specialisation, NUTS 2 units, employment data

Relative specialisation (2 digit)	1992 Kj (2 digit)	1993 Kj (2 digit)	1994 Kj (2 digit)	1995 Kj (2 digit)	1996 Kj (2 digit)	1997 Kj (2 digit)	1998 Kj (2 digit)	1999 Kj (2 digit)	2000 Kj (2 digit)	2001 Kj (2 digit)	2002 Kj (2 digit)
Central Hungary	0.46	0.43	0.44	0.45	0.41	0.40	0.40	0.37	0.31	0.29	0.31
Central Transdanubia	0.31	0.31	0.30	0.30	0.38	0.42	0.36	0.34	0.34	0.37	0.43
Western Transdanubia	0.28	0.31	0.32	0.32	0.31	0.27	0.27	0.26	0.31	0.31	0.34
Southern Transdanubia	0.36	0.36	0.34	0.35	0.35	0.35	0.29	0.27	0.25	0.28	0.26
Northern Hungary	0.42	0.42	0.43	0.42	0.39	0.35	0.36	0.35	0.29	0.27	0.22
Northern Great Plain	0.24	0.19	0.23	0.20	0.24	0.28	0.28	0.32	0.27	0.28	0.31
Southern Great Plain	0.46	0.43	0.43	0.43	0.45	0.47	0.41	0.37	0.38	0.36	0.37

Table 9.5 Absolute concentration, NUTS 2 units, employment data

Absolute concentration	1992 Hci	1993 Hci	1994 Hci	1995 Hci	1996 Hci	1997 Hci	1998 Hci	1999 Hci	2000 Hci	2001 Hci	2002 Hci
C	0.31	0.31	0.26	0.27	0.27	0.25	0.25	0.23	0.24	0.20	0.20
15–16	0.16	0.16	0.16	0.15	0.16	0.16	0.16	0.16	0.16	0.16	0.16
17–19	0.19	0.18	0.18	0.17	0.17	0.17	0.17	0.16	0.16	0.16	0.16
20–22	0.26	0.26	0.25	0.24	0.24	0.25	0.24	0.25	0.20	0.21	0.21
23–25	0.40	0.35	0.35	0.34	0.33	0.32	0.31	0.29	0.20	0.20	0.21
26	0.21	0.19	0.19	0.18	0.18	0.18	0.17	0.17	0.17	0.17	0.17
27–28	0.20	0.20	0.20	0.20	0.19	0.19	0.19	0.18	0.17	0.17	0.17
29–35	0.30	0.28	0.26	0.24	0.22	0.21	0.20	0.20	0.17	0.17	0.17
36–37	0.19	0.20	0.19	0.18	0.18	0.18	0.19	0.20	0.17	0.17	0.17
D	0.21	0.20	0.19	0.18	0.18	0.18	0.17	0.18	0.15	0.16	0.16
E	0.15	0.15	0.15	0.15	0.16	0.16	0.16	0.15	0.16	0.16	0.16

Table 9.6 Relative concentration, NUTS 2 units, employment data

Relative concentration	1992 Ki	1993 Ki	1994 Ki	1995 Ki	1996 Ki	1997 Ki	1998 Ki	1999 Ki	2000 Ki	2001 Ki	2002 Ki
C	0.29	0.27	0.18	0.18	0.17	0.15	0.16	0.14	0.10	0.06	0.05
15–16	0.04	0.03	0.03	0.03	0.03	0.02	0.01	0.02	0.02	0.02	0.02
17–19	0.03	0.03	0.03	0.03	0.03	0.04	0.04	0.04	0.04	0.05	0.05
20–22	0.02	0.03	0.03	0.03	0.03	0.03	0.03	0.03	0.03	0.04	0.03
23–25	0.10	0.09	0.09	0.09	0.09	0.09	0.08	0.06	0.03	0.03	0.03
26	0.02	0.03	0.03	0.05	0.06	0.06	0.05	0.04	0.03	0.03	0.03
27–28	0.05	0.04	0.05	0.05	0.03	0.03	0.05	0.02	0.02	0.02	0.02
29–35	0.05	0.04	0.04	0.03	0.02	0.02	0.01	0.01	0.01	0.02	0.01
36–37	0.03	0.03	0.03	0.03	0.03	0.03	0.02	0.02	0.01	0.01	0.01
D	0.08	0.06	0.05	0.04	0.04	0.03	0.03	0.03	0.02	0.02	0.02
E	0.03	0.03	0.03	0.03	0.03	0.02	0.03	0.03	0.02	0.02	0.02

Table 9.7 Absolute specialisation, NUTS 2 units, export data

Absolute specialisation (2 digit)	1995 HSj (2 digit)	1996 HSj (2 digit)	1997 HSj (2 digit)	1998 HSj (2 digit)	1999 HSj (2 digit)
Central Hungary	0.28	0.26	0.13	0.27	0.31
Central Transdanubia	0.32	0.40	0.57	0.61	0.64
Western Transdanubia	0.47	0.49	0.02	0.68	0.73
Southern Transdanubia	0.23	0.25	0.35	0.45	0.60
Northern Hungary	0.35	0.30	0.32	0.08	n.a.
Northern Great Plain	0.22	0.24	0.23	0.23	0.22
Southern Great Plain	0.27	0.27	0.26	0.22	0.20

Table 9.8 Relative specialisation, NUTS 2 units, export data

Relative specialisation (2 digit)	1995 Kj (2 digit)	1996 Kj (2 digit)	1997 Kj (2 digit)	1998 Kj (2 digit)	1999 Kj (2 digit)
Central Hungary	0.50	0.51	0.61	0.61	0.56
Central Transdanubia	0.87	0.73	1.07	0.59	0.43
Western Transdanubia	0.84	0.69	0.61	0.54	0.46
Southern Transdanubia	0.58	0.54	0.65	0.30	0.28
Northern Hungary	0.76	0.77	0.60	0.59	n.a.
Northern Great Plain	0.46	0.44	0.37	0.77	0.86
Southern Great Plain	0.99	1.01	0.82	0.84	0.82

Table 9.9 Absolute concentration, NUTS 2 units, export data

Absolute concentration	1995 Hci	1996 Hci	1997 Hci	1998 Hci	1999 Hci
C	0.33	0.30	0.38	0.35	n.a.
15–16	0.19	0.18	0.19	0.17	0.17
17–19	0.19	0.19	0.18	0.19	0.19
20–22	0.27	0.24	0.25	0.25	n.a.
23–25	0.35	0.37	0.34	0.45	n.a.
26	0.26	0.26	0.26	0.22	0.23
27–28	0.37	0.32	0.33	0.37	0.35
29–35	0.28	0.26	0.45	0.29	0.27
36–37	0.23	0.24	0.26	0.26	0.21
D	0.19	0.20	0.21	0.22	n.a.
E	0.77	0.95	0.98	0.95	n.a.

Table 9.10 Relative concentration, NUTS 2 units, export data

Relative concentration	1995 Ki	1996 Ki	1997 Ki	1998 Ki	1999 Ki
C	0.25	0.21	0.19	0.16	n.a.
15–16	0.13	0.11	0.14	0.12	0.09
17–19	0.03	0.04	0.07	0.08	0.09
20–22	0.03	0.02	0.07	0.10	n.a.
23–25	0.19	0.20	0.24	0.35	n.a.
26	0.19	0.18	0.15	0.11	0.12
27–28	0.30	0.16	0.10	0.16	0.16
29–35	0.11	0.09	0.43	0.15	0.13
36–37	0.08	0.07	0.11	0.08	0.02
D	0.12	0.35	0.48	0.52	n.a.
E	0.39	0.57	0.68	0.76	n.a.

output and export data. Missing values, however, limit the strength of the above statement. On NUTS 2 level, the decreasing trend dominates employment and export data, while in the case of output data, the picture is mixed (for details, see Tables 9.6, 9.10 and 9.14).

The reasons behind the above trends can be found – not surprisingly – in the country and policy characteristics discussed previously. The factors presented at the presentation of the article by Rédei *et al.* (2002) are, of course, valid; the most important of them – symbolising the transformation of the industrial structure in Hungary – is the increasing importance of the machinery and equipment sector.

As it can be seen from the evaluation of the results, the trends described by Rédei *et al.* (2002) are generally valid for our calculations as well. Due to the limited availability of disaggregated data, we were not able to obtain a deeper picture on the change of industrial structure. The role of machinery in the changes reflected by the figures is obvious; these figures, however, do not tell us much about what kind of machinery caused the changes in one or another county.

Quite unsurprisingly, calculations for NUTS 2 regions did not provide us much additional information. As regions consist each of 3 NUTS 3 units (except for Central Hungary consisting of 2 NUTS 3 units, one of which is the capital of the country), the special features of the constituting NUTS 3 units are counterbalanced by each other, and therefore the picture on the NUTS 2 level is much less sharp than on the NUTS 3 level. One has to remind here that NUTS 2 regions have no historical traditions in Hungary. The today existing NUTS 2 regions are territorial-statistical regions, but do not constitute organic economic entities. As a result, the analysis of NUTS 2 level data in Hungary can only have limited value added to the present research.

Table 9.11 Absolute specialisation, NUTS 2 units, output data

Absolute specialisation (2 digit)	1992 HSj (2 digit)	1993 HSj (2 digit)	1994 HSj (2 digit)	1995 HSj (2 digit)	1996 HSj (2 digit)	1997 HSj (2 digit)	1998 HSj (2 digit)	1999 HSj (2 digit)
Central Hungary	0.17	0.18	0.19	0.21	0.20	0.18	0.18	0.18
Central Transdanubia	0.16	n.a.	n.a.	0.18	0.20	0.30	0.34	0.38
Western Transdanubia	0.14	n.a.	n.a.	0.24	0.26	0.31	0.43	0.50
Southern Transdanubia	0.11	0.11	0.12	0.13	0.12	0.13	0.15	0.25
Northern Hungary	0.11	0.14	n.a.	0.17	0.15	0.15	0.15	n.a.
Northern Great Plain	0.15	0.17	n.a.	0.17	0.19	0.17	0.17	0.16
Southern Great Plain	0.24	0.26	0.14	0.23	0.23	0.23	0.19	0.27

Table 9.12 Relative specialisation, NUTS 2 units, output data

Relative specialisation (2 digit)	1992 Kj (2 digit)	1993 Kj (2 digit)	1994 Kj (2 digit)	1995 Kj (2 digit)	1996 Kj (2 digit)	1997 Kj (2 digit)	1998 Kj (2 digit)	1999 Kj (2 digit)
Central Hungary	0.57	0.54	0.52	0.59	0.56	0.49	0.53	0.54
Central Transdanubia	0.55	n.a.	n.a.	0.58	0.62	0.73	0.64	0.57
Western Transdanubia	0.43	n.a.	n.a.	0.54	0.60	0.55	0.67	0.65
Southern Transdanubia	0.47	0.45	0.50	0.53	0.53	0.51	0.39	0.29
Northern Hungary	0.32	0.36	n.a.	0.55	0.50	0.50	0.55	n.a.
Northern Great Plain	0.33	0.30	n.a.	0.37	0.46	0.46	0.56	0.56
Southern Great Plain	0.62	0.63	0.51	0.69	0.66	0.71	0.61	0.93

Table 9.13 Absolute concentration, NUTS 2 units, output data

Absolute concentration	1992 Hci	1993 Hci	1994 Hci	1995 Hci	1996 Hci	1997 Hci	1998 Hci	1999 Hci
C	n.a.	n.a.	n.a.	0.21	0.22	0.23	0.21	n.a.
15–16	0.16	0.16	0.16	0.16	0.16	0.17	0.17	0.17
17–19	0.22	0.22	0.21	0.42	0.21	0.19	0.21	0.18
20–22	0.32	0.29	0.31	0.30	0.49	0.33	0.34	n.a.
23–25	0.52	n.a.	n.a.	0.41	0.43	0.41	0.40	n.a.
26	0.20	0.19	n.a.	0.18	0.18	0.20	0.19	0.19
27–28	0.31	0.27	0.29	0.30	0.28	0.30	0.33	0.29
29–35	0.33	0.28	0.27	0.26	0.24	0.25	0.26	0.24
36–37	0.18	n.a.	n.a.	0.20	0.19	0.20	0.23	0.20
D	0.24	0.23	0.22	0.21	0.21	0.21	0.20	0.20
E	0.19	0.18	0.18	0.18	0.19	0.19	0.18	n.a.

Table 9.14 Relative concentration, NUTS 2 units, output data

Relative concentration	1992 Ki	1993 Ki	1994 Ki	1995 Ki	1996 Ki	1997 Ki	1998 Ki	1999 Ki
C	n.a.	n.a.	n.a.	0.14	0.15	0.14	0.09	n.a.
15–16	0.06	0.06	0.04	0.04	0.04	0.05	0.04	0.04
17–19	0.03	0.03	0.03	0.11	0.03	0.05	0.02	0.05
20–22	0.03	0.02	0.03	0.04	0.16	0.06	0.09	n.a.
23–25	0.17	n.a.	n.a.	0.14	0.15	0.16	0.19	n.a.
26	0.03	0.04	n.a.	0.07	0.07	0.04	0.03	0.03
27–28	0.21	0.16	0.18	0.20	0.14	0.12	0.16	0.12
29–35	0.04	0.03	0.03	0.05	0.06	0.10	0.13	0.12
36–37	0.08	n.a.	n.a.	0.05	0.05	0.06	0.04	0.02
D	0.04	0.03	0.03	0.03	0.03	0.03	0.04	0.32
E	0.03	0.02	0.02	0.03	0.03	0.03	0.04	n.a.

Conclusions

In the 1990s, the Hungarian economy went through a radical change. After the stabilisation of the economy, the country has begun to catch up to the developed countries. Rapid economic growth, however, was not accompanied by a spectacular decline of territorial imbalances within the country. In some respects, differences between different parts of the country have become bigger. In most cases, factors influencing positively the economic development of the country – e.g. FDI – contributed to the persistence or to the increase of regional inequalities.

Economic policy was able to stabilise the economy and to put it onto a rapid growth path, but specific policies – devoted at least partly to the diminution of territorial imbalances – were not effective enough to produce spectacular results. Although regional policy has gone through important changes, and as a result, it has been to a great extent "Europeanised", financial limits and administrative problems reduced its effectiveness. Industrial policy – mainly due to the rapidly changing internal economic (but also political) circumstances – was redesigned several times in the 1990s, but no real long-term concept emerged.

Now a member of the EU, Hungary has had to redefine its policies in order to use best the possibilities opened up by its accession. A new industrial policy concept is under debate now, and the open questions of regional policy will also come soon to the foreground, as planning for the 2007–2013 begins. The seven-year long financial perspective of the EU provides the possibility of (or, looking at it from another angle, necessitates) the coordination of plans and programmes in different fields and on different levels of the economy. It is very important that planning has to take into account those processes that modify the geographical location of industries. The 1990s have brought considerable changes in this respect; EU membership is another factor which can bring some new ones in the next years.

Our statistical analysis detected that absolute specialisation of the counties have been increasing in Hungary throughout the 1990s, but absolute concentration of industries showed a declining trend. Relative specialisation of the counties was declining, while relative concentration of industries was growing on average.

One of the main objectives of the present research is to detect the effects of European integration on the location of industries. In the case of Hungary – as probably of all the new member states from Central and Eastern Europe – this is highly complicated. The complexity of the issue is due to the fact that different important processes influencing the development of the economy have been going on (at least partially) parallel to each other.

The CEEC – and Hungary among them – were on the way towards their EU-accession for one and a half decades. The process of approaching the EU was longer than expected, while the period of the 1990s was also burdened by difficulties stemming from their economic transition and from the sharpening of the process of globalisation. It is very difficult and sometimes even impossible to separate integration-, transition- and globalisation-related effects from each other, which makes the assessment.

Statistical analysis does not differentiate between the reasons of the changes – it only shows changes in the regional industrial structure. In such a case, background information about the country's economic policy (and some specific policies as regional and industrial policies) can help us to estimate the various effects.

Quite obviously, European integration played an important role in formulating these policies. The design of regional policy in Hungary has become significantly more "EU-conform" in the 1990s – a clear result of the integration process. Due to the limited financial resources, however, this policy could not have decisive effects on the territorial location of different industries.

Industrial policy plays an important role in formulating the industrial structure of a country. In Hungary, in the biggest part of the 1990s, however, no real long-term industrial policy was elaborated. This was due to the very rapid change of the internal and external economic environment: industrial policy had to react rapidly on acute issues and therefore could not formulate a long-term vision. For the end of the 1990s, the prospect of EU-accession has brought changes in this respect as well; the regional factor, however, is still not decisive even in the newer concepts.

Geographic features – constituting a decisive factor in the location of industries – have become new meanings with the prospect (and, in 2004, with the realisation) of EU-accession. Beyond the role of Budapest – unique city of its category in the country – the Western territories of the country have attracted more investment, and thus produced more rapid growth and also a change towards a more modern industrial structure. Regions lying in the Eastern part of the country were (and still are) in a more difficult situation in this respect. Their situation can change as European integration goes on: the accession of Romania could provide for some of them new – easier – possibilities of cross-border cooperation. The design of future policies should also take these effects into account.

Notes

1 The source of data in the text of this chapter – if not indicated otherwise – is the Central Statistical Office of Hungary.
2 The author thanks Sándor Buzás, research fellow at the Institute for World Economics of the Hungarian Academy of Sciences, and Andrea Éltetö, senior research fellow at the Institute for World Economics of the Hungarian Academy of Sciences for their contribution to the statistical analysis, as well as for their valuable comments. Of course, the author bears the whole responsibility for any eventual mistake.

References

Bartha, A. and Klauber, M. (2000a), "Az autópályákkal kapcsolatos néhány indikátor értékének elemzése". *Ipari Szemle* 2000/6, 10–12.
Bartha, A. and Klauber, M. (2000b), "Négysávos fejlödés. Az autópályák hatása a gazdasági növekedésre". *Cégvezetés* 2000/1–2, 101–107.
Brusis, M. (ed.) (1999), *Central and Eastern Europe on the Way into the European Union: Regional Policy-Making in Bulgaria, the Czech Republic, Estonia, Hungary, Poland and Slovakia*. Center for Applied Policy Research, Munich.
Horváth, G. (1999), "Regional and cohesion policy in Hungary". *In Central and Eastern Europe on the Way into the European Union: Regional Policy-Making in Bulgaria, the Czech Republic, Estonia, Hungary, Poland and Slovakia*, edited by Brusis, M., Center for Applied Policy Research, Munich.
Horváth, G. and Illés, I. (1997), "Regionális fejlödés és politika. A gazdasági és szociális kohézió erösítésének feladatai Magyarországon az Európai Unióhoz való csatlakozás idöszakában". *Európai Tükör Mühelytanulmányok* No. 16, Budapest.
Horváth, G. and Rechnitzer, J. (2000), Magyarország területi szerkezete és folyamatai az ezredfordulón. Magyar Tudományos Akadémia Regionális Kutatások Központja, Pécs.
Hrubi, L. (2000), "A gazdasági térszerkezet változásai Magyarországon". *In Magyarország területi szerkezete és folyamatai az ezredfordulón*, edited by Horváth, G. and Rechnitzer, J., Magyar Tudományos Akadémia Regionális Kutatások Központja, Pécs.

József, L., Molnár, L. and Skultéty, L. (2000), "Az M1-es autópálya gazdasági hatásai". *Cégvezetés* 2000/1–2, 108–110.

Molnár, L. and Skultéty, L. (2000), "Autópálya-forgalom". *Cégvezetés* 2000/1–2, 110–114.

Pálné Kovács, I. (2001), Regionális politika és közigazgatás. Dialóg Campus Kiadó, Budapest–Pécs.

Rédei, M., Jakobi, A. and Jeney, L. (2002), "Regionális specializáció és a feldolgozóipari tevékenység változása". *Tér és Társadalom* 2002/4, 87–108.

Török, A. (1997), "Ipar- és versenypolitika az Európai Unióban és Magyarországon. Helyzetértékelés". *Európai Tükör Mühelytanulmányok* No. 2, Budapest.

10 Regional economic divergence patterns in the Czech Republic

Eva Kippenberg

Introduction

On 1 May 2004, ten Central and Eastern European Countries (CEECs) acceded to the European Union (EU). The task of the coming years in these countries is to assure economic integration with the EU and the improvement of regional cohesion within and between the former and new member countries. As pointed out in Chapter 3, the Czech Republic, being one of the new member states, has an economic structure that is comparably close to the EU average concerning regional specialization indices. However, some economic indicators reveal that there is still a long way to go to reach European economic standards. In 2002, the Czech Republic produced 67 per cent of the average GVA and 61 per cent of per capita GDP in purchasing power standards of the countries of the European Monetary Union (EMU). In the same year, the compensation per employee was only 25 per cent of the EMU average while the unemployment rate in the Czech Republic was 115 per cent of the EMU average. However, compared to other new EU member countries the Czech Republic performed quite well. Only Poland produced higher values in GVA and only Slovenia and Cyprus reached higher shares in GDP per capita in PPS.[1] In 2002, the Czech Republic, Poland and Hungary accounted for more than three-quarters of FDI flowing to the new member countries.[2] According to Eurostat (2002), the Czech Republic was, in 2000 with 1.33 per cent of GDP, the country with the second highest relative expenditure in R&D among the new EU member states. These indicators show that the Czech Republic as a country has performed quite well compared to other CEECs since 1993. However, taking into account the regional development within the country, the Czech Republic was subject to increasing regional economic divergence. This chapter deals with the regional economic development within the Czech Republic between 1993 and 2003 focusing on this divergence of economic indicators.

One aspect influencing the economic development of a country is the initial situation of the considered timeframe, which is itself highly influenced by the history of the country. The differing developments in the CEECs, however, result to a large part from different political decisions after 1989. Until 1940, the

Czech Republic was one of the ten most developed economies in the world, possibly explaining part of the favourable development compared to other CEECs since 1993. However, the communist rule between 1945 and 1989 lead to a thorough downturn of the economic performance of the Czech Republic as it did in other countries. According to Dillon and Wykoff (2002), the two main results of the communist rule were a forced separation from world trade and a strong decline in per capita income following transfers of financial and physical capital from Czech regions to the Slovak Republic. At the end of the 1980s, only 3 per cent of the country's net material product, the communist-era equivalent of GDP, was produced by the private sector.[3] Per capita income had declined from being close to Austria's before the war to about one-fifth of Austria's per capita income in 1990.[4]

After the Velvet Revolution in 1989, the country went through a radical reform process, beginning with the liberalization of prices for retail goods and the phasing out of state subsidies. Economic and political differences in the Czech and Slovak parts of the country eventually induced the "Velvet Divorce" in 1993, resulting in the secession of the Czech and the Slovak Republics.[5] The privatization scheme pursued in Czechoslovakia before and the Czech Republic after 1993 induced a rapid privatization process raising the share of the private sector to about 70 per cent of Czech GDP in 1995.[6] However, the privatization process was mainly maculation. The largest share of private firms was owned by funds that were themselves to a large extent owned by state-owned banks.[7] Therefore, the state remained heavily involved in business practices. The relatively low unemployment rate compared to unemployment rates in other transition countries was one indicator reflecting the low restructuring activity within private firms. The ramifications of this "pseudo-privatization" and the lack of a legal framework on ownership rights eventually lead to a strong decline in the Czech stock market, with the PX50 index reaching a historic low of 316 points in 1998.[8] The result was increasing criticism on the voucher privatization system after 1996 and the initiation of the privatization of the financial sector in 1997.

The economic development was accompanied by an increasing regional divergence, which was most strongly reflected by regional unemployment rates. In 1998, the Czech Government formulated new principles of regional policy in order to contain the increasing regional divergence. Regional policy was understood to pursue the aims of:

1   contributing to a balanced and harmonious development of Czech regions;
2   reducing the differences in speeds and quality of development between the regions;
3   improving the regional economic and social structure.[9]

In the same year, the government started accession talks with the EU. Ích and Larischová (1999) point out that the Czech government as indicated in the "National Accession Strategy, 1998" understood regional policy primarily as a prerequisite to deal with side effects of EU integration rather than an important instrument to achieve sustainable economic development in the Czech Republic. In this context, one of the main tasks of regional policy was to ensure the administrative capacity to absorb EU structural funds. As a result, regional policy in the Czech Republic developed in a way that made it fully compatible with EU regional policy. In 2001, administration structures were established in the initial 14 provinces corresponding to the regional administration units NUTS 3, which are pictured in figure 10.1. In addition, a set of priorities was specified on the basis of regional and sectoral consultation documents, which were required for the EU policy of economic and social cohesion. According to Blazek (2001), these priorities were grouped in the following six axes:

1 Strengthening the competitiveness of industry and entrepreneurial services;
2 development of a basic infrastructure;
3 human resource development;
4 protection and improvement of the environment;
5 rural development and multifunctional agriculture;
6 the development of tourism and the spa sector.

These measures aim at assisting structurally weak regions and thereby strengthening the Czech economy.

The aim of this paper is to picture the economic development in Czech regions. Due to free trade within the EU, the prospect of European integration is expected to have had some effect on the regional development in the Czech Republic. This aspect is taken into account in the interpretation of regional developments.

The remainder of the chapter is structured as follows. In the next section, the development of economic indicators in the Czech Republic and its regions are described. The economic structure of Czech regions, the economic specialization of regions and concentration of sector branches, is introduced in the next section. Special emphasis is put on the development of these indicators and the implications for leading and lagging regions.

Stylized country and regional characteristics

At the end of the 1980s, economic capacity was fairly evenly distributed over the area of the Czech Republic due to the policy of even development and reducing inequalities of the communist regime. However, in the course of transition, differences between the regions in economic development emerged. While the regions in the centre of the country showed a relative improvement in economic activity, especially the Eastern regions bordering Slovakia seemed to slowly fall behind. The following section gives some closer insight on the development of regional characteristics in the Czech Republic over the years 1993 to 2003.

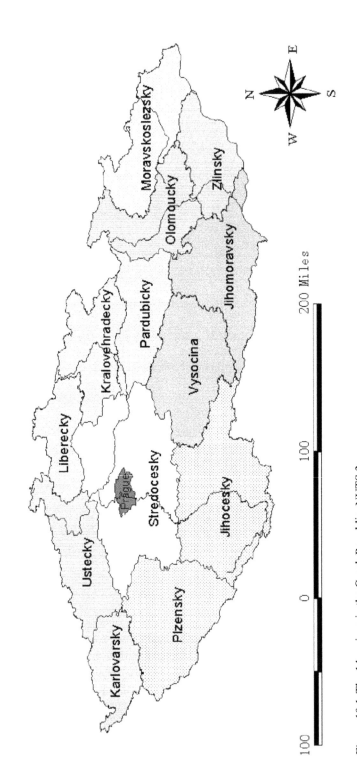

Figure 10.1 The 14 regions in the Czech Republic, NUTS 3.

Population

Population in the Czech Republic showed a slow but persistent decline from 10.3 million in 1993 to 10.2 million in 2002 and a slight increase again in 2003. The coefficient of variation of population in Czech regions reveals merely a tendency to decline. The regions with the largest population sizes, Moravskoslezsky (1.26 million), Prague (1.16 million), Stredocesky (1.13 million) and Jihomoravsky (1.12 million), experienced also the strongest declines in population. An exception to this rule was Stredocesky, which was the only region in the country registering a pronounced increase in population in the considered timeframe (by 2.1 per cent between 1993 and 2003).[10] This increase signals an increasing suburbanization of Stredocesky, absorbing to some extent the population outflow from Prague. The population density in the capital region was with 2,347 inhabitants per square kilometre by far the highest in the country in 2003. The Czech Republic as a whole had a population density of 129 persons per square kilometre in the same year. The least populated areas were those bordering Austria and Germany (Jihocesky with 62 inhabitants per square kilometre, Plzensky with 73 inhabitants per square km, and Karlovarsky with 92 inhabitants per square km) and Vysocina in the centre of the country (with 75 inhabitants per square km).

Economic activity

Economic activity in the considered timeframe was also highly concentrated in Prague. Between 1993 and 2001, GDP in the Czech Republic grew on average by 4.46 per cent annually, increasing from 29.8 billion Euros in 1993 to 63.3 billion Euros in 2001. The share of national GDP that was produced in the

Table 10.1 Area (sq. km) and population density (inhabitants per sq. km) of Czech regions, 2003

Region/kraj	Area	Population density
Prague	496	2,346
Stredocesky	11,015	103
Jihocesky	10,056	62
Plzensky	7,561	73
Karlovarsky	3,314	92
Ustecky	5,335	154
Liberecky	3,163	135
Kralovehradecky	4,758	115
Pardubicky	4,519	112
Vysocina	6,925	75
Jihomoravsky	7,065	159
Olomoucky	5,139	124
Zlinsky	3,964	150
Moravskoslezsky	5,554	227

Table 10.2 Population and population density in Czech regions, 1993–2003, summary statistics

	1993	1994	1995	1996	1997	1998	1999	2000	2001	2002	2003
Population (in thousands)											
mean	737.8	738.1	737.7	736.8	735.9	735.3	734.6	733.7	730.0	728.9	729.4
st. dev.	320.57	320.32	319.74	318.21	317.25	316.85	316.09	315.47	312.21	311.61	312.22
c.o.v.	0.43	0.43	0.43	0.43	0.43	0.43	0.43	0.43	0.43	0.43	0.43
max	1,293.5	1,294.6	1,293.8	1,287.9	1,285.9	1,285.2	1,282.9	1,280.1	1,267.8	1,264.3	1,261.9
min	304.4	304.9	305.1	305.0	304.7	304.9	304.8	304.8	304.1	304.0	304.5
max/min	4.25	4.25	4.24	4.22	4.22	4.22	4.21	4.20	4.17	4.16	4.14
Population density (in absolute numbers per sq km)											
mean	289.1	289.0	288.5	287.7	286.9	286.2	285.0	284.0	280.8	280.1	280.5
st. dev.	624.7	623.9	622.0	619.4	616.8	614.4	609.9	606.7	596.9	594.7	596.3
c.o.v.	2.16	2.16	2.16	2.15	2.15	2.15	2.14	2.14	2.13	2.12	2.13
max	2,454.0	2,451.2	2,444.0	2,434.3	2,424.3	2,415.5	2,398.5	2,386.4	2,349.4	2,340.8	2,347.0
min	62.2	62.3	62.4	62.3	62.3	62.3	62.3	62.2	62.1	62.1	62.2
max/min	39.44	39.33	39.20	39.06	38.92	38.77	38.49	38.35	37.80	37.67	37.73

capital region increased from 19.6 per cent in 1993 to 24.9 per cent in 2001. Also the surrounding region Stredocesky benefited from the economic performance and gravitational pull of the capital. The share of national GDP from this region increased from 8.6 per cent in 1993 to 9.2 per cent in 2001. In the two regions together, GDP jumped from 8.4 billion Euros in 1993 to 21.6 billion Euros in 2001. Accordingly, GDP per capita had the highest average yearly growth rates in Prague (8.2 per cent between 1993 and 2001) and Stredocesky (5.2 per cent). Over the considered timeframe (1993–2001), GDP per capita in these regions increased by 88 per cent and 49 per cent, respectively. Due to the increase in regional GDP in these already economically strong regions, the shares in national production declined in basically all remaining regions of the Czech Republic with the exception of Vysocina, where the share in national production increased by 0.06 percentage points and GDP per capita by 44 per cent. The decline in the national production shares was most pronounced in Moravskoslezsky in the East of the country (declining by 1.68 percentage points) and Ustecky in the North (−1.22 percentage points). These low increases in GDP between 1993 and 2001 (by 22 per cent and 19 per cent, respectively) were only undercut in Karlovarsky with 15 per cent. As pointed out by Ěh and Larischová (1999) and Dupal (2000), the slow growth in Moravskoslezsky and Ustecky was due to a decline in economic activity in the heavy industry and mining sectors.

The increasing regional divergence in economic activity in the Czech Republic was mainly due to the strong economic development of Prague. The coefficient of variation of regional GDP increased by 26 per cent between 1993 and 2001 and for GDP per capita it even increased by more than 75 per cent in the same time period. However, excluding Prague, economic activity rather converged in the considered timeframe as shown by the coefficient of variation for GDP, which declined by 3 per cent, and for GDP per capita, which declined by 8.3 per cent.

The national and regional development of economic activity in the Czech Republic is also reflected by labour market indicators. Between 1993 and 2003, the total labour force sluggishly declined by approximately 140,000 people. The strongest decline occurred between 1996 and 2000 following an increase in employment in the years before. In these years, the privatization of the financial sector commenced, thereby inducing the internal restructuring in the private sector. The picture emerging from employment numbers closely mirrors the development of GDP. While the central regions, Prague, Stredocesky and Vysocina, experienced average annual increases in employment in the considered timeframe of 0.09 per cent, 0.5 per cent and 0.12 per cent, respectively, the Eastern regions of Moravskoslezsky, Jihomoravsky, Olomoucky, and Zlinsky and the Northern region of Ustecky suffered the most severe annual average declines in employment with −0.9 per cent, −0.4 per cent, −0.4 per cent and −0.3 per cent, respectively. However, due to the relatively large populations, the employment numbers in Moravskoslezsky and Jihomoravsky remained well above the national average with respectively 155 per cent and

Table 10.3 Gross domestic product in Czech regions, 1993–2001, summary statistics

	1993	1994	1995	1996	1997	1998	1999	2000	2001
Summary statistics									
avg.	7,236	7,547	8,120	8,754	8,922	9,012	9,211	9,790	10,238
st. dev.	4,538	4,942	5,554	5,876	6,270	6,748	7,157	7,710	8,113
c.o.v.	0.63	0.65	0.68	0.67	0.70	0.75	0.78	0.79	0.79
max	19,891	21,626	24,491	25,679	27,619	29,672	31,493	34,019	35,717
min	2,909	2,932	3,084	3,244	3,144	3,076	3,114	3,336	3,342
max/min	6.84	7.37	7.94	7.92	8.78	9.65	10.11	10.20	10.69
Without capital region									
avg.	6,263	6,464	6,861	7,452	7,484	7,423	7,497	7,926	8,278
st. dev.	2,817	2,945	3,061	3,420	3,350	3,321	3,306	3,423	3,612
c.o.v.	0.45	0.46	0.45	0.46	0.45	0.45	0.44	0.43	0.44
max	12,208	12,821	13,450	15,030	14,651	14,014	13,785	14,174	14,863
min	2,909	2,932	3,084	3,244	3,144	3,076	3,114	3,336	3,342
max/min	4.20	4.37	4.36	4.63	4.66	4.56	4.43	4.25	4.45

151 per cent. In Prague, employment was almost twice the national average with 180 per cent in 2003.

An increasing regional divergence largely independent of the development in Prague is reflected by Czech unemployment rates. Between 1993 and 1996, the coefficient of variation jumped from 0.15 to 0.44. Subsequently, it varied around a mean of 0.39 until 2003. Excluding the capital region, the increase was from 0.15 to 0.41, subsequently varying around a mean of 0.36. In 1993, unemployment rates in Czech regions varied between 3.3 per cent in Liberecky and 5.8 per cent in Moravskoslezsky. The regions suffering the largest increases in the unemployment rate between 1993 and 2003 were the Eastern regions with an increase of almost 9 percentage points in Moravskoslezsky (reaching an unemployment rate of 14.7 per cent), 4.8 percentage points in Olomoucky (9.6 per cent), and 3.8 percentage points in Jihomoravsky (8 per cent). Also Ustecky in the North experienced an extreme increase in the unemployment rate with 8.4 percentage points, reaching an unemployment rate of 13 per cent in 2003. In contrast, the regions in the centre of the country underwent comparably small increases in unemployment rates. In Prague, the unemployment rate increased by merely 0.7 percentage points to an unemployment rate of 4.2 per cent, in Stredocesky, it increased by 0.8 percentage points to 5.2 per cent, and in Vysocina by 0.9 percentage points to 5.3 per cent.

The picture emerging from the data suggests a strong agglomeration of economic activity in the capital city and an increasing suburbanization of Stredocesky. Some share of the population leaving Prague is taken up by Stredocesky, which offers living space close to the capital without the negative effects of agglomeration such as high costs of living and congestion. The same seems to hold true for economic activity. The attraction of Prague and Stredocesky for economic activity is also mirrored at the data on FDI stocks. In 2002, almost 53 per cent of FDI stocks were located in Prague and almost 10 per cent in Stredocesky. The other regions hosted shares of between 6.5 per cent in Ustecky and 1.3 per cent in Karlovarsky. At the same time, the situation of the Eastern regions turns from being closer to the centre under the communist regime to becoming more peripheral in the European context. Declining economic activity and increasing unemployment rates reflect structural challenges in these regions. In the context of European integration, Czech regions are faced by a strong need to remodel their economic structure in order to increase economic cohesion. In the following section, the economic structure of the Czech regions and its development in the considered timeframe is described. Special focus is put on the structural difference between regions developing more favourably and regions with lagging economic performance.

Integration and structural change in Czech regions

The economic structure of the Czech Republic underwent significant changes between 1993 and 2003. A strongly declining share in primary sector

Table 10.4 Unemployment rate in Czech regions, 1993–2003, summary statistics

	1993	1994	1995	1996	1997	1998	1999	2000	2001	2002	2003
Summary statistics											
mean	4.27	4.24	3.96	3.86	4.68	6.43	8.61	8.50	7.80	7.00	7.43
st. dev.	0.65	1.13	1.22	1.68	1.95	2.17	2.82	3.45	3.00	3.08	3.09
c.o.v.	0.15	0.27	0.31	0.44	0.42	0.34	0.33	0.41	0.38	0.44	0.42
max	5.79	6.48	7.06	8.95	9.87	11.69	15.37	15.97	14.29	13.32	14.75
min	3.28	2.82	2.47	1.97	2.38	3.25	3.98	4.20	3.86	3.64	4.19
max/min	1.77	2.30	2.86	4.56	4.15	3.60	3.86	3.80	3.71	3.66	3.52
Without capital region											
mean	4.33	4.35	4.07	4.01	4.86	6.67	8.97	8.83	8.10	7.26	7.68
st. dev.	0.64	1.10	1.20	1.66	1.91	2.05	2.58	3.35	2.89	3.04	3.07
c.o.v.	0.15	0.25	0.29	0.41	0.39	0.31	0.29	0.38	0.36	0.42	0.40
max	5.79	6.48	7.06	8.95	9.87	11.69	15.37	15.97	14.29	13.32	14.75
min	3.28	3.16	2.47	2.74	3.36	4.87	6.25	5.84	5.60	4.17	5.16
max/min	1.77	2.05	2.86	3.26	2.94	2.40	2.46	2.73	2.55	3.19	2.86

Table 10.5 Sectoral employment shares (%) in the Czech Republic,[a] 1993–2003

	1993	1994	1995	1996	1997	1998	1999	2000	2001	2002	2003
Primary sector	7.7	6.9	6.6	6.1	5.8	5.5	5.2	5.1	4.8	4.8	4.5
Secondary sector	42.9	42.2	41.8	41.5	41.1	40.9	40.1	39.5	40.0	39.6	39.3
Tertiary sector	49.3	50.9	51.5	52.2	53.0	53.5	54.6	55.3	55.1	55.4	56.0

Note
a Differences to 100% are due to rounding.

employment, from 7.7 per cent of total employment in 1993 to 4.5 per cent in 2003, is observed, accompanied by an increasing importance of the service sectors from 49 per cent of total employment in 1993 to 56 per cent in 2003. The relative size of the secondary sector measured in terms of employment remained fairly stable. The distribution of economic activity across regions and patterns of regional specialization in the Czech regions are described in the following section.

The economic structure of the Czech economy and its change

The share of primary sector employment in 1993 was largest in Vysocina (18 per cent), Jihocesky (13 per cent), Plzensky and Pardubicky (each 11 per cent), but also the decline in primary sector employment was most pronounced in these regions. In Vysocina, the share had declined by 7.7 percentage points by 2003, in Jihocesky by six percentage points. However, despite the strong decline in primary sector employment, the two regions remained among the most rural regions in the Czech Republic with primary sector employment shares of 10 per cent in Vysocina and 7 per cent in Jihocesky. One more region with a similarly large share of primary sector employment in 2003 was Olomoucky with also 7 per cent. Regions with very small employment shares in the primary sector in 2003 were Prague with 0.37 per cent and Karlovarsky with 2.86 per cent.

In the regions with strongly declining primary sector shares, i.e. Vysocina, Jihocesky, Plzensky and Pardubicky, employment shed in the primary sector was to a large part taken up by increasing employment in the manufacturing sector. However, these were also the only regions with increasing employment shares in the manufacturing sector between 1993 and 2003. The increase reached magnitudes of 1.8 percentage points in Vysocina, 1.5 percentage points in Plzensky, one percentage point in Jihocesky, and 0.5 percentage points in Pardubicky. In the Czech Republic as a whole, the employment share in the manufacturing sector declined by 3.6 percentage points, but remained an important sector for employment in most regions. In 2003, the region with the lowest share in secondary sector employment was Prague with a share of 21 per cent, followed by Stredocesky with a share of 37 per cent. The largest shares in secondary sector employment in 2003 were hosted in Zlinsky (49 per cent) and Liberecky (48.7 per cent), located in the Southeast and the Northwest of the country, respectively.

The tertiary sector significantly gained in importance in the Czech Republic between 1993 and 2003. The region hosting the largest and increasing share in tertiary sector employment throughout the considered time period was Prague reaching a share of 78 per cent of regional employment in 2003. Stredocesky was the region with the second largest employment share in the tertiary sector in 2003 with 57 per cent, followed by Ustecky with 56.4 per cent and Jihomoravsky with 56.1 per cent. In these regions, the share in tertiary sector employment had increased most significantly between 1993 and 2003:

in Ustecky by 10.5 percentage points, in Stredocesky by 9.6 percentage points, and in Jihomoravsky by 7.2 percentage points. Other regions with strong increases in tertiary sector employment shares were Kralovehradecky with 8.7 percentage points and Moravskoslezsky with 7.6 percentage points, reaching shares of 56 per cent and 52 per cent, respectively.

Employment in the Czech Republic as a whole mainly shifted from the agriculture (with the employment share declining by 3 percentage points), manufacturing (2.3 percentage points) and mining sectors (1.5 percentage points) to the trade and repairs (with the employment share increasing by 2.8 percentage points), real estate, renting and business activities (1.5 percentage points) and health and social services sectors (0.7 percentage points). There seems to be a pattern that in initially rural regions employment mainly shifted to manufacturing, while in regions with initially high manufacturing employment, workers switched from manufacturing to the services sectors. The most important sectors in terms of employment shares in 2003 were the manufacturing sector with 27 per cent, the trade and repairs sector with 13 per cent, and the construction sector with 9 per cent of total employment.

The structural change in an economy is described by sectoral concentration as well as regional specialization. Therefore, the distribution of sectoral activity across Czech regions is described in detail using data disaggregated according to the NACE classification as provided by the Czech Statistics Office. Specialization and concentration indices are calculated and interpreted following the methods used by Theil, Herfindahl, Brülhart, Träger and Krugman as described in Chapter 1.

The distribution of sectoral activity across Czech regions

Probably the most highly concentrated sector in the Czech Republic in the considered time period was the mining sector. Due to missing observations[11] it was excluded from the calculations of the concentration indices, but the available data show that the shedding of employment in the sector was strongest in regions with comparably low employment shares, thereby causing an increase in the localization of the sector. The regions with the largest employment shares in 1993, Moravskoslezsky with 42.7 per cent, Ustecky with 23.2 per cent and Karlovarsky with 7.5 per cent, increased their sector shares to 47 per cent, 25.4 per cent and 10.5 per cent in 2003, respectively. In 2003, the other regions had employment shares between 4.4 per cent in Liberecky and 1.6 per cent in Plzensky.[12] However, the influence of employment in the mining sector on the overall regional economic structure was limited. Employment in the mining sector in 2003 reached merely 4.6 per cent of total regional employment in Moravskoslezsky. Overall, the share of national employment in the mining sector declined from 2.6 per cent in 1993 to 1.1 per cent in 2003.

The most concentrated sector according to the calculated indices until 2001 was the real estate, renting and business activities sector, which was also the sector with the second largest increase in relative employment. In 1993, 32 per cent of employment in the sector was located in Prague, followed by

17 per cent in Jihomoravsky and 8 per cent in Moravskoslezsky. By 2003, concentration in the sector had declined more strongly than in all other sectors. The employment share in Prague had declined by 2.25 percentage points and in Jihomoravsky by 4.5 percentage points. The most strongly increasing employment shares were seen in Stredocesky (by 3.5 percentage points to 11 per cent in 2003), Ustecky (by 1.3 percentage points to 6.5 per cent), and Jihocesky (by 1.1 percentage points to 4.7 per cent). The picture therefore to some extent supports the shift of economic activity from the Eastern border region, Jihomoravsky, towards the central regions of the country, Stredocesky and Jihocesky.

In 2002, the financial intermediation sector became the most concentrated sector, strengthening this position in 2003. The large share of employment in the financial intermediation sector in Prague (31 per cent) increased by 1.6 percentage points during the period 1993–2003. The strongest increase in employment in this sector of 2.2 percentage points was seen in Stredocesky, which hosted in 1993 already the second largest share of 9.4 per cent. Another sector with strong increases in concentration relative to other sectors in the Czech Republic (with an increase of the Theil index of 0.042 index points between 1993 and 2003) was the electricity, gas and water supply sector. The increase in concentration in this sector was due to comparably strong increases in sector shares in regions hosting already comparably large sector shares (Prague with 10 per cent of sector employment in 1993 increased its share by 2 percentage points, Jihomoravsky with 9.7 per cent in 1993 increased its share by 1.3 percentage points, and Stredocesky with 9.2 per cent in 1993 increased its share by 1.2 percentage points) and comparably low declines in other regions with large sector shares (the sector share in Ustecky declined from 13.9 per cent in 1993 by 0.2 percentage points and in Moravskoslezsky from 12.5 per cent by 0.07 percentage points). The shift of economic activity in the sector to Prague, Stredocesky and Jihomoravsky mirrors the economic and demographic development of the regions. The development of the sector shares in all Czech regions is summarized in Table 10.A2 in the Appendix.

The increasing sector share of the trade and repairs sector was accompanied by a slowly declining concentration of the sector. While the largest shares of employment in the trade and repairs sector located in Prague and Moravskoslezsky declined from 17.8 per cent in 1993 to 16.1 per cent in 2003 and from 11.3 per cent to 9.9 per cent, respectively, the sector shares in Jihomoravsky, Kralovehradecky, Ustecky and Stredocesky increased by 1.8 percentage points to 10.7 per cent, by 1.2 percentage points to 6.4 per cent, by 1.1 percentage points to 9 per cent and by 0.3 percentage points to 11.4 per cent, respectively. The strongly increasing importance of the trade sector in Czech regions is to some extent related to the increasing integration of the Czech Republic with the EU. The trade share of GDP of the Czech Republic with the EU, measured as the sum of exports and imports in per cent of GDP, increased from 0.35 in 1993 to 0.8 in 2001. The integration parameter, measured as the trade share with the EU relative to the trade share with the world, increased

Table 10.6 Integration parameter of trade with the Czech Republic, 1993–2001

	1993	1994	1995	1996	1997	1998	1999	2000	2001
Trade share of GDP with EU countries	0.35	0.36	0.55	0.53	0.57	0.61	0.66	0.78	0.80
Trade share of GDP with the World	0.83	0.82	0.90	0.87	0.93	0.95	0.99	1.19	1.23
Integration parameter	0.42	0.44	0.61	0.61	0.61	0.64	0.67	0.65	0.65

from 0.42 in 1993 to 0.65 in 2001. However, the development does not seem to be reflected in the regional distribution of the sector, indicating that proximity to former EU countries is of minor importance in the process.

The strong decline in agricultural activity was accompanied by some decline in the concentration of agricultural employment across Czech regions. The largest employment share in Jihomoravsky (14 per cent in 1993) declined by 2003 to 12.1 per cent, the employment share of Vysocina declined somewhat from 11.9 per cent to 11.7 per cent. On the other hand the already strong position of the agricultural sector in Stredocesky (12.9 per cent), increased to 13.7 per cent of agricultural employment in 2003. Especially strong increases in sectoral employment shares of two percentage points and 1.6 percentage points were seen in Kralovehradecky and Olomoucky, respectively, reaching employment shares of 7.6 per cent and 9.4 per cent in 2003.

The sector with the second largest decline in the sector share was the manufacturing sector. According to the calculated Theil and Herfindahl indices, the manufacturing sector was the least concentrated sector throughout the considered time period with even declining concentration until 2003. However, this is not very surprising and results from the fact that aggregate manufacturing data was used in the calculation. The regions with the largest sector shares, Moravskoslezsky (hosting 12.6 per cent of manufacturing employment), Stredocesky (11.6 per cent) and Jihomoravsky (11.4 per cent), all experienced a decline in their shares of total manufacturing employment, by 0.4 percentage points, 0.6 percentage points and 0.6 percentage points, respectively. Within the manufacturing sector,[13] the basic metals and fabricated metal products sector was the most highly concentrated industry in the Czech Republic in 2003. About 36.5 per cent of employment in the sector in 2003 was located in Moravskoslezsky, followed by 7.5 per cent in Jihomoravsky. A similarly concentrated sector was the transport and equipment sector, in which 32.8 per cent of employment was located in Stredocesky, followed by 13.3 per cent in Moravskoslezsky. The regionally most evenly distributed sectors in 2003 were the machinery and equipment n.e.c. and the electrical and optical equipment sectors. The largest share of employment in the machinery and equipment sector (16.3 per cent) was located in Jihomoravsky, followed by 10.8 per cent in Moravskoslezsky and 9.8 per cent in Olomoucky. Even though it is the least concentrated sector in the country, the sector – as also the strongly concentrated basic metals and fabricated metal products sector – still reveals some concentration in the Eastern regions, possibly reflecting the initially strong position of the Eastern regions in heavy industry. Manufacturing of other non-metallic mineral products were mostly located in the North of the country with 21.9 per cent of sectoral employment in Liberecky, 13.8 per cent in Stredocesky and 10.1 per cent in Ustecky, another region with initially high employment shares in mining and quarrying. The only sector revealing some degree of concentration in central regions (not taking into account the highly concentrated transport sector in Stredocesky) was the electrical and optical equipment sector. The sector was mainly located in Plzensky, Stredocesky, Pardubicky and Prague, hosting 12.6 per cent, 11.5 per cent, 11.3 per cent and 10.4 per cent of sectoral employment, respectively.

The average sectoral concentration in the Czech Republic[14] declined sluggishly until 1999 and then sluggishly increased again. Sectors with absolute increases in concentration between 1993 and 2003 were sectors reflecting increasing economic activity, such as the financial intermediation and insurance sector, the electricity, gas and water supply sector and the transport, storage and communications sector. All of these sectors experienced strongly increasing sectoral employment shares in Prague and Stredocesky and with the exception of the financial intermediation sector also in Jihomoravsky, the regions with the most favourable economic development. Other sectors with increasing concentration between 1993 and 2003 were the education and the health and social work sectors. These sectors experienced their strongest increases in sectoral employment shares in Moravskoslezsky, possibly reflecting to some degree the dealing with the deteriorating structural situation. While the regional concentration of sectors pictures the distribution of sectoral activity across regions in the Czech Republic, the sectoral composition within the regions may give some closer insight on the regional economic potential. Regional specialization indices for the Czech regions and their development are therefore described in the following section.

Regional specialization patterns in the Czech Republic

Between 1993 and 2003, most regions experienced a decline in specialization, reflecting the increasing relative importance of the service sectors in the country. According to the Herfindahl index, the region with the strongest decline in specialization was Stredocesky, which experienced strong increases in the trade and repairs sector (up 2.99 percentage points to a regional employment share of 13.1 per cent), the real estate, renting and business activities sector (up 1.8 percentage points to 5.8 per cent) and the construction sector (up 1.8 percentage points to 9.1 per cent). At the same time, the manufacturing sector lost relative regional importance, shedding regional employment share by 5.25 percentage points to 26.2 per cent. Other regions with strong declines in specialization were the formerly strong regions of Olomoucky (rank 3 in the decline of specialization according to the Herfindahl index), Ustecky (rank 4), and Moravskoslezsky (rank 5). In all these regions, the trade and repairs sector experienced comparably large increases in its regional employment share while manufacturing lost relative importance. In Moravskoslezsky and Ustecky, also the mining sector was subject to strong declines in sector share. Other sectors with increasing sector shares in these regions were the public administration sector (+3.4 percentage points in Ustecky and +1.8 percentage points in Moravskoslezsky) and the health and social service sector (+1.9 percentage points in Ustecky and +1.6 percentage points in Moravskoslezsky).

The only regions with increasing specialization between 1993 and 2003 were Plzensky, Jihocesky and Liberecky. In these regions, the manufacturing sector experienced increasing regional employment shares (by 2.9 percentage points, 2.6 percentage points and 1.6 percentage points, respectively), accompanied by strong declines in the agricultural sector (by 4.1 percentage points, 3.7 percentage points and 1.9 percentage points, respectively).

The economically most diversified region in all years of the considered time frame was the capital city, Prague. In 2003, the largest employment shares of ten of fifteen sectors were located in the capital city. Exceptions were agriculture, which had the largest sector share located in Stredocesky (13.7 per cent of employment in the agricultural sector), the forestry and fishing sector, which was mainly located in Jihocesky (13.7 per cent). Employment in the electricity, gas and water supply sector was mainly located in Ustecky (13.7 per cent), and manufacturing and mining had their largest employment shares located in Moravskoslezsky (12.2 per cent and 47 per cent, respectively). The largest sector in the capital region in 2003 was with 17 per cent of regional employment the trade and repairs sector, followed by the real estate sector with 14 per cent of regional employment and 11 per cent in the manufacturing sector. Between 1993 and 2003, the economic structure in Prague had shifted somewhat from manufacturing (−4.5 percentage points) towards real estate, renting and business activities (+2.3 percentage points), trade and repairs (+1.67 percentage points),

Table 10.7 Herfindahl indices of specialization and rank in Czech regions, 1993 and 2003

	Herfindahl	(Rank)	Herfindahl	(Rank)	Index	(Rank)
Plzensky	0.1390	4	0.1538	9	0.0148	1
Jihocesky	0.1306	2	0.1356	6	0.0051	2
Liberecky	0.1869	13	0.1911	13	0.0042	3
Prague	0.1024	1	0.1015	1	−0.0009	4
Vysocina	0.1656	9	0.1639	11	−0.0017	5
Zlinsky	0.1986	14	0.1947	14	−0.0039	6
Pardubicky	0.1688	11	0.1644	12	−0.0044	7
Karlovarsky	0.1354	3	0.1310	4	−0.0045	8
Jihomoravsky	0.1464	6	0.1333	5	−0.0131	9
Moravskoslezsky	0.1682	10	0.1523	8	−0.0159	10
Ustecky	0.1413	5	0.1251	2	−0.0162	11
Olomoucky	0.1780	12	0.1600	10	−0.0180	12
Kralovehradecky	0.1652	8	0.1415	7	−0.0237	13
Stredocesky	0.1564	7	0.1278	3	−0.0287	14

financial intermediation (+1.66 percentage points to 5 per cent), and other community, social and personal services (+one percentage point to 7.1 per cent).

Below, some indicators of economic performance and their change and the Herfindahl specialization index values and rank of the regions with respect to the development of these indicators in the considered time period are summarized. The strongest increases in per capita GDP were experienced in the capital and the surrounding region Stredocesky as well as regions bordering Stredocesky. These regions also registered the lowest increases in the unemployment rate. The slowest increase in per capita GDP and the strongest increases in regional unemployment rates were seen in the Eastern regions, accompanied by Ustecky in the North and Karlovarsky in the West. Three of these regions, Karlovarsky, Ustecky and Moravskoslezsky, still hosted the largest regional employment shares in the mining sector in 2003 and were between 1993 and 2003 hit especially hard by the shedding of labour in this sector by 42 per cent, 49 per cent and 51 per cent of formerly employed persons, respectively.[15] These evidence as well as calculated correlations offer no clear picture of the influence of increasing or decreasing specialization on regional economic performance. The most successful regions with the exception of Plzensky as well as the lagging regions all experienced declines in specialization. Also the relative importance of primary, secondary and tertiary sector employment do not seem to have an influence on the economic success of a region.

The Brülhart-Träger index and the Krugman index of relative specialization reveal that Prague was also the region with the economic structure most strongly diverging from the national average. The employment share of the financial intermediation sector amounted to 282 per cent of the national average, followed by the real estate sector with 260 per cent of the national average, 196 per cent in the other community services sector, 137 per cent in the transport and equipment sector and 130 per cent in the trade and repairs sector, while employment in other sectors such as agriculture and manufacturing reached only 9 per cent and 37 per cent of the national average, respectively. The region with the lowest divergence from the average regional economic structure in the Czech Republic was Jihomoravsky in 2003. Correlating data on GDP per capita growth and the Krugman index of relative specialization shows that neither the relative divergence from the average economic structure (i.e. the Krugman index value) nor the change of the index values are significantly correlated with growth in Czech regions. This shows that neither the degree nor the type of economic specialization in Czech regions seem to have a significant influence on regional growth or regional divergence.

The manufacturing sector was of varying relative importance in Czech regions in the considered timeframe. In 2003, the sector covered between 38.6 per cent of regional employment in Zlinsky and 10.6 per cent of regional employment in Prague. The Theil and Herfindahl indices of regional specialization in 2003 mark Moravskoslezsky as the most specialized region when it comes to manufacturing sectors. In Moravskoslezsky, the manufacturing sector amounted to 28.7 per cent of regional employment. The strong specialization of the region was caused by the strong relative importance of the basic metals and fabricated metal products sector, which accounted for 50.3 per cent of manufacturing employment in

Table 10.8 Summary of economic development in Czech regions, 1993–2003

	Population density 2003	GDP per capita in mill CZK			Unemployment rate			Employment share in agricultural sector 2003	Herfindahl index of specialization	
		2001	% growth 1993–2001	Growth rank	2003	Change in pp 1993–2003	Rank in change		2003	Change 1993–2003
Prague	2,347	30.65	87.55	1	4.19	0.74	1	0.37	0.1015	-0.0009
Stredocesky	103	11.69	49.34	2	5.16	0.79	2	4.32	0.1278	-0.0287
Vysocina	75	11.75	44.48	3	5.32	0.94	3	8.44	0.1639	-0.0017
Kralovehradecky	115	12.18	40.05	4	5.85	1.51	5	5.06	0.1415	-0.0237
Plzensky	73	13.58	39.69	5	5.31	1.26	4	4.02	0.1538	0.0148
Jihocesky	62	12.32	34.79	6	5.17	1.86	7	5.15	0.1356	0.0051
Liberecky	135	11.72	34.67	7	6.11	2.83	8	2.64	0.1911	0.0042
Pardubicky	112	11.73	33.92	8	7.60	3.36	10	5.81	0.1644	-0.0044
Zlinsky	150	11.67	33.17	9	7.53	3.34	9	2.51	0.1947	-0.0039
Jihomoravsky	159	12.73	32.62	10	8.05	3.85	11	4.10	0.1333	-0.0131
Olomoucky	124	10.84	30.93	11	9.57	4.79	12	5.66	0.1600	-0.0180
Moravskoslezsky	227	11.72	24.22	12	14.75	8.95	14	2.14	0.1523	-0.0159
Ustecky	154	11.15	19.54	13	13.00	8.37	13	2.94	0.1251	-0.0162
Karlovarsky	92	10.99	14.99	14	6.39	1.66	6	1.98	0.1310	-0.0045

the region. The employment in this sector was also very pronounced in Ustecky (21 per cent of regional manufacturing employment). In Ustecky, total manufacturing accounted for 23.9 per cent of regional employment. Both of these regions initially had strong economic activity in mining and heavy machinery and equipment industries, which had strongly lost importance after 1993. However, despite the strong employment share in the basic metal and fabricated metal products sector, Ustecky was still, according to the Herfindahl as well as the Theil index, the least specialized region with respect to manufacturing sectors. Another strong sector in the region was the other non-metallic mineral products sector, accounting for 16 per cent of regional manufacturing employment. The sector with the lowest relative importance in Ustecky was the rubber and plastic products sector with 2.9 per cent of regional manufacturing employment. Olomoucky, Pardubice and Plzensky specialized in electrical and optical equipment, accounting for 23 per cent, 32 per cent and 29.9 per cent of regional manufacturing employment, respectively. The strongest manufacturing sector in Prague was the food products, beverages and tobacco sector (29.8 per cent of regional manufacturing employment), while the surrounding region, Stredocesky, strongly specialized in the transport equipment sector (39.9 per cent of regional manufacturing employment). The specialization patterns in Moravskoslezsky, Ustecky, Prague and Stredocesky are not very surprising looking at the regional economic history and population. Unfortunately, the development over time of regional specialization patterns within the manufacturing sector cannot be analysed at the time due to data availability. This remains a topic for future research.

Summary and conclusion

This study deals with the economic development and the increasing economic divergence in Czech regions. The first part of the study describes the development of economic indicators, while the second part of the paper takes a closer look at sectoral concentration and regional specialization patterns. The data show an increasing regional divergence in economic indicators in the Czech Republic between 1993 and 2001. The increase was especially pronounced between the capital region, Prague, and the rest of the country. Eastern regions seem to fall behind in economic development despite their initially favourable positions as industrial centres. Even though regional disparities were of minor importance during the communist regime, the concentration of heavy industry in the East and the persistence of agricultural regions already set the ground for emerging regional disparities when the policy of even development and reducing regional inequalities came to an end. Due to the decline in the mining and quarrying and the heavy industries sectors, the regions with the initially best conditions were faced with unemployment rates increasing to levels above the national average. The Ministry of Regional Development confirms that the increasing regional disparities were mainly caused by the strong decline of activity in the heavy industries and mining sectors. In addition, they point out that the decline of employment in the agricultural sectors especially in rural areas and the uneven development of small and medium sized enterprises and the service sectors, which are primarily concentrated in urban areas, contributed to the increasing regional divergence.[16] This is reflected by the comparably good development of the regions surrounding the capital, which seem to benefit from spillovers of the strong development generated in Prague.

In addition to the description of economic indicators, the study provides some insight in the regional economic structure by providing specialization and concentration indices. The Herfindahl index of absolute specialization also reflects some divergence in regional specialization. However, specialization patterns as well as tertiary sector shares do not seem to have an influence on the regional economic performance in the Czech Republic. Also, there is no clear indication in the data that regions bordering Germany and Austria are better off due to their location close to the older market economies.

The rapid transition of the Czech economy from a centrally planned to a market economy was to a large extent driven by the determination of the Czech government to become a member of international trade organizations (e.g. the WTO and OECD). This way, many reforms necessary for the building up of a market economy were encouraged and guided by organizations with market experience. However, as pointed out by Ferragina and Pastore (2005), the fast speed of the progress in the restructuring of transition economies seems to have furthered strong increases in unemployment rates. The future development of regional economic indicators and the containment of regional divergence may be helped by the sensible coordination and use of structural funds. One way to deal with the issue could be to improve the regional infrastructure especially in afflicted regions. Regional specialization does not seem to be the solution to the problem in the Czech Republic. One danger for social stability is that the most afflicted regions are also regions with comparably high population density. Keeping regional divergence in check will therefore be one of the most important tasks of Czech regional policy in the future in order to prevent social unrest.

Appendix

Table 10.A1 Data sources and time coverage

Population	1996–2003	Czech Statistics Office
GDP	1993–2001	Czech Statistics Office
Sectoral employment, NACE I	1993–2003	Czech Statistics Office
Sectoral employment, NACE II	2003	Czech Statistics Office
Unemployment rate	1993–2003	Czech Statistics Office
Trade	1993–2001	EU Commission, Regular Reports 1998–2002
FDI stocks	2000–2002	Czech National Bank
FDI inflows	1993–2001	Czech National Bank

Table 10.A2 Development of the regional distribution of sectoral employment shares in Czech regions, 1993–2003

	NACE	Jihocesk	Jihomoravsky	Karlovarsky	Kralovehradecky	Liberecky	Moravskoslezsky	Olomoucky	Pardubicky	Plzensky	Prague	Stredocesky	Ustecky	Vysocina	Zlinsky
Agriculture and hunting	A 01	-4.93	-4.35	-1.76	-1.80	-1.43	-1.88	-2.77	-3.80	-4.92	-0.06	-3.61	-1.88	-7.82	-3.75
Forestry, fishing	A 02, B	-1.11	-0.13	-0.71	-0.60	-0.48	0.23	0.07	-0.51	-0.83	0.00	0.16	-0.52	0.17	-0.35
Mining and quarrying	C	-0.40	-0.83	-2.57	-1.10	-0.87	-4.68	-0.19	-0.69	-0.67	0.00	-1.36	-3.57	-1.16	0.00
Manufacturing	D	1.54	-3.55	-0.37	-5.44	1.48	-1.56	-3.29	-0.51	3.31	-4.48	-5.94	-3.96	1.88	-0.72
Electricity, gas and water supply	E	-0.55	-0.13	-1.82	-0.99	-0.63	-0.32	-0.13	-0.77	-0.28	-0.12	-0.27	-0.45	0.03	-0.46
Construction	F	0.40	1.61	1.90	0.91	-0.37	0.60	1.59	2.51	-0.84	-0.61	1.27	-0.27	1.05	-0.83
Trade and repairs	G	2.85	4.68	0.27	5.44	-0.80	1.78	3.53	1.14	2.39	1.65	2.29	5.88	1.92	3.56
Hotels and restaurants	H	0.38	-0.23	3.01	0.66	-0.45	1.48	0.67	1.01	-0.54	-0.83	1.34	0.80	0.95	0.90
Transport, storage and communications	I	-0.27	0.69	-1.75	-1.34	-1.34	-0.78	-1.68	-0.42	-0.36	-0.52	0.95	-1.46	0.80	0.06
Financial intermediation and insurance	J	0.36	0.50	0.57	0.40	0.94	0.30	0.40	0.25	0.60	1.65	0.81	0.29	0.11	0.55

continued

Table 10.A2 continued

	NACE	Jihocesk	Jihomo-ravsky	Karlovarsky	Kralovehra-decky	Liberecky	Moravskos-lezsky	Olomoucky	Pardubicky	Plzensky	Prague	Stredocesky	Ustecky	Vysocina	Zlinsky
Real estate, renting and business activities	K	1.93	0.03	1.58	1.91	2.00	1.12	1.12	0.50	0.77	2.24	2.57	2.40	1.12	0.64
Public administration and defense	L	-0.92	0.78	2.40	0.26	-0.14	1.57	0.54	0.92	-0.22	-0.17	1.32	1.76	0.30	0.47
Education	M	0.63	-0.57	-0.45	0.81	0.02	0.74	-2.42	-0.58	-1.42	-0.29	-0.73	-0.53	0.01	-1.08
Health and social work	N	-0.25	1.07	-0.22	-0.58	1.26	1.93	2.42	1.06	1.83	0.53	-0.36	0.33	0.32	-0.26
Other community, social and personal services	O	0.05	0.26	0.01	1.11	0.63	-0.59	0.02	-0.32	1.17	1.03	1.40	0.99	0.29	1.31

Notes

1 All according to data from the Cambridge Econometrics Database.
2 UNCTAD (2003).
3 OECD (2001).
4 Dillon and Wykoff (2002).
5 Dillon and Wykoff (2002).
6 EBRD (1998).
7 Dillon and Wykoff (2002).
8 Prague Stock Exchange.
9 Ch and Larischová (1999), Illner (2001).
10 The only other region also registering a slight increase in population between 1993 and 2003 was Karlovarsky in the West of the country bordering Germany.
11 Data on employment in the mining sector is missing for the regions Jihocesky, Kralovehradecky, Pardubicky, Prague and Zlinsky.
12 Numbers for employment in the mining sector in 2003 for Prague, Pardubicky, Kralovehradecky, Jihocesky and Zlinsky are missing. However, data is provided for all these regions for some years, never exceeding 2.3 per cent of sectoral employment (in Kralovehradecky in 1993).
13 The data availability allows calculating concentration and specialization indices for eight manufacturing sectors in 2003, i.e. the food and tobacco sector, textiles, rubber and plastic products, other non-metallic minerals products, basic metals and fabricated metal products, machinery and equipment n.e.c., electrical and optical equipment, and the transport equipment sectors. Within the NACE classification, these are the sectors DA, DB, DH, DI, DJ, DK, DL and DM. The other manufacturing sectors had to be excluded due to missing observations.
14 Taking into account only sectoral disaggregation on NACE I-level due to data availability.
15 See also Dupal (2000).
16 Ch and Larischová (1999).

References

Blazek, J. (2001), "Regional Development and Regional Policy in the Czech Republic: An Outline of the EU Enlargement Impacts". *Informationen zur Raumentwicklung*, 11, 757–767.
Dillon, P. and Wykoff, F. C. (2002), *Creating Capitalism*. Northampton: Edward Elgar.
Dupal, J. (2000). "Regional Planning, Policy and Disparities in the Course of Transition in the Czech Republic". *Informationen zur Raumentwicklung*, 7, 381–389.
EBRD (1998), EBRD Investment Report. United Kingdom.
Eurostat (2002), "Foreign Direct Investment within the Candidate Countries", *Statistics in Focus*, Theme 2, 55/2002.
Ch, J.H. and Larischová, K. (1999). "Regionale Entwicklungsdisparitäten und Regionalpolitik in der Tschechischen Republik". In: Brusis, M. (ed.), *Regional Policy-Making in Bulgaria, the Czech Republic, Estonia, Hungary, Poland and Slovakia*. Munich: Centre for Applied Policy Research.
Illnes, M. (2001). "Regional Development in the Czech Republic Before and After the Accession. Some Speculative Scenarios", *Informationen zur Raumentwicklung*, Heft 11/12, 751–756.
MMR (1999), *Regional Policy*. Czech Republic: Ministry of Regional Policy.
OECD (2001), *OECD Reviews of Regulatory Reform: Regulatory Reform in the Czech Republic*, Paris, France.
UNCTAD (2003), *World Investment Report*.

11 The regional economic structure of Romania, 1992–2001

Anna Iara

Introduction

Romania's pre-1989 economic policies equipped the country with a specific inheritance. In the 1980s, Romania had internationally specialized in industrial goods with low value added. The fabric of manufacturing was formed by giant enterprises, while small and medium enterprises had vanishing relevance. State control of any economic activity, that had already been high at the beginning of the decade, was further extended. At the same time, achieving economic autarky ranked first among the economic policy objectives. Due to the forced reduction of external debt, the country underwent serious economic hardship in the 1980s, including damaging underinvestment and the strangulation of domestic consumption. Though Romania concluded the Ceausescu era with zero foreign debt, the economy suffered from deferred modernization.[1]

After 1989, Romania underwent a stop-and-go regime of transition policies. During the transformation recession in the early 1990s, first steps towards a liberalized market economy were taken, including land privatization, small-scale privatization and the admission of private enterprises, and the establishment of a two-tiered banking system. The policy measures taken, however, lacked consistency and the determination to effectively combat inflation and trade imbalances or push restructuring. In 1994, steps of monetary and fiscal stabilization supported higher GDP and export growth, improvements in the trade and current account balances and receding inflation. However, while large-scale privatization was delayed and price controls and subsidies were maintained, these achievements were only transient. The country soon struggled again with increasing inflation and fiscal and trade and current account deficits respectively. A more committed stabilization programme combined with structural reforms was first undertaken by the centre-right government that replaced the post-communist administration in late 1996. These measures produced a severe recession in 1997–1998, accompanied with increasing trade imbalances and budgetary deficits that necessitated harsh austerity measures in late 1998. The centre-right government failed to maintain the momentum of the initial reforms: the late 1990s saw hyperinflation and increased risk of foreign debt default in times of low levels of FDI inflows due to hesitant privatization and the perceived instability of the policy and legal environment. At the same time, excessive inter-enterprise arrears indicated that tight budget constraints had still not been established in the business sector. Dissatisfaction with deteriorating living conditions resulted in the return of the post-socialist government in November 2000. Together with the unresolved tasks of enterprise restructuring and large scale privatization inherited from the previous legislature, the new government faced multiple policy challenges of stimulating domestic consumption and investment, combating inflation and tightening fiscal discipline, and promoting FDI by improving the business climate.

By 2001, Romania's record of transition was mixed. The share of the private sector in GDP had not surpassed 65 per cent (European Bank for Reconstruction and Development, 2001: 12).[2] On the other hand, by the end of the year, the private sector covered 77 per cent of total employment, nearly 80 per cent of turnover and around 85 per cent of exports. Important steps of trade liberalization had been taken in the preceding decade, including the assumption of WTO membership in 1995. Economic stabilization and industrial restructuring, however, had remained unresolved. By 2001, Romania displayed lowest GDP per capita in purchasing power standards and highest inflation among the ten EU accession countries. Also, financial intermediation was underdeveloped: domestic credit reached just 8 per cent of GDP, while stock market capitalization amounted to 6 per cent of GDP (European Bank for Reconstruction and Development, 2002: 188).[3] Comparatively low levels of capital inflow were related to the mistrust in the stability of the economic environment and rampant corruption. No sooner than 2003 did the European Commission judge Romania to have successfully stepped forward towards a functioning market economy (European Commission, 2003). After positive evaluations of its prepatory efforts for EU accession on behalf of the EU institutions, Romania became a member of the EU on 1 January 2007. It has, however, still a number of postponed preparatory commitments, the implementation of which is closely monitored by the European bodies. In the case of deviation from these agreements, the European Commission may involve safeguard measures, and EU funds can be withheld from the country.

With 23 million inhabitants, Romania is second largest among the countries of the Eastern EU enlargement. The Europe Agreement that provided the basis for Romania's path to EU accession was concluded in 1993 and entered into force in February 1995. By then, Romania had been a member of EFTA for two years. Romania requested EU accession on 22 June 1995; EU accession negotiations were opened five years later.[4] Accession negotiations were concluded in December 2004. Romania signed the accession treaty on 25 April 2005 and hopes for accession on 1 January 2007. A specific safeguard clause allows for the postponement of the accession by one year if important commitments for readiness are not duly implemented.[5]

As part of the Eureco project,[6] this chapter provides an account of the regional structure and development of key socioeconomic variables in Romania in the 1990s, as a specific case within the broader European picture of regional production structures and their economic outcomes. In particular we review the regional structure of population, GDP, total and sector employment, unemployment and

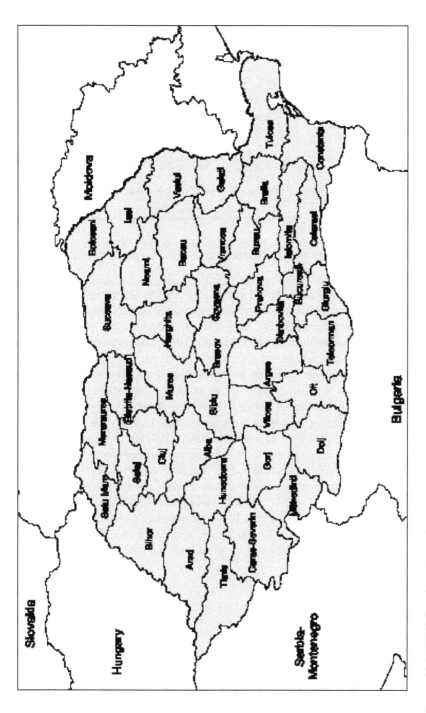

Figure 11.1 NUTS 3 regions, Romania.

Table 11.1 Key economic variables, Romania 1992–2001

	1992	*1993*	*1994*	*1995*	*1996*	*1997*	*1998*	*1999*	*2000*	*2001*
GDP growth, %				2.8	−1.6	−5.0	−6.3	−4.6	1.9	2.8
CPI growth, %	256	138	32	39	155	59	46	46	34	23
population, 1000	22,789	22,755	22,731	22,681	22,608	22,546	22,503	22,458	22,435	22,408
employment, 1000	10,458	10,062	10,012	9,493	9,379	9,023	8,813	8,420	8,629	8,563
unempl. rate, %	8.2	10.4	10.9	9.5	6.6	8.9	10.4	11.8	10.5	8.8
econ. act. rate, %	75.1	73.8	73.6	68.5	65.4	64.6	64.2	62.4	62.8	61.1

Note
These are national figures from the dataset used in the above analysis. Differences to the summary statistics presented below are due to the fact that the latter are un-weighted averages.

economic activity and render further consideration to the structure of the manufacturing industry, regional manufacturing specialization and its potential interrelations with economic growth. The basic unit of analysis is the NUTS 3 region, which is the administrative unit called "judet". The present division of Romania's territory into 40 such counties plus the capital, with the surrounding agricultural area of Ilfov (see Figure 11.1) has prevailed since 1968. The average size of a judet is 5,876 km². While most variables are available from 1992 to 2001, regional GDP data has only been at our disposal since 1995. If not indicated otherwise, the data originates from the Romanian National Institute for Statistics. Most of them are available in the *Statistical Yearbook of Romania*. Table 11.1 gives a summary of the key variables on a national level in the period under review.

The present chapter is structured as follows: the next section describes regional patterns in population, GDP, labour markets and the sector composition of employment in 1992 to 2001. The following section portrays the structure of manufacturing employment by NACE 2-digit branches and patterns of regional manufacturing specialization in the above mentioned period, and considers potential effects of specialization on economic growth. Finally, we offer a summary of the findings.

Population, GDP, economic activity, sectors of the economy

Population

In 1990, the population of Romania amounted to 23.2 million. In the following years, the number of inhabitants fell sharply, with a peak in 1991/1992 at 1.7 per cent. Until 1994, the country had lost 480,000 inhabitants, i.e. 2 per cent of its 1990 population. In 2001, Romania had only 22.4 million inhabitants (see

Table 11.1). In the early 1990s, the decrease in population was dominated by emigration; since 1995, however, more than half of the total population decrease was made up by natural demographic change.[7] Most of the decrease in the early 1990s occurred in the counties having higher shares of inhabitants belonging to ethnic minorities, especially Germans, pointing to the exodus of the ethnic Germans from Romania in the early 1990s. The loss of population over the total period of 1990 to 2001 was especially pronounced in the counties at the Northern side of the Southern Carpathian arch (Brasov, Sibiu, Hunedoara and Caras-Severin – by up to 13 per cent), but also in Teleorman. In contrast, some North-Eastern counties (Iasi, Bacau, Suceava, Vaslui, Neamt) as well as South-Western Gorj recorded positive population growth rates of 0.5 to 3 per cent. This relates to higher reproduction rates, as described below.

In terms of population, the capital region of Bucuresti (with the surrounding agricultural district of Ilfov)[8] has an outlier position: 10 per cent of the population (2.27 million in 2001) live there, while the area constitutes 0.7 per cent of the country's territory. The other counties of Romania are typically centred around one important town that absorbs around 28 per cent of their population. Counties with the largest population are the industrial centres of Prahova, Iasi, Bacau, Constanta, Dolj, Cluj, Suceava and Timis.[9] In 2001, these counties had around 700,000 to 850,000 inhabitants. The smallest counties (Covasna, Salaj, Tulcea, Giurgiu) had 230,000 to 300,000 inhabitants. The average number of inhabitants per county was 550,000 (510,000 without the capital). With a countrywide average of 93 in 2001, population density was over 1,240 inhabitants per square kilometre in Bucuresti and 84 in the rest of the country.[10]

In 1990, one-quarter of Romania's population were aged 14 and younger, 10 per cent were in the post-productive age of 65 and more. Romania's population is ageing: until 2001, the share of children in the total population dropped to 18 per cent, and the share of the elderly increased to 14 per cent. This led to a fall in the age dependency ratio from 0.54 to 0.47, which is below the EU-15 value of 0.50 in the same year. On the regional level, variation in the age structure of the population was moderate.[11] The share of the active aged population (15 to 64), 69 per cent countrywide, was fairly equal across regions. Some North-Eastern counties – Vaslui, Suceava, Botosani, Bistrita-Nasaud, Iasi, Bacau – were relatively abundant in offspring (with more than two-fifths of the inhabitants aged 14 and less in 2001), while children below the age of 15 were represented just 17 per cent of the population in industrial centres like Brasov, Timis, Cluj and Bucuresti, as well as Teleorman. The ratio of the active-aged per dependent-aged inhabitants (the latter being below 15 or above 64) varied between 1.7 and 2.6, with lowest values in the North-Eastern counties with younger population and highest values in the industrial centres of Hunedoara, Timis, Cluj, Constanta, Brasov and Bucuresti. Summary statistics of regional population data by age groups are presented in Table 11.2.

Table 11.2 Total population by age groups, Romania 1990–2001: summary statistics

	1990	1991	1992	1993	1994	1995	1996	1997	1998	1999	2000	2001
0–14												
average	24.07	23.53	22.56	21.95	21.38	20.77	20.24	19.77	19.50	19.19	18.71	18.22
st.dev.	2.38	2.39	1.86	1.78	1.71	1.67	1.63	1.61	1.61	1.63	1.66	1.67
c.o.v.	0.10	0.10	0.08	0.08	0.08	0.08	0.08	0.08	0.08	0.09	0.09	0.09
max	29.76	29.29	25.68	25.00	24.43	23.86	23.29	22.86	22.73	22.58	22.22	21.85
min	18.92	17.92	18.29	17.90	17.63	17.25	16.67	15.95	15.34	14.68	13.91	13.45
15–64												
average	65.43	65.69	66.20	66.52	66.81	67.10	67.40	67.54	67.56	67.65	67.85	68.02
st.dev.	2.25	2.32	1.33	1.38	1.48	1.61	1.71	1.83	1.94	2.06	2.18	2.26
c.o.v.	0.03	0.04	0.02	0.02	0.02	0.02	0.03	0.03	0.03	0.03	0.03	0.03
max	70.00	70.54	69.13	69.39	69.57	70.15	70.68	71.04	71.35	71.80	72.40	72.55
min	59.48	59.78	62.96	63.26	63.51	63.61	63.85	63.87	63.55	63.44	63.52	63.54
>64												
average	10.50	10.78	11.24	11.53	11.81	12.12	12.37	12.68	12.94	13.16	13.44	13.76
st.dev.	1.69	1.74	1.81	1.85	1.89	1.92	1.92	1.94	1.95	1.95	1.98	2.01
c.o.v.	0.16	0.16	0.16	0.16	0.16	0.16	0.16	0.15	0.15	0.15	0.15	0.15
max	14.89	15.39	16.35	16.81	17.23	17.69	17.95	18.34	18.65	18.84	19.24	19.67
min	6.85	7.12	7.40	7.73	8.00	8.32	8.60	8.95	9.29	9.61	9.94	10.30

GDP

In 1995, Romanian GDP was 27.3 billion euro, i.e. 71,715 billion ROL. Per capita, Romanian GDP amounted to 6.8 per cent of the EU-15 average.[12] In 1996, total Romanian real per capita GDP increased by 2.8 per cent against the previous year, this was however followed by three years of negative per capita GDP growth as high as 5 per cent in 1997 (see Table 11.1). Only in 2000 and 2001 did per capita GDP increase again, and the 1995 level was finally sur-passed in 2001. Average annual per capita GDP growth of the regions 1995 to 2001 was virtually zero, 0.29 per cent. In 1995 to 2001, positive average annual growth rates prevailed in only nine of the 41 regions of Romania: Bucuresti (8.3 per cent), Cluj and Arad (just above 2 per cent), as well as Caras-Severin, Timis, Constanta, Dolj and Prahova (below 1 per cent). Summary statistics of regional GDP per capita are presented in Table 11.3.

Relative to the national level, regional GDP per capita[13] varied between 63 and 135 per cent in 1995. Per capita GDP in the fourth quartile of the regions was 1.6 times higher on average than that of first quartile. In the following years, this ratio has increased to 1.95 (1.77 without Bucuresti – see Figure 11.2). In 2001, average regional GDP per capita was significantly lower than in 1995. However, its stan-dard variation has not significantly changed (both with and without the capital). Nevertheless, estimating a standard convergence model with annual GDP levels and growth rates respectively[14] suggests that among the regions except Bucuresti, beta convergence of the income levels has taken place after 1995: a region experi-enced the higher economic growth (the lower decline) the lower its GDP was. Con-vergence conditional on region-specific time-invariant characteristics appears particularly strong: fixed effects panel estimations produce a highly significant

Table 11.3 Regional real GDP per capita, Romania 1995–2001: summary statistics

	1995	1996	1997	1998	1999	2000	2001
All regions							
average	95.3	98.4	93.9	87.8	85.5	85.1	89.2
st.dev.	17.3	19.8	20.3	20.4	21.5	26.4	28.3
c.o.v.	0.18	0.20	0.22	0.23	0.25	0.31	0.32
max	135.3	146.4	138.5	149.5	154.5	198.6	217.8
min	63.2	62.3	63.7	58.0	55.1	46.0	48.5
max/min	2.1	2.3	2.2	2.6	2.8	4.3	4.5
Without capital							
average	94.3	97.2	92.7	86.3	83.8	82.3	86.0
st.dev.	16.3	18.5	19.2	18.1	18.6	19.4	19.6
c.o.v.	0.17	0.19	0.21	0.21	0.22	0.24	0.23
max	130.9	132.4	134.4	127.5	130.3	122.3	127.8
min	63.2	62.3	63.7	58.0	55.1	46.0	48.5
max/min	2.1	2.1	2.1	2.2	2.4	2.7	2.6

Note
National (weighted!) GDP per capita 1995 = 100.

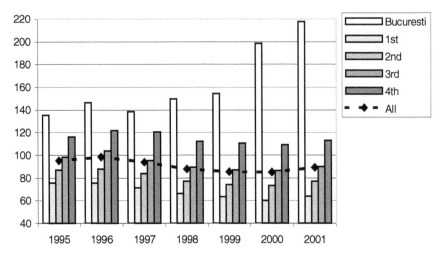

Figure 11.2 Regional real GDP per capita, Romania 1995–2001: unweighted averages by quartiles.

Notes
a National GDP per capita 1995 = 100. Bucuresti is considered separately.
b The order of the bars listed in the key corresponds to the left-to-right order they are displayed in on the graph.

Table 11.4 Annual change in per capita GDP, 1995–2000: regression results

Dep. variable: $log(GDPC_{i,t+1}/GDPC_{i,t})$	OLS		LSDV	
	coeff.	s.e.	coeff.	s.e.
log (GDPC)$_{i,t}$	−0.0521*	0.0297	−0.7079***	0.1051
Year dummies	17.23***		15.37***	
Region fixed effects			3.15***	
No. of obs.	240		240	
R²	0.19		0.50	

Note
Heteroskedasticity-robust standard errors. Constant included. *, **, *** denote significance at conventional levels.

convergence coefficient of −0.7. Assuming that time-invariant regional characteristics are constant, this means that a region having twice the income of another in a given year will have just 30 per cent higher GDP in the next so that regional income levels rapidly equalize. Obviously, region specific characteristics that change little over time – such as the geographical position of the county, its infrastructure and settlement patterns etc. – determine much of regional differences in economic performance. This is in line with the fact that relative positions of the regions have remained relatively stable: per capita GDP levels 1995 and 2001 are highly significantly correlated at 0.81; regions' relative positions in terms of quartiles were most likely to remain unchanged (see Table 11.5).

Table 11.5 Regional GDP per capita, Romania 1992–2001: regions' transition probabilities (frequencies) between quartiles (%)

	2001				
	1st	*2nd*	*3rd*	*4th*	*Total*
1995					
1st	83.3	13.9	2.8	0	100
2nd	13.8	69.0	15.5	1.7	100
3rd	3.5	14.0	68.4	14.0	100
4th	0	1.69	11.9	86.4	100
total					100

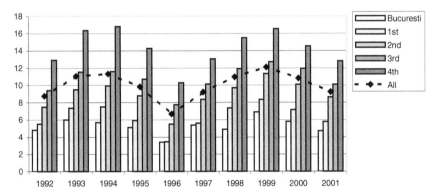

Figure 11.3 Regional unemployment, Romania, 1992–2001: unweighted averages by quartiles.

Notes
a Bucuresti is considered separately.
b The order of the bars listed in the key corresponds to the left-to-right order they are displayed in on the graph.

Employment, unemployment, economic activity

Romania experienced a massive loss of jobs in the 1990s. In 1990, the Romanian workforce (number of persons employed) comprised 10.8 million people. Over the 1990s, the workforce contracted by around 20 per cent (see Table 11.1). Employment fell steadily to 8.4 million in 1999, when the decrease halted. In 1990, 71 per cent of the working-age population were employed. Nine years later, this rate reached a minimum of 55 per cent. On the regional level, the employment losses of 1992–1999 affected 50,000 people on average. In the previous two years, on average 10,000 workers were dismissed in each region. The employment loss up to 1999 hit the regions to an extent of 7 to 29 percentage points relative to the level of 1992.[15] By 1999, the relative employment decrease was highest in Bucuresti as well as in the mining centre of Hunedoara. Aggregated to the NUTS 2 level, following Bucuresti, the regions in the South-East, South and West experienced highest employment loss by around 20 per cent, whereas the other NUTS 2 regions lost employment by 14–17 per cent only.

From virtually zero at the beginning of the 1990s, unemployment rates rapidly rose and reached nearly 9 per cent in 1992. This level was then characteristic of the following years (see Table 11.1). Particularly high unemployment of 11–12 per cent hit the country in 1993–1994 and 1997–1999, i.e. the years following various reform measures. Countrywide unemployment reached a remarkably low 6.6 per cent in 1996, and it has decreased by the end of the decade. The spatial spread of unemployment has become more equal in the 1990s: except for a sharp increase in 1996, regional variation in unemployment rates has steadily decreased from 0.41 in 1991 to 0.28 in 2000, and has slightly risen thereafter (see Table 11.6 and Figure 11.5). Regional unemployment was highly persistent: regional unemployment rates of 2001 showed strong and significant correlation with those of the mid-1990s.[16] In 2001, in addition to the capital and the county of Vrancea, very low unemployment rates of 3.1 to 6.1 per cent were recorded in some counties at the Western border. Very high unemployment of 12 to more than 15 per cent occurred in some agricultural counties of Eastern Romania and the mining region of Hunedoara.

Rising unemployment gives an incomplete picture of the breakdown of the Romanian economy. Romania also witnessed a massive withdrawal of the population from economic activity. From 75 per cent in 1992, the countrywide economic activity rate[17] dropped to 61 per cent by 2001 (see Table 11.1). The range of regional activity rates covered 65 to 83 per cent in 1992, this range shifted to 54 to 71 per cent in 2001 (see Table 11.7). Regional variation in activity rates was very low, the variation coefficient showed a tendency to increase over the 1990s but only reached 0.08. There is no simple relationship between the downsizing of employment and the withdrawal from economic activity: by years, there was typically no correlation between regional unemployment and eco-

Table 11.6 Regional unemployment, Romania 1992–2001: summary statistics

	1992	1993	1994	1995	1996	1997	1998	1999	2000	2001
average	8.7	11.1	11.3	9.8	6.7	9.2	11	12.1	10.8	9.2
st.dev.	3.04	3.85	3.94	3.35	2.78	2.91	3.42	3.35	3.05	2.83
c.o.v.	0.35	0.35	0.35	0.34	0.42	0.32	0.31	0.28	0.28	0.31
max	16.1	22.9	24.1	17.3	13.1	15	18.7	21.3	16.7	15.3
min	2.8	4.2	3.9	3.9	2.3	4	4.9	6	4.5	3.1
max/min	5.75	5.45	6.18	4.44	5.7	3.75	3.82	3.55	3.71	4.94

Table 11.7 Regional economic activity rates (%), Romania 1992–2001: summary statistics

	1992	1993	1994	1995	1996	1997	1998	1999	2000	2001
average	74.56	73.75	73.46	68.90	66.20	65.56	65.10	64.05	63.95	62.01
st.dev.	3.85	4.09	4.34	4.33	4.46	4.29	4.08	5.35	4.90	4.43
c.o.v.	0.05	0.06	0.06	0.06	0.07	0.07	0.06	0.08	0.08	0.07
max	83.14	80.80	82.73	78.68	77.41	75.78	75.23	77.53	75.61	70.94
min	64.67	65.49	64.46	59.22	57.73	56.03	56.57	47.24	53.06	53.75
max/min	1.29	1.23	1.28	1.33	1.34	1.35	1.33	1.64	1.43	1.32

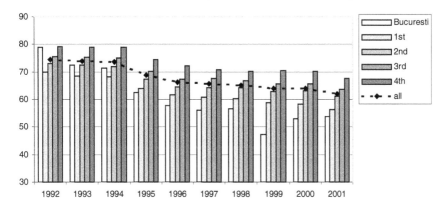

Figure 11.4 Regional economic activity rates (%), Romania 1992–2001: unweighted averages by quartiles.

Note

a Bucuresti is considered separately.

b The order of the bars listed in the key corresponds to the left-to-right order they are displayed in on the graph.

nomic activity rates. Similarly, only for few regions were economic activity and unemployment rates correlated across the years. Remarkably, while the rate of economic activity had been particularly high in Bucuresti in 1992, the withdrawal from economic activity was most pronounced: in no other region had economic activity dropped by more than 25 percentage points (see Figure 11.4).

Sector composition of the workforce

In the early 1990s, the relative majority of the workforce of Romania – 37 per cent, i.e. 3.9 million people – worked in mining, manufacturing, construction or energy-related branches (NACE sections C-F, hereafter referred to as the industrial sector). Romania then suffered severe deindustrialization. From 1992 to 2001, industrial employment dropped by nearly 40 per cent, i.e. more than 1.5 million. Since 1993 agriculture was the largest sector in Romania, it provided for 41 per cent of total employment in 2001.[18]

In 1992, regional industrial employment varied between 19 and 56 per cent. The most important industrial centres – Brasov, Hunedoara, Prahova, Sibiu and Bucuresti – formed a kinked belt between the capital and the Apuseni mountains in the West, crossing the Carpathians at the Prahova valley. Among these counties, Brasov and Sibiu were prominent locations of manufacturing activity (that accounted for more than 85 per cent of industrial employment), while Hunedoara had a large mining industry (39 per cent of industrial employment). Some counties in the South-Eastern environs of Bucuresti, together with Botosani in the very North-East, were the least industrialized. Until 2001, regions lost 13 to 56 per cent of their 1992 level of industrial employment, with moderate regional differences (variation coefficient: 0.23). With Bucuresti, some of its neighbours and North-Eastern Suceava were most affected. The employment loss was only moderate, around 25 per cent, in Tulcea, Timis and Satu Mare, while Arad had exceptionally low employment loss of 13 per cent. Except Tulcea that had been a region dominated by agriculture in 1992 already, these regions are located at the Western border. In relative terms, industrial employment dropped by 10 percentage points on average. In no region has the share of industrial in total employment increased since then. Industrial activity became relatively more widespread in the country: while in 1992, 50 per cent of the industrial workforce were concentrated in 11 regions, in 2001 the most industrialized 11 regions accounted for 33 per cent of the total industrial workforce. In 2001, Prahova, Brasov, Sibiu and Hunedoara were still among the most industrialized regions, while Bucuresti was replaced by Arges that is also bordering the aforementioned industrial area. Also, the South-Eastern neighbours of Bucuresti and Botosani continued to be the least industrialized regions. Still, the relative decrease of the secondary sector was highest in the important industrial centres, supporting the equalization of the economic structure of the country. The relative decrease of industrial employment was least severe in the aforementioned counties that suffered least from the absolute decrease of their industrial sector.

In 1992, agriculture provided for 33 per cent of total employment in Romania. Regional variation of agricultural employment shares was slightly higher than of employment in industry and services (variation coefficient: 0.3). Agriculture was the largest sector in absolute (relative) terms in seven (16) counties. Several predominantly agricultural counties formed a belt from Olt to Vrancea around the Bucuresti-Prahova industrial area. Further regions dominated by agriculture were in the South-West and the North of the country. The predominantly agricultural counties were those that were least industrialized, and vice versa.

The huge decrease of employment in the secondary sector was not met by a comparable increase in agricultural employment. From 1992–2001, agricultural employment increased by some 50,000 persons (i.e. 1.5 per cent) only, from 3.44 to 3.5 million. Nevertheless, agriculture has been the largest sector in Romania since 1993. In 2001, agriculture provided for 41 per cent of total employment. On the regional level, Arad was the only region that had not increased its agricultural employment share in 2001 as compared to 1992. Regional variation in the share of agriculture decreased slightly from 0.31 to 0.29.

In 1992, employment in the services sector accounted for 30 per cent of total employment in Romania, which implied 3.13 million persons working in this sector. Regional variation in the share of services in employment was lowest across the sectors (coefficient of variation: 0.21). In 1992, Romania had two regions with dominant services sectors in relative terms: Constanta – Romania's Black Sea port – and Bucuresti. Other regions with relatively large services sectors (28–33 per cent of regional employment) were Timis and Arad, Cluj, Mures and Sibiu, Iasi, Prahova, Dolj, Galati and Tulcea. Regions with the least developed services sectors were found in the South-Western environs of Bucuresti and in North-Eastern Romania (Dambovita, Teleorman, Calarasi, Giurgiu, Botosani and Vaslui).

Table 11.8 Regional shares of employment by NACE 1-digit sectors, Romania 1992–2001: summary statistics

Sector (NACE)	1992	1993	1994	1995	1996	1997	1998	1999	2000	2001
Agriculture (A-B)										
Average	37.72	40.94	41.4	38.62	39.39	41.54	42.21	44.77	45.53	45.10
st.dev.	11.61	12.60	12.53	11.64	11.80	12.23	12.37	12.40	12.98	12.87
c.o.v.	0.31	0.31	0.3	0.3	0.3	0.29	0.29	0.28	0.29	0.29
Max	55.08	61.93	62.42	58.67	58.47	61.88	63.00	65.35	65.69	66.40
Min	4.25	5.02	5.14	5.71	5.72	6.30	5.63	7.26	6.58	6.65
Max/min	12.95	12.34	12.15	10.27	10.22	9.82	11.20	9.00	9.99	9.98
Industry (C-F)										
Average	34.93	33.37	32.33	31.82	32.36	30.39	28.97	27.18	25.94	26.29
st.dev.	8.62	9.46	8.88	8.44	8.72	8.32	8.27	7.82	7.76	7.40
c.o.v.	0.25	0.28	0.27	0.27	0.27	0.27	0.29	0.29	0.30	0.28
Max	56.72	57.61	51.09	51.05	54.17	51.96	49.06	48.88	43.33	44.06
Min	18.76	17.05	16.14	16.76	18.54	17.53	13.30	12.97	9.80	11.40
Max/min	3.02	3.38	3.17	3.05	2.92	2.96	3.69	3.77	4.42	3.86
Services (G-O)										
Average	27.35	25.69	26.28	29.55	28.26	28.07	28.82	28.05	28.53	28.61
st.dev.	5.67	5.86	6.15	6.32	6.13	6.85	6.25	6.81	7.02	7.15
c.o.v.	0.21	0.23	0.23	0.21	0.22	0.24	0.22	0.24	0.25	0.25
Max	49.78	48.36	50.01	53.14	51.03	51.97	55.03	56.03	58.58	59.68
Min	19.80	18.26	16.95	20.77	20.29	18.41	19.85	19.71	19.22	18.26
Max/min	2.51	2.65	2.95	2.56	2.51	2.82	2.77	2.84	3.05	3.27

Table 11.9 Manufacturing industries: NACE 2-digit classification

DA	Food, beverages, tobacco
DB	Textiles, textile products
DC	Leather, leather products
DD	Wood, wood products
DE	Pulp, paper, publishing, printing
DF + DG	Coke, petroleum, nuclear fuel, chemical products, man-made fibers
DH	Rubber, plastic products
DI	Other non-metallic mineral products
DJ	Metals, metal products
DK	Machinery and equipment
DL	Electrical and optical equipment
DM	Transport equipment
DN	N.e.c. incl. furniture

From 1992–2001, employment in services decreased by 20 per cent, meaning 1.9 million fewer jobs. The share of the sector in total employment, however, slightly increased to 31.6 per cent. Due to the over-proportional job destruction in the industrial sector, since 1998 more people were employed in services than in the secondary sector. Until 2001, regional variation in the share of services increased somewhat. By 2001, alongside with Bucuresti and Constanta, Arad at the Western border had also become a region dominated by the services sector.

Manufacturing activity and specialization

The structure of manufacturing employment

In 1992, the most important industries[19] in Romania were textiles (19 per cent of manufacturing employment), machinery (16 per cent), and basic metals (13 per cent). With employment shares of 2 to 4 per cent, the leather, wood and paper groups were the least important manufacturing branches. In total, manufacturing employment amounted to 2.7 million. The division of total Romanian manufacturing employment across the 13 industries considered is shown in Table 11.10.

Total manufacturing employment in Romania fell by 40 per cent until 2001. The employment change was negative in each year until 2000. In 2001, no manufacturing branch reached its 1992 employment level. Employment contraction 1992–2001 was particularly strong in the manufacturing of machinery (−67 per cent), chemicals, plastic and basic metals (around −50 per cent), minerals and transport equipment (around 45 per cent). In the textiles (−25 per cent), wood (−19 per cent) and especially the leather industries (−5 per cent), the extent of job destruction was below average. The annual employment change by industries was typically negative. Still, some branches recorded employment growth in certain years, e.g. the wood industry 1995–1996, textiles and leather since 1998 (except 1999), and in the electrical and optical equipment industry since 2000. In 2001, the shares of the industries in total manufacturing employment did not change by more than 2.5 percentage points as compared with the 1992

Table 11.10 Share of manufacturing industries in total manufacturing employment, Romania 1992–2001; total relative to 1992 (%)

Industry	1992	1993	1994	1995	1996	1997	1998	1999	2000	2001
DA	8.6	10.1	10.4	10.9	10.4	10.8	11.5	11.5	11.1	10.4
DB	18.8	18.3	17.7	17.1	18.3	16.7	19.6	20.6	22.8	24.4
DC	3.7	3.7	4.1	3.8	3.9	4.1	4.3	4.6	5.5	6.1
DD	3.1	3.1	3.4	3.5	3.0	3.4	4.2	4.6	4.5	4.4
DE	2.0	2.5	2.3	2.2	2.3	2.4	2.8	2.3	2.4	2.4
DF + DG	6.7	7.2	7.4	7.4	7.5	8.5	6.3	6.4	6.1	5.7
DH	2.5	2.1	2.2	2.2	2.3	2.2	2.1	2.1	2.1	2.0
DI	5.5	5.3	5.6	5.6	5.5	5.8	5.4	5.5	5.5	5.3
DJ	12.7	12.3	12.4	12.3	12.0	12.6	12.4	11.7	10.5	10.5
DK	16.1	15.1	14.9	14.8	13.6	12.5	11.0	11.0	9.6	9.1
DL	5.8	5.4	5.3	5.3	5.1	5.2	4.6	4.4	5.0	5.0
DM	8.4	8.5	7.9	8.2	8.8	8.9	8.5	8.8	8.4	7.9
DN	6.0	6.6	6.5	6.7	7.2	7.0	7.0	6.5	6.6	6.7
DA-DN	100	100	100	100	100	100	100	100	100	100
Total	100	94	88	80	78	74	69	60	57	58

values. Exceptions are the textiles industry (+5.6 per cent) and the manufacture of machinery (−7 per cent). By 2001, by the shares in total manufacturing employment, the manufacture of textiles (25 per cent) and basic metals (10 per cent) were still the most important industries, followed now by the food industry.

Manufacturing employment shares typically show fairly high regional variation, especially so in the case of the manufacture of electrical and optical equipment and of leather products (coefficient of variation: 1.2–1.3).[20] Comparatively low variation (variation coefficient: 0.4 to 0.8) prevails for the textiles industry, food processing, and the "not elsewhere classified" group.

Relative manufacturing specialization

Measured with the Brülhart-Träger index,[21] in 1992–2001, the Romanian regions had an average level of relative regional specialization of 0.31 to 0.35.[22] Closest to the average was the county of Prahova in 1992: the five industries that were overrepresented as compared to the national structure accounted for 70 per cent of total manufacturing employment. In 2001, Harghita had a specialization level closest to the average: the group of overrepresented industries comprised four branches that provided for 78 per cent of manufacturing employment: the "typical" region has become less diverse. On average, the relative manufacturing specialization of the Romanian counties has steadily increased in several steps from 1992 to 0.36 in 1997 (except a slight decrease in 1995) to drop to 0.32 thereafter. Since 1998, average regional specialization has increased, but this tendency again changed in 2001. The change of the regions' specialization levels against the previous year was in some years significant only, 1995, 1999 and

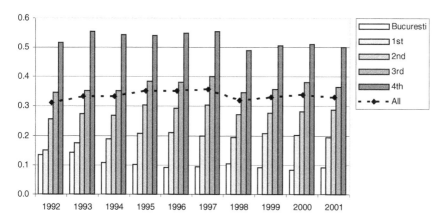

Figure 11.5 Relative manufacturing specialization of the Romanian regions: Brülhart-Träger index, averages by quartiles, 1992 to 2001.

Notes
a Bucuresti is considered separately.
b The order of the bars listed in the key corresponds to the left-to-right order they are displayed in on the graph.

Table 11.11 Regional relative manufacturing specialization (Brülhart-Träger index), Romania 1992–2001: summary statistics

	1992	1993	1994	1995	1996	1997	1998	1999	2000	2001
average	0.3127	0.3348	0.3326	0.3528	0.3520	0.3582	0.3197	0.3310	0.3381	0.3310
st.dev.	0.1486	0.1584	0.1540	0.1472	0.1494	0.1518	0.1348	0.1312	0.1334	0.1342
c.o.v.	0.4751	0.4733	0.4629	0.4172	0.4244	0.4239	0.4218	0.3963	0.3947	0.4055
max	0.7081	0.8132	0.8252	0.9113	0.8950	0.8131	0.8395	0.7235	0.7044	0.7270
min	0.0982	0.0966	0.0771	0.1014	0.0905	0.0573	0.0495	0.0769	0.0830	0.0910
max/min	7.2085	8.4169	10.7026	8.9849	9.8938	14.1973	16.9655	9.4037	8.4897	7.9921

2000. Regional variation in Brülhart-Träger specialization levels was moderate (annual variation coefficients of 0.40 to 0.47). The variance of the regions' specialization levels has not significantly changed in the period considered.

In 1992, 16 regions were specialized above average. Counties with specialization levels higher than a standard deviation above the average had specialization levels of 0.46 to 0.71. Their areas of specialization[23] were the manufacture of metals and metal products (Salaj: 42 per cent of regional manufacturing employment; Caras-Severin: 35 per cent), food products (Ialomita: 41 per cent; Tulcea: 21 per cent), machinery and equipment (Caras-Severin: 36 per cent; Gorj: 40 per cent), coke, petroleum etc. and chemical products (industries DF + DG – Valcea: 23 per cent), and transportation goods (Tulcea: 22 per cent). The regions with specialization levels that were by more than one standard deviation below the average were Constanta, Dolj, Buzau, Teleorman, Bucuresti, Mures, Sibiu and Iasi (ordered by decreasing specialization). In these regions, the largest industry provided only for 21 per cent of regional manufacturing employment on average.

In 2001, 19 regions had above average specialization levels, but only four of these were specialized more than one standard deviation above average, with Brülhart-Träger indices of 0.55 to 0.73. Their industries of specialization were metals and metal products (Galati: 53 per cent of manufacturing employment), coke, petroleum etc. and chemical products (Valcea: 34 per cent), food products (Ialomita: 55 per cent), as well as the production of machinery and equipment, other non-metallic mineral products, and rubber and plastic products (Gorj: 26 per cent, 16 per cent, 8 per cent of manufacturing employment, respectively).[24] The other regions in the fourth quartile ranked by the Brülhart-Träger index were specialized in the manufacture of textiles (Vrancea: 57 per cent of manufacturing employment; Botosani: 55 per cent), leather products (Bihor: 33 per cent), food products (Giurgiu: 42 per cent), metal products (Caras-Severin: 31 per cent), non-metallic mineral products (group DI, Botosani: 13 per cent), and transportation goods (Arges: 33 per cent). In 2001, Alba, Cluj, Sibiu, Iasi and Bucuresti were specialized below average by more than one standard deviation.

Tables 11.12 to 11.15 show the areas of specialization of the Romanian regions grouped by quartiles. This categorization allows for the following insights: first, several industries are providing the leading area[25] in both specialized and de-specialized regions. In particular, these are the manufacture of textiles, metals and products, machinery and equipment, transport equipment and "not elsewhere classified" (NACE categories DB, DJ, DK, DM, DN). In this respect, many specialized and de-specialized regions do not differ. Second, there is no leading industry that can be said to be typical of highly specialized regions. In contrast, less specialized regions cover a wider range of leading industries, including some that are less represented among the higher specialized regions, such as the manufacture of leather products (DC), of non-metallic mineral products (DI), and of paper etc. (DE). These are thus leading industries typical of regions with more diverse economic structures. Third, there is a high degree of constancy as concerns the leading industry of regions: in 18 cases, the leading industry has not changed

Table 11.12 Most specialized regions (fourth quartile by Brülhart-Träger index) by areas of specialization, 1992–2001

	DA	DB	DC	DD	DE	DFG	DH	DI	DJ	DK	DL	DM	DN
1992	Ialomita	Botosani Calarasi				Valcea			Caras-S., Salaj	Dambovita, Gorj		Tulcea	Harghita
1993	Ialomita			Harghita		Vallea			Galati, Calarasi, Caras-S., Salaj	Gorj		Tulcea Arges	
1994	Ialomita	Harghita				Valcea			Galati, Calarasi, Salaj	Dambovita, Gorj		Tulcea Arges	
1995	Ialomita	Botosani, Vrancea Calarasi, Harghita				Valcea			Galati, Caras-S.	Gorj		Tulcea	
1996	Calarasi Ialomita	Tulcea, Vrancea		Suceava		Valcea			Galati, Caras-S.	Dambovita, Gorj			
1997	Ialomita	Tulcea, Harghita	Covasna			Valcea			Galati, Caras-S.	Dambovita, Gorj			Salaj
1998	Ialomita	Vrancea		Harghita		Vallea			Galati	Dambovita, Gorj		Tulcea Arges	Marams.
1999	Giurgiu Ialomita	Vrancea, Calarasi Harghita		Suceava		Valcea			Galati, Caras-S.	Gorj			
2000	Ialomita	Botosani, Vrancea Calarasi		Suceava Harghita		Valcea			Galati, Caras-S.	Gorj			
2001	Giurgiu Ialomita	Botosani, Vrancea	Bihor			Valcea			Galati, Caras-S	Gorj		Arges	

Table 11.13 Rather specialized regions (third quartile by Brülhart-Träger index) by areas of specialization, 1992–2001

	DA	DB	DC	DD	DE	DFG	DH	DI	DJ	DK	DL	DM	DN
1992		Suceava, Vrancea			Braila	Bacau			Galati	Vaslui, Prahova	Covasna	Arges, Mehedinti	
1993	Giurgiu	Botosani, Suceava, Vrancea, Covasna								Vaslui, Satu M., Prahova		Mehedinti	Marams.
1994		Botosani, Vrancea		Neamt, Suceava		Bacau			Caras-S.	Vaslui, Prahova			Arad, Satu M.
1995		Covasna		Suceava		Bacau				Vaslui, Alba, Dambovita		Arges, Giurgiu	Arad, Salaj
1996		Botosani, Covasna, Harghita							Buzau	Vaslui, Alba		Constanta, Arges	Satu M., Salaj
1997		Botosani, Vaslui, Vrancea, Calarasi		Suceava		Bacau						Constanta, Arges, Mehedinti	Satu M.
1998		Botosani, Vaslui, Calarasi, Covasna		Suceava					Buzau, Caras-S.	Teleorman		Mehedinti	Salaj
1999	Salaj	Vaslui, Covasna	Bihor						Dambovita	Prahova		Constanta, Tulcea, Arges, Mehedinti	
2000		Marams., Salaj	Timis, Bihor		Covasna				Dambovita			Constanta, Tulcea, Arges, Mehedinti	
2001		Vaslui, Calarasi, Salaj, Harghita		Suceava					Dambovita, Olt		Timis	Constanta, Mehedinti	

Table 11.14 Rather de-specialized regions (second quartile by Brülhart-Träger index) by areas of specialization, 1992–2001

	DA	DB	DC	DD	DE	DFG	DH	DI	DJ	DK	DL	DM	DN
1992		Giurgiu				Neamt			Huneda.	Alba Brasov		Olt	Arad, Satu M., Marams.
1993					Braila	Bacau Neamt			Buzau Huneda.	Dambovita Alba, Brasov		Olt	Arad
1994	Teleorman	Covasna		Bistrita-N.		Neamt			Huneda.	Alba, Brasov		Giurgiu, Mehedinti	Marams.
1995	Teleorman			Bistrita-N. Marams.		Neamt			Buzau Huneda.	Satu M. Brasov		Constanta Mehedinti	
1996	Teleorman	Marams.				Bacau Neamt			Huneda.		Bistrita-N.	Giurgiu, Dolj Mehedinti	Arad
1997	Teleorman			Marams.	Braila	Neamt			Buzau Huneda.	Prahova Alba		Giurgiu	Arad
1998		Braila				Neamt			Olt Huneda.			Constanta Giurgiu, Dolj	Arad, Satu M., Mures
1999		Botosani	Timis		Bistrita-N.				Huneda.	Teleorman Alba, Brasov		Olt	Satu M., Mures
2000	Giurgiu Teleorman	Vaslui Braila		Neamt						Bistrita-N. Brasov	Dolj		Satu M., Mures
2001		Traila, Tulcea, Covasna		Neamt Marams.		Bacau				Prahova Teleorman	Dolj		Mures

Table 11.15 Least specialized regions (first quartile by Brülhart-Träger index) by areas of specialization, 1992–2001

	DA	DB	DC	DD	DE	DFG	DH	DI	DJ	DK	DL	DM	DN
1992		Iasi, Sibiu, Bistrita-N.						Cluj	Buzau		Timis, Bucuresti	Constanta Dolj	Mures
1993		Iasi Sibiu	Bihor			Teleorman		Cluj			Timis, Bistrita-N., Bucuresti	Constanta Dolj	Mures
1994	Braila	Iasi, Sibiu	Bihor	Buzau				Cluj			Timis, Bucuresti	Constanta Dolj	Mures
1995		Iasi, Sibiu	Bihor		Braila			Cluj	Olt	Prahova	Dolj, Timis, Bucuresti		Mures
1996		Iasi, Sibiu	Bihor		Braila			Cluj	Olt	Prahova, Brasov	Timis, Bucuresti		Mures
1997		Iasi, Sibiu	Bihor					Cluj	Olt	Bistrita-N., Brasov	Timis, Bucuresti	Dolj	Mures
1998		Iasi	Bihor, Sibiu	Bistrita-N.		Bacau		Cluj		Prahova Alba, Brasov	Timis, Bucuresti		
1999		Iasi, Braila Marams.	Sibiu		Bacau Neamt			Cluj	Buzau		Bucuresti	Dolj	Arad
2000		Iasi, Arad	Sibiu		Bacau			Cluj	Buzau, Olt, Huneda.	Prahova Alba	Bucuresti		
2001		Iasi	Sibiu					Cluj Alba	Buzau Huneda.	Bistrita-N. Brasov	Bucuresti		Arad Satu M.

Table 11.16 Regional specialization (Brülhart-Träger index), 1992–2001: regions' transition probabilities (frequencies) between quartiles (%)

	2001				
	1st	2nd	3rd	4th	Total
1992					
1st	75.8	20.2	4.0	0.0	100
2nd	21.1	52.2	21.1	5.6	100
3rd	4.4	23.3	53.3	18.9	100
4th	1.1	2.2	21.1	75.6	100
total	26.8	24.4	24.4	24.4	100

Table 11.17 Annual change in regional specialization (Brülhart-Träger index), 1992–2000: regression results

Dep. variable: $(BTS_{i,t+1}-BTS_{i,t})$	OLS		LSDV	
	coeff.	s.e.	coeff.	s.e.
$BTS_{i,t}$	−0.1274***	0.0399	−0.6192***	0.1009
Specialization: DH	0.0426**	0.0196	0.0986*	0.0383
Specialization: DI	−0.0378*	0.0197	insig.	
Year dummies	3.04***		2.40**	
Region fixed effects			3.44***	
No. of obs.	369		369	
R^2	0.15		0.38	

Note
Heteroskedasticity-robust standard errors. Constant included. Dummies included for areas of specialisation DB-DN; DA omitted. Insignificant coefficients are not reported. *, **, *** denote significance at conventional levels.

in the period surveyed; in the other cases changes of the area of specialization were also non-recurring or transitory.

Comparing specialization levels in 2001 with those in 1992, 21 regions have increased specialization while the other half have de-specialized. The extent of the specialization change has been modest though, so that the regional pattern of manufacturing specialization has remained relatively stable: specialization levels 1992 and 2001 were highly significantly correlated with a correlation coefficient of 0.64. Table 11.16 shows the transition matrix for the regions between quartiles by relative regional specialization. In two-thirds of the potential transitions, the regions have not changed their position, while one-sixth of the regions moved into a category with higher and lower specialization levels respectively.

Patterns of regional specialization change 1992–2000 are investigated in a regression framework (see Table 11.17). The results of this exercise allow to conclude the following: First, relative specialization levels of the Romanian regions have converged i.e. regional patterns of manufacturing activity have equalized: changes in the

Brülhart-Träger index were negatively related to initial values. Second, changes in regional specialization levels are characterized by regional idiosyncrasies, as shown by highly significant region specific effects. Third, there are barely any systematic patterns of specialization change specific to regions that have specialized in certain areas: dummies indicating the area of specialization are significant only for the production of rubber and plastic products and other non-metallic mineral products respectively; these relate to the regions of Buzau and Cluj in certain years.[26]

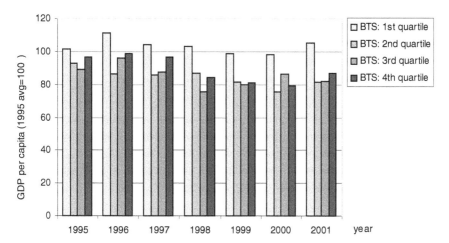

Figure 11.6 GDP per capita: unweighted averages by quartiles of relative manufacturing specialization levels (Brülhart-Träger index), 1995 to 2001.

Notes
a Bucuresti is not included.
b The order of the bars listed in the key corresponds to the left-to-right order they are displayed in on the graph.

Table 11.18 Regional specialization and growth, 1995–2000: regression results

Dep. variable: log $(GDPC_{i,t+1} / GDPC_{i,t})$	OLS		LSDV	
	coeff.	s.e.	coeff.	s.e.
log $GDPC_{i,t}$	−0.0733**	0.0366	−0.7227***	0.1098
BTS	insig.		insig.	
Specialization: DI	0.0739**	0.0344	insig.	
Specialization: DK	insig.		−0.0948**	0.0404
Year dummies	15.43***		15.28***	14.83***
Region fixed effects			3.09***	2.99***
No. of obs.	240		240	
R^2	0.21		0.52	

Note
Bucuresti is not included. Heteroskedasticity-robust standard errors. Dummies included for areas of specialisation DB–DN; DA omitted. Insignificant coefficients are not reported. *, **, *** denote significance at conventional levels.

Manufacturing specialization and economic performance

There is no simple relationship between relative specialization and economic performance. By years, Brülhart-Träger index values and real per capita GDP display significant correlation for 1999 and 2000 only, with a correlation coefficient of −0.35 and −0.27, respectively. For the total sample of regions (with or without the capital), Brülhart-Träger index levels are not partially correlated with real per capita GDP. Figure 11.6 shows however that regions with lowest relative specialization perform better: average per capita GDP is significantly higher in the first quartile of the regions defined by specialization than in the other quartiles. Among the latter, per capita GDP do not differ significantly. Introducing specialization levels and dummies for the area of specialization in the convergence regressions presented in Table 11.18 does not substantially change the regression results: specialization levels are not significantly shaping economic growth. As concerns the regions' specific areas of specialization, only regions specialized in the production of machinery and equipment are found to experience less growth than other regions when region-specific effects were taken into account.[27] The enormous employment decline in the production of machinery and equipment described above thus appears to be related to the downsizing of that industry rather than to productivity improvement from restructuring.

Conclusion

This chapter has offered a review of the main economic developments in Romania's regions during the 1990s. In particular, we portrayed regional patterns in the areas of population, economic performance, labour markets, the sector composition of the economy and the composition of manufacturing by industries. Further, we investigated the development of relative manufacturing specialization of the regions, and tentatively inquired the relationship between specialization and economic growth. Below we summarize the insights arising from this exercise.

The opportunities that emerged from the lifting of the Iron Curtain and the hardships that accompanied economic transition in Romania effectuated a sizeable decrease of the population. The country saw high emigration in particular of minority nationals, while the drop in fertility rates also contributed to the decrease of the number of inhabitants by several hundred thousand during the decade.

In the years of transition and the Western integration experience of Romania reviewed above (1992–2001), the most marked development concerning the regional economic structures of the country is the enormous decline of employment. Total employment contracted by 20 per cent during the 1990s. With a loss of 40 per cent of the jobs, the industrial sector was hit particularly hard. Although agriculture has been the most important provider of jobs since 1993, the sector could absorb only a minor share of the active aged population. Also, while unemployment in Romania remained at medium levels as compared with other Central and Eastern European transition countries in the 1990s, it does not reflect the full extent of job destruction: economic activity also suffered considerable decline.

In the manufacturing industry, the decline of employment has not been equal across regions and industries. The manufacture of machinery and equipment incurred over-proportional decline, while employment in the textiles industry underwent a comparatively favourable development. In the early 1992 levels of relative regional manufacturing specialization have been comparatively low on average. The average change in specialization was moderate and followed no steady direction. We find a tendency towards the equalization of regional specialization levels in the period reviewed. No systematic relationship could however be uncovered between regional specialization, be it in terms of the level or the area of specialization, and regional economic growth. This may suggest that the extent of restructuring of the Romanian manufacturing industry has not yet been sufficient to produce sizeable shifts in the regional economic structure of the country until 2001.

Notes

1 For extensive reviews of economic and policy trends in Romania during the period surveyed refer to Daianu (2000), Hunya (1999, 2000, 2001), as well as to various issues of the EBRD Transition Report. On economic policies in the Ceausescu era see Gilberg (1990).

2 For comparison: in Hungary, one of the more advanced transition countries, the share of the private sector was 60 per cent in 1995 and 80 per cent in 2001. In Bulgaria, these shares were at 50 per cent and 70 per cent, respectively.

3 For comparison: these values were at 31 per cent and 19 per cent of GDP in Hungary. In Bulgaria the volume of domestic credit relative to GDP was nearly twice as high as in Romania, 15 per cent, while stock market capitalization was below 4 per cent of GDP.

4 The European Union has conditioned the opening of accession negotiations with the Eastern European applicant countries on the implementation of basic structures of a functioning democracy including the preservation of human rights (the so-called first Copenhagen criterion). Romania was judged to fulfil this criterion no earlier than 1999.

5 This so-called postponement clause allows the European Commission to recommend to the Council that the entry into force of the accession treaty be delayed to January 2008 if there is clear evidence of the risk that Romania is not sufficiently prepared for membership in important areas. A similar postponement clause applies to Bulgaria.

6 The author thanks to the participants of the Eureco project for the supply of data and helpful comments and discussions. The review of draft versions of the paper by Guntram Wolff is also thankfully acknowledged.

7 Own calculations based on population data available online from Eurostat.

8 In the present chapter reference to the capital region as "Bucuresti" is meant to include the Ilfov agricultural area.

9 The capitals and industrial centres respectively of these counties are Ploiesti, Iasi, Bacau, Constanta, Craiova, Cluj-Napoca, Suceava and Timisoara.

10 On the NUTS 3 level, variations in the size of the counties give a distorted picture of variations in the distribution of population. The NUTS 2 regions are more homogenous in size – the area of the largest is times 1.3 more than of the smallest, while this ratio is 2.4 for the NUTS 3 regions (without Bucuresti). On the NUTS 2 level, the West and the Centre of Romania were most sparsely populated (around 70 inhabitants

per square kilometre), while the North-East and the South had highest population densities (around 100).

11 In 2001, even the highest variation in the shares of population by age groups (concerning the elderly) was moderate at 0.15.

12 In purchasing power standards, Romanian per capita GDP amounted to 32 per cent of the EU-15 average in 1995 (Stapel, 2000).

13 Our regional GDP data are own calculations of real GDP from Eurostat data in current euro prices where we have used exchange rates and the Romanian national GDP deflator of the wiiw database. The data may give a distorted picture of economic performance on the regional level insofar as regional price levels could not be taken into account.

14 Results of these regressions are given in Table 11.4.

15 The case of Salaj that basically kept its level of employment is a remarkable outlier. The relative size of employment loss across regions is steadily distributed in the range of 7 to 29 per cent.

16 The correlation coefficient between the regional unemployment rates of 2001 and 1995 was 0.6. Conversely, unemployment rates of 1992 and 1997 displayed a correlation coefficient of 0.5.

17 Calculated as the share of people either employed or unemployed in the total number of people aged 15 to 64.

18 Summary statistics of regional employment shares in agriculture, industry and services respectively are given in Table 11.8.

19 The present analysis covers the NACE 2-digit manufacturing industries DA to DN. DF and DG cannot be distinguished separately due to the lack of data. The 13 branches considered are listed in Table 11.9.

20 While the coefficient of regional variation in the employment share of the plastic industry was below 1 in 1992, it increased heavily to 2.3 in 1996 and reached 1.95 by 2001. These movements are related to changes in employment in this branch which are moderate in size (concerning around 100 jobs) but large in relative terms.

21 As a general form of the Theil index of specialization, the Brülhart-Träger index of regional specialization is the sum of industries' logarithmized location quotients in a specific region, weighted by industry shares in regional employment: for region i, $BTS_i = \sum s_{ij} \ln(s_{ij}/a_i)$, where s_{ij} is the share of industry j in region i and a_j is the nationwide share of the respective industry (see Bruelhart and Traeger, 2004).

22 For summary statistics of the regions' Brülhart-Träger index of regional specialization see Table 11.11. Regional average specialization levels by quartiles are presented in Figure 11.5.

23 The claim that a region is specialized in a particular industry is based on the highest addends of the Brülhart-Träger index. Remember that the addends of the index are driven both by industry shares in regional employment and the size of the respective industries relative to the national industrial structure (i.e. the location quotient). By the way the Brülhart-Träger index is constructed, regions with higher specialization levels typically have comparatively high employment shares of their largest industry and higher maximum values of industries' location quotients, as well as comparatively high correlation between industry shares of employment and respective location quotients.

24 The high specialization of Gorj was shaped by the location quotients of the industries mentioned above. In 2001, nationwide employment in the manufacture of other non-metallic mineral products and rubber and plastic products provided for 5 per cent and 2 per cent of Romanian manufacturing employment, respectively.

25 On the area of specialization see footnote 23.

26 The regression results are stable to the inclusion of the capital region. Therefore we do not report the results of the regression without Bucuresti.

27 The dummy for specialization in the NACE category DI that is found significant in the regressions not controlling for region specific effects mostly refers to Cluj.

References

Bruelhart, Marius and Rolf Traeger (2005). "An account of geographic concentration patterns in Europe". *Regional Science and Urban Economics* vol. 35, No. 6, pp. 597–624.

Daianu, Daniel (2000). "Structure, strain and macroeconomic dynamic in Romania", in: Christoph Rühl and Daniel Daianu (eds), *Economic Transition in Romania Past, Present and Future: Proceedings of the Conference: "Romania 2000. 10 Years of Transition – Past, Present and Future",* October 21st–22nd, 1999, Bucharest. Bucuresti: The World Bank and Romanian Center for Economic Policies.

European Bank for Reconstruction and Development (2001). *Transition Report 2001. Energy in Transition.* London.

European Bank for Reconstruction and Development (2002). *Transition Report 2002. Agriculture and Rural Transition.* London.

European Commission (2003). *2003 Regular Report on Romania's Progress towards Accession.* Brussels.

Gilberg, Trond (1990). *Nationalism and Communism in Romania: The Rise and Fall of Ceausescu's Personal Dictatorship.* Boulder: Westview.

Hunya, Gábor (1999). *Romania: Stop-go Transition 1990–2005, Analytical Forecast and Country Risk Assessment.* Vienna: The Vienna Institute for International Economic Studies.

Hunya, Gábor (2000). "Romania: new government plans budget expansion to support recovery", in: Leon Podkaminer *et al., The Transition Economies: Externally Conditioned Improvements in 2000, Slowdowns and Adjustments Likely in 2001: and 2002.* Vienna: The Vienna Institute for International Economic Studies.

Hunya, Gábor (2001). "Romania: economic upswing may create current account problems", in: Peter Havlik *et al., Transition Countries in 2001: Robust Domestic Demand, Concerns about External Fragility Reappear.* Vienna: The Vienna Institute for International Economic Studies.

Romanian National Institute of Statistics. *Romanian Statistical Yearbook.* Multiple issues.

Stapel, Silke (2000). *The GDP of the Candidate Countries.* Statistics in focus: Economy and Finance. Luxemburg: Eurostat.

12 Economic integration and structural change

The case of Bulgarian regions

Stoyan Totev

Introduction

Bulgaria has experienced the impact of the interacting processes of integration and transition since the early 1990s. The economic forces and dynamics generated by these two processes have had important consequences for the structural and spatial regularities of the economy. The operation of market forces and the adoption of a reform agenda in all aspects of internal organization and external relations structures has been a long and painful process of restructuring, confronted with serious difficulties. These difficulties and delays in the process of restructuring have resulted to the delayed accession of Bulgaria to the EU.[1]

The aim of this chapter is to assess the impact of the process of economic integration on the regional and structural characteristics of the Bulgarian economy. The analysis focuses on manufacturing, because of the inherent importance of this sector in the former regime and because of the changes that it has undergone afterwards. The next section presents the regional structure and inequalities of the Bulgarian economy. The level of economic performance of the Bulgarian regions is compared to the respective level of the other regions in Central and Eastern Europe. Demographic issues are also examined, since they are among the main contributors to the unfavourable conditions found in many regions. In the same section we analyse the spatial pattern of development in Bulgaria and estimate the level of regional inequalities. In the third section, the analysis focuses on the patterns of regional specialisation and industrial concentration of the economy and the relation of these patterns to development and restructuring. The last section reports the conclusions of the chapter.

Regional structure and inequality in Bulgaria

The economic performance of Bulgarian regions: a comparison to the regions of the Central and Eastern European countries

Bulgaria consists of six NUTS 2 and 28 NUTS 3 regions (Map 12.1).[2] These regions present significant economic hysteresis, despite significant growth in

Map 12.1 The regions of Bulgaria, NUTS 2 and NUTS 3 spatial levels (source: own elaboration).

real GDP in the period after the introduction of the Currency Board in 1997 (4.9 per cent in 2002, 4.3 per cent in 2003 and 5.6 per cent in 2004, the latest figures) (Totev, 2004).

In comparison to the regions of the Central and Eastern European countries (CEEC)[3] the Bulgarian regions, at both spatial levels, present figures of per capita GDP that are among the lowest (Table 12.1 and Figure 12.1). The capital region of Sofia is the only exception to this general rule.

Regional distribution of population

Bulgaria entered into a deep demographic crisis at the end of the twentieth century. After 1989 a significant population decrease is observed (accounting for 20 per cent of the population in a period of 20 years) as a result of natural decline and migration. These processes cause a negative impact on the level of regional disparities, disrupting the productive bases of the weakest regions.

Although internal migration is not intensive, it sharpens the demographic problems caused by natural decline (the respective figure for 2003 was 1.2 per cent). The number of the regions with negative internal migration is rising along with the deterioration of demographic indicators. Even though in 1994 only two Bulgarian NUTS 2 regions (North-Central and North-East) had negative internal migration, in 2001 only one Bulgarian NUTS 2 region (South-West) had positive internal migration. Analogous is the situation with

Table 12.1 Ranking* of the Bulgarian NUTS 2 regions, in per capita GDP terms (in purchasing power parity), among the NUTS 2 regions of the CEEC, 2003

Region	GDP per capita (national average = 100)	GDP per capita (EU-15 average = 100)	Ranking* (within the CEEC NUTS 2 regions)
North-West	87.7	26.1	45
North-Central	81.2	24.2	52
North-East	85.1	25.3	48
South-East	83.5	24.9	49
South-Central	82.8	24.6	50
South-West	144.7	43.0	26

Source: EUROSTAT Regio database/own elaboration.

Note

* Ranking is in a descending order (the region with rank 1 has the highest figure of GOP per capita).

the Bulgarian NUTS 3 regions: in 1994 14 regions were characterized by negative internal migration figures, while in 2001 the same trend was observed in 25 regions.

Population density is a major contributor of regional divergence in Bulgaria. The estimated linear correlation coefficient between net internal migration and population density, at the NUTS 3 spatial level, is getting stronger over time, from 0.21 in 1994 to 0.72 in 2001. The respective coefficient between population density and net revenues per employee, at the NUTS 2 spatial level, was also positive, reaching the level of 0.44 in 2001. Excluding the South-East

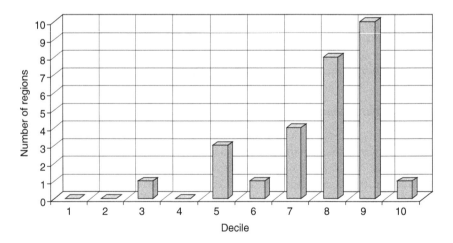

Figure 12.1 Ranking* of the Bulgarian NUTS 3 regions in per capita GDP terms (purchasing power parity) among the NUTS 3 regions of CEEC, 1999 (source: EUROSTAT Regio database/own elaboration).

Note

* Ranking is in a descending order.

region,[4] this coefficient is rising to the level of 0.67. Extremely high is the correlation coefficient between population density and per capita GDP, at the NUTS 3 spatial level, since it reaches the level of 0.84. This positive and strong relation implies that as regional population density increases, regional per capita GDP also increases due to higher productivity, which is the result of agglomeration economies.[5]

The important role of agglomeration economies in the processes of spatial development indicates that regions having a critical threshold of economic activities, allowing the operation of agglomeration economies, will be growing at a faster rate. On the contrary, regions lacking such critical scale of activities are going to face difficulties in their efforts to maintain significant growth rates. The positive and high linear correlation coefficient between per capita GDP and average annual wages, at the NUTS 3 spatial level, that reaches the level of 0.80 reveals the creation of a vicious cycle in the Bulgarian economy. Low population density contributes to low per capita GDP and to low annual wages that contribute, in their turn through migration, to low population density, increasing, thus, the level of regional disparities.

Regional inequalities in Bulgaria

An uneven spatial pattern of development seems to emerge in Bulgaria. The capital region of Sofia forms, together with the regions of Varna, Vratsa and Burgas, the developmental axis of the country (Petrakos *et al.*, 2004). Having in mind the overall hysteresis of the Bulgarian economy, the significant differences observed between the capital region and the other Bulgarian regions can lead to serious socioeconomic problems.

The level of regional inequalities in Bulgaria is estimated through a series of inequalities and agglomeration indices: the weighted coefficient of variation, the maximum to minimum ratio, the γ-density coefficient and the β-convergence coefficient.[6] The coefficient of variation depicts disparities among the regions of a country, taking into consideration their relative weight. It takes the formula:

$$CV_W = [\sum_i (X_i - X_{avr})^2 * (P_i / P)]^{\frac{1}{2}} / X_{avr}$$

where X_i is the level of per capita GDP at the regional level, X_{avr} is the level of per capita GDP at the country level, P_i is the population at the regional level and P is the population at the country level. CV_W takes values in the interval $[0, \infty]$, from absolute equality to infinitely high levels of inequality. The maximum to minimum ratio is the ratio of the richest to the poorest region in terms of per capita GDP. It is calculated by the formula:

$$MM = \frac{Y_{max}}{Y_{min}}$$

where Y_{max} is the level of per capita GDP of the richest region and Y_{min} is the level of per capita GDP of the poorest region, and it takes values in the interval $[1, \infty]$, from absolute equality to infinitely high levels of inequality. The γ-density coefficient is the slope coefficient of the regression $Y_t = a + \gamma^* D_t + \varepsilon$, where D_t is regional population density, Y_t is regional per capita GDP, a is the constant term, γ is the population density coefficient and ε is the disturbance term. The γ-density coefficient is a measure of inequality that is attributed to the operation of agglomeration economies. The β-convergence coefficient is estimated from the regression:

$$\frac{Y_{t1}}{Y_{t0}} = a + \beta^* Y_{t0} + \varepsilon$$

where Y_{t0} is the initial regional per capita GDP, $\frac{Y_{t1}}{Y_{t0}}$ is the regional per capita GDP growth, a is the constant term, β is the convergence coefficient and ε is the disturbance term. Positive and significant values of β indicate that more advanced regions grow faster than less advanced ones and regional divergence trends prevail in the country. On the contrary, a negative sign of β indicates that weak regions grow faster and therefore a process of regional convergence takes place.

Bulgaria is characterized by an increase in the weighted coefficient of variation and the maximum to minimum ratio in the period 1995–2001 (Figures 12.2 and 12.3). This general trend indicates that the market-based processes of integration and transition are accompanied by a significant increase of regional inequalities. This trend, which was evident from the early stages of transition (Petrakos, 2001), has continued to prevail in the late 1990s with an undiminished pace. The interesting point is that in a short period of time, Bulgaria reached levels of regional inequalities comparable to those of the EU-15 countries. If in the post-1989 period the market mechanism is considered to be the most important factor creating regional inequalities, a question is raised about the future evolution of inequalities (given that Bulgarian market is relatively

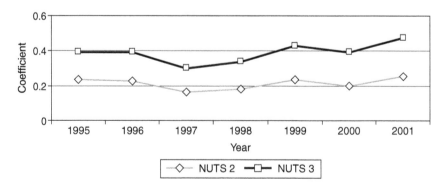

Figure 12.2 Regional inequalities in Bulgaria, weighted coefficient of variation, period 1995–2001 (source: Regio database/own elaboration).

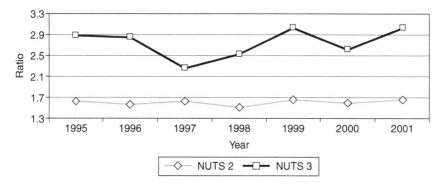

Figure 12.3 Regional inequalities in Bulgaria, maximum to minimum ratio, period 1995–2001 (source: Regio database/own elaboration.

young and not fully developed). The γ-density coefficient, for 2001, is positive (2.483) and statistically significant (p-value = 0.000). This implies that as regional population density increases, regional per capita GDP will increase also due to higher productivity, which is the result of agglomeration economies. Regions having a critical threshold of activities, allowing the operation of agglomeration economies, will be growing at a faster rate than in the past. On the contrary, regions lacking such critical scale of activities are going to face difficulties in their efforts to maintain significant growth rates. The value of the β-convergence coefficient is negative (−0.01); however, it is statistically insignificant (p-value = −0.953). This means that during the period 1995–2001 significant trends of regional convergence are not observed in the country. The divide between the rich and the poor Bulgarian regions seems to remain unaltered.

Regional specialization and concentration in manufacturing

Labour market indicators and the structure of production

Regional differences concerning employment and unemployment generate economic and social disparities and determine, to a great extent, the migration flows in Bulgaria. Unemployment problems are sharp in the areas where the share of employment in the industrial sector is low and the relative share in the agricultural sector is high. The correlation coefficient between the share of employment in industry and the level of unemployment is −0.53 and the correlation coefficient between the share of employment in agriculture and the level of unemployment is 0.45. The first coefficient reaches the level of −0.76 when two NUTS 3 regions (Sofia city and Kardzali) are excluded from the estimations.[7] Doing the same task, the second coefficient reaches the level of 0.65. These figures indicate a close relationship between labour market indicators and the structure of production at the regional level.

The recent economic situation in Bulgaria requires the restructuring of the industrial sector in order to provide a basis for growth and development. The

Table 12.2 Sectoral composition of industrial employment at the regional level in Bulgaria, 20

NUTS 3	Foods, beverages and tobacco	Textiles and wearing apparel	Leather, leather and fur clothes, footwear and products	Wood and products of wood and cork, plaiting materials	Pulp, paper and paper products, publishing and printing	Coke, refined petroleum products and nuclear fuel	Chemicals, chemical products and man-made fibres	Rubber and plastic produc
Vidin	17.2	36.5	0.5	1.3	0.3	0.0	0.0	15.9
Vratsa	14.2	27.1	0.2	1.4	3.2	0.0	13.4	0.7
Montana	21.2	24.1	2.4	3.7	1.0	0.0	1.3	4.3
Veliko Tarnovo	28.2	10.7	0.5	2.0	4.4	0.0	10.2	2.6
Gabrovo	7.6	23.1	7.7	1.7	0.8	0.0	2.4	3.2
Lovech	17.5	11.1	2.9	10.4	1.5	0.0	4.8	0.7
Pleven	22.8	27.6	3.1	0.5	2.6	6.6	0.1	1.2
Ruse	15.6	25.3	2.5	0.9	1.7	2.1	9.6	5.6
Varna	15.0	13.3	0.2	2.0	2.6	0.1	15.4	0.7
Dobrich	24.6	30.7	10.9	0.6	0.5	0.0	3.5	6.6
Razgrad	17.1	5.4	1.8	0.4	1.9	0.0	24.2	0.4
Silistra	23.3	25.2	2.6	7.6	1.5	0.0	0.0	2.6
Turgovishte	19.1	32.5	0.9	1.5	0.5	0.0	0.2	3.0
Shumen	23.1	11.6	0.9	3.4	1.8	0.1	4.4	1.6
Burgas	21.7	10.6	0.4	3.3	0.6	32.7	0.3	3.0
Sliven	22.7	31.1	0.4	4.6	1.5	0.0	0.4	0.8
Yambol	27.0	24.5	2.6	0.8	1.6	0.0	14.0	1.5
Kurdzhali	18.2	43	6.7	2.0	0.7	0.0	0.0	0.2
Pazardzhik	15.3	17.6	5.5	8.5	10.4	0.1	7.6	8.9
Plovdiv	21.1	14.6	5.0	1.4	6.5	0.1	4.5	4.3
Smolyan	13.3	48.9	5.4	9.0	0.8	0.0	6.9	1.2
Stara Zagora	15.5	13.1	0.3	1.5	1.9	0.1	7.4	0.9
Haskovo	25.8	29.6	2.6	0.9	1.7	0.0	13.1	0.5
Blagoevgrad	14.6	44.8	8.5	3.2	3.0	0.0	2.8	2.5
Kyustendil	9.4	29.1	13.2	1.3	5.3	0.2	17.4	1.2
Pernik	7.7	8.5	0.1	0.5	1.9	0.0	4.2	3.6
Sofia cap.	13.1	13.5	3.3	1.2	9.9	0.0	5.3	3.5
Sofia	17.5	15.3	1.1	3.2	9.0	0.1	3.2	3.0

Source: National Statistical Institute/own elaboration.

economic recovery, not only in Bulgaria but also in the other CEEC, is closely related to the degree of successful structural adjustment of the industrial sector (Landesmann, 2000). The inadequate economic structure is among the main factors for the lack of adaptability of the Bulgarian economy and the significant GDP decline in the 1990s. It is evident that the highest rates of unemployment are observed in the regions where industrial production exhibited the highest decline. Industrial structure and development are, thus, significant factors accounting for the economic differences among the regions. The social dimension of these differences is well expressed through differences in the rates of unemployment.

er - allic ducts	Basic metals except casting of metals	Metal products, machinery and equipment; casting of metals	Electrical and optical equipment	Transport equipment	Manufacturing n.e.c.	Total	CRS Industries	CRS Industries (1990)
5	0.0	12.1	4.6	0.0	1.0	100.0	74	53
3	7.2	19.0	4.0	0.2	1.6	100.0	69	65
	7.3	20.3	4.9	0.7	2.9	100.0	78	72
	0.6	29.7	1.7	3.1	2.3	100.0	78	63
)	0.0	34.4	7.7	1.9	3.6	100.0	82	81
5	0.0	20.8	10.1	1.7	11.0	100.0	78	63
7	0.0	20.6	5.4	1.6	2.2	100.0	81	80
	2.9	11.4	6.2	7.7	5.5	100.0	64	58
	0.0	20.6	2.3	17.9	2.7	100.0	59	57
	0.0	11.1	4.5	1.8	3.7	100.0	83	72
3	0.1	9.5	3.8	5.0	4.5	100.0	53	58
	0.0	21.7	10.1	1.3	1.5	100.0	84	82
	1.5	24.0	9.6	2.9	2.7	100.0	82	71
	7.6	9.3	2.4	9.9	4.7	100.0	64	53
	4.2	6.8	5.1	5.1	3.7	100.0	48	53
	0.0	13.6	13.0	0.3	2.2	100.0	80	75
	2.0	17.2	2.2	0.1	3.0	100.0	78	74
	11.7	12.4	2.5	0.0	1.8	100.0	85	78
	2.5	7.7	9.0	0.0	4.1	100.0	65	61
	3.4	28.9	4.1	1.3	1.9	100.0	78	68
	0.0	4.9	5.6	0.2	2.8	100.0	85	75
	0.0	49.4	5.4	0.1	2.9	100.0	85	74
3	0.0	13.8	3.0	0.1	1.5	100.0	79	79
3	0.3	7.1	6.6	0.0	5.3	100.0	86	61
	0.5	12.6	5.0	0.3	2.1	100.0	72	62
	38.5	28.0	4.0	1.2	0.5	100.0	47	42
	18.3	12.5	10.0	2.2	3.8	100.0	54	52
	9.6	16.3	10.2	3.4	3.6	100.0	64	57

Regional-industrial activity in Bulgaria

The Bulgarian regions are mainly specialized in industrial activities associated with constant returns to scale (CRS) (Table 12.2).[8] With the exceptions of the regions of Varna, Razgrad, Burgas, Pernik and Sofia capital, in all NUTS 3 Bulgarian regions these activities account, in 2001, for more than 60 per cent of the total industrial employment. Comparing to 1990, the shares of these activities have increased in almost all regions. The absence of industries associated with increasing returns to scale (IRS) is a structural deficiency of the Bulgarian economy and no easy cure seems to exist.

Absolute regional specialization in Bulgaria

The level of absolute regional specialization in Bulgaria is estimated with the application of the Herfindahl Index of Specialization (HIS) (Tables 12.3 and 12.4). HIS takes the form:

$$\sum_{i}^{n}(a_i)^2$$

where a_i is the share of the ith industry in a given region, and takes values in the interval $\left[\frac{1}{n},1\right]$. The upper limit of the interval indicates complete regional specialization, while the lower level indicates no specialization at all.[9]

The levels of the HIS are very low – the average index (unweighted arithmetical average) rose from 0.104 in 1990 to 0.125 in 2001 – and almost equal for all Bulgarian NUTS 2 regions, as the maximum to minimum ratio is 1.1. With the exception of the South-West region, a process of moderate increase of the values of HIS is observed in all regions. The figure of the South-West region is the lowest in the country (only 0.104 in 2001) and the only one that presented a decreasing trend during the studied period. The levels of the HIS are moderate concerning the Bulgarian NUTS 3 regions – the average index was 0.165 in 2001. During the studied period, an increase in the levels of the HIS was recorded, with the exception of three regions (Pazardzhik, Sofia capital, Sofia region) where a decrease was observed. The indicators of variation verify this trend.

A strong relation between the level of absolute specialization and the levels of per capita GDP, share of industry in GVA, population density, FDI per capita and other macroeconomic indicators cannot be settled since the estimated coefficients of correlation were found to be insignificant. The only case where it is possible to speak about some kind of relation is between the level of absolute specialization and the number of firms with foreign participation. This relation is strong and significant in border regions. The lack of obvious relation between the level of absolute specialization and the main macroeconomic indicators suggests that the process of specialization cannot be considered synonymous to the level of regional economic performance. However, the differences observed in the level of the HIS have their economic explanation; lagging-behind regions present relatively higher levels of specialization, whereas this is not the situation for the country's urban regions (i.e. Sofia, Varna, Ruse, Burgas).

Relative regional specialization in Bulgaria

The level of relative regional specialization in Bulgaria is estimated with the application of the Krugman Index of Specialization (KIS) (Tables 12.5 and 12.6). KIS takes the form:

$$\sum_{i}^{n}|a_i - b_i|$$

Table 12.3 Absolute regional specialization at the NUTS 2 spatial level in Bulgaria, Herfindahl index, 1990 and 2001

NUTS 2	1990	2001
North-West	0.097 (6)	0.125 (6)
North Central	0.108 (2)	0.131 (2)
North-East	0.099 (5)	0.121 (5)
South-East	0.106 (4)	0.127 (3)
South Central	0.109 (1)	0.141 (1)
South-West	0.107 (3)	0.104 (4)
Average	0.104	0.125
Coefficient of variation (%)	4.5	9.0
Minimum	0.097	0.104
Maximum	0.109	0.141
Maximum/minimum	1.1	1.4

Sources: National Statistical Institute/own elaboration.

where a_i is the share of the ith industry in a given region and b_i is the share of the ith industry in a reference economy, and takes values in the interval [0, 2]. The lower limit of the interval indicates regions with completely identical structure with the reference economy, while the upper limit of the interval indicates regions with a completely different industrial structure between the regional and the reference economy.[10]

Two types of regions are observed; the first type consists of the North-West, the North-Central and the South-Central regions that have low levels of relative specialization (i.e. these regions have industrial structure similar to the country's average) and the second type consists of the North-East, the South-East and the South-West regions that are relatively more specialized. The regions that belong to the second type are the ones with the lower industrial GVA and industrial employment. This divide exists throughout the studied period and it becomes more significant over time.

The comparison between the rankings of the rate of changes in terms of absolute and relative specialization at the NUTS 2 spatial level is negative as the high and negative (−0.90) Spearman's coefficient of correlation, for 2001, indicates. However, this is not the situation at the NUTS 3 spatial level. The respective coefficient of correlation is positive, although not high (0.30), showing that the increase in the ranking in terms of absolute specialization is accompanied by an increase in the ranking in terms of relative specialization. The explanation for these differences is based on the fact that at the NUTS 2 spatial level the regions that have higher levels of relative specialization are those that have levels of absolute specialization higher than the country's, whereas at the NUTS 3 spatial level the regions that have higher levels of relative specialization are those that have levels of absolute specialization lower than the country's. This indicates that the NUTS 2 regions with better economic indicators than the county's average have higher levels of relative specialization since they managed to retain their specializations (or to create

Table 12.4 Absolute regional specialization at the NUTS 3 spatial level in Bulgaria, Herfindahl index, 1990 and 2001

NUTS 3	1990	2001
Vidin	0.180 (2)	0.213 (4)
Vratsa	0.104 (27)	0.128 (22)
Montana	0.111 (22)	0.139 (20)
Veliko Tarnovo	0.126 (11)	0.193 (7)
Gabrovo	0.155 (4)	0.171 (11)
Lovech	0.115 (18)	0.122 (24)
Pleven	0.135 (8)	0.164 (15)
Ruse	0.102 (28)	0.105 (25)
Varna	0.113 (20)	0.140 (19)
Dobrich	0.113 (20)	0.172 (10)
Razgrad	0.125 (13)	0.173 (9)
Silistra	0.122 (15)	0.155 (18)
Turgovishte	0.114 (19)	0.205 (6)
Shumen	0.129 (9)	0.134 (21)
Burgas	0.144 (7)	0.179 (8)
Sliven	0.155 (4)	0.170 (13)
Yambol	0.128 (10)	0.157 (16)
Kurdzhali	0.126 (11)	0.242 (3)
Pazardzhik	0.108 (24)	0.095 (28)
Plovdiv	0.117 (17)	0.156 (17)
Smolyan	0.125 (13)	0.171 (11)
Stara Zagora	0.185 (1)	0.286 (1)
Haskovo	0.120 (16)	0.165 (14)
Blagoevgrad	0.148 (6)	0.207 (5)
Kyustendil	0.109 (23)	0.128 (22)
Pernik	0.179 (3)	0.244 (2)
Sofia cap.	0.108 (25)	0.105 (25)
Sofia	0.106 (26)	0.104 (27)
Average	0.129	0.165
Coefficient of variation (%)	17.9	27.3
Minimum	0.102	0.095
Maximum	0.185	0.286
Maximum/minimum	1.8	3.0

Sources: National Statistical Institute/own elaboration.

new ones) in absolute terms. This was, obviously, not the situation concerning the NUTS 3 regions that have higher levels of relative specialization.

As in the case with the absolute specialization, an attempt was made to specify relations, at the NUTS 3 spatial level, between relative regional specialization and per capita GDP, share of industry in GVA, population density, FDI per capita and other macroeconomic indicators. Only FDI per capita exhibits a moderate negative relation (the correlation of coefficient is −0.40). There are two types of regions that present high levels of KIS; the first type includes regions (i.e. Burgas and Stara Zagora) that have strong industrial activity as a result of the development of some main branches and the second type includes

Table 12.5 Relative regional specialization at the NUTS 2 spatial level in Bulgaria, Krugman index, 1990 and 2001

NUTS 2	1990	2001
North-West	0.275 (4)	0.279 (5)
North Central	0.242 (6)	0.201 (6)
North-East	0.417 (3)	0.406 (3)
South-East	0.451 (1)	0.600 (1)
South Central	0.243 (5)	0.291 (4)
South-West	0.424 (2)	0.473 (2)
Average	0.342	0.375
Coefficient of variation (%)	26.3	35.7
Minimum	0.242	0.201
Maximum	0.451	0.600
Maximum/minimum	1.9	3.0

Sources: National Statistical Institute/own elaboration.

regions (i.e. Vildin, Razgrad, Shumen, Smolyan and Kardzhali) that have weak industrial activity with only specific industrial branches to present some kind of development. In these regions, the level of FDI per capita is low (since it goes only to specific branches, when FDI are present in a region) and constitutes a negative relation with the level of the relative specialization.

The discriminant analysis (Huberthy, 1994) is showing that there are some regional characteristics (the share of the branches with constant returns to scale, the share of population that did not complete the primary education and the share of the persons employed in the agriculture) that would favour an increase in the (future) levels of specialization. Obviously, existing levels of regional specialization at early stages of economic development do not provide evidence for the formation of regional clusters. However, the tendencies in the Bulgarian regions, during the last years, provide a basis for the hypothesis that the process of specialization will be intensified in the future, allowing for the formation of regional clusters.

Absolute manufacturing concentration in Bulgaria

The level of absolute manufacturing concentration in Bulgaria is estimated with the application of the Herfindahl Index of Concentration (HIC) (Tables 12.7 and 12.8). HIC takes the form:

$$\sum_{i}^{n} (a_i)^2$$

where a_i is the share of the ith region in a given industry. The index takes values in the interval $\left[\frac{1}{n}, 1\right]$, where the upper limit of the interval indicates complete manufacturing concentration and the lower limit indicates no concentration at all.[11]

The level of absolute manufacturing concentration, at the NUTS 2 spatial level,

Table 12.6 Relative regional specialization at the NUTS 3 spatial level in Bulgaria, Krugman index, 1990 and 2001

NUTS 3	1990	2001
Vidin	0.810 (1)	0.807 (4)
Vratsa	0.430 (19)	0.496 (21)
Montana	0.329 (26)	0.297 (28)
Veliko Tarnovo	0.417 (20)	0.536 (18)
Gabrovo	0.625 (7)	0.557 (14)
Lovech	0.433 (18)	0.501 (20)
Pleven	0.543 (13)	0.432 (23)
Ruse	0.236 (28)	0.382 (26)
Varna	0.522 (14)	0.597 (13)
Dobrich	0.473 (16)	0.639 (11)
Razgrad	0.708 (3)	0.862 (2)
Silistra	0.411 (21)	0.455 (23)
Turgovishte	0.373 (24)	0.537 (17)
Shumen	0.686 (4)	0.645 (10)
Burgas	0.758 (2)	0.799 (5)
Sliven	0.563 (10)	0.811 (3)
Yambol	0.498 (15)	0.468 (22)
Kurdzhali	0.647 (6)	0.753 (7)
Pazardzhik	0.464 (17)	0.531 (19)
Plovdiv	0.287 (27)	0.423 (25)
Smolyan	0.552 (12)	0.770 (6)
Stara Zagora	0.555 (11)	0.709 (9)
Haskovo	0.566 (9)	0.557 (14)
Blagoevgrad	0.603 (8)	0.714 (8)
Kyustendil	0.398 (23)	0.634 (12)
Pernik	0.674 (5)	0.881 (1)
Sofia cap.	0.399 (22)	0.551 (16)
Sofia	0.348 (25)	0.379 (27)
Average	0.511	0.597
Coefficient of variation (%)		26.1
Minimum		0.297
Maximum	0.810	0.881
Maximum/minimum	3.4	3.0

Sources: National Statistical Institute/own elaboration.

was low during the studied period. The average level increased slightly from 0.263 in 1990 to 0.286 in 2001, while the maximum to minimum ratio remained almost unchanged. Analogous is the situation at the NUTS 3 level of spatial aggregation. The average level increased from 0.117 in 1990 to 0.134 in 2001. A slight increase of concentration is observed in the majority of manufacturing branches.

Relative manufacturing concentration in Bulgaria

The level of relative manufacturing concentration in Bulgaria is estimated with the application of the Krugman Index of Concentration (KIC) (Tables 12.9 and 12.10). KIC takes the form:

$$\sum_{i}^{n} |a_i - b_i|$$

where a_i is the share of the ith region in a given manufacturing branch and b_i is the share of the ith region in the sector of manufacturing. The index takes values in the interval [0, 2], where the lower and the upper limits indicate respectively completely identical to completely different industrial structure between the manufacturing branch and the manufacturing sector.[12]

The average level of the KIC, at the NUTS 2 spatial level, was 0.395 in 1990 and 0.422 in 2001. It is evident that the most concentrated branches, relative to the manufacturing sector, were the same (paper and paper products, refined petroleum, basic metals and transport equipment) at the beginning and at the end of the studied period. During this period the recorded changes (increases) were rather moderate for the majority of manufacturing sectors. Analogous is the situation at the NUTS 3 spatial level. Though the values of the KIC are higher, the tendencies are the same (the average value of the KIC was 0.643 in 1990 and 0.719 in 2001). There are some branches (wearing apparel, leather and wood) that present increasing relative concentration. The reason for this trend is the

Table 12.7 Absolute manufacturing concentration at the NUTS 2 spatial level in Bulgaria, Herfindahl index, 1990 and 2001

Branches	1990	2001
Foods, beverages and tobacco	0.185 (15)	0.201 (14)
Textiles	0.207 (8)	0.202 (13)
Wearing apparel	0.200 (11)	0.217 (10)
Leather, leather and fur clothes, footwear, etc.	0.239 (6)	0.280 (5)
Wood and products of wood, cork, plaiting mat.	0.202 (10)	0.207 (12)
Pulp, paper, paper products, publishing & printing	0.308 (3)	0.336 (3)
Coke, refined petroleum products and nuclear fuel	0.667 (1)	0.685 (1)
Chemicals, chemical prod. & man-made fibres	0.206 (9)	0.219 (8)
Rubber and plastic products	0.190 (14)	0.217 (11)
Other non-metallic products	0.193 (13)	0.200 (15)
Basic metals except casting of metals	0.425 (2)	0.514 (2)
Metal prod., mach. and equipm.; casting of met.	0.219 (7)	0.238 (6)
Electrical and optical equipment	0.249 (5)	0.237 (7)
Transport equipment	0.258 (4)	0.325 (4)
Manufacturing n.e.c.	0.198 (12)	0.218 (9)
Average	0.263	0.286
Coefficient of Variation (%)	47.0	46.6
Minimum	0.185	0.200
Maximum	0.667	0.685
Maximum / Minimum	3.6	3.4

Sources: National Statistical Institute/own elaboration.

Table 12.8 Absolute manufacturing concentration at the NUTS 3 spatial level in Bulgaria, Herfindahl index, 1990 and 2001

Branches	1990	2001
Foods, beverages and tobacco	0.051 (13)	0.056 (15)
Textiles	0.055 (11)	0.059 (14)
Wearing apparel	0.050 (15)	0.060 (12)
Leather, leather and fur clothes, footwear, etc.	0.079 (6)	0.093 (5)
Wood and products of wood, cork, plaiting mat.	0.051 (13)	0.065 (10)
Pulp, paper, paper products, publishing & printing	0.136 (3)	0.152 (4)
Coke, refined petroleum products and nuclear fuel	0.663 (1)	0.674 (1)
Chemicals, chemical prod. & man-made fibres	0.066 (8)	0.073 (9)
Rubber and plastic products	0.085 (4)	0.083 (6)
Other non-metallic products	0.056 (10)	0.060 (12)
Basic metals except casting of metals	0.187 (2)	0.253 (2)
Metal prod., mach. and equipm.; casting of met.	0.066 (8)	0.076 (8)
Electrical and optical equipment	0.071 (7)	0.079 (7)
Transport equipment	0.080 (5)	0.168 (3)
Manufacturing n.e.c.	0.053 (12)	0.065 (10)
Average	0.117	0.134
Coefficient of variation (%)	129.0	114.2
Minimum	0.050	0.056
Maximum	0.663	0.674
Maximum/minimum	13.4	11.9

Sources: National Statistical Institute/own elaboration.

concentration of these branches in the country's border regions with Greece. There are some other branches, however, (transport equipment, basic metals and manufacturing n.e.c.)[13] that present increasing relative concentration as a result of the decline of their activities in many regions.

Conclusions

The restructuring of the Bulgarian economy is accompanied by an increase in the level of regional inequalities. The less urbanized regions, and the peripheral regions of the country, are among the most adversely affected ones. In contrast, the more urbanized regions, which had a relatively good economic performance in the past, are the ones that will probably fare better in the future. These regions have the ability to attract FDI, exploiting the benefits of the existence of infrastructure and communications networks. Low labour cost, by itself, is proved to be insufficient. The process of regional divergence is expected to create intense differences concerning the economic development of the Bulgarian regions; these differences are already higher compared to the respective EU standards.

The analysis outlined as a main factor for the creation of regional inequalities the industrial structure of the Bulgarian regions. The regions that have higher levels of per capita GDP are the ones that have lower levels of specialization.

Table 12.9 Relative manufacturing concentration at the NUTS 2 spatial level in Bulgaria, Krugman index, 1990 and 2001

Branches	1990	2001
Foods, beverages and tobacco	0.201 (12)	0.165 (14)
Textiles	0.276 (8)	0.261 (8)
Wearing apparel	0.065 (15)	0.094 (15)
Leather, leather and fur clothes, footwear, etc.	0.209 (11)	0.324 (7)
Wood and products of wood, cork, plaiting mat.	0.131 (13)	0.166 (12)
Pulp, paper, paper products, publishing & printing	0.516 (4)	0.525 (4)
Coke, refined petroleum products and nuclear fuel	1.447 (1)	1.486 (1)
Chemicals, chemical prod. & man-made fibres	0.221 (10)	0.229 (10)
Rubber and plastic products	0.365 (6)	0.166 (12)
Other non-metallic products	0.378 (5)	0.420 (5)
Basic metals except casting of metals	0.791 (2)	0.933 (2)
Metal prod., mach. and equipm.; casting of met.	0.266 (9)	0.339 (6)
Electrical and optical equipment	0.293 (7)	0.247 (9)
Transport equipment	0.635 (3)	0.775 (3)
Manufacturing n.e.c.	0.130 (14)	0.206 (11)
Average	0.395	0.422
Coefficient of variation (%)	86.0	86.2
Minimum	0.065	0.094
Maximum	1.447	1.486
Maximum/minimum	22.1	15.9

Sources: National Statistical Institute/own elaboration.

Table 12.10 Relative manufacturing concentration at the NUTS 3 spatial level in Bulgaria, Krugman index, 1990 and 2001

Branches	1990	2001
Foods, beverages and tobacco	0.340 (14)	0.298 (15)
Textiles	0.543 (9)	0.618 (8)
Wearing apparel	0.423 (11)	0.596 (10)
Leather, leather and fur clothes, footwear, etc.	0.586 (8)	0.720 (5)
Wood and products of wood, cork, plaiting mat.	0.462 (10)	0.678 (7)
Pulp, paper, paper products, publishing & printing	0.709 (4)	0.747 (4)
Coke, refined petroleum products and nuclear fuel	1.741 (1)	1.751 (1)
Chemicals, chemical prod. & man-made fibres	0.702 (5)	0.689 (6)
Rubber and plastic products	0.601 (7)	0.559 (11)
Other non-metallic products	0.608 (6)	0.610 (9)
Basic metals except casting of metals	1.071 (2)	1.173 (2)
Metal prod., mach. and equipm.; casting of met.	0.399 (12)	0.555 (12)
Electrical and optical equipment	0.372 (13)	0.444 (13)
Transport equipment	0.775 (3)	0.965 (3)
Manufacturing n.e.c.	0.311 (15)	0.386 (14)
Average	0.643	0.719

continued

Table 12.10 continued

Branches	1990	2001
Coefficient of variation (%)	54.6	48.0
Minimum	0.311	0.298
Maximum	1.741	1.751
Maximum/minimum	5.6	5.9

Sources: National Statistical Institute/own elaboration.

The Bulgarian regions being exposed to international competition have been experiencing great difficulties in comparing with their European counterparts. These difficulties restrain the industrial structure of the Bulgarian regions, forcing them to be specialized mainly in labour-intensive activities. Development related to competitiveness based on innovation which is improving the quality of the products is still not observed, although the capital region of Sofia is probably the exception to this rule. The less advanced regions are expected to develop mainly labour-intensive activities, increasing in this way their levels of absolute and relative specialization. Despite its drawbacks, this process of specialization may be considered as the most feasible economic growth path for these regions at this stage of development.

Notes

1 Bulgaria joined the EU on 1 January 2007.
2 NUTS: Nomenclature of Territorial Units for Statistics.
3 These are the EU new member states (Estonia, Latvia, Lithuania, Poland, Hungary, Czech Republic, Slovakia, Slovenia, Bulgaria and Romania).
4 There are certain reasons to exclude the South-East region from the estimation of this relation; the presence of big oil processing corporations is the main source of net revenues in this under populated region.
5 A higher population density at the regional level implies that there is a higher concentration of activities. This concentration favors horizontal and vertical interaction among firms, or favours the creation of new services. In either case, it increases productivity (Petrakos *et al.*, 2004).
6 See Petrakos *et al.* (2004) for details.
7 Kardzali is a special case due to the presence of a Turkish minority and Sofia city is the country's metropolitan centre. In both regions, the relation between the shares of employment in industry and in agriculture to the level of unemployment is weak.
8 CRS are the sectors of food, textile, leather, wood, paper, rubber and plastic, non-metallic products (part), metal products (part) and manufacturing n.e.c. See Pratten (1988) for details.
9 See Bode *et al.* (2003) for further details.
10 See Bode *et al.* (2003) for further details.
11 See Bode *et al.* (2003) for further details.
12 See Bode *et al.* (2003) for further details.
13 This branch included (among others) part of the military production of the former Eastern bloc; the military production actually collapsed in Bulgaria after the collapse of the bloc.

References

Bode, E., Krieger-Boden, C. and Soltwedel, R. (2003), *Comprehensive Theoretical and Methodological Framework*, Contribution to EURECO Project, http://www.zei.de/eurec/eureco.htm.

Huberty, C. (1994), *Applied Discriminant Analysis*, New York: John Wiley & Sons.

Landesmann, M. (2000), Structural Change in the Transition Economies, 1989–1999, *United Nations Economic Survey of Europe*, n. 2/3, pp. 95–123.

Petrakos, G. (2001), Patterns of Regional Inequality in Transition Countries, *European Planning Studies*, n. 9, vol. 3, pp. 359–383.

Petrakos, G., Psycharis, Y. and Kallioras, D. (2004), Regional Inequalities in the EU New Member-States: Evolution and Challenges, in: Bradley, J., Petrakos, G. and Traistaru, I. (eds), *The Economics and Policy of Cohesion in an Enlarged European Union*, New York: Springer, pp. 45–64.

Pratten, C. (1988), A Survey of Economies of Scale, in Commission of the European Communities: *Research of the "Cost of Non-Europe"*, Studies on the Economics of Integration, vol. 2.

Totev, S. (2004), Regional Economic Differences in Bulgaria and the Other Countries Applying for Membership of the EU, *Economic Thought* n. 2, (in Bulgarian).

13 The location of multinational enterprises in Central and Eastern European countries

Laura Resmini

Introduction

After the fall of the Berlin Wall and the start of the transition from a centrally planned to a market economy, foreign direct investment (FDI) inflows to Central and Eastern European countries (CEECs) increased substantially throughout the 1990s. This phenomenon has been seen as a beneficial one, since FDI had brought into the countries the financial resources, the new technologies and the know-how necessary for transforming CEECs in successful open market economies. According to the theory, the beneficial impact of FDI on economic performance is more likely when the social capabilities (i.e. education level, technological capabilities, good legal systems, etc.) and absorptive capacity (i.e. capital intensity, skilled labour force, R&D activity) of the host economy exceed a certain threshold (Kokko, 1992). With its well-educated labour force and existing industrial infrastructure, CEECs are believed to have a very good absorptive capacity. Therefore, FDI has been considered as a fundamental ingredient for economic growth and prosperity (Sinn and Weichenrieder, 1997).

Given the importance and the novelty of the phenomenon, a huge literature on FDI in Central and Eastern Europe has been developing since the beginning of the transition phase. It focuses mainly on the determinants and consequences of FDI at aggregate country or industry level,[1] while little or no attention has been devoted to the spatial aspects of the activity of foreign firms. This chapter tries to fill this gap, by focusing on the location patterns of foreign firms in some Central and Eastern European regions.

Several reasons explain the importance of this issue. In particular, FDI inflows into transition countries show a lot of variation not only across but also within countries, due to the diversity of economic development levels recorded in the area. This implies that while FDI is able to exert a positive effect at national level, this effect may be different at regional level, thus triggering regional economic inequalities. Studying where multinational enterprises (MNEs) locate should then help understanding how the benefits generated by FDI spread across regions in Central and Eastern Europe. Besides the obvious implications for regional policies, a regional approach to foreign firms' location patterns allows to point out several interesting features concerning the determinants of FDI

(Pusterla and Resmini, 2007). A better comprehension of the mechanism behind the location decision of multinationals may thus help policy-makers improve the attractiveness of laggard regions.

Existing evidence on MNEs' location in Central and Eastern Europe at sub-national level is quite scarce, often limited to country studies and provides contrasting patterns. For example, Cieslik (2005) shows that foreign capital in Poland is highly concentrated in a few regions. This uneven distribution has reinforced the existing West-East divide inherited from the past. Boudier-Bensebaa (2005) shows for Hungary a skewed distribution of FDI towards the capital city and the Western and Central Trasdanubia regions, i.e. the region bordering with Austria. On a comparative basis, Altomonte and Resmini (1999) investigate the sectoral and geographical patterns of location of FDI in the Czech Republic, Hungary, Poland and Romania during the 1990s. They demonstrate first of all that multinational enterprises were initially concentrated around the capital cities and that they have tended to be more dispersed over time. Second, these patterns of geographical location vary across countries and sectors, with the manufacturing sectors less concentrated than the service ones.

The primary aim of this chapter is not to test a particular theory but, more simply, to examine facts and relationships concerning FDI and regional development in five Central and Eastern European countries, namely Bulgaria, the Czech Republic, Hungary, Poland and Romania. These countries capture most of the variety that characterizes Central and Eastern Europe in terms of size of the countries, degree of economic development, progress made in the transition phase and the integration process with the EU. How much do regions vary in terms of absolute and relative concentration of FDI? How important is FDI for the growth prospects of the hosting regions? Does the distribution of foreign firms across manufacturing sectors in a region matter? How does the sectoral composition of FDI affect regions' performance? Those and other questions are examined by employing basic statistical tests and indicators. In-depth analyses of particular hypotheses are the subject of other papers.[2]

The core dataset is an update version of the PECODB database, a firm level dataset on foreign firms in CEECs. In its present version, it includes information on about 4,600 manufacturing foreign investments which have been undertaken in the above mentioned Central and Eastern European countries during the 1990s.[3] For each investment transaction the database lists four digit Nace Rev. 1 industry codes, name and country of origin of the foreign owner(s), location by cities and regions, and the date of incorporation. The primary geographic units used in the analysis are regions at NUTS 2 level, while at sectoral level the analysis concentrates on the manufacturing sector.[4] The focus on the manufacturing branches is not casual, but it responds to precise research objectives. First of all, the manufacturing sector has, as a whole, collected about 50 per cent of total foreign investment in the CEECs (Lovino, 2002). Second, in this sector of economic activity location decisions are mainly affected by the so called "second nature characteristics", i.e. those attributes which are more inherent to the functioning of economic interactions – on both the demand and supply side – and that, in theory, are able to generate different development patterns even across initially similar regions (Ottaviano and Pinelli, 2005).[5]

The next section of this chapter focuses on foreign firm patterns of location. It compares the geographical and sectoral distribution of foreign firms at the beginning and at the end of the transition phase, highlighting the existence of clusters among foreign firms at both regional and sectoral level. It goes on to explore the possible impact of FDI on the economic performance of the hosting regions, showing that there is a divide between the regions hosting the capital cities and the other regions in terms of the role played by FDI and its sectoral composition in affecting local economic performance. A final section provides a summary and conclusions.

The location patterns of MNEs

Location of MNEs in CEECs

Table 13.1 shows some measures of FDI penetration in the CEECs in 2001. Foreign firms have been defined as firms with a foreign share in the total capital of at least 10 per cent. According to the dataset, 34.5 per cent of multinationals' location took place in Romania, followed by Poland (26.8), Hungary (22.5), and Czech Republic (13.4), while Bulgaria lags behind with a modest 2.8 per cent. Therefore, the results seem to confirm the leading role played by Hungary, Poland and the Czech Republic as main recipients of FDI in CEECs. Altogether, these three countries account for about 62 per cent of foreign affiliates established in Central and Eastern Europe over the 1990s.

Countries with large economies, however, may have more firms in general, and foreign firms in particular, than countries with smaller economies. Therefore, it is instructive to calculate size-adjusted measures of FDI penetration. The last part of Table 13.1 shows each country's number of foreign firms per million of inhabitants. The leading countries according to this measure are now Hungary and the Czech Republic, followed by Romania and Poland, while Bulgaria is confirmed as the less attractive country.

At sectoral level, Table 13.1 shows that the sectors that have attracted the largest number of foreign affiliates are on average those with a low and a medium-low technological intensity, which collect all together about 72 per cent of the total. The remaining 28 per cent encompasses medium-high and high-tech manufacturing sectors. Within the first group of sectors, food, beverages and tobacco (17.2 per cent), textiles and clothing (11.4 per cent) and wood, wood products, pulp and paper products (9 per cent) emerge as leading sectors. Within the second group of manufacturing sectors, basic metal and fabricated metal products (9.5 per cent), rubber and plastic (7 per cent), chemicals (6.5 per cent) and machinery and equipments (6.7 per cent) collect the largest number of foreign affiliates.

These shares vary substantially across countries. The percentage of foreign affiliates in low-tech sectors ranges from 68.3 per cent of Romania to 30 per cent of the Czech Republic, which however accounts for the largest percentages of

Table 13.1 Distribution of MNEs by manufacturing sector and country, 2001

Nace Rev. 1 industry code	Number of multinationals						Percentages						Per 1,000,000 inhabitants					
	BG	CZ	HU	PL	RO	Total	BG	CZ	HU	PL	RO	Total	BG	CZ	HU	PL	RO	Total
High-tech																		
24	14	47	70	100	71	302	10.7	7.6	6.7	8.1	4.5	6.5	1.77	4.26	6.86	2.58	3.17	3.34
30		4	8	5	21	38	0.0	0.6	0.8	0.4	1.3	0.8	0.00	0.36	0.78	0.13	0.94	0.42
32	1	33	50	33	23	140	0.8	5.3	4.8	2.7	1.4	3.0	0.13	2.99	4.90	0.85	1.03	1.55
33		16	21	14	12	63	0.0	2.6	2.0	1.1	0.8	1.4	0.00	1.45	2.06	0.36	0.54	0.70
	15	**100**	**149**	**152**	**127**	**543**	**11.5**	**16.2**	**14.4**	**12.3**	**8.0**	**11.7**	**1.90**	**9.07**	**14.61**	**3.92**	**5.67**	**6.01**
Medium–high																		
29	8	61	108	77	57	311	6.1	9.9	10.4	6.2	3.6	6.7	1.01	5.53	10.59	1.98	2.54	3.44
31	15	41	62	65	48	231	11.5	6.6	6.0	5.2	3.0	5.0	1.90	3.72	6.08	1.68	2.14	2.56
34	2	52	52	73	2	181	1.5	8.4	5.0	5.9	0.1	3.9	0.25	4.72	5.10	1.88	0.09	2.00
35		9	7	9	1	26	0.0	1.5	0.7	0.7	0.1	0.6	0.00	0.82	0.69	0.23	0.04	0.29
	25	**163**	**229**	**224**	**108**	**749**	**19.1**	**26.3**	**22.1**	**18.1**	**6.8**	**16.2**	**3.17**	**14.78**	**22.45**	**5.77**	**4.82**	**8.29**
Medium–low																		
23		5		1	5	11	0.0	0.8	0.8	0.1	0.3	0.2	0.00	0.45	0.00	0.03	0.22	0.12
25	2	39	93	111	78	323	1.5	6.3	9.0	9.0	4.9	7.0	0.25	3.54	9.12	2.86	3.48	3.58
26	9	73	47	108	55	292	6.9	11.8	4.5	8.7	3.4	6.3	1.14	6.62	4.61	2.78	2.45	3.23
27	4	17	26	15	32	94	3.1	2.7	2.5	1.2	2.0	2.0	0.51	1.54	2.55	0.39	1.43	1.04
28	3	36	129	79	101	348	2.3	5.8	12.4	6.4	6.3	7.5	0.38	3.26	12.65	2.04	4.51	3.85
	18	**170**	**295**	**314**	**271**	**1068**	**13.7**	**27.5**	**28.4**	**25.3**	**17.0**	**23.1**	**2.28**	**15.42**	**28.92**	**8.09**	**12.09**	**11.82**

Table 13.1 continued

Nace Rev. 1 industry code	Number of multinationals						Percentages						per 1,000,000 inhabitants					
	BG	CZ	HU	PL	RO	Total	BG	CZ	HU	PL	RO	Total	BG	CZ	HU	PL	RO	Total
Low-tech																		
15	21	73	154	252	267	767	16.0	11.8	14.8	20.3	16.7	16.6	2.66	6.62	15.10	6.50	11.92	8.49
16		3	7	12	7	29	0.0	0.5	0.7	1.0	0.4	0.6	0.00	0.27	0.69	0.31	0.31	0.32
17	9	25	37	30	125	226	6.9	4.0	3.6	2.4	7.8	4.9	1.14	2.27	3.63	0.77	5.58	2.50
18	14	4	22	57	204	301	10.7	0.6	2.1	4.6	12.8	6.5	1.77	0.36	2.16	1.47	9.10	3.33
19	5	4	15	8	97	129	3.8	0.6	1.4	0.6	6.1	2.8	0.63	0.36	1.47	0.21	4.33	1.43
20	8	11	27	40	193	279	6.1	1.8	2.6	3.2	12.1	6.0	1.01	1.00	2.65	1.03	8.61	3.09
21	6	24	29	44	36	139	4.6	3.9	2.8	3.6	2.3	3.0	0.76	2.18	2.84	1.13	1.61	1.54
22	7	27	42	50	66	192	5.3	4.4	4.0	4.0	4.1	4.2	0.89	2.45	4.12	1.29	2.95	2.13
36	3	15	32	56	94	200	2.3	2.4	3.1	4.5	5.9	4.3	0.38	1.36	3.14	1.44	4.19	2.21
	73	186	365	549	1089	2262	55.7	30.0	35.2	44.3	68.3	48.9	9.25	16.87	35.78	14.15	48.60	25.04
total	131	619	1038	1239	1595	4622	2.8	13.4	22.5	26.8	34.5	100.0	16.60	56.13	101.76	31.94	71.18	51.17

Notes

15 = food and beverages; 16 = tobacco; 17 = textiles; 18 = clothing; 19 = leather products; 20 = wood and wood products; 21 = paper and paper products; 22 = publishing and printing; 23 = coke and refined petroleum products; 24 = chemicals; 25 = plastic and rubber products; 26 = non-metal mineral products; 27 = basic metal; 28 = fabricated metal products; 29 = machinery and equipments; 30 = office machinery and computers; 31 = electrical machinery and apparatus; 32 = radio, television and communication equipments; 33 = medical, precision and optical instruments; 34 = motor vehicles; 35 = other transport equipment; 36 = furniture, manufacturing n.e.c.

foreign firms in both high and medium-high tech sectors. Hungary accounts for the largest percentages of MNEs in the medium-low tech sectors. However, when one considers size-adjusted figures, Hungary is the undisputed leader in all groups of sectors, with the exception of low-tech sectors where Romania accounts for the largest number of foreign affiliates per million of inhabitants.

Overall, these results indicate that during the 1990s Central and Eastern Europe has been particularly attractive for foreign firms operating in the less technologically advanced manufacturing sectors. Moreover, a sectoral divide seems to emerge, with high-tech foreign firms located in the more advanced countries and low-tech foreign affiliates mainly located in the laggard countries.

Table 13.2 shows the number of MNEs by NUTS 2 regions and macro-sectors at the beginning and the end of the 1990s. Again, the cumulated number of foreign firms has been size-adjusted using population.

Generally speaking, the figures confirm the leading role that Hungary, Poland and the Czech Republic have been played in attracting FDI since the beginning of the transition phase. However, while Hungary and the Czech Republic have accumulated an impressive number of manufacturing foreign firms within their national boundaries, Poland does not seem to have benefited from this initial advantage. At the end of 2001, in fact, the spatial distribution of FDI was more similar to the Romanian one rather than to that of the other two leading countries. Romania's catching up process is particularly impressive for low-tech foreign firms, though the Timis region (RO05) shown in 2001 has a higher number of foreign firms per inhabitants than Warsaw's region (Mazowieckie, PL07). Bulgaria is still lagging behind.

On the other hand, Table 13.2 indicates that at the end of the 1990s, foreign firms were less geographically concentrated than they were at the beginning of the transition phase. A few regions, in fact, did not host any foreign firms in 2001. The dispersion of MNEs across regions is however less pronounced in high-tech than in low-tech manufacturing sectors. Despite that, some regions or groups of regions seem to be characterized by a strong agglomeration of foreign firms. These privileged territorial units are:

- the capital districts or the regions hosting the capital cities.[6] This preference is however more apparent for high-tech rather than low-tech foreign firms, with the exception of the Sofia region (BG04);
- the three North Western regions lying between Budapest and the Austrian border in Hungary (HU01–HU03) as well as the three North Western Romanian regions close to the Hungarian border (RO05–RO07);
- regions hosting important industrial poles, as Poznan (Wielkopolskie, PL15) and Wroclaw (Dolnoslaskie, PL01) in Poland, Varna (Severoiztochen, BG03) in Bulgaria and Timis (Vest, RO05) in Romania.

Finally, it is worth noticing that, in Czech Republic the spatial distribution of foreign firms seem to be less concentrated than in the other countries of the sample. This is true for all manufacturing macro-sectors.

In Poland and Bulgaria the regions bordering with the former EU-15 countries (PL04 and PL16, and BG05, respectively) do not seem to be locations particularly attractive for foreign firms. If some clustering does occur, it involves mainly medium-low and low-tech foreign firms.

It is instead quite clear that the most penalized regions in terms of FDI are those located along the Eastern border. This phenomenon is relatively more apparent for Poland (see regions PL03, PL09 and PL10), mainly at the beginning of the transition period, and Romania (see regions RO01 and RO02), not considering low-tech foreign affiliates, which seem to be more dispersed than foreign affiliates producing in more technological intensive sectors.

Multinational agglomeration patterns

In order to better emphasize possible patterns of agglomeration among MNEs, the geographical (size-adjusted) distribution of foreign firms across regions can be compared with the sample average. Table 13.2 the results obtained for the four groups of sectors in 1992 and 2001.

What emerges is that FDI has largely flowed into just a few regions, with differences across sectors limited to countries rather than regions. In particular:

*   The preferred locations for high-tech foreign firms are, besides the capital districts, a few regions belonging to the Czech Republic and Hungary, with the exception of Timis region (RO05) in Romania.
*   Medium-high tech foreign firms concentrate the most in Hungary and the Czech Republic. Outside these two countries, the concentration of this kind of foreign firms is above the sample average only in the Timis region (Romania) and Dolnoslaskie, Poland (PL01).
*   Medium-low tech foreign firms follow more or less the same patterns of location as medium-high tech foreign firms, with a few differences, concerning Mazowieckie (PL07) in Poland and Centru (RO07) in Romania. However, while the former does not show a concentration of foreign firms above the sample average, the latter emerges as a favourite location for foreign firms.
*   Several Romanian regions take the lead as preferred location for low-tech foreign firms. It is worth noticing that Czech regions are now below the sample average, with the exception of Prague.
*   Bulgaria plays a very marginal role in attracting any kind of FDI. During the 1990s, its regions host a number of foreign firms below the sample average in all the considered manufacturing macro-sectors.

Over time something has changed, mainly in Poland and Romania. While in the former the number of regions showing a concentration of foreign firms above the sample average has decreased in all manufacturing sectors but high-tech ones, in the latter the number of regions with a concentration of foreign firms above the sample average has increased in all manufacturing sectors, though the phenomena is particularly apparent for low-tech foreign firms.

Overall, these results seem to indicate that sector specific factors affect the distribution of foreign firms' across countries with high and medium-tech foreign firms preferring Hungary and the Czech Republic, and low-tech foreign firms concentrating in Romania. Moreover, they confirm the marginal role played up to now by Bulgarian regions in the FDI attraction tournament and that Poland has lost position in favour of Romania.

The next section is devoted to the analysis of the main consequences of these patterns of location on the economy of regions.

FDI and regional growth

In order to assess the impact of foreign firms on local development and growth prospects, this section explores the relationships existing between GDP per capita, its growth rates and the geographical and sectoral distribution of FDI. The GDP per capita appears in many previous empirical studies on firm location as one of the most important explanatory variable (Resmini, 2000; Bekes, 2004; Woodward *et al.*, 1998). It can have both demand and supply side interpretation. On the demand side, it reflects the potential demand in a region, while, on the supply side, it can be considered as a good proxy for host location's capacity to absorb FDI productively (Nunnenkamp and Spatz, 2003).

Figure 13.1 plots the number of foreign firms per capita in each region on the vertical axis and regional GDP per capita on the horizontal axis. Both variables have been measured in 1995 and 2001 and normalized by the respective national averages in order to account for size effects. According to the figures, there seems to be a positive relationship between GDP per capita and FDI. This indicates that foreign firms prefer to locate in the more advanced regions. The importance of GDP per capita as factor of attraction is country-specific, but not time-specific. It appears in Hungary, Poland and Romania, though with different intensity but not in Bulgaria and the Czech Republic, and it seems to be persistent over time.

Another striking characteristic highlighted by Figure 13.1 is the role played by the regions hosting the capital cities, which almost everywhere appear as outliers. These are of course the most urbanized regions of each country, hosting the largest agglomeration of economic activity, and accounting for no less than one-fifth of each country's GDP and one-tenth of population.[7] The outlying position of the capital regions further reinforces over time. During the second half of the 1990s, the capital cities/regions show an increase in their GDP per capita and a decrease in the concentration of FDI, with the exception of Prague. Both phenomena contribute to exacerbate the divide with the rest of the country. No other region seems to be able to compete with the capital regions, at least in terms of FDI penetration and GDP per capita. Only few noticeable exceptions enjoy values of both variables above the national average.[8]

The divide between the capital cities and the other regions in the CEECs is further marked by the analysis of the regional growth patterns. Figure 13.2 clearly indicate that patterns of divergence emerge within Central and Eastern European regions only when the capital cities are included in the sample. On the

Table 13.2 The distribution of FDI by region and sector, 1992–2001 (number of foreign firms per million of inhabitants)

High tech sectors				Medium high tech sectors				Medium low tech sectors				Low tech sectors			
1992		2001		1992		2001		1992		2001		1992		2001	
BG01	0	BG01	0	BG01	0	RO01	1.04	BG06	0	BG06	0	BG01	0	BG01	0
BG02	0	BG05	0	BG02	0	BG06	1.26	PL03	0	PL03	0.44	PL03	0	RO03	3.08
BG03	0	BG06	0	*BG04*	0	BG05	1.52	BG02	0	BG02	0.84	PL10	0	RO04	3.41
BG04	0	PL03	0	BG05	0	PL10	1.71	PL10	0	PL10	1.71	PL13	0	RO05	3.67
BG05	0	PL08	0	BG06	0	BG01	1.88	BG01	0	BG01	1.88	BG06	0	RO07	3.78
BG06	0	PL10	0	PL09	0	PL09	1.89	BG05	0	BG05	2.03	PL12	0.34	RO06	4.45
CZ03	0	PL13	0	PL10	0	PL14	1.98	BG03	0	BG03	2.3	BG03	0.47	BG05	4.6
CZ04	0	RO02	0	PL13	0	PL06	2.09	RO04	0	RO04	2.92	PL09	0.48	PL03	4.73
CZ07	0	PL05	0.38	RO01	0	PL03	2.2	RO01	0	RO01	3.39	BG05	0.53	RO01	5.08
CZ08	0	RO04	0.42	RO02	0	RO02	2.39	PL09	0	PL09	3.79	CZ07	0.68	RO02	5.36
PL03	0	PL12	0.85	RO03	0	PL02	2.88	PL16	0	*BG04*	4.29	PL06	0.72	BG03	5.38
PL05	0	RO03	0.87	RO04	0	PL13	2.94	*BG04*	0.34	PL06	5.08	CZ08	0.77	BG02	6.32
PL08	0	PL11	0.89	RO06	0	BG03	3.07	*RO08*	0.43	PL05	6.01	BG02	1.06	PL12	6.7
PL09	0	PL06	0.9	*RO08*	0	PL08	3.63	PL06	0.46	PL16	6.17	PL01	1.17	BG06	7.34
PL10	0	*BG04*	0.95	RO07	0.37	BG02	3.92	PL05	0.48	PL13	6.61	PL11	1.31	PL10	10.18
PL13	0	PL09	0.95	PL02	0.45	PL04	4	PL13	0.48	RO02	6.82	PL08	1.46	CZ07	11.8
RO01	0	PL04	1	BG03	0.72	*BG04*	4.29	RO02	0.72	PL11	7.08	RO04	1.52	CZ08	12.94
RO02	0	PL15	1.49	PL04	0.85	RO07	4.55	PL11	0.77	*RO08*	7.71	PL05	1.71	*RO08*	13.9
RO03	0	RO07	1.52	PL03	0.96	PL11	4.87	PL12	1.33	PL12	7.85	CZ04	1.76	PL13	14.25
RO04	0	BG02	1.67	PL08	0.97	RO03	5.2	PL02	1.42	PL02	8.15	PL14	1.77	PL09	14.54
RO05	0	PL01	1.67	PL15	1.17	PL05	5.26	*PL07*	1.54	*PL07*	8.17	PL16	2.06	PL01	14.58
RO06	0	PL16	1.68	RO05	1.43	RO04	5.43	HU06	1.61	HU06	8.31	*BG04*	2.3	*BG04*	16.21
RO07	0	CZ04	1.78	CZ07	1.46	CZ07	6.7	*CZ01*	1.65	*CZ01*	8.77	CZ02	3.4	CZ05	16.9
RO08	0	RO05	1.92	PL06	1.52	PL15	7.79	RO03	1.76	RO03	8.96	CZ06	3.49	CZ04	17.04
PL15	0.29	PL02	1.98	PL05	1.53	PL12	8.8	PL04	1.95	PL04	9	HU06	3.8	PL06	17.27
PL12	0.35	PL14	2.09	PL14	1.6	PL16	9.33	PL14	2.28	PL14	9.92	CZ03	4.87	PL08	17.89
PL06	0.38	RO06	2.11	PL11	1.61	CZ08	10.23	RO06	2.54	RO06	10.56	HU05	5.38	PL11	18.42

PL11	BG03 0.54	PL16 2.3	PL15 2.01	PL04 10.42	PL15 2.56	CZ02 10.72	PL02 5.41	PL02 18.7
PL16	CZ08 0.67	PL12 2.37	**Average 2.66**	PL02 10.89	CZ08 3.15	PL05 11.85	CZ05 5.75	CZ05 22.24
PL01	CZ07 0.69	CZ08 2.44	PL01 3.05	PL14 11.02	**Average 3.2**	**Average 12.61**	PL15 5.99	PL15 22.63
HU07	HU07 0.72	PL01 2.9	CZ08 3.43	PL15 12.64	PL01 3.51	PL14 12.69	**Average 7.21**	**Average 23.01**
Average	HU04 0.76	**Average 3.01**	***PL07 3.61***	**Average 12.85**	CZ03 3.87	PL15 13.63	RO03 7.91	RO03 23.13
HU05	**Average 0.76**	HU06 3.55	HU07 3.9	PL16 15.21	***CZ01 4.01***	HU06 15.52	PL04 8.45	PL04 23.99
PL14	HU06 0.8	HU05 3.84	CZ06 5.35	PL01 15.83	CZ06 4.46	PL04 15.83	***PL07 8.52***	***PL07 24.32***
CZ01	CZ03 0.82	***PL07 4.26***	CZ04 5.4	HU06 16.03	HU07 5.2	PL16 15.94	RO02 8.69	RO02 25.58
PL04	CZ02 0.85	CZ06 4.45	HU05 5.67	HU04 16.89	CZ05 5.93	CZ06 17.52	HU02 8.91	HU02 25.88
CZ02	HU05 0.9	HU07 4.61	RO05 5.77	CZ05 17.22	HU04 6.81	***PL07 18.04***	HU04 9.83	HU04 28.07
HU03	CZ06 0.99	CZ02 5.48	HU04 8.11	HU07 19.04	RO07 7.21	PL02 20.08	HU07 9.9	HU07 30.43
HU04	***PL07 0.99***	CZ04 6.33	CZ03 8.14	CZ06 20.44	RO05 8.1	CZ03 20.17	RO01 11.45	RO01 30.75
PL02	CZ05 1.35	CZ05 6.74	***CZ01 9.36***	CZ03 22.41	CZ02 8.59	HU05 20.46	***CZ01 11.46***	***CZ01 43.96***
CZ05	RO05 1.7	CZ03 7.87	***RO08 10.02***	CZ02 24.19	CZ04 9.91	HU02 22.26	***HU01 11.66***	***HU01 49.8***
HU06	HU03 1.95	***CZ01 10.96***	CZ02 10.69	HU05 25.8	HU05 11.46	***CZ01 23.03***	RO06 17.27	RO06 64.77
PL07	***RO08 3.66***	HU04 12.32	CZ05 10.87	CZ04 26.96	HU07 12.79	HU07 28.61	RO07 17.3	RO07 65.56
CZ06	HU02 4.05	HU02 16.06	HU03 15.25	***HU01 33.87***	***HU01 12.8***	HU04 33.43	HU03 17.79	HU03 70.73
HU02	***HU01 4.49***	HU03 16.25	HU02 17.9	HU02 38.37	***RO08 20.63***	***HU01 56.21***	RO05 26.27	RO05 80.18
HU01	***CZ01 7.41***	***HU01 22.41***	***HU01 20.2***	HU03 39.91	HU02 23.87	HU03 62.76	***RO08 34.81***	***RO08 124.93***

Note:
Regions hosting the capital cities are in bold and italics. Regions are numbered according to the Nomenclature of Territorial Units for Statistics published by Eurostat in 1999.

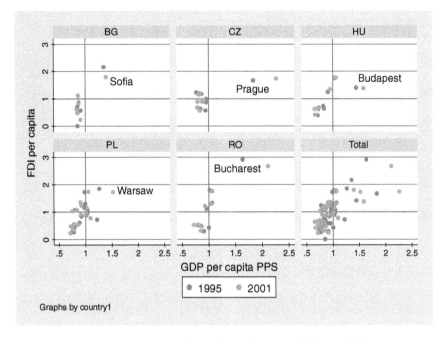

Figure 13.1 GDP per capita vs. FDI by region and country, 1995 and 2001.

contrary, no clear pattern of growth can be identified among regions not hosting the capital cities. In conclusion, the capital regions appear as the true winners of both the transition process and the FDI tournament.

With the distribution of foreign firms skewed towards the capital regions within each country the positive impact of foreign affiliates in terms of technology transfer, capital inflows and knowledge diffusion may be limited to the already well developed regions and the existing regional disparities may further exacerbate.

Figure 13.3 explores this issue by plotting the number of foreign firms per inhabitant in 1995 in each region on the horizontal axis and the average GDP per capita growth rate in the period 1995–2001 on the vertical axis. It provides clear evidence of a FDI-led growth, though the correlation between FDI and the economic growth becomes less significant when the capital regions are not considered.[9]

Besides differences in the relative concentration of foreign firms, two other important factors may explain this fact. First of all, social capabilities and absorptive capacity might be above the threshold level in the capital regions only, thus making more difficult the transmission of the benefits MNEs are supposed to generate to local economy outside these regions. Second, we earlier demonstrated that the sectoral composition of foreign firms differs between the capital cities and the other regions in their respective countries, with the former hosting mainly high-tech foreign firms. Therefore, industry characteristics and, mainly, technology intensity, are likely to shape the growth impact of FDI in various ways.

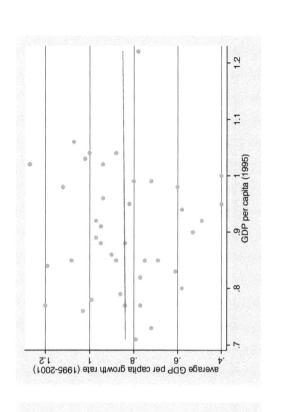

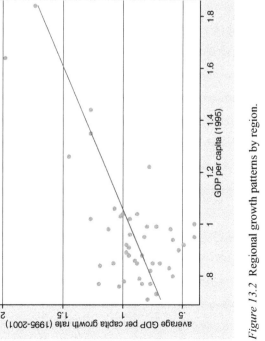

Figure 13.2 Regional growth patterns by region.

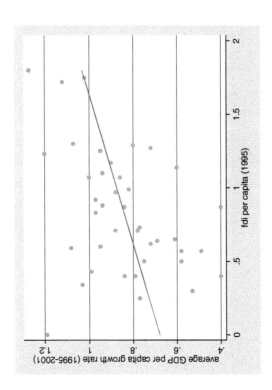

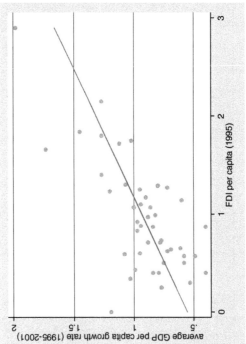

Figure 13.3 The contribution of FDI to GDP growth.

In order to understand the role of industry characteristics and their interplay with host-location characteristics in shaping the growth impact of FDI, measures for relative concentration of foreign firms in the four different groups of manufacturing sectors has been computed for each regions. Such a measure is very closed to the Hoover's localization index and measures the localization of foreign firms belonging to industry j in location i relative to the localization of foreign firms as a whole in i, that is:

$$LQ_{ji} = \frac{N_{ij}}{\Sigma_i N_{ij}} \left/ \frac{\Sigma_j N_{ij}}{\Sigma_i \Sigma_j N_{ij}} \right.$$

The location quotient allows comparisons across different groups of industries. $LQ_{ij} > 1$ indicates that foreign firms in industry j have a share of total FDI in location i larger than the same share measured at national level. The opposite happens when $LQ_{ij} < 1$.

These indexes, computed for the initial year, have been put in relation with the average GDP per capita growth rate of the 1995–2001 period. Figure 13.4 shows the results, according to which the contribution of FDI belonging to different manufacturing sectors to growth, is not very clear. The correlation between FDI and GDP per capita growth rates is negative, though not statistically significant, for medium-low and medium-high tech foreign firms, positive but not significant for low-tech foreign firms and positive and statistically significant for high-tech foreign firms. Therefore, it is possible to conclude that regions enjoying a concentration of high-tech foreign firms above the national average are those recording GDP per capita growth rates above the national average.

A final consideration concerns the role played by the regions hosting the capital cities. Figure 13.4 clearly indicates that they play a crucial role in shaping the relationship between the concentration of high-tech foreign firms and GDP per capita growth rates: excluding them from the sample would yield to a less intensive association between high-tech foreign firms and GDP per capita growth rate.

Overall these results indicate that benefits arising from FDI, though they are more likely to occur in presence of technologically advanced foreign firms, are not automatic. They are able to enhance growth only in locations well endowed with social capabilities and absorptive capacity, as the metropolitan areas. Outside these regions, foreign firms are more similar to "cathedrals in the desert" rather than catalysts for local development.

Conclusions

This chapter analyses some striking characteristics concerning the location of multinational firms in CEECs and their contribution to growth prospects both across and within countries. In particular, low-income candidate countries have lagged behind Central European new member states in their ability to attract

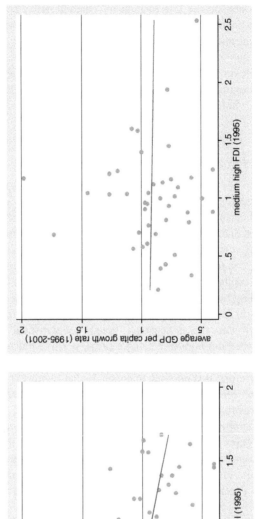

Figure 13.4 Regional growth patterns and the contribution of FDI by sector.

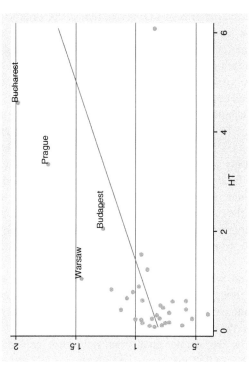

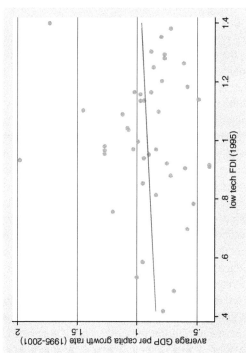

Figure 13.4 continued.

FDI. Similarly, sectoral patterns of FDI reveal that CEECs represent a favourite location mainly for low-tech foreign firms, who found there a skilled and cheaper labour force as well as experienced domestic firms operating in upstream and downstream manufacturing sectors. High-tech FDI represents less than one-third of the total number of foreign affiliates and concentrates the most in the more developed countries and or regions of the sample.

This uneven distribution has further exacerbated the income gaps between and within countries. Economic growth and FDI seem to interact in a virtuous cycle: regions with a GDP per capita above the national average have attracted a share of foreign firms above the national average. During the 1990s, these regions have grown faster than the other ones, thus increasing inequalities.

This group of winner regions includes almost exclusively the capital cities or the regions hosting the capital cities. Therefore, in each of the considered countries there is an increasing divide between the capital city/region and the other regions, which with a very few exceptions are developing along very similar patterns of growth.

FDI is not neutral with respect to these patterns of growth. The chapter demonstrates that foreign affiliates have positively contributed to regional growth, but the intensity of such a relationship is higher in the capital cities/regions than in the other regions of the sample.

More interestingly, the chapter shows that only high-tech foreign firms are able to positively affect GDP per capita growth rates, while the contribution of less technological intensive FDI is nil or negative, though not significant. Therefore, only regions with a strong concentration of high-tech foreign firms seem to possess the necessary conditions for reaping the benefits generated by foreign firms. Unfortunately, these regions coincide with the capital city/regions.

These results, though preliminary and functional for further analyses, raise some policy concerns. A first concern regards the *sectoral composition of FDI*. According to the results presented in this chapter, it seems to be too unbalanced towards low-tech manufacturing sectors. Besides the obvious implications in terms of technology transfer, low-tech foreign firms are more footloose and less embedded into the local economy than high-tech foreign firms. This is due to the fact that cost advantages and, mainly, labour cost advantages, reduce over time, because of the improvement in the general standards of living in the CEECs. In the short-medium run, this might become a problem for Romania and Bulgaria. Attracting an increasing number of new investments is important, mainly if the existing pool of investments is rather limited. However, in terms of growth prospects what matters the most is the *quality* of FDI, i.e. a "large employer, with a highly skilled, productive and high-wage workforce, and a high level of local purchases to generate macro multiplier effects" (Mudambi, 1998).

Second, the chapter demonstrates that FDI alone does not suffice to foster regional growth and generate convergence processes within countries. Foreign firms can offer a positive contribution to growth only if supported by good infrastructures, a well-developed local labour market, business facilities, financial services etc. In other words, they need to find a fertile economic environment in order to become a potential source of growth, provided that they are technologically advanced. Thus, in order to attract high-quality FDI, laggard regions have to improve all these factors.

Notes

1 Campos and Kinoshita (2003), Merlevede and Schoors (2004), Resmini (2000) and Pusterla and Resmini (2007), among many others, explore the determinants of FDI at country, sector and region level. Resmini (2007), Jensen (2002) and Smarzynska-Javorcik (2004), instead, exemplify possible impacts of FDI on the host economy in terms of industry location, industrial restructuring and domestic firms' productivity, respectively. UNECE (2001) provides an extensive survey on the consequences of FDI on growth, at both macro and microeconomic level.
2 See Young *et al.* (1994) and, more recently Pavlinek (2004) for an extensive theoretical analysis of the regional development implications of foreign direct investment in CEECs.
3 For further details on the origin of the dataset, its sources and contents see Alessandrini (2000) and Pusterla and Resmini (2007).
4 It is important to notice that the dataset at the base of this work is not exhaustive, since it does not cover all foreign firms that had set up a production plant in the CEECs during the 1990s, the main reason being that small transactions usually escape any type of official registrations at both macro- and micro-level. Despite that, the results presented here provide patterns of MNEs in the CEECs that are, on average, consistent with previous empirical evidence (Pusterla and Resmini, 2007).
5 First nature characteristics include natural resource endowment, climate and morphological conditions. Therefore they are important for location decisions concerning resource-based activities, such as agriculture, mining and quarrying, tourism, etc. The distinction between first and second nature characteristics is due to Cronon (1991). The location of service activities, instead, is mainly affected by proximity with consumers. Needless to say, the functioning of the economic activity may be changed by the economic agents and policy-makers, while first nature characteristics do not. This explains why the understanding of location processes in manufacturing is more important than in other economic sectors.
6 The cities of Budapest, Prague and Bucharest are independent administrative units both at NUTS 2 and 3 level, while Warsaw and Sofia are independent administrative units at NUTS 3 level only.
7 These figures are much more impressive for Budapest – which accounts for about 40 per cent of the country's GDP and 30 per cent of the country's population – and Sofia, whose shares in the country's GDP and population are about 35 and 25 per cent, respectively.
8 They are Nyugat-Dunantul in Hungary, i.e. the region bordering with Austria; Timis's region (Vest) in Romania; Dolnoslaskie and Wielkopolskie in Poland.
9 This result does not depend on how GDP, its growth rate and FDI are measured. Very similar trends have been detected by using total GDP instead of GDP per capita and different measure of FDI, such as total number of foreign firms, regional share of total foreign firms, measured both in absolute and in relative terms.

References

Alessandrini, S. (2000), *The EU Foreign Direct Investment in Central and Eastern Europe*, Milan: Giuffré.

Altomonte, C. and L. Resmini (1999), "The geography of foreign direct investment in transition countries: a survey of evidence", in Tavidze, A. (ed.), *Progress in International Economics Research*, New York: Nova Science Publishers, pp. 1–36.

Bekes, G. (2004), "Location of manufacturing FDI in Hungary: how important are business to business relationship?", mimeo.

Boudier-Bensebaa, F. (2005), "Agglomeration economies and location choice. Foreign direct investment in Hungary", *Economics of Transition*, vol. 13, n. 4, pp. 605–628.

Campos, N. and Y. Kinoshita (2003), "Why does FDI go where it goes? New evidence from the transition econonomies", IMF working paper n. 03/228.

Cieslik, A. (2005), "Regional characteristicfs and the location of foreign firms within Poland", *Applied Economics*, 37, pp. 863–874.

Cronon, W. (1991), *Nature's Megalopolis: Chicago and the Great West*, New York: Norton.

Jensen, C. (2002), "Foreign direct investment, industrial restructuring and the upgrading of Polish exports", *Applied Economics*, 34, pp. 207–217.

Kokko, A., (1992), *Foreign Direct Investments, Host Country Characteristics and Spillovers*, Stockholm: Stockholm School of Economics.

Lovino, I. (2002), "Foreign direct investment in the candidate country: sector and country composition", Eurostat, Theme 2, *Statistics in Focus*, n. 55.

Merlevede, B. and K. Schoors (2004), "Determinants of foreign direct investment in transition economies", mimeo.

Mudambi, R. (1998), "The role of duration in multinational investment strategies", *Journal of International Business Studies*, vol. 29, n. 2, pp. 239–262.

Nunnenkamp, P. and Spatz, J. (2003), "Foreign direct investment and economic growth in developing countries: how relevant are host-country and industry characteristics?", Kiel working paper no. 1176.

Ottaviano, G. and D. Pinelli (2005), "A 'new economic geography' perspective to globalization", *The Italian Journal of Regional Science*, vol. 4, n. 1, pp. 71–106.

Pavlinek, P. (2004), "Regional development implications of foreign direct investment in Central Europe", *European Urban and Regional Studies*, vol. 11, n. 1, pp. 47–70.

Pusterla, F. and L. Resmini (2007), "Where do foreign firms locate in transition countries? An empirical investigation", *The Annals of Regional Science*, Vol. 41 n. 4, pp. 835–856.

Resmini, L. (2000), "The determinants of foreign direct investment into the CEECs: new evidence from sectoral patterns", *Economics of Transition*, vol. 8, n. 3, pp. 665–689.

Resmini, L. (2007), "Regional patterns of industry location in transition countries: does economic integration with the EU matter?", *Regional Studies*, vol. 41, n. 6, pp. 741–764.

Sinn, H.W. and A. Weichenrieder (1997), "Foreign direct investment, political resentment and the privatization process in eastern Europe", *Economic Policy*, vol. 12, n. 24, pp. 178–210.

Smarzynska-Javorcik, B. (2004), "Does foreign direct investment increase the productivity of domestic firms? In search of spillovers through backward linkages", *American Economic Review*, 94, pp. 605–627.

UNECE (2001), "Economic growth and foreign direct investment in the transition economies", *Economic Survey of Europe*, n. 1, pp. 185–225.

Woodward, D., R. Rolfe, P. Guimaraes and T. Doupnik (1998), "Taxation and the location of foreign direct investment in Central Europe", mimeo.

Young S., N. Hood and E. Peters (1994), "Multinational enterprises and regional economic development", *Regional Studies*, vol. 28, n. 7, pp. 657–677.

14 Structural change and regional policy

Concluding remarks

Edgar Morgenroth and George Petrakos

Introduction

Since the foundation of the EEC in 1957 there has been an ongoing process of deepening and widening of economic integration. This process was accelerated in the 1990s through the introduction of the Single European Market (SEM) and European Economic and Monetary Union (EMU), which culminated in the introduction of the euro. Simultaneously, with the collapse of the communist regimes in Central and Eastern Europe (CEE), a process of enlargement of the EU, which was unprecedented in scale, was set in motion, which culminated with the accession of ten new member states (NMS) into the EU in 2004.

The enlargement of the European Union towards the transition economies of Central and Eastern Europe is likely to change the international and interregional division of labour and the location of industry, increase the diversity and affect the regional cohesion in Europe. Existing evidence indicates that trade reorientation towards the European Union has taken place among all member states, albeit with different magnitudes. In the NMS, integration accelerated in the run-up to the entering into force of the Europe Agreements. It is however unclear whether and to what extent patterns of industrial location and regional specialization have changed due to increasing economic integration with the EU and what impact this change has had on regional income and cohesion in the NMS.

As is highlighted in the EU Cohesion Reports, economic activity is not spread evenly across space within the EU, and indeed the heterogeneity within countries is often greater than that between countries, especially for the old member states (EU-15). According to the European Commission, large regional disparities remain, and, at least with respect to unemployment, they increased substantially since the late 1970s (Martin, 1998). During the whole integration process and despite longstanding and substantial policy efforts, some Mezzogiorno-type problems appear to be rather tenacious. Given the recent enlargement it is important to consider whether some regions of the NMS might also fall into such an underdevelopment trap. Moreover, there is a lack of knowledge with respect to some aspects of the regional impacts of integration. In particular, the specific effects on the division of labour between European regions and on industrial location and regional specialization have not been addressed sufficiently and in-depth so far.[1] Exceptions to this are a number of studies that attempt to investigate the determinants of manufacturing location across countries: Amiti (1999); Haaland *et al.* (1999); Midelfart-Knarvik *et al.* (2000); characteristics of spatially concentrated industries are analysed in Brülhart and Torstensson (1996) and Brülhart (1998).

Indeed, an empirical analysis of these effects is also warranted since alternative theoretical approaches yield very different results so that one cannot say a priori what the likely impact will be. According to the neoclassical trade theory, economic integration fosters the division of labour according to comparative advantages, which raises the overall welfare as well as the welfare of each country or region involved in the process, and equalizes factor prices. In this analytical framework, it was taken for granted that convergence of countries and regions is to be expected. Thus, regional policy could only speed up a convergence process, which would presumably happen anyway. Otherwise the role for government is merely to ensure that markets work well.

However, more recent strands of economic theory like the new trade theory, the new economic geography (NEG), or the new strand of theory on the role of foreign direct investment (FDI) which allow for market failures and externalities, often predict a lack of convergence and persistent differences in income per capita which can only be overcome by more substantial policy interventions. In these models factor prices do not equalize and while free trade is globally welfare improving, not all regions will gain.

The overall scientific objective of this book is to identify and explain in a cross-country analysis the impact of European integration and enlargement on regional structural change and cohesion. An important innovation in this book is the use of more disaggregated data with respect to both the sectoral and spatial level of disaggregation. The lack of disaggregation in the few previous studies severely reduces their usefulness for policy analysis since specialization is a very localized phenomenon and cannot be picked up at the national level or macro-region level.

The analysis conducted in this book provides empirical evidence about the relationship between industrial location, regional specialization and regional income per capita in the context of European integration and EU enlargement. These findings are summarized in this report. Furthermore, this report highlights the policy conclusions and recommends policy interventions and changes to existing policy.

The continual enlargement of the EU is reflected in the sample of countries that are analysed in this study, namely Austria, Bulgaria, the Czech Republic, France, Germany, Greece, Hungary, Ireland, Italy, Poland, Portugal, Romania and Spain. These countries joined the EU at different points in time. Countries such as Italy, West Germany and France were founding members in 1957. Ireland joined in 1973 and Greece in 1981. Both Portugal and Spain joined in 1986. Finally, Austria joined in 1995. All these countries are referred to here as EU-15. Among the new member states the Czech Republic, Hungary and

Poland, joined the EU in 2004 while Bulgaria and Romania joined on 1 January 2007.

Summary of results

The analysis in the introductory and the country chapters has revealed a number of interesting structural characteristics of the European regions. This section attempts to identify common regional trends and processes related to structural change, setting the framework for a meaningful discussion about the implications of structural characteristics and processes for regional policy.

Patterns of regional inequality and regional specialization in Europe

A number of studies in this volume confirm earlier reports indicating that regional inequalities have increased in the 1990s in a number of EU countries. This trend is more apparent in the new member states where inequalities have increased significantly due to the superior performance of metropolitan and Western border regions.

One of the driving forces of increasing disparity at the regional level is the continuing change in the productive structure of the European economy. Although in most of the advanced Western EU members structural change has been modest, this is not the case in many member states in the East and the South. In the latter, the 1990s have been a period of significant structural change characterized by a general shift of output and employment from agriculture and industry to services.

During this period, manufacturing has been the most severely affected sector with a significant reduction in output (in the East) and employment (in almost all EU countries). Inside manufacturing at least two different structural patterns seem to exist. In the old EU-15 members a core-periphery model may be in place, as more advanced core countries tend to concentrate a relatively higher share of capital and knowledge intensive sectors, while less advanced peripheral ones tend to concentrate a relatively higher share of labour and resource intensive sectors. Within the member states of the most recent accession a similar divide tends to take place among Central European countries, like Hungary, Slovenia or the Czech Republic and the less advanced states in the Baltic Sea and the Balkans.

The direction of structural change in the 1990s is also an important element of the integration process of most countries and regions in the East and the South. Dissimilarity tests have shown that many regions in the East are developing industrial structures that are increasingly different from that of the EU-15 average, providing an indication of a defensive structural change taking place in their productive base. On the contrary, many regions in Central Europe are developing industrial structures that are increasingly similar to that of the EU-15 average. While the latter seem to successfully converge towards the economic structure of the EU core, the former seem to follow a different structural trajectory, converging towards the economic structure of the old EU periphery.

The speed of structural change and adjustment seems to differ significantly among countries and regions. A general pattern appears where the less advanced countries and regions are usually the ones undergoing structural change at a faster, and in most cases beyond their control, pace.

The structural change induced by the process of integration in the new member states has affected significantly their regional specialization and industrial concentration patterns. In general, the levels of specialization are moderate and declining. Many regions have experienced a decrease in their levels of specialization due to the collapse of a significant part of their industrial base in the early 1990s. However, other regions have managed, with various degrees of success, to develop new activities, primarily in services, but also in manufacturing. In this environment of rapid structural change, the rule is that capital regions, their satellites and Western border regions are the least specialized regions or the ones with more diverse industrial bases.

Structural change and growth performance

One of the factors behind the increase in regional inequalities in the EU new member states is the structural characteristics of their regions. On the one hand, many highly specialized or mono-structure regions experienced a collapse in output and employment in the early years of transition. On the other hand, the more diversified core regions have experienced a better performance.

As mentioned before, during the 1990s some regions in Central and Southern Europe have managed to develop a more similar industrial structure with that of the EU-15 average. These regions are typically characterized by a better performing industrial sector and combine successfully structural convergence towards the EU-15 with convergence in terms of GDP per capita. On the other hand, the majority of the regions in the East and many regions in the South have experienced pressures from the new economic environment that have led to a divergence from the EU-15 average structure. It is exactly these regions following a different structural path that find the greatest difficulties to converge towards the EU-15 development levels.

What is behind the relation of structural characteristics to development prospects in the European regions? In other words, which characteristics are found to be more conductive to a strong growth performance? In the EU-15 the evidence shows that regions are typically characterized by low and declining levels of industrial specialization and limited intra-industry structural change over time. In general, there is no clear overall relation between levels of regional specialization and performance. However, the evidence tends to indicate that high levels of regional localization tend to be associated with inferior performance especially when they involve resource intensive, footloose or IRS sectors.

In the new member states it seems that a general pattern of specialization arises where core and advanced or Western regions have a more diversified industrial structure than less advanced regions. The evidence shows that regions with relatively higher levels of specialization experienced slower growth in the 1990s. This implies that regions with a more diversified industrial base have recorded a better growth performance in the 1990s.

Overall, regional specialization increases as we move from the core to the peripheral countries and regions of Europe. The core regions tend to be highly diversified, while the periphery experiences higher levels of specialization.

In addition, the evidence seems to indicate that regions with higher employment shares in capital-intensive sectors have done better in terms of growth performance. In fact there is a great amount of overlapping between the two groups of regions (specializing in capital-intensive sectors and having a diverse industrial base), as the presence of (hard to develop everywhere) capital sectors contributes to greater diversity.

In any case, the evidence seems to indicate that the structural patterns of specialization and change tend to reinforce the existing spatial patterns of development, favouring more advanced regions and increasing inequalities. Therefore, regional inequalities increase due to the higher growth performance of the more advanced regions, which are typically specialized in capital intensive sector, have a more diverse industrial base, usually benefit from a central location in the European market and have developed significant metropolitan functions. This pattern is further reinforced by FDI, which is typically directed to the more advanced countries and regions, contributing in several instances to the enrichment and diversification of their economic base and increasing further regional inequalities.

Structural change and the regional policy context

The return of polarization trends and increasing regional inequalities in many EU countries in the 1990s is to a large extent an unavoidable by-product of the ongoing and interacting processes of economic integration and structural change. This reinforces the need for policies in favour of the less advanced and structurally weak regions. As regional inequalities increase or remain high, there will be a continuous need for a better designed, adequately funded and more efficiently implemented regional policy.

Structural change may impose significant adjustment in the composition of employment in ways that many regions are not prepared to cope with. Although structural change affects all regions, the weaker ones have limited control on these changes and face tremendous difficulties to take advantage of them in a creative way.

Although comparative advantage will continue to be the basis for the development of new activities, excessive regional specialization and dependence on a limited number of industries may not be a successful policy for long-term growth. In this context, regions hosting IRS industries may benefit from their location in terms of employment and income, run, however, a possibly greater risk to face employment pressures by the next wave of technological and structural change.

This may be an indication that regional development policies favouring variety and differentiation through external economies of scale (for example clusters of interacting activities) may be more promising than policies favouring specialization through internal economies of scale. In general, regions will have to find a delicate balance between locally established advantages in specific sectors and a need to increase the diversity of their productive base. Local development initiatives more and more frequently face the question whether existing or pursued types of specialization will be able to resist the upcoming waves of deeper integration, greater competition and faster structural change, in order to contribute to long term growth.

Regional policies will have in the future to address more frequently the structural characteristics of the regions. As regional output and employment shift from industry to services, new tasks emerge for regional employment policy. On the one hand, tertiarization leads to a greater segregation of the labour force and increases the gap between "white" and "blue" collar workers. On the other hand, the decline of industry sets continuous pressures for an innovative and effective use of national and EU funds for the retraining of the labour force.

In general, as the structural component of inequality and weak performance will become more and more evident, regional policy will have to respond by restructuring its own portfolio. The emphasis may have to shift from infrastructure to measures related more directly to the productive structure and the direction of activities and resources to sectors and processes that are likely to have a greater contribution to endogenous growth. In addition, regional policy will need to improve its structural component and its capability to lead regions through a rapidly changing economic environment to adaptation and change that is gradual, smooth and does not result in abrupt effects and negative shocks in the local labour markets.

A diverse economic base is more likely to protect labour markets from turbulence in times of unwanted or externally driven structural change. Specialization, on the other hand, is likely to be more beneficial in periods coinciding with the beginning of a product cycle and a new period of expansion.

Finding over time a working balance between specialization (in the right sectors) and diversification is one of the most difficult tasks of regional policy. In general, it is more difficult to successfully address the structural problems of the regions rather than provide basic infrastructure. Perhaps the tendency in the least advanced regions to put more emphasis on infrastructure projects is partly the admission of the difficulty to design an appropriate policy mix addressing the structural weaknesses of their economy.

Finally, we should keep in our minds that each region is a unique case. Despite common trends and processes, regions follow their own growth trajectories where initial conditions have a crucial role in indicating the type of policies that are more likely to have a significant impact. As a result, regional policies designed at the EU and national level should leave enough room for a regionally determined mix of actions and interventions, avoiding the convenient, but not very effective, one-size-fits-all policy approach of the recent past.

Review of existing policies

The research findings that are outlined in this book and which have been summarized in the section above have important policy implications. However, these policy implications can only be identified in the context of existing policies. This section provides a brief review of relevant regional, national and EU policies.

Policy environment

The developments of the industrial structure do not, of course, occur in a policy vacuum. At the regional, national and EU level, a variety of policies have been pursued that have a direct or indirect effect on structural change and regional income and thus have an impact on cohesion. It is therefore important to consider what policies have been in place and what their impact has been. The latter is of course a difficult task since this book was not concerned with the evaluation of policy, and thus we have to draw on the available literature to determine the effect of policies.

Regional and national policies

First, it is useful to consider the general economic policies that have driven the development of the countries under investigation. A brief review shows that the policy approaches have been quite heterogenous. For example, West Germany has been subject to a relatively non-interventionist regime since the Second World War. West Germany fully embraced free trade which, given the relatively high productivity in the past, resulted in high export volumes and thus greater prosperity than would otherwise have been the case. Nevertheless, some sectors have continued to be supported, such as the heavy subsidization of the coal mining industry.

In France there has traditionally been a tendency to enact policies that were aimed at reducing uncertainty mainly through the production of plans (*planifica-tion*). Thus, firms and other agents received ex ante information, which allowed them to plan ahead. Nevertheless, France has been an open economy with substantial trade flows and integration into the wider world economy. On the other hand Greece, Portugal and Spain had a somewhat different economic history mainly due to their political situation, as these countries were subject to dictatorships. In the case of Portugal and Spain the Salazar and Franco regimes aimed at increasing the degree of industrialization as the two countries were largely agricultural at the end of the Second World War. At the same time as they pursued industrial promotion policies they followed the infant industry-protectionist policies that were common in postWar Europe. These protectionist policies were also followed in Ireland until the late 1950s. Following a prolonged period of relative economic isolation Ireland opened up its trade to international competition during the 1960s and became a member of the European Economic

Community (EEC) in 1973. This meant that the indigenous firms that grew up under the protection of tariff barriers were exposed to international competition.

The new member states and East Germany were part of the COMECON. They were thus subject to non-market plan-economics where supply and thus production was centrally determined. With the fall of communism these countries have pursued a path of transition towards market-driven systems, through a set of economic and legislative reforms. While the reforms were introduced at different speeds the general direction of policy in these countries has been similar. Of course the case of East Germany forms a special case since all changes took place all at once, which means that the regions of East Germany were subjected to a sudden policy shock. The resulting restructuring through privatization and widespread plant closures was supported by substantial financial transfers from West Germany.

Structural policies

West German industrial policy traditionally focused on subsidies for private enterprises rather then on public ownership as main instruments. Nevertheless, the state does hold substantial shares in a number of major publicly quoted companies such as Volkswagen. The focus of the subsidies was concentrated on traditional sectors like coal mining, agriculture and construction. The federal political structure of the country has always ensured that regional policy has been important. At the heart of this is a scheme of fiscal equalization between the Federal States, which seeks to eliminate the fiscal effects of any disparities across Federal States. Furthermore, an investment grant scheme for lagging regions exists, where support is granted both to infrastructure projects of communities as well as to investment projects of private enterprises, usually from the manufacturing sector. While these policies are mainly aimed at lagging regions, old industrial areas with major restructuring problems and high unemployment also benefit from this policy.

In France, Portugal and Spain, the industrial policies focused more on state-owned enterprises (SOEs). In all three countries many large industrial enterprises were state-owned. Portugal started socialist nationalizations after the revolution of 1974. Spain, after 1976, transformed the Franco-created state-owned holding company INI (Instituto National de Industria) into an "enterprise hospital" that acquired several large private firms in trouble. France in 1982 experienced a number of nationalizations after the socialist party came into power. However, these policies were reversed in the 1990s, as all three countries embarked on a policy of privatizing state owned enterprises. The aim here was to save these firms in the short-run and to restructure and modernize them in order to make them more competitive, which was successful in at least some cases. Nevertheless, there is still a higher willingness of governments in these countries to intervene and bail out firms that are in trouble. However, given the relatively strict EU rules regarding state aid, opportunities to bail out firms have diminished substantially.

More generally, subsidies in these countries tended to be directed towards:

1　industries that used to be regarded as being important for a strong and self-sufficient economy, and that are now ailing, like agriculture, iron and steel and shipbuilding;
2　industries regarded as being modern and growth-promoting like aeronautics, nuclear industries and telecommunications.

Also, subsidies tended to favour large firms. Regarding regional policies, the three countries used a range of policy instruments at hand (regional incentive schemes, SOEs, indicative planning, installation and support of high-technology parks) with the main objective of trying to decentralize the economy.

In Ireland, industrialization was initiated by the state in the 1930s through the foundation of major state-owned companies. Furthermore, a protectionist policy was enacted until the late 1950s in order to support infant industries. As this was replaced by a more open trade policy, support for industries has slowly declined, but even today certain sectors can avail of subsidies, e.g. the tourism sector, which of course is more important in remote areas. The general thrust of industrial policy has shifted progressively towards the promotion and attraction of more high-tech sectors.

Postwar Irish regional policy has constantly evolved and indeed the importance of regional issues has varied. During the 1960s the idea of growth centres was promoted although no specific policies to promote growth centres were enacted. However, this was superseded by the Regional Industrial Plans, which aimed at dispersing industrial development rather than concentrating it in a few growth centres. During the 1980s regional issues diminished in importance as unemployment soared. Throughout, the policies of the Industrial Development Agency (IDA) were pursued through industrial grants, which were available on investment. More recently these grants were subject to strict job creation targets and indeed some companies had to pay back grants if these targets were not achieved.

In Greece regional policy was also aimed at enhancing the industrial activity at the regional level. This policy was implemented through subsidies and tax exemptions at the firm level, and through more general public investment, which has also been aided by the EU through the Structural Funds. In general it appears that the policy had some success in attracting investment into the regions, even though this was typically in labour intensive industries. More recently the focus has shifted towards start-up firms.

All EU-15 countries under observation intervene in the process of regional structural change, mainly by industrial policies, and therefore mainly aimed at large, ailing industries in highly industrialized regions. Support for growth-intensive industries with new technologies was usually less important. Regional policies were mainly aimed at lagging regions, thus trying to counterbalance at least partially the rather centripetal stance of the industrial policies.

In contrast, in the former COMECON countries investments for its state-owned enterprises were largely centrally directed. There was a general focus on heavy industries. Rather than allowing a range of companies to grow up production was concentrated in large vertical combines. Compared to the capitalist systems of the EU-15 production of consumer goods was neglected. On the spatial level, this policy focused on locating at least one industrial complex in every region including the most remote ones. Thus, their location was not chosen by underlying economic forces, but rather the location was determined by technocrats. Transition in the new member states has resulted in the decline of the industrial base.

EU policy

Apart from national policies, the EU has also pursued various policies, which have important implications for both regional development and regional specialization. Principally, the Structural Funds have been targeted at the lagging regions and those undergoing structural change. Furthermore, in the run-up to EU membership the accession countries were eligible to pre-accession Structural Funds. While these instruments constitute direct regional policy, it is obvious that the integration process itself, which has been accelerated through the introduction of the Single Market and the euro have a significant indirect impact at the regional level.

Rather than simply transferring resources in an untied manner, the Structural Funds have to be spent on certain types of activities and according to the principles of concentration, partnership, additionality and programming. The general aim of the Structural Funds is to improve the economic structure of the regions that receive funding through the development of infrastructure, the improvement of human resources through education and investment in the productive sector. For the period 2000–2006 the EU is making available a total of €213 billion.

Structural Funds, as the name suggests, is made up of a number of different funds. These are:

- European Social Fund (ESF) encompasses support for active labour market policy, specifically training and recruitment aid in order to re-integrate the long-term unemployed back into the workforce.
- European Regional Development Fund (ERDF) is concerned with basic infrastructure, also with education and healthcare infrastructure projects, job creating investments and aid for small firms.
- European Agriculture Guarantee and Guidance Fund (EAGGF-Guidance), is concerned with rural development measures and aid to the farming sector. These two aspects are particularly concentrated on the so-called disadvantaged areas. The EAGGF is closely linked to the Common Agricultural Policy of the EU.
- Financial Instrument for Fishery Guidance (FIFG) is specifically aimed at modernizing fishing fleets.

Separate from the Structural Funds is the Cohesion Fund. This fund was set up in 1993 in order to help Greece, Portugal, Ireland and Spain in their preparations for the Single Currency by further improving the economic environmental infrastructure in these countries and thereby strengthening their economic structure. For the period from 2000 to 2006, the annual budget of the Cohesion Fund amounts to €2.5 billion, or €18 billion over seven years.

In addition to Structural Funds there is a Trans-European network programme, which is designed to improve transport links throughout Europe by improving designated transport routes. Furthermore, the EU has become involved in spatial planning through the formulation on the European Spatial Development Perspective.

During the pre-accession stage the EU Commission recognized the need to also help these countries, which were aiming to become EU member states, especially as the process of preparation for EU membership imposes costs on these countries. As a consequence the EU put in place the so-called Pre-accession Structural Funds to help the then applicant countries (Estonia, Latvia, Lithuania, Poland, the Czech Republic, Slovakia, Hungary, Slovenia, Romania, Bulgaria) prepare for the accession. These included the following measures:

- The Instrument for Structural Policies for Pre-accession (ISPA) has been in place since January 2000. It comprises a co-financing of big-scale (minimum €5 million) investment projects in the transport and environment sectors. The EU covers up to 75 per cent of the cost of projects that are submitted by the national governments or the private sector. Overall there is a budget of €7 billion over the period (€1 billion per year).
- Poland and Hungary Assistance for Economic Recovery programme (PHARE)[2] was aimed at financing reforms in economic development, administration, social change and legislative work. This is expected to help the candidate countries meet the criteria for membership of the EU particularly in the area of institution building. The programme that was started in 1989 will end when candidate countries (except Malta, Cyprus, Turkey) have become EU members. The financing is 100 per cent.
- Special Accession Programme for Agriculture and Rural Development (SAPARD) was the community support for pre-accession measures for agriculture and rural development in the applicant countries of Central and Eastern Europe in the pre-accession period. A new programme was initiated early in 2000, and will run until 2006. The EU co-finances up to 50 per cent of the total costs of the profit-making projects and up to 100 per cent of other projects. It also requires national government co-financing at least 25 per cent. The total budget for this is €3,640 million.

Structural Funds evaluation

Given the size and significance of the EU aid package, legislation in the form of the Council Regulation No. 1260 of 26.06.99 requires the appraisal of the

Structural Funds as well as a regular reporting on the economic and social cohesion in the EU. Analysis of the impacts of the EU regional policies is a crucial aspect in reforming the EU structural policies in order to maximize their benefit following enlargement. However, such a review must take into account that regional development in the CEECs is likely to be different due to the specific features of the transition economies.

Despite the existence of numerous empirical studies of EU regional convergence, the insights that policy-makers can gain from them is limited since there are a number of problems which are common to the majority of existing empirical research that address policy evaluation. First, until recently a lack of a sound EU-wide regional database limited the analysis to small selection of regions and time periods, which might bias the results that can be drawn from the analysis.[3] Second, the EU has been developing gradually, with integration occurring steadily between various states at various times. This leads to evolving convergence benchmarks and blurs the assessment of policy impacts. Third, as was outlined above most of the countries have implemented independent regional policies prior to introduction of EU structural and cohesion funds in 1994, which makes it almost impossible to identify the impact of EU regional policy independent of these other policies. This difficulty appears to be even more serious given different objectives pursued by national regional policies and given the long-term impacts of regional policies.

On the methodology side, five evaluation approaches are commonly used to assess the effectiveness of EU regional and cohesion policies: case studies, Input-Output (I-O) models, Computable General Equilibrium (CGE) models, single equation econometric models and multi-equation econometric models (see Ederveen et al., 2002, for review of some of the evaluation techniques). Evaluation based on fully specified macroeconomic models is discussed, e.g. in Bradley et al. (1995), Roeger (1996) and Bradley et al. (2005). The main advantage of such model-based evaluations is that they allow estimating policy impacts compared to the base-line scenarios that assume no policy intervention. Of course the theoretical underpinnings of these models play an important role in determining the size of the impacts.

Overall, the empirical evidence of the success of the EU structural and regional policies has been mixed. In addition to the methodological factors already mentioned, conclusions regarding the effectiveness of EU regional and cohesion policies depend crucially on how the policies are defined in terms of their targets and instruments used to measure the EU contributions. Furthermore, extracting impacts of other factors and policies that can be captured in the regression analyses (e.g. structural change in rapidly developing cohesion countries) can alter results significantly. Another element of difficulty is the definition of geographically relevant regional units, as this involves interpretation of policy objectives.[4] Analysis that focuses on too disaggregated regions may pick up natural heterogeneity as a lack of policy success, or vice versa. Therefore, most of the empirical evidence on policies' effectiveness should be treated with caution and certain degree of scepticism.

In contrast to the cohesion countries, the CEECs have not only a development gap towards industrialized countries, but also more pronounced disparities among the regions within the country. Nearly all the CEE countries have experienced a drastic microeconomic adjustment during the initial years of transition that hit particularly severely the more industrialized regions. The economic integration with the EU, loss of traditional export markets and distortion of the vertical linkages resulted in a slump in highly specialized regions of the CEECs that were a part of a planned production structure. This increased regional disparities, promoting the growth in the capital city and border regions that had good access to the EU market and EU-originated FDI while stagnating economic development of the peripheral regions.

Structural Funds reform

Enlargement is likely to speed up a reform of the EU regional and structural policy framework due to both the specific features of the transition economies policy-makers will have to address and the budgetary pressure associated with increased number of countries that are eligible to aid. Already, EU policies have been evaluated qualitatively, and a number of academic studies pointed at weaknesses in the existing framework that can be addressed and improved without necessarily increasing the current levels of public financing (see e.g. Weise, 2002).

Inevitably reform will require a shift of resources towards the NMS and away from the recipient regions in the EU-15. Another change to the Structural Funds is a change in the terminology. The financial allocations that were previously designated by the term "Objective 1" are now designated under two headings: the *Convergence Priority* (previously termed the Structural Funds) and the *Cohesion Fund*.

The impact of this reorientation has been evaluated by Bradley *et al.* (2004) using the familiar HERMIN modelling framework for the next (post-2006) round of expenditure on cohesion policy. In order to assess the impact the analysis is conducted with and without the cohesion policy interventions subsumed in Community Support Frameworks (CSFs). Thus, the counterfactual against which the policy is evaluated involves running the models in the absence of cohesion policy, which is highly artificial since in the absence of cohesion policy member states may enact at least some similar policies.

Importantly the study made a clear distinction between the short-run demand effects of convergence and cohesion policy expenditures (i.e. the effects generated during the implementation of the actual policy programmes) and the longer-run supply-side effects. Given the range of outputs and the fact that it is long run impact that are of key interest, the results were summarized in a cumulative multiplier, which is defined as the cumulative percentage change of GDP due to the CSF, divided by the cumulative CSF as a percentage of GDP. Clearly only if this multiplier is larger than one is there a positive impact of the Structural Funds. The highest impacts were predicted for the Czech Republic, Estonia,

Slovenia, Poland and Portugal. Particularly poor impacts are predicted for Greece, East Germany and the Italian Mezzogiorno. These results appear to support the shift of emphasis towards the NMS.

Policy recommendations

The key aim of national and EU regional policies is to decrease the disparities between regions, while at the same time maintaining the highest possible level of economic activity in all regions. The rationale for regional policies can be supported through a number of arguments, discussed below.

First, if regional disparities become too large, a political entity such as a country or indeed a supranational body such as the EU could be destabilized, as the inhabitants of the poorest regions are unlikely to be satisfied with this situation. This is of course not an economic argument for policy interventions but a political argument, but this makes it no less important. Second, if disparities become too large, regions may fall into a poverty trap, from which they might not be able to escape using their own resources. For example the new economic geography (NEG) models suggest a process of cumulative causation. The models suggest that, if some sectors are facing increasing returns to scale and transport costs, market size differences will lead to a progressive relocation of the IRS industries to the core. As more and more firms locate in the core, the periphery becomes progressively less attractive for firms in these sectors. Similarly, the endogenous growth literature suggests that convergence will not take place without well-targeted policy interventions. Indeed that literature suggests that due to externalities investments in human capital, R&D or infrastructure can substantially increase growth. But of course to reap the benefits of these externalities countries need to devote resources to this investment, which naturally favours those countries that are already better off. Conversely, poor countries and regions may not be able to achieve these higher growth rates as a lack of resources constrains the amounts that can be invested in these key areas. This latter argument suggests that, with some assistance, lagging regions may be able to escape this trap, resulting in higher incomes and thus higher purchasing power, which would benefit all regions. Thus, overcoming disparities might be a Pareto optimal move in the long-run. Finally, if regional disparities are due to market failures, then any regional policies that tackle the market failures are obviously called for and such a policy will be welfare-improving in all regions. This rationale is more in line with the neoclassical growth and trade theories, which predict convergence once all markets are working properly.

Finally, core-periphery patterns could be optimal from a welfare point of view if policies to reduce disparities would reduce overall welfare. Even if this could be proven there would still be a rationale to enact policies that enable the efficient functioning of markets.

Given the above discussion, it is also important to consider at which level policies should be enacted. Depending on the nature of the problem that policy is trying to address, different policy actors are better placed to deliver the policy.

For example if the key issue is simply that a lack of resources to invest is constraining some regions, policies should be enacted at the national or supranational (e.g. the EU) level. Here it is noteworthy that in the analysis for the Single Market, the Ceccini report highlighted the fact that poorer countries and regions may lose and thus counteracting policies were necessary. Of course poor regions may be located in poor countries suggesting that in this case the supernational level is more appropriate. A similar argument can be made if equity issues are at the heart of the policy. The EU has always had a policy of increasing cohesion, that is to reduce disparities, and this has been a major driving force behind the Structural Funds. Finally, ensuring that markets function properly may require interventions at different levels of government. Given that market failures are cross-country market failures there is a clear role for the EU to get involved alleviating such problems. However, often the problems occur within a country and may be difficult to identify at a supernational level, so that there is a clear role for national and regional governments.

While there is real convergence between regions within the EU-15, the disparities within the EU are still considerable and with enlargement the difference between the richest and poorest regions have increased significantly. For example the poorest region in Romania has a GDP per capita which is just 17.2 per cent of the EU-15 average. On the other hand, Brussels has a per capita GDP that is over double that of the EU-15 average. This suggests that on equity grounds alone policy interventions might be needed. However, simple large-scale transfer payments that are not aimed at improving the economic structure of the poorer regions are unlikely to have any long-term impact. Indeed there is evidence that if the underlying economic and institutional conditions are not right structural policies are likely to fail. It is important to note that policies that make the better off regions worse off while not generating any sustainable increase in living standards in the poorer regions are clearly sub-optimal.

Given that many NMS regions have lost out through the transition and integration process and since there are large disparities among EU-15 regions, a role for regional policies remains. However, what is important is to consider the causes of these disparities. The focus of this book was to investigate to what extent the integration process has impacted on the degree of regional specialization, which in turn might impact on regional economic performance and thus influence disparities.

While there is weak evidence for the NEG models, the predicted catastrophic relocation of economic activities to the centre is not apparent. Nevertheless, central regions have a more favourable industrial structure to ensure their future success since they tend to be more specialized in knowledge-intensive sectors. Evidence for emerging core-periphery patterns is apparent in the NMS, where regions that have border to non-EU countries have been subject to negative structural change. Particularly regions that have a high specialization in primary activities tend to perform badly and have low incomes.

The EU-15 regions appear to be converging in terms of industrial structure and per capita GDP, the slow changes of the degree of specialization appears to be supporting convergence. Given the slow speed of diversification it is reasonable to consider that policies be introduced that speed up the convergence of industrial structures since this could benefit the speed of convergence. This conclusion also corresponds with the observation that those regions that are more focused on the primary sector, which implies a significant difference from the average industrial structure, have performed poorly. Thus, rather than focusing substantial funds on the support of the agricultural sector, a reorientation of these resources towards more advanced sectors could help reduce regional disparities. Similarly, regions that are specialized in resource-intensive industries appear to be performing poorly, and instead of supporting these industries, policies that deal with the transition costs for the reorientation of regions towards more sustainable industries, should be pursued. An important focus of this reorientation should be placed on training and other labour market initiatives that would overcome hysteresis effects.

In general, at least for EU-15 a more diversified industrial structure appears to be more beneficial than one that is highly specialized. In the NMS the converse appears to have been the case. This is due to the fact that in several cases the decline in specialization is the outcome of the collapse of the industrial bases of regions highly specialized in vulnerable sectors. As a result the collapse of monostructure industrial bases appears as an increase in diversification. In reality, the relation between structural diversity and performance in the NMS is the same as that found in the EU-15. The regions that were able to truly diversify their economic base (like the metropolitan regions) have managed to have an overall a better growth performance.

Since 1988 the EU Structural Funds have been the main EU regional policy. These are provided on a programme basis for a planned period so that there is certainty of funding for some time. In general these have been focused on three particular aspects, namely infrastructure, human resources and aids to the private sector. Both the infrastructure and human resource aspects of the Structural Funds are aimed at improving the underlying potential of the regions, while the aids to the private sector provide subsidies to various private sector activities including marketing and R&D.

Our analysis does not provide any evidence about the underlying potential of the regions and thus cannot make recommendations on the infrastructure and human resources parts of the Structural Funds other than to recommend that these should be supportive of diversifying the economic structure. In relation to the aids to the private sector, more clear-cut recommendations can be made. First, for the EU-15 these should not be focused on traditional resource-intensive industries, which are declining. Rather, they should aim to diversify the industrial structure and in particular aim to promote knowledge-intensive activities (which should be supported by appropriate human resource and infrastructure investments).

Summary and conclusions

This chapter has summarized the results of the other chapters and explored the policy implications of these results. Since the policy implications can only be drawn out in the context of the rationale for policy this was discussed extensively. Furthermore, it is important to consider the findings of our analysis with reference to the international literature, which was also outlined.

Regional policy can be justified on the grounds of poverty traps due to cumulative causation processes, market failures and equity considerations. The former two can be derived from alternative theoretical frameworks, namely the new economic geography and traditional trade and growth theory frameworks. The new economic geography models generally predict agglomeration of certain economic activities provided transport costs are within a reasonable range. These agglomerations occur in locations, which have an initial advantage, which is reinforced through circular causation. Thus, some regions which do not have an initial advantage can be left behind, and this disadvantage can only be overcome by appropriate policies. The traditional economic frameworks suggest that convergence will take place provided that markets work efficiently. Since market imperfections are common, convergence may be slow or may not come about at all. Thus, government policies need only ensure that markets work properly to achieve eventual convergence. Finally, if the gap between richer and poorer regions is excessive, territorial cohesion within an economic union such as the EU can be undermined. This latter political economy argument appears to have been the rationale for EU regional policies, which after all are referred to as Cohesion Policies. However, since the term Structural Funds is also commonly used, the rationale is also derived from the other two strands of reasoning.

This discussion is also important in identifying the appropriate level of government, which should enact policies. If disparities are either of the equity (political economy) or poverty trap type, policy will need to be instigated at the national or supranational (EU) level. If however they are of the market failure type then the source of these will determine the level at which policy should be enacted. There is however a role for the EU and/or the member states in ensuring that the necessary action is taken.

The primary regional policy tool of the EU is the Community Support Framework (Structural Funds, Cohesion Fund, Pre-accession Structural Funds). The CSF focus on investment in infrastructure, human resources and aids to productive sector. However, other EU policies such as the Common Agricultural Policy, Competition Policy and the Internal Market also have regional impacts.

The "Structural Funds" have been assessed in a number of studies. Given the resources expended this is an important task. Some studies find significant impacts while others do not but these differences are to a large extent due to the methodologies that are utilized. Those methodologies that best incorporate the mechanisms through which the CSF operate tend to find positive impacts. In general a number of factors make CSF evaluation a more difficult task than should be the case. The lack of comprehensive EU-wide regional databases seriously constrains the analysis especially as the impact may be quite local and can therefore only be identified at a NUTS 3 level. The EU has been developing gradually, with integration occurring steadily between various states at various times. This leads to evolving convergence benchmarks and blurs the assessment of policy impacts. Independent regional policies have been implemented by the member states, which makes it difficult to disentangle the impact of the CSF independently of other policies.

Regarding national regional policies, a variety of such policies have been enacted by the national governments and regions in the EU-15 and in many countries regional policy has a long tradition. However, the impact of these policies appears very patchy with some regions such as Bavaria in Germany significantly improving their relative economic position while other such as the Italian Mezzogiorno remaining underdeveloped for an extended period despite much policy effort.

Our results regarding the link between the integration process and specialization in the EU-15 indicate that institutional integration does not appear to be associated with specialization. However, the link between economic integration and specialization is difficult to establish in empirical work. There is no catastrophic relocation and agglomeration of increasing returns to scale (IRS) industries, which is predicted by the new economic geography literature. Nevertheless, a weak core-periphery pattern was found. In general there appears to be slow convergence of specialization degrees and industrial structure in the EU-15. A more diverse industrial structure is associated with the better-off regions suggesting that excessive specialization may not be good unless that specialization is in the few very high performing industries. Regions that are focused on heavy industries and the primary sector are performing poorly.

A number of linked processes have impacted on specialization in the new member states. These are political restructuring, trade reorientation, integration and they have had a differentiated impact. In general there appears to be divergence between the regions in the NMS, with a more defined core-periphery pattern. Regions with external borders perform less well economically and they also tend to be more specialized. Manufacturing and the primary sectors have declined strongly in most NMS regions with strong growth in services. Regions that have had the most structural change have not performed well. A shift from capital intensive heavy industry to labour-intensive industries (comparative advantage) is evident in many regions. Nevertheless there is a positive relationship between high IRS-capital intensive industries and GDP.

FDI has changed the pattern of industrial location across and within the NMS. Some countries have benefited more (e.g. Hungary and Estonia) in that they have attracted a larger volume of inward investment. An interesting location pattern can be observed where distance from the core determines the type and level of FDI inflow. Thus regions that are closer to the core, e.g. in Hungary, have received a higher level of inward investment and this investment is in more high-tech sectors, while more remote regions have attracted smaller volumes of low-tech inward investment. Apart from the level and nature of the investment, the links to local firms are important in determining the impact of FDI. In this respect relatively weak linkages between foreign and indigenous firms are observed. There appears to be some agglomeration of foreign firms. Thus, it is not surprising that while FDI has positively impacted on regional growth it has not led to convergence.

Overall then our findings show that regions that are heavily focused on the primary sector (EU-15 and NMS) have not performed well. Similarly those with a specialization in heavy resource-intensive industries in the EU-15 have not performed well. More diverse regions have done better. There are weak core-periphery patterns with, capital city regions doing better, and regions with external border do worse.

If a diversified industrial structure appears to aid the level and growth of GDP then a natural policy conclusion is that policies should support diversification. Similarly, if specialization in the primary sector and resource-intensive industries is associated with low per capita GDP then policies should support restructuring. Given that EU-15 industrial structures and per capita GDP are converging slowly, an increase in structural convergence may also increase GDP convergence.

Consequently, the CSF and in particular the aids to the productive sector need to be focused on diversification and away from primary and poor growth secondary sectors. Other CSF interventions need to be targeted accordingly. For example investments in human resources need to complement the restructuring effort. Given that the CSF has a differentiated impact across countries and regions, it appears that the underlying institutional and economic structure is an important determinant of the success of the CSF. In cases where the impact is likely to be low these constraints need to be tackled first.

The NMS are getting more dissimilar compared to EU-15. This may have a negative long-term impact by locking the NMS into more labour intensive industries, which are only competitive as long as wages are low. In this respect the role of FDI is important in moving up the value chain. However this will only be a successful strategy if linkages to indigenous firms are fostered.

Notes

1 While there are many studies on the degree of industrial specialization, these studies have by-in-large not focused on the underlying determinants of specialization.
2 In French the programme was called "Pologne, Hongrie Assistance à la Reconstruction Economique" and thus became known as PHARE. It was extended to cover all accession states.
3 Data limitations are described, for example, in Midelfart-Knarvik and Overman (2002).
4 This is a type of problem that is usually referred to as the modifiable areal unit problem. This refers to the possibility that an empirical analysis that is carried out over different levels of spatial aggregation will find differing results.

References

Amiti, M. (1999) "Specialisation Patterns in Europe", *Review of World Economics*, 135(4), pp. 573–593.

Bradley, J., K. Whelan and J. Wright (1995) "HERMIN Ireland", *Economic Modelling*, 12(3), pp. 249–274.

Bradley, J., J. Gacs, E. Morgenroth and G. Untiedt (2004) "A Study of the Macro-Economic Impact of the Reform of EU Cohesion policy", report submitted to DG Regional Policy.

Bradley, J., T. Mitze, E. Morgenroth, and G. Untiedt (2005) "An Integrated Micro-Macro (IMM) Approach to the Evaluation of Large-Scale Public Investment Programmes: The Case of the EU Structural Funds", *ESRI Working Paper, No. 167*. Dublin: ESRI.

Brülhart, M. (1998) "Trading Places: Industrial Specialization in the European Union", *Journal of Common Market Studies*, 36 (3), pp. 319–346.

Brülhart, M. and J. Torstensson (1996) "Regional Integration, Scale Economies and Industry Location in the European Union", CEPR Discussion Paper No. 1435.

Ederveen, S., H. De Groot and R. Nahuis (2002) "Fertile Soil For Structural Funds?", *Tinbergen Institute Discussion Papers*, 02–096/3.

Haaland, J., H.-J. Kind, and K.-H. Midelfart (1999) "What Determines the Economic Geography of Europe?", CEPR Discussion Papers: 2072.

Martin, R. (1998) "Regional Dimension of Europe's Unemployment Crisis", in: P. Lawless (ed.) *Unemployment and Social Exclusion: Landscapes of Labor Inequality*, London: Routledge.

Midelfart-Knarvik, K.H., H.G. Overman, S.J. Redding and A.J. Venables (2000) "The Location of European Industry" report prepared to the Directorate General for Economic and Financial Affairs, European Commission. Economic Papers 142, ECFIN/318/00-EN.

Midelfart-Knarvik, K.H. and H.G. Overman (2002) "Delocation and European Integration: Is Structural Spending Justified?", *Economic Policy: A European Forum*, no. 35, pp. 321–351.

Roeger, W. (1996) "Macroeconomic Evaluation of the Effects of Community Structural Funds with QUEST II", Mimeo, European Commission, GDII.

Weise, (2002) "How to Finance Eastern Enlargement of the EU: The Need to Reform EU Policies and the Consequences for the Net Contributor Balance", ENEPRI Working Paper No. 14.

Index

www.ingramcontent.com/pod-product-compliance
Ingram Content Group UK Ltd.
Pitfield, Milton Keynes, MK11 3LW, UK
UKHW020859280225
455677UK00006B/106